TWO KINGDOMS, TWO LOYALTIES

Mennonite Pacifism in Modern America

PERRY BUSH

THE JOHNS HOPKINS UNIVERSITY PRESS

BALTIMORE AND LONDON

© 1998 The Johns Hopkins University Press
All rights reserved. Published 1998
Printed in the United States of America on acid-free paper

9 8 7 6 5 4 3 2 1

The Johns Hopkins University Press
2715 North Charles Street
Baltimore, Maryland 21218-4363
The Johns Hopkins Press Ltd., London
www.press.jhu.edu

Library of Congress Cataloging-in-Publication Data

Bush, Perry.
Two kingdoms, two loyalties : Mennonite pacifism
in modern America / Perry Bush.
p.   cm.
Originally presented as the author's thesis (doctoral)—
Carnegie Mellon University.
Includes bibliographical references and index.
ISBN 0-8018-5827-5
1. Mennonites—United States—History—20th century.
2. Pacifism—Religious aspects—Mennonites—History of
doctrines—20th century.   I. Title.
BX8116.B87   1998
261.8′73′088287—dc21   97-44233
                                          CIP

A catalog record for this book is available
from the British Library.

Contents

Acknowledgments

There will be, I suspect, much blame and some credit assigned to this book when it appears. The blame is mine alone, but the credit should be shared around a bit.

First of all, I would like to thank my parents, to whom this book is appropriately dedicated. I would never have been able to undertake a project such as this one without their love, support, and encouragement. My father, in particular, has provided for me a model of careful, committed scholarship and an unswerving dedication, both scholarly and personal, to the pursuit of truth. In doing so, he has left me engulfed in a sea of affection and with a debt of gratitude that I can never hope to repay.

This book began as a doctoral dissertation at Carnegie Mellon University and was substantially shaped by faculty there. My own accomplishments as a scholar are due, in no small measure, to their tutelage and care. In particular, I want to thank by name the members of my committee who saw this study through from a vague idea to a completed dissertation. Peter Stearns did his best to work into me the skills, methodologies, and orientation of social history. Lizabeth Cohen reinforced these lessons, ever reminding me not to forget the stories of ordinary people that social history tries to recapture. Finally, I could not imagine a more dedicated and properly critical principle dissertation advisor than John Modell, who provided a steady stream of thoughtful, encouraging, constructive criticism of my work. Whatever contributions to a larger dialogue this book makes are due in great part to him.

This book has undergone heavy revisions and rewriting beyond the dissertation stage, and I have received a great amount of assistance from a number of scholars in this process. George Marsden, Martin Marty, and Mark Noll graciously consented to read and critique the finished dissertation with an eye to publication in book form and came up with pages of constructive suggestions for revision. While I did not follow all of their advice, it is no fault of theirs; nonetheless, I hope they will be pleased with what they find in the final product. Secondly, it will be apparent to anyone reading Mennonite scholarship that the Mennonites have, in their ranks, a busy and talented community of historians, sociologists, and theologians, who have done much to shape, interpret, and reinterpret their own tradition. I wandered into this community quite by accident, merely by virtue of the dissertation topic I had chosen. Gradually I began to follow, and finally to participate in, the fascinating and creative dialogue of the Mennonite academic community.

This book has made ample use of that community's rich resources. Robert Kreider—who is not only a skilled scholar of Mennonite history but also an active and important leader of it—read and critiqued the first four chapters in page after page of thoughtful, informed suggestions and insight. Jim Juhnke, Rachel Waltner Goossen, J. Denny Weaver, J. R. Burkholder, and Jim Satterwhite all read and commented on portions of the manuscript. In a like manner but more informally, my thinking was shaped by conversations with Denny Weaver, Beulah Hostetler, Al Keim, and Theron Schlabach. Elmer Neufeld, Winfield Fretz, Loris Habegger, Greg Luginbuhl, J. R. Burkholder, Noah Good, and Paul Landis all agreed to oral interviews. I very much appreciate the hours of time and energy all these people have invested in this work. In a similar manner, I spent a portion of one hot summer afternoon in conversation with the late Guy Hershberger six months before his death in December 1989. Given what I realized was the extent of his influence on twentieth-century Mennonite history and ethics, it was an exciting few hours. And as he has done for so many younger students of his church tradition, Jim Juhnke has indelibly shaped my own understanding of recent Mennonite history. My intellectual debt to him should be clear to anyone reading these pages.

It would be hard to find more amenable and friendly subjects of study than Mennonites. More than once they copied my name off archival bulletin boards or campus newsletters and opened their homes to me; they loaned me keys to archives; they hunted down obscure citations on my behalf. In the course of this study, some of these people have made the transition, for me, from courteous archival and library staff and busy college professors to warm personal friends. Specifically, I need to thank Harold Huber and the staff of Menno Simons Historical Library at Eastern Mennonite University; Carolyn Charles Wenger and her staff at Lancaster Mennonite Historical Society; David Haury, Kathy Schrag, and John and Barbara Thiesen of Mennonite Library and Archives at Bethel College; and Janet Shoemaker of Mennonite Historical Library at Goshen College. The staff at the Archives of the Mennonite Church at Goshen repeatedly went out of their way to aid my research in a wide variety of ways and did so with remarkable warmth and good humor that rendered their archives such a pleasant place to work. I need to extend my personal thanks to Leonard Gross, Dennis Stoez, and J. Kevin Miller. At home, I relied heavily on the efforts of local librarians who pointed me to titles I had missed and patiently handled my many requests on inter-library loan. I want to make sure to extend my gratitude to Rick Sayre and Wileta Larrison of Zollars Memorial Library at Phillips University; Harvey Hiebert and Robert Tiessen of Musselman Library at Bluffton College; and Anne Hilty of Mennonite Historical Library at Bluffton. Art Shelly of Bluffton College was very helpful in printing out the manuscript. This study was also greatly aided by George Thompson, Douglas Armato, and the staff with John Hopkins University Press. I am especially grateful to Elizabeth Yoder, who skillfully copyedited the final manuscript.

In the course of research trips, I enjoyed the warm hospitality of Gladys Beyler, Leonard and Irene Gross of Goshen, and Jim and Anna Juhnke of Newton. While researching in Lancaster, I stayed for several weeks at the home and dairy farm of Hershey and Evie Hostetter, where I became the beneficiary of what emerged into an informal but very unequal arrangement. Their friendship, warmth, and good cooking by far outweighed my pitiful assistance with the afternoon milking. Such research trips were made possible by research and travel monies I received from the History Department of Carnegie Mellon University and from the Bluffton College Study Center.

A number of people aided this study in a variety of other ways. For their hospitality away from home, their help with computers, their functioning as a sounding board for my ideas, and most of all for their friendship, I want to thank Ellis Leslie, John Adgate, Tim and Kim Kelly, Susan Ambrose, and Ed Hostetter. Likewise I benefited from the warm collegiality and insights offered by faculty colleagues: Rick Lowery of Phillips University, and Denny Weaver, Jim Satterwhite, Gerald Schlabach, and Loren Johns of Bluffton College. Faye Kiryakakis of Phillips University helped tirelessly in a bulk of the secretarial chores required.

Finally, last but not least, in the course of research, writing and completing this book I benefited in countless ways from a few individuals whose love, encouragement, and support deserve so much more than a few lines here. In numerous fishing trips and in passionate conversation, my brother Preston Bush has vastly aided the construction of an Anabaptist vision of my own. To my great joy and appreciation, my daughters Kerry and Cassidy and my son Jackson have done their best to distract me from this entire project and to remind me of more important things than books and citations. When they are old enough to read it, I hope this book will one day help explain to them where I was and what I was doing so much of the time when they were very young. And finally, in her love, her encouragement, and her unfailing sense of humor, Elysia Caldwell Bush has done more than merely make this book possible. Her partnership in all things has functioned as my intellectual and emotional foundation. In trying to summarize what she has meant to me in the years I have been laboring on this book, I am possessed with a gratitude and affection which I have difficulty putting into words.

TWO KINGDOMS,

TWO LOYALTIES

CHAPTER 1

Introduction:
Two Kingdoms,
Two Loyalties

L ynn Liechty's world had always been a Mennonite world. As he grew up in the small town of Berne, Indiana, in the 1930s, the calling of a Mennonite heritage was never far below the surface of his life. At home, the family often conversed in Swiss German, though the three Liechty boys knew less of the tongue than did their parents. Liechty absorbed Mennonite religious and ethical precepts quite naturally. His father and uncles, self-employed founders of Liechty Brothers Plumbing and Heating, often turned the shop talk to issues of peace and Christian faith. In accordance with church teaching inherited from their Anabaptist ancestors, Liechty's father and uncles had all been conscientious objectors (COs) in the First World War. This unpopular public stand provided more recent, modern examples of Mennonite persecution for matters of faith. One of his uncles had even been imprisoned for such convictions in Fort Leavenworth, Kansas, during the war. Thus, there was always a great deal of discussion around the plumbing shop, which, as Liechty remembers, "was never known as a very patriotic place." When conscientious objectors came home on furlough from their service in World War II, the shop was the only public place in town where they were welcome to congregate. On Easter Sunday 1942, town vandals painted yellow swastikas on the shop windows.[1]

As a high school student, Liechty listened politely to his uncles' stories but did not pay much attention to events in Europe. "I was so busy with sports," he remembers, "and a good time." Not long after graduation in

1941, world events broke into his life with an urgency he could no longer ignore. While he was engaged in a surreptitious card game with several Mennonite friends one Sunday afternoon, the radio suddenly began blaring news of Pearl Harbor. One buddy rubbed his hands with glee, exclaiming, "We'll brush off the Japanese before breakfast and go over and get the Germans!"

Although the draft decision might have been easy for some, for Liechty it occasioned what he remembers as one of the great struggles of his life. On the one hand, there was his family's teaching and example. The Liechtys were a strong pacifist family, and Lynn was thus known as an antiwar Mennonite. There were the lessons he had absorbed in Sunday school at his Mennonite church, where several influential teachers had stressed the traditional Mennonite stance of pacifist nonresistance. On the other hand, the entire community championed the war effort; it seemed the perfect example of the good war, the just war. As an accomplished and popular high school athlete, Liechty felt especially vulnerable to community pressures.

Even more telling in Liechty's final decision was the attitude in his church, First Mennonite of Berne. His particular denomination, the General Conference Mennonite Church, counseled conscientious objection and spoke against participation in the military in either combatant or noncombatant roles. Yet First Mennonite's pastor, Rev. C. H. Suckau, privately counseled the noncombatant position in which you could join the army but be assigned to noncombat roles. You could remain true to Jesus' example but also "prove you're not a coward." When two Sunday school superintendents from First Mennonite entered the army as noncombatants, they reinforced the message to the church's young men that "that was the way to go." Many of Liechty's Mennonite high school friends opted for this position, along with a majority of the young men from First Mennonite. Of the 150 draft-age men from this large church, only 20 braved the unpopular but traditional Mennonite stance of conscientious objection.

Liechty was not one of them; in the end, he chose noncombatant service. In doing so, he hoped for the best of both worlds: he could remain true to his family's teaching and example yet maintain community acceptance; he could satisfy both God and country. Drafted into the Army Air Service in 1943, he would spend much of the next two years wondering if he had satisfied either. His family was disappointed, his father "heartbroken." Liechty found the army physical "wrenching" and saying goodbye even harder. His father drove him to the bus station and, as emotional as Liechty had ever seen him, told his son, "I wish I was going instead of you . . . Dare to be a Daniel."

Liechty soon discovered that it was hard and risky to be an Old Testament prophet like Daniel in the U.S. Army. "I knew I wasn't in the right place," he remembers. "I did not enjoy one day of my three years." In basic training, he was "determined to be a CO"; and in one particularly frightening experience, he and three others disobeyed an order to step forward and accept wooden rifles in a training exercise. Standing in place, they resolutely informed the sergeant, "We are COs and will not take the rifle." The sergeant, Liechty recalls, did not know what a conscientious objector was. Though the men were soon reassigned without further trouble, Liechty could not come to peace with his military service. Bouncing around from one army camp to another, he "lived with frustration and guilt . . . I knew what the Bible said."

Trained as a dental technician and finally attached to a new B-29 bombing squadron being formed in Texas, Liechty, along with his unit, arrived in Guam in December 1944. Each morning and evening he watched the bombers take off and return, engaged in the firebombing of Japan. Eight or so months later, one of the crews in Liechty's bomber wing—in a plane named the *Enola Gay,* after the pilot's mother—took off from the nearby island of Tinian for the Japanese city of Hiroshima, where they dropped the first atomic bomb. Liechty and his fellow medics did not realize the significance of this at the time. They merely "felt good that the war was going to be over."

After the war, Liechty returned home to Berne to work in his father's plumbing shop. He and several others refused to accept the Indiana Veterans' Bonus, calling it "blood money." As Liechty remembered later, "We did not want to be paid for something we hated to do."

To a large degree, Lynn Liechty's trials encapsulate those of his church for much of the twentieth century. A large number of Mennonites found themselves similarly caught between two conflicting sources of authority and obligation. On the one hand, there was the church. Although the religious traditions of many other denominations minimized possible grounds of conflict with the state, the weight of Mennonite history and tradition rendered such an accord much harder to achieve. Throughout their history, the Mennonite churches have wrestled with their relationship to the state, attempting to make clear to their members where the state's sphere of authority ends and that of God begins. The churches repeatedly reminded their members of their preeminent loyalty to this higher calling, an obligation reinforced in many cases by the social bonds of a Mennonite ethnoreligious community.

On the other hand, however, there was the state. Throughout this century few Americans could avoid the call of American nationalism or the more seductive supplications of American culture. Mennonites have always been good Christians, but at the same time, they have nearly always wanted to be good citizens. As Mennonites in the twentieth century weakened the walls of separation they had maintained between themselves and outside society, the status of citizenship grew all the more alluring. The process intensified with the state's turn to total war and the ideological pull that this entailed.

Thus it was that the Liechtys' struggles exemplified those of many others. The church would do its best to define a sense of acceptable Mennonite citizenship for its members, an endeavor that would take on a variety of institutional manifestations in the postwar years. As this study outlines, however, when the twin callings of good citizenship and good discipleship inescapably diverged, the church would reassert its fealty to the latter.

On the individual level, the conflicting obligations between church and state proved even more exacting, and a fair number of Mennonites in various ways reached an easier accord with the state than official church counsel taught. Still, as Liechty's case illustrates, this often did not occur without a good deal of religious pressure and resistance. And as the church faced a host of social and economic changes in the postwar years, the whole question of what to do with the state—when to say yes, when and how to say no, even how and when to "witness" to the state—became a topic of ever-increasing importance and discussion.

This study explores the Mennonites as an example of a church group wrestling with the conflicting obligations of God and country in the historical context of mid-twentieth-century America. This discussion, moreover, must necessarily be removed from wholly ethereal, intellectual patterns of discussion and be rooted firmly in the less equivocal soil of recent American social history. For the nature of the recent American security-state and the weight of Mennonite history and life have inexorably and repeatedly collided over the past fifty years. In this friction, these competing spheres issued questions of loyalty and authority that few church members could consider abstractly. The young man filling out his draft papers; his parents laboring at their tax forms; their congregation considering a call to register their dissent against military draft measures or the Vietnam War: these situations required decisions that could not always be weighed in safe, academic terms. Above all, this is the story of individuals and congregations trying to remain faithful to a long-standing ethnoreligious tradition while responding to the contending demands of citizenship in twentieth-century America.

NONRESISTANCE, THE STATE, AND SOCIAL CHANGE: AN INITIAL EXPLORATION

Because Mennonites struggled with competing obligations in a particular historical context and because history is never static, their relationship to the state underwent profound reevaluation and change in the 1935–75 period. So fundamental was this transition, in fact, that much of this study serves to explain how Mennonites went from one position to the other. Between these polar positions, this reworking ebbed and surged.

By the spring of 1941, American Mennonites had succeeded, along with the other two members of the Historic Peace Churches, the Church of the Brethren and the Friends, in working out a delicate arrangement with the federal government for its treatment of wartime conscientious objectors. Instead of uncompromisingly drafting objectors into the army as it had done during World War I, the state agreed to set up a series of unpaid labor camps for objectors in a program called Civilian Public Service (CPS). Though ultimate control would remain with the government, these CPS camps would be administered by the three church groups.

Mennonite leaders left little doubt about how they viewed the settlement. The Mennonite Church's Peace Problems Committee, for instance, relayed to the larger church in 1941 its complete satisfaction with the CPS arrangement. "That our government, in the midst of a world tendency toward totalitarian and dictatorial methods," the committee reported happily, "should make generous provisions for the consciences of nonresistant Christians, should be a matter of appreciation and deep gratitude by the entire church."[2]

These church leaders arrived at such a church-state compromise through their understanding of their relationship to the state, encapsulated in the term *nonresistance*. This relationship, in turn, registered how Mennonites defined themselves for outside society and understood themselves as a people. Taken together, the two conceptions demand some attention.

Just as nonconformity governed Mennonites' relationship with outside culture, nonresistance characterized their outlook toward forms and expressions of power commonly but not always located in the state.[3] *Nonresistance* was a sticky term, one that Mennonite scholars themselves had trouble clarifying. Though slanted more toward conservative understandings, John Mumaw's phrasing probably held some currency beyond conservative "old" Mennonite circles. According to Mumaw, nonresistance "holds that violence should not be resisted by force. It forbids taking vengeance, prescribes peaceable living with people, advocates the suffering of wrongdoing, and practices the submission to the powers that be within the limits of conscience."[4] It was a tough ethic, a hard ethic, and Mennonites readily admitted that it was not for everybody.

Strictly understood, nonresistance must be viewed in light of a "two-kingdom" ethic and theology that lies at the heart of Mennonite attitudes toward outside society. This dualistic understanding of church-state relations has exercised a paradigmatic hold on Christian history and theology not only for Mennonites, but also for many other Christian thinkers. A summary of this set of theological understandings runs something like this. Although sovereign over both, God endowed two orders, two kingdoms, for the ruling of human society. One sphere of activity was the world of secular activity and culture of all humans, to be ruled over by the state. Thus, as Romans 13 declared, God endowed human government with divine sanction for the purpose of maintaining order in the secular world. The second kingdom was the church, the world of spiritual activity, mission, and discipline. In this kingdom, Christians carried out the divine mandates applicable only to themselves as citizens of this second, spiritual realm. Christians thus had a foot in both realms; they were to be "in the world, but not of the world."[5]

Although many different Christian groups have accepted this basic two-kingdom understanding, the relationship that these different groups have had with the state has varied widely, and each group has modified this two-kingdom theology accordingly. Established or state churches, enjoying a cooperative relationship with the reigning government, have often seen these two realms, each with its own limitations, as two equal spheres of God's activity. Martin Luther, for instance, carefully defined these two kingdoms and the Christian's roles in each. Both kingdoms had their own ethic and expectations, and Lutheran theology has generally mandated Christian obedience to both the ecclesiastical and the secular as divinely inspired sources of authority. Christians owed their supreme obedience to the latter, but Luther envisioned them as cooperative rather than competing sources of authority. Calvinist "Transformationism" took this even further, arguing that the state could be a positive aid to the Christian in living the Christian life. The state, and human cultural activity in general, could even exercise divine purposes.[6]

For groups having a more hostile relationship with the state, however, two-kingdom theology was modified to emphasize separation, not church-state cooperation. Not surprisingly, the theology of nonresistance that Anabaptist reformers passed on to their Mennonite descendants stressed the latter course. Given that the governments of their day had vilified, hunted, drowned, and burned them at the stake, Anabaptists bequeathed a negative view of the state, a state from which Christians could expect great evil. At the same time, however, Anabaptists taught a more positive view of the state in an ideal sense. Like other Christians who read the thirteenth chapter of Romans, they believed that the state had been endowed by God and that Christians were to obey its directives quite submissively. With modern twentieth-century notions of democratic citizenship way beyond their grasp, of course, Anabaptists were expected to act as loyal subjects, dutifully obeying state directives unless they violated the higher obligations Christians owed to their God.[7]

Mennonite theology took such two-kingdom prescriptions to heart. On one hand, God had set up the state for the maintenance of law and order, Mennonites agreed, and thus "nonresistant Christians must be the most law-abiding citizens of the state." At the heart of their worldview lay an older, medieval notion of state residents not as citizens but as subjects. While the suppression of evil was the purpose and function of the state, God's people, embodied in God's church, were to have a different orientation. When individuals accepted Christ and joined the church, Mennonites reasoned, they accepted the harder and more demanding ethic of Christian love and suffering exemplified in the nonresistant tradition to which Christians owed ultimate obedience, even in the face of terrible persecution. So deep was the separation Mennonites defined between the affairs of the church and the affairs of the state that they traditionally saw state matters as simply none of their business. Instead, Christians should have, in Mumaw's formulation, "other-worldly interests." They would not push forceful peacemaking, but rather practice passive nonresistance to state aggression, just as loyal, dutiful subjects would. In the words of one

Mennonite bishop in 1837, they would be "ready and willing, as loyal subjects, to submit to government doctrines in all things lawful, that do not
oppose the doctrine of Christ and the dictates of consciences."[8]

Mennonites, therefore, were not to engage in protest. "The Nonresistant Christian has no interest in thwarting the government in any of its
activities," Mumaw argued. Because of such reasoning, large numbers of
Mennonites traditionally refused to vote. Similarly, although jobs in functional activities such as road building were permissible, most governmental
offices involved a degree of coercion and were thus off-limits for proper
Christians. One could neither serve as a policeman, wielding violence on
behalf of the state, nor as the mayor or governor directing the police, nor as
the legislator appropriating the funds for police or militia activities.[9] This
line of reasoning has led Mennonites to regard the legal profession with
some distrust. Because of the close association of lawyers with the coercive
functions of the courts, they have likewise often refused to sue in court.
And because of this fear of being involved in coercion, they have also traditionally refused to join labor unions.[10]

Finally, because Mennonites viewed the state as established by God for
the maintenance of order in the secular realm, they have traditionally
looked with some disfavor on groups and movements interpreted as threatening this order. By the time of the Second World War, for instance, for
many this had come to mean the Social Gospel and liberal pacifism. These
movements, Mennonite leaders argued, tried to create a kingdom on earth
without taking into account the full depths of human sin. "Believers in Biblical nonresistance find the social gospel pacifism of religious liberalism
inadequate," argued Guy F. Hershberger in 1943, "because they have a
wrong conception of sin, of Christianity and of the kingdom of God . . .
The kingdom is made up only of those who have been redeemed from, and
called out of, the sinful society." Similarly, for the General Conference
Mennonites, Donovan Smucker scored modern pacifism for its simplistic
optimism, its attempt to "Christianize" the social order, and its easy substi-
tution of nonviolent coercion for nonresistant love.[11]

Many of the Mennonite leadership of the war years deeply resonated
with Reinhold Niebuhr and his school of "Christian Realists." Like Niebuhr, many Mennonites agreed that God decreed a different ethic for the
kingdom of the church than for the kingdom of the world. To attempt to
apply one to the other, to naively hope for the establishment of God's kingdom in history through confident human action and "progress," was naive
optimism at its best and heresy at its worst. Even as they began to do battle

with Niebuhr on other issues, this Mennonite aversion to change and disorder continued into the postwar years and found its firmest expression, with monumental implications, among the laity. (For example, as increasing numbers of Mennonites began to vote in the post–World War II years, like other rural white Protestants, they tended to favor conservative Republicans). Altogether, throughout most of Mennonite history, on a behavioral level Mennonite nonresistance has amounted to an antistatist, let-us-alone variant of conservatism, for some even an altogether reactionary outlook.[12]

Such a withdrawn relationship with the state expressed an equally cautious sense of peoplehood. The Mennonite nonresistant identity has always oscillated between two tensions, two alternative visions of what it means to be a Mennonite. The stance that has received the dominant weight over the centuries has been the Mennonite identity as *Die Stillen im Lande* (the Quiet in the Land). This was a self-perception inherited directly from their Anabaptist ancestors, "the non-complaining people of the land," summarized one Mennonite writer, "the people who bore their suffering patiently, faced their persecution without complaint, and went to their death quietly." These were humble people who "avoided self-display in equipment, in living, and in dress."[13] It was an ideal that their American descendants took very much to heart. American Mennonites quite intentionally fashioned a mirror-image identity as *Die Stillen im Lande*—quiet, backroads farmers who neither gambled, swore, nor drank; who avoided legal issues, paid their taxes, refrained from proselytizing their neighbors, and asked only to be left alone to serve their God in their own way. For centuries, Mennonite two-kingdom theology reinforced their sociocultural isolation by branding cultural incursions and political activism as "worldly" and sinful. Like good children, they were seen but not heard. This was the primary identity that the tradition of nonresistance had forged.

So ran the traditional Mennonite theology and self-perception, a worldview that Mennonite leaders such as Guy F. Hershberger and Harold Bender, endeavoring to help the church withstand the pressures of world war and social transformation, consciously redefined and fortified in the early 1940s. Indeed, in two classic formulations appearing during the war years—Bender's "The Anabaptist Vision" and Hershberger's *War, Peace, and Nonresistance*—these men reintegrated two-kingdom theology into Mennonite history in such a way as to articulate a reinforced identity for Mennonites in the new mosaic of American denominations that they had begun to enter.[14]

But no sooner had church leaders articulated such a stance than Mennonite interaction with the social changes of the postwar years plunged it into
serious reevaluation. The most revealing sign of such a reworking was the
curious gap that soon appeared between Mennonite practice and Mennonite preaching. By the 1950s, Mennonite leaders had begun quite clearly
telling the government what to do, first on matters that primarily concerned Mennonites, like conscription and the draft, and then on matters
that did not, such as race relations and Vietnam. As Mennonite mediation
in a postwar process of acculturation transformed their conception of their
church community, it widened their field of social responsibilities as well.
New theological formulations followed along directly.

Altogether, this process of religious brokering of social change led directly to the second polar position, encapsulated once again by a quote.
Thus it was that not forty years after the expression of Mennonite appreciation quoted above, Mennonite Church delegates found themselves
confronted by a collection of long-haired Mennonite young people at their
biennial churchwide conference in 1969. These students argued persuasively that "the Vietnam war and the continued military conscription have
prompted us to examine our individual and church relationships with the
Selective Service System. By cooperating with this agency, we are in effect
sanctioning its actions." Though they plunged the conference into controversy, in the end the young people won the day. The church delegates finally voted to "recognize the validity of noncooperation as a legitimate
witness."[15]

Even though such a stance decisively broke with the patterns of uneasy
collaboration that church leaders had established with the state and although it emerged as a result of a long theological, behavioral, and political
reevaluation, this new position did not lie outside the parameters of the
older nonresistant tradition. For there had always been one way in which
nonresistance could take on overtones of outright radicalism and could, in
the state's eyes, transform these rural conservatives into dangerous subver-
sives. Mennonites were gladly willing to concede state authority as long as
it exercised that authority in its proper sphere. They could endorse the
dualistic Christian obedience to two kingdoms as long as Christians were
always clear about where their higher loyalty lay. "When the state reaches
into the realm of religion, conscience and the home," Hershberger warned,
"it is demanding what does not belong to it."[16] In those instances, Mennonites repeatedly demonstrated their determination to line themselves up
with New Testament apostles, proclaiming that "We must obey God rather

than men" and then submitting meekly to the inevitable consequences from the state. Soundly conservative in most aspects, Mennonites were ✓ willing to countenance a radical civil disobedience—to them, a holy obedience—when the state tried to cross the boundary line between the two kingdoms. There were just some areas of life, Mennonites insisted, in which the authority of the state had little or no bearing.

Whether or not they were forced to disobey depended on where the state tried to push its authority. The crucial issues that led to so much martyrdom were the Anabaptists' refusal to pledge oaths of political allegiance and, most importantly, the peculiar but terrible rage engendered in European Protestant church-states when Anabaptists (literally, "rebaptizers") insisted on adult, as opposed to infant, baptism. What rebaptism represented to the sixteenth-century state, young Mennonite radicals suggested in the late 1960s, issues such as draft and tax resistance represented to its twentieth-century counterpart.[17]

There was, moreover, an alternative self-perception, also bequeathed by Anabaptist forebears, that coexisted with the quiet identity, sometimes in a good deal of tension. The humble Anabaptists who went off to their martyrdom singing hymns should not have been much surprised at the waves of persecution descending on them. For these "non-complaining people" had shown a marked penchant for penetrating social and religious criticism of the prevailing Protestant establishment, a stubborn refusal to compromise their principles no matter the severity of the consequences, and a passionate missionary zeal that, if allowed to proceed unchecked, threatened to conquer continental Europe. Their Mennonite descendants thus also inherited a heritage of prophetic dissent, of devout agitation, and of missionary fervor. For most of Mennonite history, this identity had been overridden by the predominant, quiet pose outlined above. Yet it existed as a continual undercurrent and broke out into the Mennonite mainstream not long into the postwar period.

For as Mennonites became gradually acculturated, they looked around at the evils occurring in larger society and began to ponder the price of their silence. Prophetic voices of their own arose to help them in this process. "Can we be still," asked one Mennonite in 1959, "when atomic tests cause dangerous radioactive fallout . . . when the nations are engaged in a mad armaments race?" African American Mennonite pastor Vincent Harding did much to trigger an awakening on issues such as race relations and the Vietnam War. In 1958, for instance, Harding reviewed American racial oppression in the pages of *The Mennonite* and asked, "Can Mennonites afford

to be 'Die Stillen im Lande' in the face of today's tragedy? Is it possible for
any group which takes seriously its Christian faith to be silent in such a time
as this?" As the Vietnam crisis heated up, people such as Harding began to
suggest that it was time to recapture this alternative, prophetic Anabaptist
vision of Mennonite identity, though the costs, they were clear, would be
substantial. Seen in this light, the calls for draft resistance by young Mennonites in the late 1960s do not appear as a rejection of the nonresistant
tradition, but instead as an effort to emphasize a long-neglected vision of
the Mennonite identity: as the City on a Hill, as prophets banging on the
gates, as Anabaptist Witnesses to the Truth.[18]

Thus, the Mennonite reinterpretation of their nonresistant tradition lies
at the center of the story we are about to trace. So, too, does a process of
socioeconomic change battering at the church throughout this era. Historically an isolated, rural people devoted primarily to agriculture, Mennonites in these years began moving to urban areas, partaking much more
heavily in higher education, and branching out into a variety of occupations, including an especially strong move toward professional callings.
Though still remaining more rural overall than the general American population, and markedly more prosperous (a reflection of unmistakable patterns of Mennonite social mobility), Mennonites in the postwar years increasingly began to resemble their non-Mennonite neighbors in a variety
of ways.[19]

Even more important than these socioeconomic changes was their increasing acculturation. For throughout this century, and especially in the
last four to five decades, Mennonites have rapidly discarded the patterns of
speech, dress, and consumption that marked their rural communities to
adopt, nearly wholesale, the trappings of larger American culture. As Mennonites began to change their relationship with the state, articulated in
Mennonite terminology as *nonresistance*, so too did they change their relationship with outside culture, something they had traditionally characterized as *nonconformity*. The two processes were deeply interrelated, as
church leaders repeatedly observed with alarm. Particularly in the largest
Mennonite group, the Mennonite Church, this process of rapid acculturation triggered a desperate rearguard struggle by many leaders to preserve
the venerable old cultural separation (just as many also fought to maintain
a strict adherence to the older, political separation of the two kingdoms).

Perhaps such leaders would have tempered their alarm if they could have
foreseen that this was clearly a case of ethnic acculturation, but not assimilation. In his classic articulation of the concept, Milton Gordon character-

ized assimilation as a one-way, linear process in which the group discards all of its own cultural traits and replaces them with those of the host society.[20] Quite plainly this has not been the case with American Mennonites. Instead of discarding their cultural tradition in total, they have—as Gordon's definition of acculturation suggests—de-emphasized aspects of it and borrowed from the larger society other cultural elements, such as evangelicalism, that could be integrated into an adaptable yet strengthened Mennonite cultural worldview.

Needless to say, such changes would register a deep impact on the Mennonite peace position. Withdrawn, isolated farmers wanting only to be left alone felt the calling of American citizenship less than did Mennonite urban professionals anxious to participate fully in American life. As Mennonites began to ease the cultural barriers between themselves and larger society, the pressures toward full citizenship intensified. Much of the twentieth-century Mennonite story revolves around this shift, from an isolated enthnoreligious people still retaining medieval notions of themselves as subjects, to full participants in American society trying to accept in a Mennonite way the expectations and responsibilities of modern American citizenship. Indeed, it was precisely the escalating attractions of citizenship that gave the Mennonite reaction to Vietnam some of its particular agony. It is also important to note that not only did acculturation affect the Mennonite relation to the state, but an inverse relationship existed here as well. By scattering thousands of young Mennonite COs around the country and around the world, the state itself began to serve as an effective acculturating agent.[21]

In sum, the Mennonite relationship with the state in the 1935–73 period was shaped in the interaction of a complex religious ideology and tradition with the larger forces of social change and the state. In this interaction, however, lie some larger meanings for other people.

CHRISTIAN PACIFISM AND
THE RISE OF THE MODERN WARFARE STATE

On the basis of raw numbers, it is hard to award the Mennonites much significance in the larger panoply of American religion. In 1972, for instance, the thirteen American Mennonite, Amish, and Hutterite denominations totaled barely two hundred thousand baptized members.[22] By a numerical analysis, Mennonites qualify neither as a major denomination nor as a major ethnic group. These considerations, especially when seen in light of traditional Mennonite separatism, certainly relegate them, in the minds of many scholars, to the margins of American history. The Mennonite story in the twentieth century moves from the periphery to the center of recent American history, however, when the focus shifts to include the modern warfare state, the partner and principal antagonist in their recent history. Indeed, for much of this century, these two parties have been locked in a delicate dance, a parry-and-thrust that has taken some strange and ironic turns.

Recent Mennonite history illuminates the implications that the larger American drift toward total war, modern war, has meant for dissenters in particular and for the quality of American democracy in wartime in general. It is unnecessary to review here the development of the modern state or Max Weber's paradigmatic assertion that violence lay at the roots of it. The modern military apparatus and the modern state have been deeply related historically; to a large degree they have created each other. What Eisenhower called the "military-industrial complex" has been, according to Ekkehart Krippendorff, the "very mid-wife of the modern state." Hence the predominant characteristic of modern war has been, in Krippendorff's words, "the collective and total mobilization of violence organized within the framework of the bureaucratic industrial state."[23]

This total mobilization of violence, and its delivery upon the totality of the enemy population without regard for whatever moral distinctions still remained in early modern warfare, has been driven by two principal sorts of factors. The first revolved around the emergence of mass armies and the type of warfare made possible by the industrial revolution and demographic growth in the West in the nineteenth century. According to Samuel Finer, mass armies did not really make their entrance onto the world stage until this era, due to several related developments. These included expanding national populations providing the necessary manpower for such forces and the technological advances in weaponry, such as the rifled musket and artillery, steam-powered warships, and the machine gun, with which such mass armies were armed. The nineteenth-century industrial revolution led to the quick adaptation to warmaking of new technologies such as the railroad and telegraph and also to the mass production of these new goods. Finally, the emerging central and managing role of the state was a necessary precondition for mass armies, as well as an obvious cause. The modern state pays, equips, and directs troops; and it has become responsible for the national war economy, technology, and even the creation of propaganda.[24]

The rise of such huge industrial armies has revolutionized the way modern wars have been fought. New tactics and strategies emanated from an emerging economic superstructure for warfare. Given the amount of human and material resources demanded by such mass armies, ultimate victory for a belligerent no longer depended so much on individual acts of heroism—if indeed, these mattered at all—as much as it depended on the degree to which that society mobilized its total resources. Modern wars, such as World Wars I and II, necessarily became "gross national product wars" in which, in Russell Weigley's words, "the contest did largely turn upon the question of which rival coalition of powers could outproduce the other." In such warfare, the old moral "Just War" distinctions between combatants and noncombatants have been quickly disregarded as a matter of deliberate war policy. If the enemy nation had involved its entire population in the war effort, a mobilization that had become key to its chances of ultimate victory, then enemy civilians appeared just as much a legitimate target for attack and destruction as enemy soldiers. Under this new reality, nations engaged in modern warfare rather quickly developed tactics of ever more effective naval blockading, wanton destruction of homes and factories, saturation bombing, and finally nuclear deterrence, which transformed enemy civilian populations into targets of attack. As one of the architects of the firebombing of Japan in 1945, U.S. Air Corps General Curtis LeMay grasped this point quite clearly. "There are no innocent people," he recalled after the war. "You are fighting a people, you are not trying to fight an armed force anymore. So it doesn't bother me to be killing the so-called innocent bystanders."[25]

One set of factors giving birth to modern war is socioeconomic; a second emerged, as the above suggests, in ideological developments of the late nineteenth and early twentieth centuries. For much of Western history, asserts Finer, civilians have resisted going off to war; it was a dangerous, tedious, and thoroughly unattractive enterprise. Nor have they generally willingly contributed their resources toward it. Warmaking rulers have thus been left with two ways of obtaining the human and material resources they needed: coercion or persuasion. The latter option was much more effective than the former; indeed, if a population could be sufficiently persuaded to fully support the war effort, they would willingly furnish the necessary people and supplies far beyond what naked coercion could ever hope to accomplish. By the early twentieth century, the state found two mechanisms through which citizens could be rendered willing, even anxious, to go to war: the twin ideologies of nationalism and popular sovereignty. From 1900 to 1945, these ideologies worked beautifully. Popular sovereignty, in which citizens were "represented" by their national legislatures, awarded long-hated measures, such as conscription, a new popular legitimacy. This was accompanied by a reinforcement of the trend from voluntary to universal military service so that every citizen, soldier or not, was expected to participate in the war effort.[26]

So skillfully did modern nation-states learn to exploit the ideological dimension that military service emerged as central in the modern concept of citizenship altogether. Beginning with the American and French Revolutions, Morris Janowitz postulated, willingness to serve in the armed forces became "an integral aspect of the normative definition of citizenship." So much did battlefield sacrifice become the ultimate guarantee and expression of citizenship that American minority groups suffering from discrimination have periodically clamored for the right to serve in the military in order to obtain it. The ideological machinery of total war could be eminently functional for the warmaking state in another way as well. With popular wrath aroused to a fever pitch, home populations could be induced not only to endorse the destruction of enemy civilians but to do so with relish.[27]

The new turn to modern war, in which a nation employs the totality of its resources to destroy the totality of its enemy's resources, has deep implications for people who dissent from the war effort. Individuals who felt compelled to remain uninvolved in the national enterprise began to encounter a host of new problems. With the state now endeavoring to enlist its entire productive capacity in the conflict, it became increasingly difficult to remain immune from the war effort. Even a group of isolated and withdrawn farmers such as the Mennonites met with great troubles in this regard. Conflicts only intensified for them with the pace of acculturation. Was it still sufficient, for example, to imagine oneself as uninvolved in the sin of war when the government urged people, as it did in the First World War, to "Win the War with Wheat," or when it proclaimed "Every Garden a Munitions Plant"? In the Second World War, the state found farming such an essential war industry that it issued widespread military deferments for farmers. Involvement in the total war effort was nearly inescapable. For reasons such as these, argued the *Christian Century* in 1942, "The Christian pacifist is in the fight with all the rest of us. He has no alternative. He accepts the war as his war and fights for victory." How does one retain conscientious scruples against war in a nation at total war? Pacifists would have to wrestle with this question with increasing vigor in the twentieth century.[28]

Moreover, the ideological aspects of modern war issued other, equally thorny problems that people of peace would have to solve. Even if pacifists had found a way to extricate themselves from modern conflicts economically, the ideological intensity accompanying total wars would surely have largely precluded it. Twentieth-century wars have not tolerated dissent very well. American civil liberties came under severe attack in the crusade-like atmosphere of World War I, for instance, as measures such as the Espionage and Sedition Acts of 1917 did much to silence domestic opposition. Although such measures were perhaps a bit excessive, from the state's perspective, the efforts to whip up popular enthusiasm were more than merely functional: they were indispensable for the maximum productivity essential to victory. Lynching, mob action, and curtailment of civil liberties were only unfortunate by-products of this public ardor.[29]

Similarly, while they might have been pacifists, Mennonites and other people of peace also felt the call to proper citizenship as did other Americans. Yet given their refusal to offer the models of sacrifice on the battlefield that emerged as the supreme embodiment of proper citizenship, this call plunged pacifists into a dilemma. They would labor hard to demonstrate their willingness to sacrifice in other ways, searching desperately for what philosopher William James called the "moral equivalent of war."[30]

While pacifists faced their problems about how to maintain their opposition, the state confronted its own dilemma about how to best handle dissent in wartime. In the United States, the solution that has historically emerged from this conflict of interests—though not entirely agreeable to either side—has been conscientious objection. The roots of this notion lay in the particularly American concept of the citizen-soldier. Unlike a number of other nations, Americans have viewed warmaking with suspicion and have, throughout most of their history, avoided a professional military establishment. Accordingly, the development of military service in the United States was marked by a corresponding emphasis on egalitarianism. To set off certain groups or people as not subject to military service has been seen as running counter to the values of an egalitarian society. As the debate over student deferments in the 1960s illustrated, to attempt to do so had dangerous class implications (except in the obvious cases of racial minorities and women, who for most of American history were not subject to the military call because they were widely held to be unequal).[31]

Given that the egalitarian impulse in American political culture stressed universal military service in time of war, the government's ability or willingness to excuse certain groups or individuals for reasons of conscience has appeared rather tenuous, especially as it moved toward the economic and ideological imperatives of total war. The U.S. Constitution awarded conscientious objectors (COs) no particular sanction. Instead, arrangements for them were, in the words of longtime Selective Service Director Lewis B. Hershey, "an indulgence extended to a few." With the new mandates of total war, it became essential to enroll pacifists in the war effort in one way or another. President Wilson attempted to draft COs into the army in World War I. On their refusal, many, including large numbers of Mennonites, were sentenced to long prison terms.[32]

By the late 1930s, the government had begun to rethink this policy of repression. In its official account of conscientious objection in World War II, the Selective Service System admitted bluntly that disallowing it might have produced "considerable opposition to Selective Service operations" and also a "lessening of national unity" (something now so integral to the war effort). The CO systems that resulted—Civilian Public Service (CPS) for World War II and the I-W program for the 1950s and 1960s—were congruent with American political values and in themselves reveal much about the tolerance for dissent in wartime. Because of a clearly limited public tolerance for COs, the concept of egalitarianism would need to override all other considerations. To ensure that objectors underwent an experience somehow commensurate with that of GIs, they would be placed in unrewarding, low-paying (or, in the case of CPS, nonpaying) jobs, far from their homes. This would avoid all appearances of their being "coddled" and would not tempt the insincere draftee to opt for pacifism. Far from detracting from American ideals, officials like Hershey worked to integrate this legitimizing of COs into the American democratic tradition, in this case evidence of American tolerance of minority dissent. To Hershey it was a matter of pride "that today we live in a country where a small minority can enjoy freedom of conscience, and not be placed in concentration camps on account of their belief."[33]

For people of peace, conscientious objection appeared as only a partially satisfactory solution, and one that raised a host of troubling issues. On one hand, a small but important alliance of church groups have repeatedly battled hard to preserve this "indulgence." These were the Friends, the Brethren, and the Mennonites, who by the time of World War II had begun calling themselves the "Historic Peace Churches." Each had its own but not dissimilar reasons for refusing to fight and battled hard for conscientious objection throughout much of this century. While the Friends took the lead in the legislative battles, Mennonites provided the vast majority of actual conscientious objectors, thereby doing much to account for the survival of Christian pacifism into the late twentieth century.[34]

Yet these churches were also increasingly quick to recognize the shortcomings of the alternative service arrangements that they had jointly created with the state. Historian Lawrence Wittner has explored the walkouts, strikes, and other forms of resistance to CPS by objectors unhappy with such aspects as its forced, unpaid nature and the church administration of the camps. While Mennonites were generally much more supportive of the arrangement than the more radical Friends, some of this unhappiness spilled over into their ranks. Moreover, what kind of effective witness was this against war, wondered many of them, when done so conveniently at the government's request and in accordance with the military's wishes? Was this really any kind of dissociation from warfare? Perhaps the whole arrangement was too much of a compromise with the state, pacifists began to argue. For pacifists it was, as one Mennonite pastor cried in 1962, "a course that respects their conscience but costs them nothing and effectively silences their protests against preparations for mass murder." Yet what other course was there? How does one witness against warfare in the economic and ideological milieu of modern war?[35]

WHO ARE THE MENNONITES?

Before further exploring the interplay between social change and church-state relations among the Mennonites, it is necessary to unravel some of the complexities of the Mennonite world. For by the twentieth century, the forces of social change had been at work on them long enough that the appellation of "Mennonite" is really only an umbrella term, covering a wide variety of theological, political, and behavioral understandings among a myriad of related peoples.

To fully understand the Mennonites, it is necessary to reflect at least briefly on their spiritual—and, for many of them, genealogical—ancestors, the Anabaptists. The Anabaptist movement emerged quite early in the ferment and turbulence of the Protestant Reformation, originating in Switzerland in 1525 and then spreading rapidly throughout much of Germany and Holland. Caught up with Luther's attacks on Catholicism, youthful leaders such as Michael Sattler, Conrad Grebel, and Felix Manz found these protests too limited and immediately set out to reform the reformers. Rejecting the state church conceptions of both Catholicism and emerging Protestantism, they called for a voluntary association of believers committed to mutual sharing, a refusal to swear oaths, and pacifism. Though most of the early leaders were martyred soon thereafter, other leaders survived their twenties to maintain and enlarge the group's teaching. One of these, a former Dutch priest named Menno Simons, exercised such an influence that his Anabaptist followers began calling themselves Menists, which later evolved into Mennonites.[36]

The reigning authorities might have ignored these enthusiastic religious dissenters, except that so many people found their vision an attractive one. Calvin Redekop asserts that Anabaptists became "one of the fastest growing religious movements in early modern times," radiating rapidly across the continent. Yet their repeated polemical attacks on both church and secular authority highlighted what appeared as blatant heresy. Not long after the movement had begun, both Protestant and Catholic establishments determined to stamp it out, and the ensuing persecution produced Anabaptist martyrs in staggering numbers. In the movement's first ten years, authorities put more than five thousand of the dissenters to death, including most of the early leaders.[37]

In the end, sustained persecution achieved two main results, both with deep implications for later Mennonite history. First, the persecution finally broke the evangelization efforts among Swiss/South German Anabaptists, who were the most harassed. Predominately an urban movement at first, these Anabaptists finally fled for safety into rural regions, where they developed a much stricter separationist ethic than their church brethren in Holland and North Germany. Correspondingly, in these isolated upland valleys, Mennonites began to make the connection, so influential later, between spiritual purity and agricultural occupations. Here were the roots of the enthnoreligious separation between what later evolved into the two largest Mennonite groups in the United States: descendants of rural-oriented Swiss/South Germans on the one hand, and the more urban, institutionalized, Dutch/North Germans, on the other. The other long-lasting effect of Anabaptist persecution was, of course, massive migration from the centers of maltreatment, a flight that in the eighteenth century began to bring large numbers of Swiss/South German Mennonites to North America.[38]

It is unnecessary to trace here the many migrations made by Mennonites throughout Western and Eastern Europe, Central and South America. Suffice it to say, the bulk of North American immigrants can be divided into essentially these two different streams, a fact that had deep implications for later life in America. One stream consisted mostly of Swiss/South

Germans, descendants of the heavily persecuted Anabaptist group who emigrated to Pennsylvania in the late seventeenth and eighteenth centuries and then filtered westward from this "Pennsylvania heartland." The second stream, which emigrated later, in the 1870s, 1920s, and 1940s, involved mostly Dutch/North Germans who had made generations-long stops in Prussia and South Russia. Even in America this basic geographical distinction continued, with the bulk of the first group oriented toward the eastern states, and the majority of the Dutch/North Germans settling in the Great Plains. So dissimilar were these two streams, and so fundamental are the implications for later Mennonite life, that Mennonite historian James Juhnke characterized North American Mennonites as a "bipolar mosaic." Indeed, Juhnke sketched out a major new reading of the Mennonite experience in America, rooted in a recognition of these two fundamentally different groups.[39]

Accordingly, this study structures itself along these lines of dissimilarity. The persecution-induced Mennonite diaspora sparked a fragmentation of Mennonite church bodies, as noted above, but so also did a developing Mennonite tendency toward internal schisms. The most notable example of such a schism occurred among the Swiss/South German group in the 1690s, when Mennonite leader Jacob Amman began to demand a stricter Mennonite discipline and then excommunicated all who disagreed with him. His followers soon cast off Menno's name and adopted his, becoming known as the Amish. By 1972, such developments had resulted in no less than thirteen duly constituted Mennonite bodies in the United States alone. Eight of these groups had less than ten thousand baptized members. Only two (discounting the Old Order Amish, who, despite sharing common Anabaptist roots, draw a distinction between themselves and present-day Mennonites) had membership totals over twenty thousand.[40] To attempt to give equal weight to every such small group would introduce a labyrinthine complexity that is plainly beyond the scope of this study. Instead, this work limits itself to an examination of the two largest Mennonite groups, which, conveniently, orient themselves around the two major poles of Juhnke's bipolar mosaic.

One major group, the Mennonite Church or "old" Mennonites (henceforth abbreviated as MC or OM)[41] descends from the Swiss/South German emigration stream and is the oldest Mennonite group in America. With more than 89,000 baptized members by 1972, they are also the largest, with a membership total over twice that of the next largest group. With these characteristics, it is easy, but not entirely accurate, to characterize the "old" Mennonites as a kind of Mennonite mother denomination, a perception that the group itself did little to undermine when it began referring to itself as "The Mennonite Church" in the postwar years. As noted above, this group of Mennonite emigrants had several attributes that proved foundational for their life in America: a strong separationist stance, including a marked two-kingdom theology; a strict insistence on Mennonite nonconformity; and an orientation toward agricultural pursuits. In light of this separationist orientation, for two centuries "old" Mennonites wrestled with pressures wrought by outside influences that brought an inescapable splintering. Their relative success in withstanding these changes triggered over twenty-five schisms, either by subgroups unhappy because the OMs had not guarded the tradition carefully enough, or by groups such as General Conference Mennonites, described below, who felt that the Mennonite Church had not changed enough with the times.[42]

"Old" Mennonites did change in response to outside influences, sometimes in accordance with church blessings and sometimes not. Slowly the group fanned out westward, maintaining a geographical heartland in Pennsylvania-Virginia-Ohio-Indiana but establishing a fair number of congregations further west in midwestern states such as Kansas and the Dakotas, and even on the Pacific coast by the early twentieth century. In this geographical dispersion, church leaders found it ever harder to regulate change. After at least a century of theological and cultural stagnation, OM leaders adopted a number of innovations from the evangelical fervor sweeping the nation in the late nineteenth century. In what later leaders referred to as a Mennonite "great awakening" (or, in Theron Schlabach's phrase, a "quickening") of 1880–1910, the Mennonite Church burst forth with missionary endeavors and philanthropic activities as quiet Mennonites became aggressive revivalists. In addition, like other American church groups the "old" Mennonites established patterns of denominationalism at about this same time, creating church-wide committees for education, publishing, and evangelism and finally pulling the disparate OM congregations into a loose denominational structure called the Mennonite General Conference in 1897. While these adoptions from American Protestantism did induce many Mennonites to begin to separate ethics from salvation— and thus paved the way for substantial inroads of Protestant fundamentalism among them—they also demonstrated a new interaction with outside culture.[43]

The second major Mennonite group, the General Conference Mennonite Church (abbreviated as GCMC or GC), did not experience as much of this sort of internal agony over acculturation, mainly because they perceived acculturation in much less negative terms. It was exactly because they found such readiness lacking in the "old" Mennonites that sixteen Mennonite ministers, led by John Oberholtzer, split away from the parent body in the years before the Civil War. These eastern Pennsylvania dissidents demanded a more open and progressive Mennonite church, one that would include such innovations as Sunday schools, mission work, Christian literature, and the formal training of ministers. Gathering other like-minded Mennonite congregations in Ontario, Ohio, and Iowa, in 1860 they formed the General Conference Mennonite Church, with the ultimate goals of uniting all Mennonites, sharing spiritual resources for mission work, and cooperating with non-Mennonite denominations for world mission endeavors. Thus, from the beginning, the GCMC was ecumenical and mission-minded. Moreover, they placed a special emphasis on congregational polity. Congregations, not bishops boards or conference structures, would be the locus of authority, the GCMC decided. The purpose for any denominational structure would not be to enforce hierarchically determined church standards, but to facilitate cooperation in common mission endeavors. They placed their emphasis, as Kauffman and Harder have pointed out, on Mennonite cooperation rather than on "uniformity of behavior." As phrased by a number of church leaders over the years, the GCMC motto would be "unity in essentials, liberty in non-essentials, and love in all things."[44]

Although the GCMC founding congregations originated in the ranks of the "old" Mennonites, the church would be dominated, not long after its founding, by members of a differing ethnic group, the second stream of Juhnke's bipolar Mennonite mosaic. In 1873, the threat that the Russian government might go back on its promise of permanent Mennonite military exemption triggered a large Mennonite exodus.[45] These were originally Dutch/North German Anabaptists who had gradually, over two centuries, settled in Russia when conditions in their host countries grew unfavorable. Now they would move again, about eight thousand succumbing to eager Canadian invitations to settle in Manitoba and ten thousand others in the United States. Accepting promises from U.S. government officials and different railroad companies of military exemption and cheap land, they settled in Minnesota, South Dakota, Nebraska, and especially in Kansas.

Not only did they bring with them the famous Turkish red wheat, which would revolutionize prairie agriculture, but they also arrived with firm institutional inclinations, reflecting their relative autonomy in Russia, where they had functioned as a "state within a state." They thus brought with them a more positive view of governing authority, including a greater willingness to vote and a greater openness to outside society and culture. Long-standing Mennonite thrift had produced a wealth that enabled them to realize their institutional visions. Quickly establishing settlements with schools, hospitals, and newspapers, these German-speaking Dutch-Russian Mennonites soon found the ecumenically minded GCMC much to their liking. By 1964, the descendants of these Russian Mennonites would account for two-thirds of the GCMC's membership.

Because their own group of Anabaptist ancestors, as outlined above, did not suffer as much from persecution and prospered in urban centers in Holland and North Germany, the GCMC did not draw as strict a line against acculturation as did the "old" Mennonites. Still, as Juhnke pointed out, the church did possess and preserve a marked set of ethnic characteristics, including strong mechanisms of boundary maintenance centered in a low-German dialect and other measures of Mennonite culture.[46]

Thus, the General Conference Mennonite Church would remain the most outward-focused of the Mennonite denominations. It united a wide variety of rural and local churches and recent immigrant groups and directed them into mission efforts. Its congregations would allow no Mennonite bishops to maintain a rigid sectarian separation from the world. The GCMC would have no authoritarian patterns of any kind, and its Dutch-Russian majority brought perceptions of openness to outside society stemming back to Anabaptist days. Yet it would not be long into the World War II and the postwar years before GC congregations would discover that such an unrestricted openness had its drawbacks too. Decentralized patterns of authority made it difficult to maintain common Mennonite understandings, as the decisions of Lynn Liechty and many other GC draftees would demonstrate. Diversity was a blessing, but it could also be a curse. By the 1930s, GC congregations ranged from ones steeped in theological/political fundamentalism to neighboring ones receptive to the more liberal understandings of the social gospel. How could they hold to liberty in nonessentials while still hoping to find unity in essentials? Indeed, who would define essentials and nonessentials? Perhaps General Conference Mennonites could avoid the Mennonite Church's bitter battles over nonconformity, but they ran into religious quagmires of their own in the midcentury decades.

These sketches illustrate the degree to which both major Mennonite groups were involved, by the 1940s, in intense internal struggles over outside influences. Caught in the delicate process of brokering these social changes for its people, the church suddenly faced the incursions of the state, with its innumerable military pressures and priorities and its succession of military adventures from the Second World War to Vietnam. The following chapters will trace the story of this confrontation.

CHAPTER 2

Challenges to
Mennonite
Peacemaking,
1914–1939

A few days after Christmas, 1937, Dr. E. L. Harshbarger, Chair of the Peace Committee of the General Conference Mennonite Church (GCMC), sat down to write Rev. A. J. Neuenschwander, the committee's secretary. "This Christmas has been a joyous one in our family," Harshbarger reflected, "but I have felt somewhat depressed with the condition of the world. Furthermore, it doesn't seem to me that we Mennonites are doing very much, either to prepare ourselves for a possible war, or to prevent that war." Looking ahead to the coming year, he added "What can you suggest?"[1]

In his discouraged musing, Harshbarger managed to put his finger on perhaps the two central thrusts of Mennonite peace activity in these interwar years. Shaken by their ordeal in World War I, Mennonite peace committee leaders determined not to be caught so nearly completely by surprise the next time. Accordingly, in the interwar period they would invest a good deal of new energy in their peace program. Their experience in the war produced other positive developments as well. In breaking down Mennonite isolation and in stimulating Mennonite philanthropic activity as their grounds for citizenship, the World War I established patterns the church would draw on again in the next world war.

Moreover, with the war having focused a good deal of their attention on their own peace position, a few Mennonites began to feel that others might benefit from such a perspective. As the cultural and social boundaries they had long constructed between themselves and outside society began to ease, they began to think that perhaps it was time to bring the Mennonite light out from under its cultural bushel. Yet as Harshbarger and his colleagues would discover, Mennonite cultural permeability would admit other, less desirable aspects too. Let loose among both branches of Mennonites, these theological and behavioral currents would considerably complicate the task of preparing themselves for the next world cataclysm.

WORLD WAR I AND ITS AFTERMATH

The First World War hit American Mennonites with considerable force and brought a sense of trauma that would last for a generation. As Europe broke out into the convulsions of war in 1914, Mennonites at first began to stress their Germanic heritage and their identity with the fatherland. The cultural ties with Germany were particularly strong for GC Mennonites in the Great Plains states. Indeed, as the boundaries between themselves and outside society lessened, an increased Germanic identity had begun to function for the GCMC in much the same manner as increased emphasis on nonconformity did for "old" Mennonites: it helped to furnish a sense of separate peoplehood. In such mechanisms as (low) German newspapers and private Mennonite schools conducted in German, many GC Mennonites fashioned a much greater cultural and political identity with the fatherland than their ancestors ever did under the czars.[2]

As world events slowly drew the nation closer to war, however, Mennonites began to consider the more practical matters of life in a nation devoted to waging total war, and they quickly learned that the national war hysteria would not countenance any such pro-German sympathy. Admittedly, the nation's larger Mennonite group, the "old" Mennonites, exhibited little Germanic sympathy; they held much more firmly to Swiss and neutral prescriptions. Still, both groups were pacifist; and for a nation engaged in a holy crusade to "make the world safe for democracy," that was enough to mark them for persecution. The resulting repression focused on these German-speaking pacifists both at home on their farms and also in the military camps.[3]

Thanks to the maneuvering of the secretary of war, who assured Mennonites that their young men would never be forced to violate their consciences, and the misplaced trust in such promises by Mennonite leaders, Mennonite draftees obediently registered for the draft and reported to the camps as instructed by their elders. Once in camp, however, young pacifist draftees found themselves subject to military, not civil law. There military officers had at their disposal more direct and effective mechanisms of persuasion, and many young men who held fast to their convictions suffered severely. Forty-five Mennonite draftees at Camp Travis, Texas, for example, refused an officer's order to don military uniforms. A court martial sentenced them all to life imprisonment at hard labor. Repeatedly, resisting COs were beaten with fists and hoses, forced to stand for hours in the sun, threatened with execution, and reduced to bread and water diets. Ultimately, more than two hundred objectors were unjustly imprisoned. In the end, in the rough compromise that pacifists worked out with military officials, most COs accepted noncombatant status but were furloughed to farm labor work. All imprisoned objectors were released soon after the war.[4]

As the nation embarked on a vicious and high-strung wartime crusade against Germany, a popular wrath at these Germanic, pacifist people extended beyond the military camps to the Mennonite community. Local patriotic watchdogs crusaded to eliminate the German tongue from schools and church services; in Newton, Kansas, the local loyalty league stamped out the teaching of German at the GCMC's Bethel College. Altogether, dozens of individual Mennonites suffered from mob actions during the war. Mobs burned Mennonite churches to the ground in Inola, Oklahoma, and Fairview, Michigan. At numerous locations around the country, Mennonite communities were coerced into buying war bonds through the threat or presence of physical violence by mobs of angry "patriots." In other places, mobs entered Mennonite church services and hung American flags behind the pulpit as the congregation watched in silence or smeared Mennonite churches and homes in yellow paint. At the very least, these and other experiences effectively plunged Mennonites into what historian James Juhnke called the "moral agony of discovering that they were not acceptable as American citizens." In a time when being an American inescapably required full-scale support of the war effort, most Mennonites chose to remain somewhat beyond the pale.[5]

Following the war, in the years of normalcy, it became clear that the abuses of overly zealous officers and the campaigns of the loyalty leagues had effected some lasting changes in Mennonite life. First, whether in retrospect they should have gone or not, thousands of young Mennonite men returned home from army camps having seen a great deal of the outside world. Furthermore, Mennonite leaders had cooperated with each other and with other peace church leaders to an unprecedented degree. While attempting only to remain faithful to Anabaptist teaching, many of these leaders had received another kind of baptism, a baptism by fire in tough political negotiations with cynical, self-serving officials. In this bruising experience, they had at least learned a number of lessons that would prove helpful the next time the church faced such a crisis. In sum, the war years had done much to rub down the edges of Mennonite isolation.[6]

Second, somewhat paradoxically, the persecutions of the great American crusade had in other ways lengthened the distance between Mennonites and outside society. To put it another way, theologically Mennonites emerged from the war with vivid reminders of why their Anabaptist ancestors had spoken so balefully about the dangers of the evil world and had expected the church to be a persecuted, faithful remnant. The experience plainly strengthened the two-kingdom doctrine. Conservatives arguing for Mennonite separation from the world could add a great many painful, recent examples to their arsenal.[7]

Third, and maybe most important, World War I revitalized Mennonite philanthropic activity. Admittedly, Mennonites gave more because they had, in the war years, more to give. Like other farmers, Mennonites benefited directly from the war-induced agricultural prosperity sweeping American rural areas in the late teens and early 1920s. Europeans had turned to fighting rather than farming, and with wartime demands rapidly increased on American suppliers, farm prices escalated dramatically. With consciences rendered uneasy by profits seemingly derived from war, Mennonites poured these surplus funds into church and secular relief agencies. The MC Mennonite Board of Missions and Charities reported receiving $86,000 in gifts in 1917 and $391,000 in 1919. The GCMC's total reported contributions leapt from $360,000 in 1917 to $734,000 in 1920. The massive extra monies made possible a host of new mission and relief activities.[8]

The most important and long-lasting Mennonite relief effort to emerge from the war's turmoil focused on Mennonite concerns and efforts. In 1920, devastated by the war, Mennonites in the Ukraine sent a delegation to seek assistance from their brethren in the West. Encountering the usual plethora of Canadian and American Mennonite groups, all eager to help, the Russian Mennonites requested a single committee to deal with. After a series of careful negotiations in Chicago, Newton, Kansas, and Elkhart, Indiana, North American Mennonites emerged with a new inter-Mennonite agency, the Mennonite Central Committee (MCC), to oversee relief efforts in the Ukraine. Faced with the starvation of thousands of Russian Mennonites, the ecumenical administrators of the new agency threw themselves into the work, funneling Mennonite money and dispatching American volunteers to the Ukraine just in the nick of time. From March

1922 to August 1923, MCC fed 75,000 people, including 60,000 Mennonites. By 1924, Mennonite relief to Russia in the form of food, horses, and
tractors totaled $1.2 million. The initial MCC efforts in Russia lasted until
1925 and saved an estimated 9,000 Mennonites from starvation.[9]

Certainly, Mennonites responded to the social dislocations of war out of
a genuine sense of Christian concern and commitment. Yet it is also clear
that through such benevolent efforts Mennonites expressed their aspira-
tions to citizenship when, because of the calling of the Mennonite heritage,
the accepted routes of fighting and dying for their country were closed to
them. They would overcome the negativity of their military refusal by their
sacrificial giving and service; their good works would prove their worthiness as Americans. As expressed by the Mennonite Brethren leader P. C.
Hiebert, the executive secretary of MCC, here was unmistakable testimony
that Mennonites seized the chance "to disprove the charges of cowardice
and selfishness made against the conscientious objectors, and to express in
a positive, concrete way the principles of peace and goodwill."[10]

Nor was it only Mennonites who turned to sacrificial service as a means
of defining a sense of acceptable pacifist citizenship in wartime. Pacifists of
all stripes also began to express the sacrificial ideal as a demonstration,
short of war, of their patriotism. Three years before Mennonites gave birth
to MCC, activist Friends created the American Friends Service Committee, which sent hundreds of Quaker volunteers to France and Germany.
There they labored diligently in war reconstruction work, attempting to
demonstrate, as did Mennonites, that pacifists would do more than simply
declare their opposition to war and then withdraw. Instead, with the nation
demanding the engagement of all its citizens in the new enterprise of total
war, people of peace would serve in some way that approximated the sacrifices demanded of those in the military. Beyond these impulses in Mennonite efforts, and before Reinhold Niebuhr began to issue his cutting broadsides against pacifist social irresponsibility, such commitments began to
drive the elaboration of a pacifist social ethic in the larger pacifist community and to function as an inducement to social reform.[11]

Finally, beyond an expression of American nationalism in pacifistic
ways, Mennonite postwar philanthropic energies moved markedly toward
the creation of a new Mennonite identity in the midcentury years. In defining a positive image for themselves as citizens, Mennonites also began
to recast their image of themselves as Mennonites. No longer did being
Mennonite mean an inwardly focused orientation on the theological and
cultural patterns of the isolated Mennonite world. Instead, Mennonitism

involved an active, caring aspect as well—an image of compassionate concern for the needy. Otherwise ordinary church members testified straightforwardly to this new momentum. "These are days of sacrifice and suffering," wrote one "old" Mennonite to his local mission board in 1918. It was not right, to him, "that the followers of Jesus . . . should live in pleasure and ease as long as our fellow men are in misery." Altogether, the Mennonite experience in World War I did much to set the stage for the Mennonite response to the next world cataclysm. The starving Mennonite brethren in the Ukraine and the war-induced cultural rejection sparked Mennonites to a whirlwind of activity that would prove foundational for their relationship with the state later in the century.[12]

Certainly Mennonites responded to outside forces with answers that were consonant with their own tradition. Nonetheless, their responses also indicated their increased involvement with outside society, for the process of acculturation gradually intensified in the interwar years. As the Goshen College Bible professor Edward Yoder observed in 1935, "Modern society . . . is becoming increasingly more closely knit and integrated and compacted in a hundred ways." As noted above, beginning in the late nineteenth century Mennonites acquiesced to this pull into national society through various routes partly because they realized that through such influences they could do much to revitalize their own religious traditions. Denominational bureaucracies, Sunday schools, revival meetings, mission agencies—Mennonites seized all these innovations as a means of refashioning their own sense of peoplehood.[13]

In the interwar years, however, they also adopted another outside influence that paradoxically would work both for and against this sense of peoplehood. In particular, it functioned to undermine Mennonite peace understandings. This was the Mennonite adoption of Protestant fundamentalism. Historian George Marsden has argued that fundamentalism emerged in the latter part of the nineteenth century as a mechanism for reassessing the relationship between Christianity and culture in a time of rapid modernization. Beyond a merely theological reaction, fundamentalism had deep cultural reverberations for many Americans. By resolutely turning back to "the Fundamentals," a number of American evangelicals hoped to reverse the "worldly" trend of American culture and to return to a perceived religious rooting.[14]

This interpretation of fundamentalism as a reassessment of cultural and theological issues certainly rang true for American Mennonites, Paul Toews has noted; only for Mennonites it assumed a paradoxical cast. Like

many other Americans, Mennonites grew alarmed over what they perceived as the spread of theological modernism, and they ruthlessly stamped
out whatever vestiges of it appeared in their own ranks in the 1920s and
1930s.[15] Yet Mennonite fundamentalism targeted enemies other than theological modernists, who, in spite of these squabbles, remained relatively
scarce in Mennonite ranks anyway. Instead, theological fundamentalism
among Mennonites reinforced and fed a growing cultural conservatism.[16]

Fundamentalism surfaced in somewhat different manifestations in the
two major Mennonite groups. We will examine both in turn.

THE MENNONITE CHURCH, PEACE PREPARATIONS, AND THE SEARCH FOR A MIDDLE WAY

The expressive link between theological and cultural conservatives becomes clearest among the "old" Mennonites. Certainly, the Mennonite
"great awakening" of the latter nineteenth and early twentieth centuries
had found much of larger Protestantism useful. In this opening-up process,
many Mennonites had imbibed theological conservatism as well. They resonated with the national religious movement that was attempting to turn
the nation back to "the Fundamentals" and to drive out liberal modernism,
root and branch. Although they were glad to join the antimodernist campaign, however, Mennonite fundamentalists identified other dangers even
closer to home. By the 1920s, many culturally conservative OM leaders began to feel that the borrowing had gone on long enough, and they mobilized
to draw the line against further cultural change. Fundamentalism fit like a
glove in this reaction. "If the awakening was an opening up process for MC
Mennonites," Toews maintained, "fundamentalism was a buttoning-down
process." Mennonite Church cultural conservatives, armed with the theological brickbats of fundamentalism, increasingly levied prohibitions
against the Mennonite adoption of the dress styles of ordinary Americans
and their participation in unions, fairs, horse races, and the like. Yet the
paradox in this reaction glitters irresistibly. As conservatives set out to re-
build the mechanisms of separation from outside society, they did so with
implements that they had borrowed from the outside. Primary among
these was an aggressive, polemical fundamentalism, a theology that put a
premium on salvation ahead of ethics—a theology that appeared light-
years away from the humble, nonresistant gospel of peace.[17]

Yet the fundamentalist momentum in the Mennonite Church was reflected and channeled by the emergence of several new and remarkably able
leaders, who would continue to guide the denomination's peace testimony

FIGURE 2.1. *Harold S. Bender,*
April 1, 1946. Mennonite Library
and Archives, Bethel College,
North Newton, Kansas.

into the 1960s. The first of these was Harold S. Bender, perhaps the single most influential and dominating Mennonite leader of this century. Careful, sometimes calculating, but usually brilliant, Bender was a scholar, not a preacher. He would make his greatest contributions to his peoples' identity by focusing on history rather than theology. Even so, his leadership emanated from his uncanny ability to navigate the shifting seas of Mennonite cultural and theological complexity and to unite these sometimes fractious people behind a central vision.

Bender came from fine "old" Mennonite stock. Born to an influential church deacon in Elkhart, Indiana, in 1897, he aimed early at a life in scholarship, graduating from the denomination's flagship college in Goshen, Indiana, in 1918 and then pursuing graduate work at Princeton Seminary. There he studied under the fundamentalist theologian J. Gresham Machen and other Princeton conservatives, who further molded his theological understandings in conservative evangelicalism. Following a strategically important marriage in 1923 to Elizabeth Horsch, daughter of the "old" Mennonite antimodernist publisher and activist John Horsch, he wangled a Princeton fellowship for a year of further study at the German University of Tubingen. Whatever academic gains he acquired there were far overshadowed by his many pilgrimages to the Swiss cities of Zurich, Bern, and Basel, the cradle of MC Anabaptism. In these visits, Bender steeped himself in Anabaptist-Mennonite history and nurtured a notion that a recaptured sense of this history could prove integral to the identity and self-understanding of contemporary Mennonites. Returning from Germany in the fall of 1924, he accepted an invitation to teach history and to manage the library at Goshen College, where he would make his home for the rest of his life.[18]

Though he tended to be domineering in the considerable authority he came to wield in the Mennonite Church, Bender was not interested in power and position for its own sake. Instead, they were only suitable vehicles for the manifestation of a broader vision he cherished for the church. This "Anabaptist Vision" will be detailed below, but for now it is only necessary to realize that Bender found in Anabaptist and Mennonite history the key to a revitalization of the entire Mennonite movement in North America, and he began to act on this intuition by the late 1920s. Even as chair of the Young People's Conference in 1923, he had pushed the study of Mennonite history as the medium for the "enthusiastic and loyal rallying to the historic principles of Mennonitism." A year later at Tubingen, he suggested to the church hierarchy a new publication as a counter to the more liberal *Christian Exponent*. In 1927, now an established leader in his own right, Bender moved to make this happen. The first issue of the *Mennonite Quarterly Review* appeared that January with an ambitious agenda on its title page. There Bender expressed a growing generational consciousness for the young leaders who had emerged from the war and now stood poised to guide the church into the future. Addressed "To the Youth of the Mennonite Church," Bender declared that "the heritage is yours . . . the future is yours. Get the vision . . ." To what seemed to some a tired people, squabbling over theology and riveted on issues of dress and doctrine, Bender proclaimed that "the Golden Age of the Mennonite Church" awaited them. And this "coming generation," embracing this "sound heritage," would take Mennonites, Bender declared, toward a "pure New Testament Church." Along with a number of committed visionaries, Bender would spend much energy in the ensuing years defining such a church. Yet already it was clear that this church would be rooted in ideals of peace and service.[19]

By the early 1930s, Bender had begun to work closely with another Goshen College professor who would indelibly stamp the Mennonite relationship with the state in the twentieth century. Even above the others, he would formulate the bedrock Mennonite ethic on peace and social justice. This was the historian, church leader, and peace activist Guy F. Hershberger. Originally from Iowa, Hershberger was a Mennonite farm boy who went on to teach in rural schools. Newly married in 1920, Hershberger and his bride Clara pointed themselves toward church service. During the war, they had yearned to go to France and engage in relief work with the Quakers. Now married, the couple dreamed of life on the mission field in India, and toward this end they enrolled at Hesston College, an OM school near Newton, Kansas. As Hershberger finished at Hesston and began teaching there, S. C. Yoder, his pastor, bishop, and mentor from Iowa, received the next appointment as president of Goshen College, following the purge of the modernists and closing of the school for a year in 1923–1924. Yoder resolved to take the talented young history teacher with him. Good teachers, he coaxed Hershberger, were even scarcer than good missionaries. After finishing a treatise on Anabaptism and receiving a master's degree from the University of Iowa in 1925 (he would finish a doctorate from the same institution in 1935), Hershberger joined Bender, teaching history and sociology at Goshen.[20]

By nature noncombative and conciliatory, Hershberger studiously avoided theological wrangles. As a concession to cultural pressures in the church, for much of his adult life he donned the required "plain coat"(coat without lapels), though usually only half hiding a more "worldly" necktie beneath it. He more sincerely embraced a conservative evangelical theology that rejected "accretions" such as premillenialism and dispensationalism. At the same time, he gravitated toward issues of peace and justice, firmly believing that these concerns had an application this side of heaven as well. When Hershberger arrived at Goshen College in 1925, Bender began urging him to take up research and writing on peace matters. As early as 1927, Hershberger began to warn of the dangers of American nationalism in the pages of the *Mennonite Quarterly Review*; and that same year, he represented the Peace Problems Committee at a larger meeting of liberal pacifists in St. Louis. He returned firmly convinced of the need to work together with larger pacifism, and by the mid-1930s, he had begun to think deeply about plans for alternative service.[21]

A third comrade in these causes was a young Mennonite named Orie Miller. Though four years older than Bender, Miller shared a number of similarities. Like Bender, Miller grew up in Elkhart County, Indiana, graduated from Goshen College, and aspired to leadership and service within the Mennonite Church. Like Bender, Miller managed to marry well; his bride, Elta Wolf, had a father with a thriving shoe factory in Akron, Pennsylvania, in the midst of the conservative Lancaster Conference. Miller moved there, came aboard as a business partner, and thereby acquired an

FIGURE 2.2. *Orie O. Miller and Family, about 1933. Back row, left to right: Orie, Elta, Lois, Albert. Front Row: John, Daniel. Orie O. Miller Collection, Archives of the Mennonite Church, Goshen, Indiana.*

economic means that left him plenty of time for church work. Originally, Miller had yearned to be a minister like his father. In Lancaster, however, the Lord and the bishops still chose the minister by use of the "lot." In 1918 and twice more in the next decade, the lot fell to someone else and the Lord passed Orie Miller by.[22]

Disappointed but undaunted, Miller applied his gifts as a lay worker. Hearing of a chance to administer war relief in Syria in 1918, Miller eagerly applied to go, leaving his wife and infant daughter for a year. There he wandered aghast among the rubble and devastation left by recent warfare. This deepened the connection in his own mind between the mandates toward peace and service. Writing for an Ohio Mennonite newspaper back home, Miller explained that "since our conscience and [the] doctrine of our church forbid us to take an active part in war, something should be done by our people to show the world the sincerity of our stand." It was not enough, Miller avowed, to simply refuse to participate in war: "In some practical way it should be shown that our religion has life, and the power to minister to the good of humanity."[23]

This did entail taking some risks, however, and in 1920 Miller had an especially close call. The fledgling MCC had sent him and another youthful volunteer, Clayton Kratz, to the Ukraine to begin relief efforts among Russian Mennonites. Soon thereafter, Kratz fell into the hands of the Red Army and disappeared without a trace into the maelstrom of the Russian Revolution, never to be heard from again. Only a chance errand to Constantinople had saved Miller from Kratz's martyrdom.

Meanwhile, Miller proceeded to finish up the work in Russia and embark on a career as MCC's administrator par excellence. He ultimately served for much of his life as MCC's executive secretary and brought the organization's offices to his home property in Akron, Pennsylvania. By 1925, Miller had negotiated in Washington on behalf of Russian Mennonites, attended disarmament conferences, and politicked with Quakers. He had become convinced that his own people had a substantial contribution to make to hopes for world peace.[24]

Ever the activist, Miller moved directly to actualize his own particular vision for the church, part of it located in a renewed denominational peace committee. The Mennonite Church had formed its Peace Problems Committee (PPC) during the trials of World War I to manage the emergency negotiations with governmental officials over the shape of noncombatant service. With the war over and the crises eased, Mennonites felt "completely worn out," a leader remembered. Like the rest of the nation, they eased down to enjoy the years of normalcy. Accordingly, at the "old" Mennonites' churchwide conference in the summer of 1925, leaders had planned to disband the old peace committee. Miller received the news with alarm. "Other wars are coming," he told the chair. "This is no time to let your committee die." Miller made the rounds through the conference and persuasively argued for the committee's continuation. The reorganized committee rewarded his efforts by electing him to serve on it and installing him as committee secretary. Miller would hold the position for the next twenty-eight years.[25]

Miller thus obtained the stature and platform to begin shaping the denomination's peace agenda. In a series of articles in the denominational organ, The Gospel Herald, in 1926–29, Miller emphasized three central tasks for the reconstituted committee. First, Mennonite men returning from the army camps had almost unanimously agreed that the church had not sufficiently prepared them for the trials of wartime. Other peace churches, noted Miller, had a body of their own literature to help inculcate their people in the way of peace; "old" Mennonites could not turn to "a single book devoted exclusively to such ends." Thus, one task for the PPC would be to better nurture the church in its peace position. Secondly,

Miller argued for an increased ecumenical orientation. For four centuries, Mennonites had expressed nonresistance but had been satisfied to "hold this light for ourselves and our children." It was time, Miller maintained, to begin the dialogue with other churches about this tradition. Thirdly, as his efforts in Washington on behalf of Russian Mennonites had taught him, the committee needed to keep open the channels of communication with government.

For conservative ears, Miller and other progressive leaders would phrase this last effort innocently in terms of merely "keeping the government informed." At other times, they outlined broader conceptions of Mennonite-state relations. For instance, consider carefully a revealing clause in the PPC's 1927 report to the Mennonite General Conference meeting. In 1925 the reorganized committee had launched its program with the three points outlined above: (a) peace education in the church; (b) "keeping government informed of our peace position"; and (c) witnessing and conversing on peace with other Christians. In the 1927 report, the committee explained point (b) as

> To represent the church and her position on this doctrine before any departments of our state, provincial and national governments which have to do with legislation or the enforcement of legislation affecting our status as nonresistant Christians *and to encourage officials wherever possible in a wider application of the policy of goodwill rather than that of force and war.*[26] (emphasis added)

Even though the report admitted that on point (b) "very little has been accomplished" and that "neither has much been done" on point (c), it soon became clear that Miller's energy had reinvigorated the committee and had set the tone for forward-looking and quietly aggressive Mennonite Church peace work.

In the next few years, Miller's reshaped Peace Problems Committee would begin to act on the program they had enunciated in 1925. A few examples of the committee's efforts to manifest point (b) should suffice to convey the texture of "old" Mennonite peace witnessing in the interwar years. For instance, in a 1927 letter to William Borah, chairman of the Senate Foreign Relations Committee, these quiet activists touched on a variety of matters. They noted "with much satisfaction" such developments as Borah's 1926 senate resolution proposing the outlawing of war and Coolidge's overtures to other military powers toward another disarmament conference. They expressed concern over such items as "our present relationships with Mexico and Nicaragua" and the growing spread of college military training. The 1928 Kellogg-Briand Pact occasioned a bustle of activity. With the encouragement of denominational peace activists, Mennonite students in the new Goshen College Peace Society sent a letter to Mennonite teachers endorsing the pact, condemning recent defense appropriations in Congress, and calling for letters and petitions to Congress to express Mennonite concerns on such matters. By 1933 the PPC had gone so far as to have disbursed church funds to such secular peace groups as War Resisters International and the Committee Against Militarism in Education.[27]

Of course, all this activity rang warning bells for OM fundamentalists, on watch for any innovation as a possible sign of modernism. "I am more convinced than ever that Orie is a dangerous man," fulminated Lancaster bishop John Mosemann to antimodernist leader John Horsch in 1927. "That man gets machinery in motion that it will take some power to stop." Usually, but not always, Miller could disarm such suspicions with ample doses from an apparently inexhaustible reservoir of traditional Mennonite submissiveness and humility. Nonetheless, in spite of Miller's meekness and Bender's political maneuvering, by the late 1920s the "old" Mennonites rapidly found themselves divided between the moderate progressives[28] dominating their peace committee and their scholarship, and a noisy, influential wing of fundamentalists neadquartered especially in the Lancaster and Virginia Conferences. It was an inauspicious set of circumstances with which to begin to prepare for peace in a nation veering again toward total war.[29]

Caught up in their dualistic worldview, OM conservatives could interpret anything but the most apolitical, salvation-centered activities as a Trojan horse for creeping modernism. They especially railed against the burgeoning national peace movement of the late 1920s and 1930s. Perceived Mennonite association with such a movement appeared particularly threatening. According to Mosemann, for example, the modern peace movement was "nothing less than a Satanic delusion, a mighty and deceptive force intended to deceive the Church of Christ and lead her headlong into the clutches of modernistic and liberalistic leaders." Mennonites should keep their distance from the likes of Harry Emerson Fosdick, Shailer Matthews, and other "semi-infidels." Even other HPCs were suspect. While individual Quakers, Brethren, and "liberal" Mennonites appeared orthodox and well-meaning, reasoned conservatives such as Mosemann and Horsch, their leaders were dangerously compromised with modernism.[30]

Admittedly, OM fundamentalists were men who turned to fundamentalism, not as a basis for an increased ecumenical orientation with biblically correct non-Mennonites, but as a reinforcement for their separatist impulses. Even so, from the beginning of Miller's efforts to lead the church into a quiet Mennonite peace activism, he began to encounter increasing resistance from such vocal and energetic conservatives.

In August 1926, Mosemann wrote Miller a lengthy letter, arguing that "war is part of the government's duty, a means of carrying out justice," and then moving on into a long premillennial explication designed to show that world peace would only arrive in the last days. At any rate, Mosemann argued that peace activities are irrelevant in the present age, that "the whole world lieth in wickedness, that the devil is loose and not bound in this dispensation." Miller replied respectfully a week later, answering Mosemann's objections point by point and asking, "What would be legitimate work for a Mennonite peace committee?" Legitimate work for the PPC, came Mosemann's prompt reply, would be to "keep in touch with any pending legislation" that might concern their people and to "show the utter fallacy of the modern peace movement." Beyond this, the bishop wrote, their efforts should devolve on preaching the gospel and having no illusions that "the golden era of world peace will be brought to pass by the efforts of men." Indeed, in the premillennialist mindset accepted by Mosemann, efforts to improve the world through humanitarian reform might even delay the return of Christ. The PPC's letter to Senator Borah filled the bishop with foreboding. Such prescriptions of policy to the state plainly contradicted, to him, the separation God had intended between the two kingdoms, the dark world and saved church.[31]

In such differing perspectives, particularly on the degree to which they demanded Mennonite withdrawal from the pain and problems of outside society, lay the fundamental lines of cleavage between fundamentalists like Mosemann and Virginia Conference bishop George R. Brunk on one side, and more engaged OM peace leaders on the other. It is important to recognize that these "progressive" peace leaders were no wild-eyed disciples of Gandhi or even of Harry Emerson Fosdick. They were profoundly conservative men. A member of the Lancaster Conference, Miller adhered carefully to the traditional conceptions of the Mennonite dress code, donning the Mennonite "plain coat" for most of his adult life. Son-in-law to the Mennonite antimodernist crusader John Horsch, Harold Bender clung so closely to theological orthodoxy that, as head of Goshen College's Bible Department, he could once accuse no less than arch-fundamentalist

George Brunk of modernism. Hershberger disagreed with religious liberalism, not because he did not respect people such as the social gospel crusader Walter Rauschenbush, but because liberal prescriptions did not square with conservative evangelical theology, a theology dear to the heart of these peace leaders. Political reforms would not usher in the kingdom of God, Hershberger argued, because they did not take into account the depths of human sin. These men, particularly in these years, remained firmly wedded to Anabaptist two-kingdom understandings.[32]

Rodney Sawatsky has assembled an interesting case that, in response to fundamentalist pressures, PPC leaders dramatically modified their definition of nonresistance to a passivistic, apolitical conception. At times, to be sure, OM peace leaders appeared to slightly modify their positions in the 1930s in order to suit their more conservative brethren or to phrase their terms in more traditional Mennonite language. In 1929, for instance, Miller aired his belief that Mennonites are "nonresistants rather than pacifists; biblical objectors rather than conscientious objectors." Any peace activity "aside from an all-inclusive Christian program," stated Miller, "has seemed to us largely futile in its ultimate results." Likewise, Hershberger, then a young history professor at Goshen College, offered a conception of nonresistance as "altogether nonpolitical in faith and practice." Yet to interpret such statements as a wholesale collapse by the Peace Problems Committee to the forces of OM fundamentalism appears at times to be a somewhat selective reading of the evidence.[33]

For in spite of such conservative predilections—or perhaps because of them—MC peace leaders continued to work toward a responsible Mennonite peace activism throughout the 1930s. In other words, they began to grope toward what a later generation would call a "third way"—between a salvation-focused fundamentalism on one hand, and a religious liberalism espousing political reforms on the other. Sometimes this meant some practical concessions to the fundamentalists, like agreeing to wear the plain coat. Men like Brunk and Mosemann pulled heavy weight in the church, and the committee would need to try to placate them. Mennonites had historically been a fractious people, and church schisms had occurred over lesser issues than these. Accordingly, as Miller's activism came under increasing fire from conservatives in the later 1920s, he moved to soothe fundamentalist fears. Since Mosemann and others interpreted the Continuation Committee of the Conference of Pacifist Churches as a dangerous liaison with modernism, Miller promptly resigned from the committee—and then continued to diligently work with it as an official "observer."

When Mosemann warned Miller that his innovations might cause him to "lose out in Lancaster County," Miller disarmed him with his own humility. "I am sure I want to do right and try to serve obediently and submissively the Master and His Church," Miller wrote. "Will you pray for me that I may be kept more faithful and more watchful yes and more humbly submissive in life, attitude and mind?"[34]

Thus while sometimes widening their distance from liberalism, activists such as Miller and others continued efforts to stake out a moderately progressive peace stance. The best early example of a search for such a middle ground occurred at a "Mennonite Conference on War and Peace" convened at Goshen, Indiana, in 1935. A number of church leaders advanced their respective fundamentalist/activist positions at this conference, and they differed on now-predictable lines of fracture.

More noteworthy are several newer stances aired by the relatively progressive wing in the conference papers and discussions. In his considerations of "Is alternative service desirable and possible?" Hershberger introduced a concept that would receive increased Mennonite attention and discussion in the years ahead. Particularly striking was his endorsement of absolute refusal to serve in the military. "Indeed, this is the only course of action which a nonresistant people can take consistently," he declared, unless the government provided some kind of alternative service. Clearly they had learned a few lessons from the First World War. Moreover, Hershberger equally as plainly laid out the task ahead, discerning that "the position of nonresistant Christians in time of war promises to become increasingly difficult unless they themselves provide some means to relieve the situation." Sketching out a conscientious objector program that would resemble in many ways what ultimately came to life in Civilian Public Service (CPS), Hershberger thus provided what one scholar termed the "intellectual articulation of what would be the Mennonite negotiating position."[35]

The most important and far-reaching address came from Harold Bender, a scholar who now stood positioned to speak to both camps. After an introduction framing his thoughts in Mennonite history, Bender outlined some of the goals the church should keep in mind when addressing the state. Certainly, he reasoned, the church should "present the truth of God to the powers that be," even to the extent of informing rulers "of the will of God for their conduct in office." While Bender immediately sought to qualify such notions—such presentations would not involve "pressure" from the church, "the church should not 'lobby'"—clearly he subtly planted the seeds for a notion of witnessing to the state. Altogether it was a masterful address. Bender managed to outline a role and function for a Mennonite peace witness that awarded it some initiative but at the same time included enough qualifiers to avoid triggering the wrath of denominational conservatives.[36] The following year, Bender replaced E. L. Frey as chair of the Peace Problems Committee, a position he would hold for most of the next twenty-five years.

In 1937, peace activists moved to manifest their moderately progressive stance by formulating and obtaining conference approval for a new conference peace statement. The committee offered the statement because of "the present troubled state of world affairs, with wars and rumors of wars threatening the peace of the world." In such perilous times, as Sawatsky has noted, the committee felt the need to unify the conference once again on the issue. In presenting the statement, which was largely written by Bender, the PPC made it quite plain that they were not springing any new creed on the church. The statement was clearly a reaffirmation of the traditional Mennonite position against war. It reviewed the thick bundle of scriptural injunctions upon which Mennonites had always based their nonparticipation in warfare. From these scriptures, the statement declared forthrightly, "We believe that war is altogether contrary to the teaching and spirit of Christ and the gospel, that therefore war is sin, as is all manner of carnal strife; that it is wrong in spirit and method as well as in purpose, and destructive in its results."[37]

From this general position, the statement went on to specifically lay out its implications. This foundational Mennonite understanding ruled out, for instance, participation in the military in either combatant or noncombatant roles. Hence, the church "must consider members who violate these principles as transgressors and out of fellowship with the church." Equally as precisely, the statement denounced wartime participation in such activities as the YMCA and the Red Cross, purchasing war bonds, working in armaments manufacturing, or partaking in college military training programs. If Mennonites inadvertently made "a profit out of war," they should donate such gains to relief and mission work. The statement also underscored the Mennonite service orientation that had developed in previous wars, affirming that "we are willing at all times to aid in the relief of those in need, distress, or suffering." Furthermore, the Mennonite wartime attitude should be "a meek and submissive spirit," avoiding war-induced hysteria or cries of revenge and "being obedient unto the laws and regulations of the government in all things, except in such cases where obedience to the government would cause us to violate the teachings of the scriptures."

Surely conservative Mennonites of all stripes could sign onto such pre-scriptions. Finally, in its efforts to produce a statement that all church members could rally behind, the statement carefully avoided avowed direc-tions to government that could evoke fundamentalist censure. The closest it came was a rather innocuous "desire to endorse the policy of neutrality and nonparticipation in the disputes between other nations." This phrase was framed within bounteous expressions of patriotism and national appreciation.[38]

The conference rewarded the committee's careful work with an easy and wholehearted approval of the statement, an endorsement that was soon fol-lowed by similar approval in district conferences. The only place where the statement ran into any modification was, predictably, Virginia. There the fundamentalist-oriented bishops added several provisions. One expressed their displeasure at the associations Miller and others were making with liberal pacifists. Another relayed the conference's dissatisfaction with the PPC's meek prescriptions about neutrality, declaring, "We do not favor giving advice to the government in any way." Still, even the Virginians en-dorsed the statement, a significant achievement for the PPC. The church's position had been phrased carefully and conservatively enough that it could unify the church behind it and obtain common agreement for a founda-tional OM statement on warfare. Indeed, the statement would prove quite useful beyond their own ranks. For their denominational peace statement in 1941, the General Conference Mennonite Church simply extracted most of it verbatim from this 1937 MC statement.[39]

Overall then, MC peace leaders had good reason to be satisfied with their efforts as the horror of war once again broke out in Europe in 1939–1940. Throughout the interwar period they had successfully articulated a peace witness that was broad and carefully stated enough to unify at least a large bulk of the church behind it. Moreover, they had done much to inculcate their flock in this peace position in the face of a determined and vocal fund-amentalist dissent from their own ranks. Whether the committee had done enough along these lines would be seen in the war that loomed menacingly by 1940.

GENERAL CONFERENCE MENNONITES, PEACE PREPARATIONS, AND THE PERILS OF CONGREGATIONAL POLITY

Like the MC Peace Problems Committee, the Peace Committee (PC) of the General Conference Mennonite Church was completely in the hands of the church's more activist leaders from its inception. Also like their MC brethren, these GC progressives would face an opposition informed and shaped by patterns of interwar fundamentalism. Beyond these basic similarities, however, the differences between the experiences of these two Mennonite groups are striking. The congregational polity of the GCMC presented its peace committee with a veritable kaleidoscope of theological/cultural nuances and subtleties that influenced the shape of the denomination's peace position at nearly every turn.

The Peace Committee received its official impetus in 1926 when the GCMC, meeting in Berne, Indiana, appointed it to replace the wartime Committee on Exemption. Initially, the PC consisted only of three people, who devoted themselves to the tasks of producing peace-oriented Sunday school materials and participating as they could with the larger Christian and secular peace activities of the era. In the ecumenically oriented GCMC, such wider peace collaboration triggered no separatist-minded conservative uproar. In fact, part of the committee's founding mandate specified cooperation "with other pacifist churches and other peace organizations." Admittedly, one committee member, the prominent Rev. H. P. Krehbiel, insisted that the committee distinguish between religiously and politically motivated pacifism. Krehbiel articulated the decisions of one important sector of the church to pursue "Christian peace," rooted in an "unfaltering acceptance of Jesus' teaching" and rejecting "any and all political admixture." Yet it was this same pastor who almost single-handedly convened the meeting of the Historic Peace Churches at Bethel College in 1935, arguing that it was time for the "friends of peace" to end a self-imposed sectarian isolation and work together on their common tasks.[40]

By the later 1930s, new leaders had emerged to continue in such a forward-looking orientation. Professor of history at Bethel, Dr. E. L. Harshbarger succeeded H. P. Krehbiel as the Peace Committee chair in 1935 and guided it until his premature death in 1942. Harshbarger came from a Swiss/South German Mennonite background, which placed him somewhat at odds with the Dutch/North German tenor of much of the rest of the church. Moreover, while holding onto the Mennonite religious tradition, Harshbarger's commitment to pacifism did not stem as much from scriptural injunctions as from an analysis of international relations, the focus of his doctoral program at Ohio State. With such an orientation, Harshbarger balanced his committee work around frequent trips to Chicago and Washington to meet with other pacifist groups and did much to move the committee toward a more overtly political focus.[41]

Harshbarger's activist outlook was continued by the committee's new secretary in 1938, the Rev. Ernest J. Bohn from eastern Pennsylvania. Bohn fully believed in "the power of nonresistance," a term that MC peace leaders would have found internally contradictory. As expounded in his pamphlet, *Christian Peace*, published by the committee in 1938, Bohn offered "an active nonresistance which somehow exercise(s) a wonderfully positive influence which is irresistible when used against opponents." The concept appeared to owe much to Gandhian nonviolence, influences Bohn underscored by his reference to Richard Gregg's *The Power of Nonviolence*.[42]

Beyond Bohn's and Harshbarger's plainly political and activist conceptions, the broad GCMC framework encompassed even more direct-action oriented Mennonites. Such a man was Carl Landes, who formed his Mennonite Peace Society, a "Peace Fellowship" of roughly 150 members, in 1936. A GC minister who moved comfortably in Friends circles, Landes would provide a role model for many young Mennonites who yearned for a more hands-on approach to poverty and injustice. From his home in a Friends home-mission site among poor miners in southwestern Pennsylvania, Landes and his members doggedly plugged away at peace education efforts within the GCMC and larger peace witness activities beyond it. As Landes outlined in the pages of *The Mennonite*, the denominational weekly, he had seen much "demoralization" among Mennonite youth in the First World War because the church had "told them 'not to fight' but did not tell them 'what else to do.'" "With that picture in mind," Landes declared, "we need to share with the world our testimony of peace."[43]

These brief sketches make abundantly clear the wide scope of political outlook and cultural behavior coexisting under the common roof of the Mennonite peace position in the interwar years. Indeed, the wide variation seen here makes it problematic even to refer to a single "Mennonite peace position." In their understandings of the larger peace movement and proper Mennonite political activity and behavior, Mennonites such as Harshbarger, Bohn, and Landes were plainly light-years away from Bishop Mosemann or even Orie Miller. Moreover, these GCMC peace leaders certainly had comparably much more latitude for such sentiments, for in their denomination, they faced no organized body of theological/cultural resistance demanding strict Mennonite separation. Such an organized body of dissent would have had a hard time forming in the heavily pluralist GCMC, for the very nature of the GCMC inhibited such groups.

Instead, the Peace Committee would hear objections and suggestions from all sides of the political spectrum in accordance with the widely varying outlooks in the congregations. In fact, it is arguable that the absence of any conflicting centers of authority within the GCMC—or any structures of authority altogether, beyond the authority of the congregation—made things even harder for the denomination's Peace Committee. For the committee faced currents of opposition to its program from many GC churches, and the locus of authority within the congregations left church leaders with few weapons to combat that opposition, outside of efforts at persuasion through several channels. At times this resistance would take identifiable shape in coalitions of individual pastors and churches. At other times, the aversion to the GCMC peace program ebbed and flowed through individual, scattered congregations or even in factions within congregations. Yet ideologically and theologically, this resistance primarily stemmed from a substantial segment of the GC Mennonite body who were attracted to fundamentalism.

A number of sources speak to the influence of fundamentalism on GC Mennonite nonresistance. In the Midwest, such influences seemed to radiate primarily out of Chicago's Moody Bible Institute. Henry Fast, employed as the Peace Committee's executive secretary in 1940, testified to this fundamentalist infiltration into GCMC churches. Peace education, Fast wrote to Donovan Smucker in 1940, has been "pretty largely neglected" in the Northern District (primarily Minnesota and the Dakotas). The fundamentalist influence was so pronounced in this district that Fast termed it "the Bible Institute Area." In Fast's estimation, Mennonite peace beliefs fared little better in other districts for similar reasons. Writing to Bluffton College professor Russell Lantz, he observed that "the middle district" (roughly Illinois, Indiana, and Ohio) as well as the Eastern District (eastern Pennsylvania) "has a few individual ministers who do not hold our historic Mennonite position toward war. They are almost invariably men who have drunk deeply from the well of the Bible institutes." Bohn underscored Fast's comments for his home district in eastern Pennsylvania. There, Bohn admitted, "The Mennonites of the General Conference in the Eastern District have been out of touch with peace teachings so long, that some of them have come to think of it as a radical modern doctrine."[44]

While fundamentalism thus made extensive inroads into many GC congregations, it is important to note that this was a theological current without most of the attached aspects of cultural conservatism common among the "old" Mennonites. With the relative openness to outside culture inherited from their Dutch/ Russian forebears, GC Mennonites did not spawn these same fundamentalist voices organizing to battle Mennonite cultural drift or waging high-strung campaigns to enforce nonconformity. Instead, fundamentalism took shade among GC pastors and congregations in the same way it did among many Protestants in general: in a near-exclusive focus on salvation as the only way to peace. Influenced somewhat by touches of premillenialism, in this formulation biblical peace was exclusively derived from a saving relationship with Jesus. Thus, one should direct one's premier efforts toward evangelism and not toward this-worldly and temporary pacifistic matters. Harshbarger provided a concise, contemporary summary of this perspective, complaining in 1936 to Landes that local, district peace committees "have done nothing" except "bark up the same old tree: stressing the peace principle of Mennonitism and the scriptural references to individual peace as the only way to secure world peace."[45]

Like their MC comrades, GC fundamentalists found that such a theological conservatism easily lead to an extreme political conservatism as well. For many of them, this political conservatism followed along the lines of cultural inheritances in the larger GCMC world, in this instance calling not for separation, but for affection for the old fatherland. As in the years before World War I, cultural affinities toward Germany ran especially deep among the GC descendants of German Mennonite colonies in Russia. At times, GC publications demonstrated an avowed pro-German attitude in these years. John Thierstein, editor of *The Mennonite* from 1937 to 1941, regarded growing American disfavor toward Germany as an "unfortunate situation . . . for our country owes much to Germany and its citizens of German extraction." "As for her Nazi government," Thierstein continued, "if that suits her, let her try it out." By the late 1930s, certain Mennonites even evinced a willingness to go along with some of Nazism's special horror. While in 1938 Rev. P. H. Richert condemned Hitler's Jewish persecutions as "absolutely unscriptural and unchristian," he judged Hitler's campaign against "Bolshevist Jews" a different matter: "Who would not give him credit for that, even if one cannot approve of the method he uses."[46]

Sympathy for fascism overseas could extend more widely to semifascist sympathies at home. The propaganda and politics of the right-wing evangelist Gerald Winrod, for instance, touched chords of support among many Kansas Mennonites in the late 1930s. They had shown a marked proclivity to supporting maverick politicians with a moralistic aura, as evidenced in their pronounced enthusiasm for LaFollette progressivism in

1924 and for the evangelical, antipolitical campaign of gubernatorial candidate John Brinkley in 1930. Similarly, the heavy Mennonite support for Winrod's 1938 campaign for the U.S. Senate from Kansas stemmed not from attraction to Winrod's anti-Semitism or to his wild conspiracy theories. Instead, the political naiveté of Mennonites rendered them ripe for the picking by such a wily, evangelical anti-Semite who could offer a vote for public morality and religion and against political machinations. Kansas Mennonites awarded 60 percent of their votes to Winrod in 1938.[47]

Harshbarger and his colleagues on the Peace Committee had their work clearly cut out for them if they were to somehow help their nonresistant people resist the pressures to fight that drew ever closer with the coming war. They labored on a number of fronts. Harshbarger offered a regular stream of peace articles in the denominational organ. They nurtured the work of peace committees in different districts and individual congregations, and they struggled to raise monies for their work. Most importantly, in 1940 the committee had the good sense and the funds to employ Dr. Henry Fast as a full-time executive secretary. This move would have more beneficial results than either Fast or his employers realized at the time.[48]

In obtaining Fast's services, the Peace Committee found a man almost uniquely suited for the nearly overwhelming task at hand. Fast had been one of the few WWI draftees to emerge from the camps and rise to positions of church leadership. Graduating from Bethel College in 1917, he had pastored congregations in Newton, Kansas, and Hartford, Connecticut, before obtaining a doctorate in New Testament from Hartford Theological Seminary. From 1936 to 1940, the GCMC had employed him as a "field secretary" and sent him visiting congregations all over the United States and Canada to speak of missions and other denominational concerns. There he developed a firm rooting in the congregations and a wealth of personal contacts. Moreover, in contrast to the scholarly Harshbarger, Fast had a biblical rooting and an effective presence in the churches. He could preach convincing and biblically sound peace sermons; he could write a persuasive letter to a fundamentalist doubter. In June of 1940, the Western District's peace committee signed him up as a special "Peace Secretary," an assignment that lasted until September when the GC Peace Committee took over Fast's services for similar functions. Immediately, Fast plunged into the work, visiting churches to preach nonresistance, responding to questions from anxious young Mennonites concerning the coming draft, and organizing a Mennonite dissent to the looming draft legislation. More

FIGURE 2.3. *Henry Fast as he returned from CPS administration to serve as Professor of Bible at Bethel College, 1943. Mennonite Library and Archives, Bethel College, North Newton, Kansas.*

FIGURE 2.4. *Elmer Ediger as a sophomore in the Bethel College yearbook, 1938. Mennonite Library and Archives, Bethel College, North Newton, Kansas.*

FIGURE 2.5. *Robert Kreider, finishing his administrative work with CPS, 1945. Mennonite Library and Archives, Bethel College, North Newton, Kansas.*

fundamentally, along with Harshbarger, Fast began making regular trips to Washington in the mounting negotiations over what would become the CPS Program.[49]

Another bright spot emerged in March of 1939, when Harshbarger received a note from "a group of us young Mennonites . . . eager to aid in some way the furtherance of the basic principles of our church." The group felt that "our Mennonite doctrine of nonresistance is needed in this world" and believed that "an expression of this doctrine should be made now, in time of peace, as well as wartime." They were aware, the group members declared, that merely opting for a conscientious objector position "is not enough to give the world our message of Christian love." Thus, the group asked Harshbarger for suggestions of practical means by which it might concretely express "our Christian peace principle now."

To be sure, GCMC youth had appeared to be especially interested in peace and service work earlier than 1939 and in places other than Bethel. When Carl Landes began his work in 1936 focusing on peace enthusiasm among Mennonite youth, Harshbarger relayed to him that April, "There is considerable interest among the young people, that is those who are alive and thinking." Yet by the late 1930s, a small nucleus of future peace leaders had collected at Bethel and had led the campus into a hubbub of peace and service activism that would not appear on Mennonite campuses again until the 1960s. Because of their later influence on the development of a renewed peace ethic in the postwar years, a few of these young activists deserve a brief introduction here.[50]

One of these was Elmer Ediger. Son of a GC Mennonite farmer and preacher, Ediger arrived at Bethel in the mid-1930s and studied history and politics under Professor Harshbarger. By nature an organizer and activist with an ache for social justice, Ediger quickly associated with the national Student Christian Movement and its models of Christian activism. One aspect of this movement was pacifism, a position that fit well into his Mennonite tradition. Another aspect was socialism. "All through my years at Bethel College we were strong socialists," Ediger remembers, "that wasn't exceptional." Upon graduation in the summer of 1941, Ediger went directly to the "Harlem Ashram," a communal living arrangement organized by a Gandhian disciple in conjunction with the Quakers in the ghettos of New York City. There he came into contact with a number of religious activists, including the young Bayard Rustin, and a number of Union Theological Seminary students who would soon be imprisoned for refusing to register for the draft. There, too, Ediger deepened his understanding of Gandhian nonviolence, helping to organize what the ashram's leader J. Holmes Smith characterized as a "non-Violent Army." Ediger had a heady time in New York City, picketing with the War Resisters League, visiting different pacifist groups, and even, he reported home excitedly, "getting into a town hall meeting and thus cornering the one and only R Neibur [*sic*]." He returned to Newton that fall determined to form similar Mennonite work camps for maximizing social justice. A quickly formed group took their idea to the president of the GCMC, who was cautiously receptive to the notion, though emphasizing that it should occur through formally trained missionaries. "Throwing this out to anybody who wanted to participate was an entirely new, strange kind of concept," recalled a compatriot, Esko Loewen.[51]

Robert Kreider was another young activist who would fill a number of important administrative and educational posts for the church and exercise considerable influence on its peace ethic. The son of a Bethel professor, Kreider cut his intellectual teeth on concepts of nonresistance and pacifism, in particular stories of Mennonites like Orie Miller feeding the hungry in the Ukraine. "I always knew I was a CO," Kreider remembered later. He rallied around these ideas quite naturally when he arrived at Bethel in 1935. Like Ediger, he studied carefully under Harshbarger, embraced the Christian socialism of Norman Thomas, and participated in Quaker work camps. Together these campus organizers pushed the local peace club into high gear, wrote activist columns in the school paper, and explored hands-on peace work in local service projects.

Bethel College, to be sure, was home to a number of students from the opposite viewpoint. Much more missions oriented and focused on evangelism, these students downplayed their pacifism and entered into a good many arguments with the campus activists. Still, it appears that at least in the prewar years, this theological/political conservatism was a pronounced minority position at Bethel. A campus poll in 1938 turned up 129 students who pledged their refusal to fight in any war, only 21 declaring their willingness to go abroad to participate in a declared war. Even more revealing, in a straw poll oriented around the 1936 presidential election, Socialist candidate Thomas emerged as the clear Bethel student preference, finishing ahead even of Alfred Landon, the Kansas governor and Republican candidate.[52]

Certainly the budding peace and service commitments of such Mennonite young people gladdened the hearts of Dr. Harshbarger and other hard-pressed members of the GC Peace Committee. It is unfortunate that

Harshbarger's death in 1942 kept him from being able to watch the impressive performance of several of these young men in important administrative posts in the CPS program. Such a knowledge would have been particularly uplifting after the discouraging years of the late 1930s. For in the acid test of its effectiveness in inculcating the peace position, the preliminary signals received by Harshbarger and others could give them little solace.

It was clear that there was confusion in the minds of the young men who would soon face the draft. At a gathering of draft-age young men, a California minister wrote to the conference president in 1939, he asked the fellows what they would do when the draft call came. "Well, as I expected," the minister relayed with much alarm, "these young Mennonite men said they did not know what to do. We talked more about it and it proves anew to me that our church and conference is failing to enlighten our young men on our stand in matters of carrying arms, and killing." The pastor had never even heard of the GC Peace Committee.[53] Others, who had, appeared similarly bewildered and concerned. A young Mennonite wrote to Fast in July, 1940, for instance, to ask what he and other such men should do in light of the imminent passage of the Burke-Wadsworth Bill (the draft legislation). Though acknowledging that "some religious or civil relief service would be much more acceptable to me and many other young men with whom I have spoken," this possible draftee listed noncombatant work in the army "as a second 'sensible alternative.'"[54] Evidently a great deal of confusion existed among young people as to what the church deemed acceptable, even at this late date. One Nebraska pastor wrote Fast the same month seeking his advice as to the permissibility of military-related flight training that two of his young men had enrolled for, while relating that another had joined the naval reserve. Reports of comparable uncertainty in the Dakotas came to Harshbarger. In a congregation there, revealed an informant, numbers of young Mennonites had begun to enlist in noncombatant service. Knowing little about conscientious objection, and with the World War I precedent in mind, by early enlistment they at least hoped they could choose their form of service.[55]

The Peace Committee had labored hard and faithfully to teach a consistent peace position through the interwar period, yet they faced a great number of obstacles in this endeavor. Most of them were rooted in the fact that the deeply pluralistic GCMC had no central authority figures to define the essentials of their faith. Certainly, scholars and pastors such as Harshbarger, Bohn, and Fast commanded a great deal of respect and influence among many GC Mennonites. Yet when these distant leaders counseled one course and one's own pastor urged another, which had the greater credibility? For a common answer, it is unnecessary to look farther than the response of Lynn Liechty.

It is clear that as Mennonites emerged from the trials of World War I, they enjoyed no period of denominational respite and recuperation. For the pressures on the Mennonite community accelerated accordingly, and increased cultural permeability admitted new theological and cultural currents that registered deep reverberations in Mennonite ranks. As the 1930s wore on, moreover, this increasingly appeared an inauspicious time in which to work out such tensions. With the state's record of repression in the last war and telling signs that it was capable of worse in the next one, Mennonites could ill afford much divisions in their ranks.

Preparations for the next total war proceeded apace in the interwar years. Even amidst the high tide of American isolationism, Franklin Roosevelt had begun to press for large increases in American defense expenditures by the later 1930s. Though nowhere near matching the military preparations of Germany or Japan, American aircraft production, for instance, nearly doubled between 1937 and 1938; and the navy received massive new monies enabling a similar expansion. The army, meanwhile, formulated plans to mobilize a vast force in the event of war. If the reality, moreover, at all matched the theory, the next conflict would wreak a human devastation and destruction beyond even that inflicted by the last. It was during these years, argue scholars such as Ronald Schaffer and Russell Weigley, that military planners developed the foundations of the air war doctrine that would be perfected in the saturation bombing of Japan in 1945. Articulated first by the fascist Italian general Giulio Douhet and popularized in this country by the controversial Air Service general Billy Mitchell, this doctrine focused on mass indiscriminate bombing of civilian areas as the preeminent path to quick victory in the next total conflict. With their morale destroyed, societies thus terrorized would simply collapse, the theory held, and so would their ability to make war.[56]

Mennonites obviously did not attend the Air Corps Tactical School where these theories were absorbed by future air war leaders, nor is there evidence that they noted Mitchell's more widespread writings. Nonetheless, they did recognize that the kind of world that gave birth to such theories posed increasing dangers for people of peace. In 1935, for example, Hershberger compared the situation of American Mennonites to that of European Mennonites in the late nineteenth century. The nonresistance of

European Mennonites had eroded rapidly in the climate of nationalism and new mass armies that ensued. In the event of another total war, he warned, even in this country the state would probably only offer two options to "nonresistant people"—the military or prison. As the international crises escalated later in the decade, the GC historian C. Henry Smith took a similarly pessimistic view. In 1938, fearing that as the First World War experience had indicated the American state had begun to mirror totalitarian ones in designating itself as the locus of ultimate loyalty and worship, he worried that it would be even more difficult to secure the right of dissent in future conflicts. A year later, H. S. Bender also read the signs of the times. "It is becoming increasingly clear to all of us that the next war will become a totalitarian war in which all the resources of the nation will be harnessed to the supreme goal of winning a complete victory," he anticipated. "Thus our own native America may still be the scene of a serious conflict between the Mennonite church and the state."[57] This conflict drew ever closer as the shadows of the coming war lengthened.

CHAPTER 3

The Mennonite
Leadership
and a Line of
Least Resistance

World War II clearly caused deep reverberations in the recent history of American Mennonites. In these years, Mennonites wrestled hard and directly with the questions of where and how to say yes and no to the state, questions that the government pressed on them in an undeviating and inescapable manner. As Ernest Bohn exclaimed in early 1941, "The testing time for the peace testimony of the Mennonite Church has come." Not only did this testing process produce patterns of church-state cooperation unparalleled in Mennonite history, but it also planted the seeds for the later dissolution of this arrangement. Similarly, other developments in the war years did much to shape postwar formulations of Mennonite life and identity. Social historians have long recognized the tremendous changes that World War II wrought on domestic American society. So too, the war did much to shape the historical experience of American Mennonites.[1]

Like all wars confronting pacifists, World War II presented Mennonite leaders with the same tough choice between two demanding sources of authority. Ever resourceful and pragmatic, they drew on the lessons they had so painfully learned in the last world conflict to plot a path that minimized possible grounds of conflict with the state while ultimately attempting to remain faithful to the dictates of the nonresistant conscience. As they negotiated with the state over the creation of the Civilian Public Service (CPS) system, Mennonite leaders set the precedent for the larger course they would map out for their people in this time of crisis. The accommodations they made to the state's demands enabled Mennonites to survive the war not only relatively intact as a people but also with many of their fundamental theological and ideological commitments reaffirmed. The compromises would also have some unintended consequences, however, that would nudge the churches into unexpected directions in the years ahead.

More immediately, leaders discovered that the matter of where and how to draw the line with the state was doubly difficult in the early 1940s. For this process happened in a nation fully engaged in the economic and ideological pressures of total war.

THE IMPERATIVES OF MODERN WAR, 1941–1945

"The essential economic aim" of World War II, writes Alan Milward, "was to outproduce the enemy, however long it took." Indeed, given the advancements of industrial warfare since the last world conflict and the enormous mass armies now mobilized to fight it, this crucial strategy of outproducing the enemy became even more critical, if possible, than before. The breakthrough weapon of World War I had been the machine gun, and the U.S. government had enlisted four million soldiers to fight. Twenty years later, new developments included the tank, the long-range bomber, and the aircraft carrier, used by an armed force of sixteen million mustered by the United States alone. A nation wielding such a force necessarily had to draw on its entire productive capacity to wage war successfully. Two days after Pearl Harbor, President Roosevelt apprised the nation that "every single man, woman and child is a partner in the most tremendous undertaking of our American history."[2]

Even before the United States' entry into the war, the nation had begun gearing up its war machine to monumental proportions. During the summer of 1940, Congress approved the first peacetime draft in American history, and the Quartermaster Corps began building new camps to house a million soldiers. The Japanese attack in Hawaii sent war production levels soaring, with industry beginning to run the factories around the clock, seven days a week. Economic production at the level required for victory necessitated the maximum use of the nation's human resources; therefore, groups previously largely excluded from industrial production, such as women and racial minorities, were now grudgingly welcomed into the common enterprise. By the end of the war, the number of working Americans had jumped from 45 million to 66 million. When morale lagged as a mechanism for inducing the necessary output, new government agencies introduced draft deferments as a tool to channel civilians into work of pre-eminent military need.[3]

Fully aware that a mass enthusiasm for the war could spell the difference between victory or defeat, the state quickly moved to intensify the second key aspect mandated in a nation at total war: the ideological dimension. Pearl Harbor, of course, supplied ample motivation for many Americans. Secretary of War Henry Stimson's first feeling, upon hearing the news, was one of relief "that a crisis had come in a way that would unite all our people." For many Americans, avenging the attack became their primary inducement to fight, ration their goods, engage in scrap drives, or work diligently in war plants. Officials at the Bureau of Intelligence realized in 1942 that such feelings of revenge were pivotal for high morale; in one poll, 67 percent of Americans preferred that the military focus the bulk of its efforts on the Japanese, whereas only 21 percent thought Germany should be the primary target.[4]

Mindful of the rhetorical excesses and mob hysteria of the first world conflict, Roosevelt initially opposed the creation of a governmental propaganda machine. The issue of high morale, however, rapidly led him to change his mind. The Office of War Information was created in June of 1942. Even though the official function of this agency was merely to report war news, this task furnished a multitude of ways of shaping the news. In deciding which facts to play up and which to slight, these agencies substantially reworked the content of "the truth" about the war received by the general public. This, combined with a rigorous federal censorship that banned casualty lists from newspapers and realistic combat footage from theaters, restricted certain radio broadcasts, and issued "suggestions" to Hollywood film makers demonstrated, in Paul Fussell's words, the government's "unique obsession" with considerations of morale.[5]

Such a climate would have unpredictable ramifications for dissenters from the war. On the one hand, the nation had seemingly made great strides forward from the crusade-like atmosphere of World War I. Contrary to the anti-German aura of that conflict, this war generally lessened nativist hostility (with the not inconsiderable exception of intense hatred for Japanese Americans) and hastened the assimilation of diverse ethnic groups. Indeed, as historian Richard Polenberg has pointed out, festivals celebrating American pluralism and the contributions made by different immigrant groups were so common that they "became something of a ritual" during the war. Immigration restrictions of the twenties had eased nativist tensions before the war; now, with so much at stake in "national unity," few American leaders would countenance ethnic hate-mongering. The vast bulk of Protestant and Catholic churches endorsed the war but refused to bless it with the type of holy war sanctifications they had issued twenty years before. Roosevelt continually reminded his war bond and propaganda officials to shun strong-arm or bullying tactics that might precipitate the ugly mob violence of the last conflict. Perhaps as a result, some polls surfaced during the war that suggested public tolerance even for pacifists. While rejecting CO beliefs, a firm majority of people surveyed felt objectors were entitled to remuneration, dependency aid, and important work assignments, including foreign relief work.[6]

However, that was only one side of the picture. Other incidents and data suggest a less magnanimous treatment of dissent. The Smith Act of 1940, the first sedition law passed in peacetime since 1798, made it a federal crime to say or do anything to incite disaffection among military personnel or to promote the overthrow of government. In the words of a song from the era, "We're gonna find a feller who is yeller and beat him red, white and blue." Communists suffered once again; in December 1941, authorities in Minneapolis trundled eighteen convicted Trotskyites off to ten-year jail sentences for "having wicked and revolutionary ideas." Jehovah's Witnesses fared even worse. Their seemingly pacifist theology created a rather hard lot for them in a nation at total war. Because they proclaimed their readiness to fight in the final battle of Armageddon, Witnesses generally had a hard time qualifying as COs or obtaining ministerial deferments. Consequently, they often found themselves in prison when drafted; ultimately, over four thousand of them landed in jail. Considering American reactions to their antiwar stance and their refusal to salute the flag (a "graven image"), prison was probably the safest place for them to be. Outside, they frequently found themselves targets of mob violence. More than fifty mob attacks on Witnesses in 1939–1940 resulted in injuries to over 500 people, many of them women and children.[7]

These economic and ideological considerations of total war soon combined to exert a horrifying influence on military tactics that even an isolated and nonresistant people would have to think about. Simply put, the logic of modern war meant that while maximizing one's own economic production and civilian morale, one concomitantly tried to destroy those of the enemy. As outlined by historians such as Ronald Schaffer and Michael Sherry, in the beginning of the war the Royal Air Force had aimed at specific military and economic targets; but stung by German attacks on British residential areas, they began to retaliate in turn. Early in 1941, the British government officially abandoned "precision" bombing (which had never been especially precise anyway) and began regular nighttime bombing of German cities. The hope was to disrupt the German economy by displacing and killing workers and by terrorizing the general population. This would damage enemy morale to the point that ultimately they might give in. Gradually the American Air Corps joined in this tactic.[8]

With fire insurance company officials working with the War Department to create new incendiary bombs that would catch the atmosphere on fire and consume everything underneath, the Allies thus embarked on a course that led quickly to the firebombing of Hamburg, Berlin, and Dresden and then to the saturation bombing of Japan in the spring and summer of 1945. On a single night of sustained firebombing of a working class section of Tokyo on March 10, 1945, for instance, a fleet of American B-29 bombers incinerated over 100,000 Japanese, most of them civilians. The Army Air Corps high command then leveled comparable assaults on a number of other populous Japanese cities such as Kobe, Nagoya, and Osaka, culminating in the atomic bombing of Hiroshima and Nagasaki. By the end of the war, such tactics had damaged 66 of Japan's largest cities, destroyed 2.3 million dwellings, and left 330,000 to 900,000 dead. Meanwhile, given the ways of wartime hatred at home, large numbers of Americans greeted such developments with glee. In 1945, *Time* magazine gloated that the Tokyo raid was "a dream come true," demonstrating that "properly kindled, Japanese cities will burn like autumn leaves." Responding to the atomic bombings, another poll in late August 1945 found 22 percent thinking that "we should have quickly used many more of the bombs before Japan had a chance to surrender." In such a way did the economic and ideological considerations of total war lead many to a hearty endorsement of genocide as a legitimate undertaking in war.[9]

It was a difficult time for the peace movement—or what remained of it. The great wave of liberal pacifism had crested in the mid-1930s and then begun to decline in the face of rising fascism in Europe and Asia. With Pearl Harbor, Lawrence Wittner has argued, "the tottering American peace movement collapsed." Outside of pacifist religious groups, only a relatively small core of committed activists remained to buck the tide of popular nationalism.[10]

A similar story played itself out in the ranks of Christian pacifism. In the debate over American intervention in 1939–1941, the issue of pacifism occasioned a tremendous amount of divisiveness in the major Protestant churches. While fundamentalists had consistently rejected pacifism as yet another face of the larger modernist enemy, their ranks soon swelled with a number of defecting liberals. This group of "Christian Realists," as they styled themselves, still very much shared the ache for social justice that had characterized liberal Protestantism since the social gospel movement. Yet they now insisted that in international affairs, as in domestic ones, the concern for justice would have to take precedence over the demand for peace. With Pearl Harbor, nearly all of the mainline churches rallied to the cause, though many with reluctance and foreboding. In the words of *Christian Century* editor Charles Clayton Morrison, himself a recently stalwart pacifist, they joined the fight as a "guilty necessity."[11]

This, then, is what total war entailed for participants in it in the mid-twentieth century. What it entailed for people of peace remained less clear. Yet if it is possible to let one thinker speak for many, this was a society that had designated a particular theological place for Mennonites. At least, they were awarded such a special function in the thinking of Reinhold Niebuhr. In his pragmatic acceptance of warfare as the lesser evil in a world of tragedy, Niebuhr had done more than merely pave the way for the conversion of a significant number of liberal Protestants to a nonpacifist position. In many ways he had engineered the transformation of political and religious liberalism itself. The older, social-gospel liberalism was optimistic and absolutist and tended toward pacifism, observed Paul Carter; whereas the emerging liberal orientation, more pessimistic and relativistic, gravitated toward nonpacifism. As the principle architect of this shift, Niebuhr would soon be embraced as the theological high priest for a coming generation of liberal warriors and politicians who would dominate American politics for half a century. Even before the war, he had carved out a peculiar role for Mennonites in this new order.[12]

Mennonite theology appealed to Christian Realists for several reasons. At the very least, both groups partook in a similar denunciation of the naively optimistic and absolutist nature of liberal pacifism. Its attempt to apply perfectionist moral considerations within the realm of political considerations was nothing less than heresy, charged Niebuhr. By overlooking the power of human sin, liberal pacifists nurtured foolish illusions about the essential goodness of human nature. "There is a sinful element in all the expedients which the political order uses to establish justice," Niebuhr argued, an element that remained unavoidable. Like continental theologians in Europe, Niebuhr thus began to reassert an understanding of human sinfulness, something that international events of the 1930s spoke to anew. Christians who aspired to social responsibility needed to recognize, as Niebuhr reasoned in 1940, that "an ethic of pure non-resistance can have no immediate relevance to any political situation." Instead, such Christians would necessarily have to strip themselves of romantic illusions, realizing that conflict, coercion, and violence were part of the character of human existence. The world did not offer simple, absolutized choices between good and evil; instead, the inescapable coercion inherent in almost all social relationships offered a choice only between relative evils. Such a world, argued Niebuhr, was a world of tragedy from which Christians could not excuse themselves. To do otherwise, and to offer up a shallow faith in nonviolence as the needed antidote for social injustice (for which "there is not the slightest support in scripture") betrayed the cause of justice and promised to leave millions defenseless in the face of stark evil.[13]

While denouncing most contemporary forms of pacifism, however, Niebuhr identified one variant of pacifism that was not heresy at all. In fact, this type had historically been a "rather valuable asset for the Christian faith." It was typified in his thought most centrally as a variant of "sectarian perfectionism," "the type of Meno Simons [*sic*] for instance." Such groups, he argued, were perfectly willing to accept their own political irrelevance. Among Mennonites, "the effort to achieve a standard of perfect love in individual life was not presented as a political alternative. On the contrary, the political problem and task were specifically disavowed." The Mennonites' absolutist ethic of love was fine as long as they applied it to no one but themselves. With their eschatological hopes lying outside history, Niebuhr explained, Mennonites focused on creating small communities as simple examples of the kingdom of God. In doing so, they performed a real service for the church at large, reminding less "ascetic" Christians that "the relative norms of social justice, which justify both coercion and resistance to coercion, are not final norms."[14]

In short, in Niebuhr's thinking, people such as Mennonites were good to have around. As long as they kept quietly to themselves and did not expect the state to operate by their utopian "norm of love," they performed a valuable duty in merely reminding more socially engaged Christians that such norms existed. Furthermore, they helped to keep alive an uneasy Christian conscience about participation in warfare. Of course, the minute such nonresistant Christians began to prescribe values to government or to expect the state to operate in accordance with their absolutist claims, they joined their liberal pacifist colleagues in heresy. Niebuhr thus accepted radical Mennonite two-kingdom doctrine as wholeheartedly as any Lancaster Conference conservative. One did not tell the state what to do; nonresistant Christians should not expect a wicked state, keeping order among the wicked, to subscribe to the values of the kingdom of God.

Yet even in this legitimation of Mennonite nonresistance, Niebuhr half hid a stinging rebuke that would shock whatever tendencies Mennonites might have toward complacency and register deep ideological reverberations in Mennonite social ethics in the years ahead. "It is a good thing," he wrote in 1937, to have such a group in the church "which seeks to symbolize the absolute ideal of love." Yet that group should always realize its own irrelevancy and irresponsibility: "Let it regard the problem of social justice as something that does not concern it directly . . . Let such pacifism realize," Niebuhr concluded, "that it is a form of asceticism and that as such it is a parasite on the sins of the rest of us, who maintain government and relative social peace and relative social justice."[15]

As defined by Niebuhr, Mennonites could rest easy as the society around them bent its energies to the tasks necessary in total war. The state geared up its economy into a war machine that would envelop the vast majority of its people and attempted to stimulate these citizens into a fever pitch that would keep them working hard for victory. With economic production fully mobilized and morale high, good citizens even lent support to war operations aimed at disrupting enemy economic production and morale through tactics that now approximated genocide. As long as they dutifully tamped down any pangs of conscience that these developments might cause them, nonresistant dissenters need not fear for their survival in such a society. Indeed, at least in Niebuhr's scheme, groups such as the Mennonites performed a valuable service for the entire church by safeguarding the ethic of absolute love while everyone else cast it aside. All a nonresistant people had to do was stay in their place. But would they?

GOING THE SECOND MILE WITH THE STATE

Much of the Mennonite story in the twentieth century, as well as a vast bulk of the energies of church leadership, is found in a Mennonite wrestling with how to answer this question. For it directly involved the fundamental matter about where to draw the line between the two kingdoms, a decision that has always involved a delicate balance. Mennonites needed to outline their relationship with the state in a manner that both demonstrated fidelity to the Anabaptist heritage and Mennonite principles and at the same time secured group survival in a state positioning itself as the focal point of all civil loyalties.

The 1940s, in fact, appeared to be a particularly precarious time in which to try to satisfy both goals. Here Mennonites found themselves enlisted as citizens in a state that had casually drafted their young men into the military twenty years before. Now it demonstrated a ready willingness to incinerate hundreds of thousands of people in its drive for the unconditional surrender of its enemies. As the nation had veered toward war in the 1930s, Mennonites had realized they faced a coming conflict between the state and their church. Now the conflict was apparently at hand.

During the war years, not surprisingly, Mennonites worked the hardest at defining their place in outside society. Their most direct ideological responses were found in two new constructs that emerged in the winter of 1943–1944. Together, they would exert a profound hold on Mennonite self-understandings and on the course of the Mennonite ethic on peace and social responsibility for several decades after the war. More immediately, they would set a course the church could follow in pursuing the ways of peace in a time of ruthless war. Although they quickly garnered a broad affirmation that cut across Mennonite denominational lines, both were formulated by MC leaders, Harold Bender and Guy Hershberger.

New Ideological Responses

The first of these ideological constructs emanated from the reaffirmations of Anabaptist-Mennonite history that Harold Bender had been engaged in since his arrival at Goshen College in 1927. For almost two decades, he and other Goshen progressives had labored at building a Mennonite "usable past" through articles in the denominational press and especially in the *Mennonite Quarterly Review.* Now Bender would attempt to express this historical reworking in a single, memorable phrasing. It came in his presidential address to the American Society of Church History meeting in December 1943, in a paper entitled "The Anabaptist Vision." There were no Mennonites present the night Bender delivered his address in New York City, but its ripples influenced them most of all and continued to reverberate in the church for decades afterward.

Bender redefined Anabaptism around three central teachings. First, for

Anabaptists, he asserted, the essence of Christianity revolved around a life of discipleship patterned on the teachings and example of Christ. Second, the church was a true brotherhood of believers dedicated to complete non-conformity with the world. And third, also crucially important in Anabaptist practice was "the ethic of love and nonresistance as applied to all human relationships." The stance for Mennonites that emerged from this redefinition was one that paradoxically reinforced Mennonite separatism but that also strengthened their mission and service impetus toward the outside world. Bender held up the model of Anabaptism as applicable for all, not just for Mennonites, but he also concluded by reminding Mennonites of the strict limitations that the Anabaptist legacy leveled on their participation in larger society. "The Christian may in no circumstance participate in any conduct in the existing social order which is contrary to the spirit and teaching of Christ," Bender stressed. Instead, Christians must "consequently withdraw from the worldly system and create a Christian social order within the fellowship of the church brotherhood." In sum, as Bender mediated the instructions passed down by Anabaptist ancestors, Mennonites would live in the proper balance demanded by their two kingdoms.[16]

As several scholars make clear, Bender's formulation, along with a number of supporting studies, rested on a somewhat selective reading of the Anabaptist movement, and it has remained a target for historical revision ever since.[17] Nonetheless, this reading of their history and of the vision of their ancestors as "evangelical Anabaptists" performed a decisive function for an entire postwar generation of Mennonites in both inward and outward directions. Inwardly, this conception of their ancestors as a dedicated band of peaceful brothers and sisters, driven by the common call of discipleship toward the Way of Jesus, would serve, according to historian Paul Toews, as "the identifying incantation for North American Mennonites." For thousands, this articulation of their heritage suddenly and majestically defined what it meant to be a Mennonite. While the vision was not new, its freshness and impact lay in the chord it touched within the Mennonite people. In the coming years, the statement would be critiqued for its apparent sanction to withdrawn passivity and its reinforcement of church bureaucratic structures. Yet despite these problems, Bender provided for the next generation a lasting and viable model of a usable past. Outwardly, Bender's vision functioned as a kind of ideological frontispiece for Mennonites in their relationship with larger American Protestantism. As Mennonites emerged from rural isolation to take a place in the mosaic of American religious denominations, this vision of "evangelical Anabaptism" would define their place in the religious community, a kind of "third path" apart from both fundamentalism and liberalism.[18]

Moreover, the vision came at a crucial time. For the Mennonite churches, the discovery of a usable Anabaptist past served as a new sort of ideological glue that could hold them together as they made the painful transition into modern America. As a host of church leaders embarked on poor-relief efforts and negotiated conscientious objector programs with the government, as they deepened and extended the church institutional and authority structures, they discovered that this reading of history could be used to affix legitimacy to such efforts among an ethno-religious people traditionally conservative and resistant to change.[19]

In a like manner, Guy Hershberger understood the power of history. In 1944 he published a book of history, theology, and political analysis that would define Mennonite thinking on peace and social concerns for a generation. Actually, his *War, Peace and Nonresistance* had been in the works for some time; it had emerged directly out of the middle ground that Goshen progressives had been enlarging for nearly two decades. The Peace Problems committee had, in fact, originally commissioned the study in 1937. Following along the lines of this conceptual inheritance, Hershberger clearly expressed the political and intellectual strategy mapped out in the hard battles with church conservatives. While agreeing with the essentially apolitical nature of the proper Christian relationship with outside society, Hershberger carefully tacked on a prophetic qualifier that would speak to the present-day activists and spell out the difference in the years to come. At the very least, Hershberger had produced the definitive Mennonite statement of nonresistance.[20]

Hershberger devoted his energies to three main aspects in the text: a biblical exegesis; a history of Christian pacifism as it originated in the early church and then continued through Anabaptist-Mennonite history; and finally, a strategic positioning of "Biblical nonresistance" in its relationship to other ethical currents. In other words, ultimately he aimed his words at people beyond the Mennonites. Here was a Mennonite response to militaristic fundamentalists, liberal pacifists, and "neo-orthodox dualists, represented by Reinhold Niebuhr." Hershberger dismissed the fundamentalist sanction of war with his biblical exposition, arguing that while God might have permitted warfare in the Old Testament, in the new covenant represented by the gospel, God clearly forbade it.[21]

Hershberger's response to the other two schools of thinking entailed a bit more complexity. He began with a reaffirmation of two-kingdom theology. As laid out in the New Testament, the state's function was to maintain order in an evil society. "The state is an agency for the administration of justice with the aid of force in an evil society," Hershberger declared, "and is not motivated by Christian love." Therefore, nonresistant Christians should not be part of the state or have much to say about how it should conduct its affairs, for "the outlook of the New Testament is entirely unpolitical." Instead, Christians were to operate by an entirely different ethic. In lines sure to be further disagreeable to liberal pacifists, he reminded them that "the Sermon on the Mount is not a piece of legislation for a secular state in a sinful society. It is a set of principles to govern the sons of the kingdom of heaven."[22]

Hershberger thus agreed with Niebuhr about the power of sin in human society and the necessity of a strong, amoral state to restrain it. Correspondingly, Hershberger resonated fully with Niebuhr's critique of liberal pacifism: "It has confused the kingdom of God with mere moral improvements within sinful society, and in so doing has identified the kingdom of God with the sinful order itself." He castigated nonviolence as non-Christian coercion, and even quoted Niebuhr approvingly on this point. Instead, the Mennonite way to a better world would be to simply *do* justice, rather than *demand* it. Here, in sum, was the Mennonite social ethic: not to demand justice or engage in vast reforms of society, because Christians could not expect a secular state to operate by their values. "The mission of nonresistant Christians, therefore, is not a political one," he wrote. It was however, "a curative mission." Instead of social demands, Mennonites would have social programs; instead of demanding justice for the oppressed, they would simply minister to them. Hershberger went on for pages spelling out contemporary Mennonite efforts in war relief and reconstruction work. Like religious liberals, Mennonites were very much interested in the social problems of the day, Hershberger insisted; but "they work on them with a different technique, namely, through regeneration and discipleship, rather than through education and reformation." As Jesus commanded, they would be the salt of the earth; they would work for justice through a mission of healing and mercy.[23]

Thus, Hershberger underscored the growing Mennonite service consciousness and identity that had emerged during World War I and now blossomed even more fully in the second world conflict. Yet one troubling issue remained. At times it sounded suspiciously like Hershberger had signed on not only to Niebuhr's critique of liberal pacifism but also to his

patronizing dismissal of the Mennonites to their own little corner. After
all, in explaining their "curative mission," Hershberger had reasoned that
the world greatly needs "the ministry of nonresistant Christians whose
light, set on a hill, stands as a glowing witness to the way of truth." While
much of Hershberger's analysis of the place of the nonresistant Christian
in society dovetailed with Niebuhr's, a complete endorsement meant swal-
lowing that cutting analysis which branded these nonresistant people as
parasites.[24]

Of course, Hershberger insisted that healing societal ills and pointing to
a better way than war were deeds of true benefactors of society, not parasites. Yet beyond this obvious rejoinder there was something more, another
key angle that would one day lead to the transformation of this entire formulation of the Mennonite-state relationship. A light cannot shine, Hershberger maintained, unless it positions itself where people can see it. Thus,
the nonresistant Christian was responsible to "testify to all men concerning
the truth as he understands it." Similarly, while refusing to engage in certain of the state's activities, as members of the "national community," such
Christians have "an obligation to testify to officials of state and to [their]
fellow citizens, by both word and deed, concerning the way of love as taught
by Jesus Christ." Their testimony would not come in some future dispensation, as suggested by the fundamentalists, or in some misplaced attempt
to force the values of God's kingdom on the state, as Mennonite traditionalists charged church activists with recommending. Mennonites needed to
speak to the state, Hershberger suggested, out of an obedience to a larger,
single moral law that God posited for all people, in both the church and
the world. Maybe God did not have two sets of values for two different
kingdoms; maybe God had only one. These ideas appeared in midtext, almost as an afterthought, and were framed innocently enough so that OM
fundamentalists raised no objections. But in a day not too far off, this legitimation of witnessing to the state would ultimately provide other Mennonites with the key to recapturing a more radical and prophetic Anabaptist
vision.[25]

The success of such arguments appeared in the reception of this text.
The Mennonite Publishing House reissued it twice, in 1953 and in 1969,
to eager audiences. Like Bender's Anabaptist Vision, *War, Peace, and Nonresistance* satisfied a wide range of Mennonites. OM fundamentalists focused their main complaints at Hershberger's interpretation of war in the
Old Testament. Meanwhile, the GC activist Don Smucker reviewed it in
glowing terms for his denomination in *The Mennonite*. To Smucker it was

"the authoritative text in the field," "epoch-making," offering "a new *Biblical* social gospel" (emphasis his). Even more significantly, together with Bender's Anabaptist Vision, Hershberger's formulations helped to unify the church around the central themes of peace and service. These two ideational constructs provided a pivotal expression of normative Mennonitism for a church caught up in the throes of social transformation.[26]

Moreover, the visions laid out by Bender and Hershberger reinvigorated the dedication and church loyalties of talented young people whose passion for justice and social change might have sent them elsewhere. While they might have been frustrated with the restrained call for social justice and prophetic witness in Hershberger's book,[27] recalled Robert Kreider years later, he and his fellow GC young radicals at least "had to wrestle with him seriously" and could not just dismiss him out of hand as they did with the fundamentalists of the Virginia Conference. Esko Loewen, who went on to a useful career as a GC pastor, college dean, and peace leader, remembers that as he graduated from Bethel College in the late 1930s, he had not planned on staying a Mennonite. What answers did they have for the problem of social injustice? Yet with the war revealing "the dark side and the fallen nature of man," he fell back on his Mennonite heritage. In the writings of Bender and others, he found something that could "sustain" him. In the long run, Bender's and Hershberger's ideological offerings would bear much fruit for the church. More immediately, they expressed the kind of ethic that was presently coming to fruition in the Civilian Public Service system.[28]

MCC and the Creation of Civilian Public Service

In March 1939, representatives of seven Mennonite groups, including Miller, Bender, and Hershberger of the "old" Mennonites, and Harshbarger and Landes of the General Conference, met together in Chicago to plan future cooperative peace activity. Already a common understanding had begun to form, born of meetings of the historic peace churches in the 1930s and of Hershberger's musings in 1935. They would need to come up with some sort of plan for alternative service. Pressure from below drove these discussions to a large degree; for many of the young people in their flock, the question of the draft was no abstract issue. In August 1940, Hershberger wrote Miller to inform him of the confusion and questions among Mennonite youth, claiming that "if the program can start at once there ought not to be very many of our young people taking noncombatant military service." Similarly, a month later Hershberger voiced his concern to Miller that the program would come "too late—that is after young people have already made up their minds the wrong way."[29]

At the group's next meeting that September, discussion and points of view coalesced enough to lead to several concrete developments. First, the delegates and guests arrived at a common "plan of action in case of war" based on some kind of alternative service for duly recognized objectors to war. The types of service envisioned by the delegates included war-relief work, forestry or soil reclamation service, and health service efforts. All of these types of service, the plan stated, would have to be under church administration and direction. Yet the plan also took pains to frame those petitions in proper patriotic and submissive language. The principle of Christian conscientious objection, said the delegates, "is not only compatible with a genuine love for country . . . but represents a high type of Christian patriotism which makes possible a constructive contribution to the spiritual and material welfare of our native land." Finally, though some had later regretted such early moves in the last war, the plan countenanced no deliberations on the wisdom of draft registration. The plan clearly directed that "all those subject by law to registration should register when called to do so," though they should clearly indicate their conscientious objector claims.[30]

Initial overtures to government officials concerning these plans raised Mennonite expectations that the whole program could take shape without much governmental interference. Quite soon, however, Mennonites and their historic peace church colleagues discovered the unpredictable nature of pliant cooperation with government. The ensuing negotiations between peace church representatives and government officials around the final shape of the CO legislation and the creation of CPS have been covered in detail by a number of scholars and do not require careful explication here.[31] In spite of the president's apparent initial enthusiasm for an alternative service arrangement, the draft legislation introduced into Congress in June 1940, the Burke-Wadsworth Bill, said nothing about alternative service for conscientious objectors and instead proposed designating them for non-combatant service within the army. In other words, the legislation paralleled almost exactly the completely unacceptable and troublesome arrangement of World War I. Suffice it to say, intense peace church lobbying efforts in the summer of 1940, spearheaded mostly by Paul French of the AFSC, managed to get the draft bill legislation changed into more acceptable language by its final passage in mid-September. As agreed upon by Congress and signed by the president, the bill recognized a class of conscientious objectors who would work under civilian, as opposed to military, administration on designated, nonmilitary work of national importance. Contested cases would be appealed within the Department of Justice, and violators of the act would face trial under civilian authorities. The bill left much to be worked out. For instance, it neglected to define "work of national importance." But this was only the most glaring omission in what emerged as a vast sea of ambiguity. Still unanswered were questions such as: Who would fund the program? Who would run it? What would be the shape of this alternative service?[32]

To address such questions and a host of others, innumerable meetings began to take place between peace church representatives and government officials from such agencies as Selective Service and the Departments of Interior and Agriculture. French remained in Washington to lead these efforts, and in September he was joined by Fast. The central organizing body for such efforts came together that October when Selective Service asked for a single church agency to deal with, rather than a number of separate groups. Obediently, the churches pulled together a large agency, finally known as the National Service Board for Religious Objectors (NSBRO). An executive committee of seven people took initial charge of the board and defined its purpose as furnishing information to constituent groups and providing a coordinated approach to Washington officials.[33]

The system that ultimately emerged from the negotiations took shape essentially as a compromise arrangement with the government holding all the cards. Though initially created as temporary, the set of agreements hardened into permanency after Pearl Harbor. Given Roosevelt's firm opposition to any sign of leniency, it quickly became clear to peace church negotiators that the churches would need to both finance and administer the program. The work designated as being of "national importance" would entail mostly soil conservation and forestry projects. Different federal agencies agreed to provide shelter (mostly in abandoned CCC camps), tools, and transportation for the COs and would also supervise them in forestry and soil reclamation projects. The NSBRO, in turn, would be responsible for the day-to-day running of the camps, including the responsibility of feeding and maintaining the men. Given the pressures on them to produce a program while concurrently mobilizing their people behind it, the peace churches had no choice but to agree, even though many CPS men and the larger pacifist community would later denounce the "slave labor" aspects of the arrangement. It was only the best they could get at the time from a recalcitrant government gearing up for total war. Admittedly, the costs of such a program would be enormous, and at least a few Mennonites expressed their reservations. The Virginia bishop George Brunk, for instance, cautioned that they needed to be careful "or we will find ourselves with something on our hands we cannot handle." Yet most others disagreed. The benefits of this CO system seemed so plain and its opportunities so glimmering compared to the arrangement in the last war that Miller undoubtedly spoke for many in his pledge that Mennonites "would gladly pay their share of the bill . . . even though every Mennonite farmer had to mortgage his farm."[34]

Meanwhile, peace church young men obediently began registering with the rest of the nation. On May 22, 1941, the first Mennonite CPSers pulled into Camp Grottoes, near Luray, Virginia, in the Shenandoah Valley. These COs quickly plunged into what would be the vast bulk of CO work: soil conservation, land reclamation, and forestry work in projects that ultimately spread all over the nation. By July 1942, for instance, 1,275 Mennonites labored in CPS camps out of a total CPS population of 3,458. At the system's peak in September 1945, 3,754 Mennonite young men worked in CPS camps and projects. MCC set up a special "Peace Section" to oversee Mennonite peace concerns.[35]

The State's Perspective

As Mennonites squared off against the state in the early 1940s, the government came to be personified most centrally in the new director of Selective Service, a red-headed, agnostic military bureaucrat with the typically Mennonite name of Hershey. Roosevelt gave Hershey wide latitude in running the alternative service program, and for most COs and CPS administrators, Hershey's opinion remained the final one this side of heaven. Not that Hershey was altogether hostile. He seemed to have some vague personal commitments to the fundamental principle of conscientious objection. To Hershey it was ultimately "an experiment in democracy . . . to find out whether our nation is big enough to preserve minority rights in a time of national emergency." He defined "religious training and belief"—the crucial definitive variable in qualifying for CO status—in a relatively broad way. The theological net he thus cast stretched wide enough to admit large numbers of religious objectors beyond the traditional Historic Peace Churches; consequently, COs in World War II consisted not just of Mennonites or even Methodists, but of Molokans as well. In the more than 1,500 "presidential appeals" by CO applicants that he decided, Hershey awarded CO status to over 90 percent of the applicants.

Many Mennonites felt a particular bond with Hershey, and not simply because of the ancestral tie. Joseph Weaver, a young Mennonite CO who worked carefully with Selective Service officials in the NSBRO office in Washington from 1940 to 1946, remembers that without Hershey's support "we would have never gone through the war as intact as we were as a peace organization." More than once, Hershey faced down groups hostile to COs such as the American Legion, defended objectors' rights in Congress, and fought off a congressional attempt to do away with the CPS system.[36]

Still, as a career army officer, Hershey had two main functions—to obey orders and to win the war—and nearly everything he did or ordered in regard to conscientious objectors seemed to devolve from these considerations. Indeed, at times this reasoning seemed to underlie much of his commitment to conscientious objection. Arguing against a congressional bill to end CPS, for example, Hershey reminded senators that "no commanding officer would want to go into battle with a conscientious objector." By defining conscientious objection in the manner he did (mandating a belief in a transcendent God and prohibiting what would later be called "selective" conscientious objection) and by assigning objectors to unglamorous, unpaid work, Hershey had assured that their numbers would remain small and that they would pose no ultimate danger to the nation's personnel needs.[37]

Even so, COs could pose a larger threat to the crucial issue of national morale and would need to be handled carefully and in certain firm ways. For the very existence of protected COs in a nation that sent off so many young men to fight and die rubbed raw against the sensitive American nerve of equity. As Mitchell Robinson has pointed out, if a democratic people resort to conscription as the means of furnishing soldiers for their army, then toleration for conscientious objectors demands the widespread belief that the arrangement is fundamentally fair. In such a society, Tocqueville argued, the clamor for equity sometimes overrides the belief in liberty. The political antennae of Hershey's Selective Service were especially attuned to such considerations. In his first annual report, for example, Hershey informed Americans that objectors "should be neither favored, nor punished because of their beliefs, but as far as the law allowed, they should undergo the same inconveniences and receive the same benefits as the men in the service." Even beyond Selective Service, congresspersons and the public at large repeatedly demanded that objectors be subjected to some kind of service equivalent to that of men in the military.[38]

This was all well and good, and if Selective Service had been able to structure CPS so that objectors experienced the same sacrifices and benefits as soldiers and sailors, it seems doubtful that the system would have received the intense criticism from all sides that it did. The basic problem was that the inconvenience of military life—at least that suffered by the minority of GIs who saw combat—by far outweighed any comparable conditions in CPS. Objectors may have labored hard in forest work, volunteered as medical guinea pigs, and parachuted into forest fires, but they were not shot at. With complete equity of service elusive, Hershey's solution for COs, Robinson has noted, was to maximize their inconvenience and minimize their benefits. Inconvenience could serve as a substitute for equity, a maxim that appeared to guide many Selective Service directives in regard to CPS. Take, for example, the issue of pay for COs, a proposal Hershey blocked every time it emerged. Admittedly, political realities partly dictated such a course. The president would never have agreed to CPS in the first place had the arrangement included a provision for pay. Moreover, Hershey believed—with some good reason, in the wartime political climate—that a bill to pay CPS men could well provoke a congressional reaction that might endanger the system altogether. The sacrificial nature of CO work, he was convinced, remained the major reason that the public tolerated it. Yet even beyond this, Hershey believed that objectors did not undergo the same sort of risks as GIs and thus did not deserve the same kind of compensation.[39]

Unlike GIs, then, objectors would not receive pay; nor were they, in the larger interests of equity, entitled to aid for their dependents, compensation for injuries suffered in service, or any kind of governmental assistance after the war. At the same time, they would need to be subjected to conditions that approximated those of soldiers in as many ways as possible. While Congress prohibited COs from engaging in relief work overseas, Hershey mandated that objectors serve at least one hundred miles from their homes. They needed to work roughly the same hours and have the same restricted leave policies. Even the course of their demobilization followed that of soldiers (only it came generally later). Facing CO demands for more meaningful work, Hershey reminded the Quaker leader French that millions of men labored in the military "without any choice of the kind of work they did," and that certainly many of them "had a real sense of frustration at the menial tasks given them to do." And all along, Hershey and his comrades knew that this was not abstract issue; the preservation of equity involved matters of vital importance in a nation at total war. Repeatedly, Hershey reminded politicians that "a great deal of harm would be done in public relations" if COs did not receive congruent treatment. In other words, the issue involved morale.[40]

This, then, was the larger political climate in which people of peace, Mennonites among them, had to plot the path of their dissent during World War II. The national demands for equity rendered the privilege of conscientious objection altogether tenuous, to such a degree that at times dissenters had to rely on unfamiliar allies like General Hershey to preserve it for them. For the fundamental problem lay in exactly this phrasing: conscientious objection was only a privilege, not a right. These were the political conditions that would inform the struggle of dissenters pledged to resist the ramifications of modern war—and even the struggle of a people pledged to nonresistance.

"Second-Mile" Philosophy

In the larger pacifist community, the limits of public toleration imposed by society's commitment to equity quieted pacifist unhappiness with the implicit compromises of the CPS arrangement only for a time. Initially, many pacifists accepted the system because it was temporary and because it was simply the best the state would grant. Moreover, at first the scheme appeared to offer a perfect chance to once again express their desire to contribute positively to their country in time of crisis. Here was an opportunity to physically demonstrate love in a world seemingly lost in hate. Frank Olmstead, chair of the War Resisters' League, proclaimed, for example, that CPS stood as "the most effective argument for pacifism which the antiwar forces of the country can offer." It was, to him, "a reservoir of liberty." Even the issue of unpaid service raised few hackles in the beginning; many peace leaders agreed that only by laboring voluntarily could peace people most clearly evidence their desire to work sacrificially.[41]

As the war wore on, however, the limitations of the program quickly became apparent, and pacifist resistance escalated. Congress would not consider pay for them or even aid to their dependents; the labor itself emerged as piddling busy work, devoid of meaning. Church administration of the camps appeared to many activists as an inexcusable compromise with evil, rendering the peace churches a veritable arm of the military. As a young Methodist CO wrote to Mennonite CPS administrator Albert Gaeddert, "For some time I have felt as many others are coming to feel that the C.P.S. program is Selective Service operated with the religious agencies acting simply as liaison representatives." Ultimately, enough Quakers agreed with this analysis that the AFSC withdrew from camp administration in March 1946. Long before that, however, hundreds of radical COs began to walk out of the camps to sit out the duration of the war in prison. Many of those that remained engaged in work slowdowns, strikes, and campaigns of Gandhian *satyagraha* in an effort to hammer at the system from the inside.[42]

Mennonites had traditionally viewed such activities with suspicion, and the church leadership entirely disagreed with such expressions of dissent. Drawing the Mennonite line against war, not conscription, the leadership embarked on a policy of ready cooperation with the state in all requests that stopped short of participation in violence. Nonresistance in this case meant a line of least resistance. While the Friends might choose to withdraw from camp administration, MCC (and also the Church of the Brethren) resolutely refused to do so and dutifully managed a large numbers of camps until CPS came to an end in 1947. More than once, Mennonites saw fit to remind the state of their gratitude for the privilege of CPS. In August, 1941, for example, the Mennonite Church's general meeting approved a resolution to Hershey bubbling over with appreciation and declaring their firm determination "to cooperate loyally with you and the Selective Service Administration in carrying forward the civilian public service program in such a way that the requirements of the government may be fully met and that we as nonresistant Christians may continue to enjoy freedom of conscience and religious liberty in accord with the historic ideals of our American democracy."[43]

As Albert Keim has persuasively argued, the CPS program was not a "marriage of convenience" between the Mennonites and government but only the best they could get, though far short of ideal. Nor was it foisted on the church by farsighted and overly-powerful leaders or unloaded on them by government. The documents leave little doubt as to the satisfaction with which most Mennonites greeted the system, a delight that leaders did little to downplay. Fast waxed enthusiastic in *The Mennonite* in January 1941: "If the people in our churches can catch a vision of the wonderful opportunity God, through this arrangement of the government, has placed at their disposal to work out together with their young men . . . they will thank God for the opportunity and undertake it with the determination to make the most of it."[44]

A number of different sources fueled this potent enthusiasm and general policy of Mennonite cooperation with the state in World War II. Certainly, the vivid memories of their ordeal in World War I informed the perspective of many Mennonites. "We need only to look back at the discomforts and persecution of those of our belief in past times to appreciate Civilian Public Service now," observed one Mennonite CPSer. Moreover, many Mennonites accurately read the political climate, realizing that public toleration for the privilege of objection depended on the appearance of equity. Why press issues such as the lack of pay and the nature of the work? Thus Fast carefully instructed Mennonite CPSers in 1942 against joy-riding in cars or taking too many weekend leaves to visit home. They had enjoyed a good amount of tolerance so far, he cautioned, and "the whole future of the CPS program is dependent on whether this public good will continues."[45]

Nor did the Mennonite leadership see the program merely as a series of negatives they worked to escape. Indeed, in taking vast numbers of young men and placing them in the hands of church officials for a number of years (at least in their off-work hours), CPS appeared as an unparalleled chance to shape the minds of an entire generation of young Mennonites. For the leaders, this was enough reason in itself to reject financial remuneration for the objectors. "Where the government pays they also take control," Fast remembered later. "And if we wanted to control the program—the life of the boys in camps—then that was about the choice we had." The dangers of an alternative arrangement seemed clear enough at the time. If the churches did not fund the system, realized Bender in October, 1941, "the Government will take over the program and operate it."[46]

As it stood, the leadership made the most of their golden opportunity. The major thrust of the educational effort took shape in a series of six small booklets, published by MCC in 1942, that constituted the "Mennonite Heritage Course." MCC's educational secretaries (Robert Kreider in 1942, followed by Elmer Ediger a year later) urged Mennonite draftees to take the course their first quarter in camp, a suggestion that many MCC camps and draftees followed. In this course, which comprised the core of the educational program in many MCC camps, Mennonite draftees received a careful introduction to the new ideational constructs of the war years. For instance, in his pamphlet entitled *Mennonite Origins in Europe*, Bender outlined his Anabaptist Vision, while Edward Yoder and the GC Historian C. Henry Smith instructed readers in the Mennonite history and heritage in America. Meanwhile, in *Christian Relationships to State and Community*, Hershberger sketched out the new ethic that he would shortly publish in more detail in *War, Peace, and Nonresistance*. Even beyond this basic course, MCC offered relief training schools, preparing a host of Mennonite relief workers for postwar service work. Hershberger, Winfield Fretz, and others extolled the simplicity of the Mennonite rural community in four "Farm and Community Schools" offered in 1945.[47]

Mennonites' appreciation for CPS and their generally cooperative stance with the state also devolved from their theology and philosophy. Given strict two-kingdom understandings, conscription unquestionably remained within the state's purview. As Hershberger wrote, nonresistant people "recognized a certain amount of compulsion as a proper function of the state for the maintenance of order in a sub-Christian society." Indeed, even making war could be legitimized under such a rationale; one Mennonite reasoned in the *Gospel Herald* in 1937 that "the Lord has a sword and uses it. And what is more, He often uses it in the hand of man." Similarly for the General Conference, Walter Dyck advised in 1942 that resisting the state's laws "is to despise government and deserves a penalty." As taught by Anabaptist ancestors (and now echoed by Niebuhr), many Mennonites did not question the state's right to conscript, wage war, or engage in any other activity that it needed to maintain order in a wicked world, as long as it excused Mennonites from participation. "We do not feel called to remind government of any moral obligation," Miller explained to the AFSC's French in 1941, "or even to suggest that they should feel such obligation."[48]

During the war, however, the teaching did not stop there; cooperation was further enhanced by a new ideological twist, something leaders referred to as the "philosophy of the second mile." Jesus enjoined his disciples to turn the other cheek, to give not only your tunic but your cloak as well. If one member of the occupation forces you to carry his pack one mile, he instructed, carry it a second mile. Certainly, admitted GC Donovan Smucker in 1944, complaints about lack of pay, meaningless work, and military supervision of CPS carried some weight. Yet "the overwhelming majority of Mennonites have rejected" such arguments, he asserted, "in favor of what they rightly believe is a more truly Christian conception of 'second-mile' obligations in relation to a generous (and divinely ordained!) government." Likewise, Bender admitted that while it "is not fair that our boys work without pay . . . who are Christians to insist upon justice? We are not to take too much account of justice. We have our testimony to give in the spirit of Christ." MCC instructed Mennonite campers that for Mennonites, CPS is "doing what they feel Christ meant for them to do when He spoke of a second mile."[49]

Finally, CPS received such a ready Mennonite endorsement because it seemed an ideal mechanism for once again proving the Mennonite worthiness of citizenship at a time when the supreme avenue for proper citizenship was sacrifice on the battlefield. Pacifists were not often allowed to forget during the war what true citizenship entailed. Consider what First Lady Eleanor Roosevelt had to say as objectors' clamor for compensation reached public ears. In comments that still appear uncharacteristically thoughtless, she opined in the *Ladies Home Journal* in 1944 that "the conscientious objector is not performing any service for the country and therefore is not entitled to pay." In response to the cries of hurt reaching her ears from the pacifist community, she conceded that while COs performed "a good record of work," this was not the most important work the country required, and thus objectors were "not the same kind of citizens as the men in the armed forces."[50]

Mennonites could only work hard and faithfully to suggest otherwise. The vision of thousands of Mennonite conscientious objectors laboring voluntarily without complaint and funded by a steadfast church back home would function as their own moral equivalent of war. The documents furnish innumerable examples of such sentiment. A 1941 editorial in the *Gospel Herald*, for instance, referred to Mennonite war-relief contributions, civilian bonds, and CPS as mechanisms for proving Mennonite patriotism in light of their refusal to participate in conventional defense drives. They would make up for the negativity of their refusal of military service with an unblemished offering of "positive service." And H. S. Bender declared that in this "time of crisis," Mennonites would "contribute to the national welfare to the best of our ability and resources . . . we wish to provide constructive alternative contributions as obedient, loyal and productive citizens." Moreover, here was another way to counter the unpleasant characterization offered by Niebuhr. As Goshen Bible professor Howard Charles instructed Mennonite COs at a special "conscription institute" in 1945, "We are obligated to render a positive contribution to society, and if we fail to perform it we deserve to be called parasites on society." The men in the camps agreed. "CPS satisfactorily fulfills our basic beliefs and desires to refrain from military service but still serve the country we love," offered one CPSer in camp near North Fork, California.[51]

Correspondingly, Mennonites turned again to increased benevolent activity as another measure of their willingness to sacrifice. In this manner, CPS functioned as a means for the continued redefinition of Mennonites as a people of service. From 1941 to 1947, MCC received over $3 million from Mennonites for CPS work as a whole. Mennonites poured out another $4 million into civilian bond purchases, a Mennonite equivalent of war bonds but used for nonmilitary purposes. These were hefty contributions from a group of roughly only a hundred thousand people. This growing service orientation penetrated to sectors of the church beyond the level of the CPS camps. Women's groups in hundreds of different congregations labored diligently throughout the war to sustain CPS: sewing new clothing and repairing old; stitching together quilts and linens; canning vegetables, fruit, and meat. In the fall of 1943 alone, for instance, the CPS distribution point at Camp Dennison, Iowa, reported receiving over 32,000 quarts of fruit and vegetables from Mennonite congregations in Illinois, Minnesota, Nebraska, and Iowa. A rail shipment from Pennsylvania was expected that would increase this total by another 30,000 quarts.[52]

Thus, viewed on the level of general American Mennonitism, the Mennonite response to the war, particularly in CPS, appears to be a stunning triumph of the principle of nonresistance. Yet there was a strange irony underlying this ready Mennonite cooperation with a state making total war. Keim stated it best. "Among those most consciously attempting to remain aloof from government," he observed, "the Mennonites by force of circumstances found themselves in one of the most intimate relationships ever established between church and state in American history, and with the military arm of the government at that."[53] Indeed, Civilian Public Service set a firm precedent for the Mennonite strategy in the war years. As in their firm embrace of CPS—an agency, after all, that remained under the ultimate command of an army general—Mennonites would take a conservative stance on a variety of issues in a cautious blend of submissiveness and pragmatism. Remembering their experience in World War I, they remained faithful to the dictates of the nonresistant conscience, but they did so in a way that maintained the survival of their communities and the health of their young men.

Cooperation in Practice

The leadership quickly defused several potentially explosive issues of conscience in wartime that, had they decided differently, would have provoked an infinitely destructive crisis with the state. By 1940, Fast, Miller, and others had decided upon a course of draft registration, and very few young Mennonite men disobeyed this advice. Upon a suggestion from Attorney General Francis Biddle in June 1940 that a tallying of Mennonite workers might be helpful to the government, MCC undertook a detailed accounting of a number of Mennonite demographic indicators and compliantly

FIGURE 3.1. *Canning meat for MCC relief work, First Mennonite Church,
Bluffton, Ohio, early 1950s. Courtesy of Mennonite Historical Library,
Bluffton College.*

turned them in to government officials, though Quakers balked at the request. Similarly, though some Mennonites two decades later would argue otherwise, a general agreement prevailed that paying taxes, which the state would then use for war purposes, presented no difficulties for the Mennonite conscience. Given the apparent New Testament approval, Hershberger contended that refusing to pay taxes amounted to revolution, something that no devotee of biblical nonresistance could countenance.[54]

War bonds, which Hershberger described as a voluntary loan to the state for making war, were something else, however. As the government embarked on a star-studded advertising campaign to sell war bonds, pacifists once again began to feel the pressure. Soon the MCC Peace Section began receiving inquiries from Mennonites anxious about when a nonresistant alternative would materialize. Remembering the grief that bond hysteria had caused them twenty years before, church leaders sprang to create a solution equivalent to CPS. By late 1941, Miller and MC bishop John E. Lapp joined Quakers in meetings with Treasury Department officials to create a civilian bond program, which emerged the following July after what the Peace Problems Committee reported were "long and wearisome negotiations." Like CPS, civilian bonds were a compromise. Hoping for an entirely separate set of bonds earmarked for an entirely separate set of civilian purposes, pacifists received a system in which these special civilian bonds, though bought separately from war bonds, ended up in the same government coffers from which Congress drew war appropriations. Altogether, it was a very shaky accommodation for people of peace. While admitting that "the plan is not altogether what was desired," Bender tried to put the best face possible on it for the MCC, presenting it as "a step far in advance as anything achieved before."[55]

Mennonites bought civilian bonds eagerly; by 1946 they had purchased nearly $5 million dollars worth, accounting for four-fifths of all civilian bond sales. And no wonder: for the bonds, though "civilian," took community pressure off. MCC's sincere entreaties to the contrary, local war bond drive organizers commonly counted these purchases in the county quota. Hence, no Mennonites were mobbed for their refusal to buy war bonds during World War II; nor were Mennonite churches burned down. At the same time, however, like other good citizens they sent their tax and bond monies off to the treasury for the state to use as it saw fit.[56]

Another potentially troublesome issue was working in war industries, which numerous church statements prohibited for obedient Mennonites. The problem was that as nearly every American industry began to contribute in some way to military production, it became increasingly difficult to find ways of making a living that were not military related. What about a plant, the Peace Problems Committee recognized, that is primarily devoted to production of civilian items such as clothing, but gradually begins to produce uniforms? As what point does conscience necessitate new employment? The committee refused to set up any firm rules, insisting only "that a clear witness is maintained against war and that the labor of a man's hands goes primarily into peaceful civilian needs."[57]

For many Mennonite young men, this was not an abstract matter of conscience. Draftees who had accepted employment in war-related industries found that when the draft call came, they had a hard time convincing their draft boards of their pacifistic convictions. Galen Koehn, for instance, had studied at Bethel College and had dutifully registered as a conscientious objector. After college, he found employment with a manufacturing firm in Peoria, Illinois, that gradually started to accept war contracts. Koehn's convictions evolved accordingly, and he realized that to remain completely nonresistant he should quit. Instead, his draft number came up, and he joined the navy. On the other hand, Darvin Luginbuhl had obediently headed off to the CPS camp near Luray, Virginia, when he was drafted; but then he realized that his position was still a bit inconsistent. For he was maintained in CPS by funds from his sister, who was making good money working in a war plant back home in Bluffton, Ohio.[58]

Work in war industry appeared seductive for a large number of Mennonites beyond the youth. Menno Schrag, who served as editor of the *Mennonite Weekly Review* in Newton, Kansas, during the war, remembers "a good number" of local Mennonites commuting to Wichita to work at the Boeing plant there. In a survey of its membership in 1943, the MC district conference in Ohio discovered 66 members employed in defense plants. Even in the conservative Lancaster Conference, bishops had to remind their people three times about the prohibitions against it, ruling in 1943 to withhold communion from those who refused to sever their employment in war industries. Sometimes such disciplinary measures backfired. Asked to comment on why one young man from his congregation joined the military, an MC pastor from Shanesville, Ohio, reasoned that he was "rebellious because church officials kept him back from communion because he worked in a defense plant."[59]

In accordance with the Mennonite theology of nonresistance, church leaders thus tried hard to guide their people into activities and livelihoods that remained untainted by any association with the war effort. This was difficult to do in a nation at total war, and it necessitated some compromises. Uneasy to always follow then, these accommodations left an ambiguous legacy to evaluate today. Certainly, in such matters as their ready cooperation in CPS and their resigned acceptance of the civilian bond deal, the Mennonite leadership of the war years charted a passage that minimized possible grounds of conflict with the state. Properly defined and explained, none of these compromises discredited the nonresistant conscience; in them, Mennonites could function as good and useful citizens in a nation at total war while managing to remain somewhat disassociated from that war. Their options remained necessarily limited, perhaps because there was no way to escape being involved in the war effort in one way or another in a nation at total war.

Still, the ultimate acceptance of these stipulations by the mass of the Mennonite people required the leadership to keep a tight lid on prophetic stirrings in the Anabaptist heritage. This task was something leaders such as Bender had to work at consciously in a few precarious moments during the war. If much of that had gotten loose in the churches, the church might have suffered the conflict with the state that Bender had forecast in 1939. Instead, Mennonite denominations by and large escaped such a destructive confrontation with their society. For an example of what might have otherwise occurred had church leaders not managed things so carefully, Mennonites needed to look no further than what happened to Jehovah's Witnesses.[60]

Yet during the war, the leadership faced other dangers and rough spots that emerged closer to home.

DANGERS CLOSER TO HOME

For both Mennonite groups, fundamentalist dissent continued to be a major problem. For MC conservatives, the dangers to their conception of pure Mennonite nonresistance seemed greater in wartime than ever before. Yet they located the major perils not in a warmaking state, but rather in the close associations with other pacifists that alternative service forced them into. In a blistering 1941 letter to Virginia Conference ministers, a young fundamentalist dissident named Ernest Gehman charged that they were "being unequally yoked with many unbelievers, including liberal Mennonites, modernists, socialists, and communists." Gehman had been listening closely to right-wing congressman Martin Dies; in Gehman's mind, as in Dies's, groups like the Fellowship of Reconciliation (FOR) were communist front outfits. Moreover, MC fundamentalists feared that even if MCC eliminated the FOR/pacifist influence, the worldly ways of GC conscientious objectors would rub off on OM young men. These "liberal groups," Sanford Shetler complained in the fundamentalist organ the *Sword and Trumpet*, had accepted practices such as "secret orders, mixing into politics, movie attendance, (and) modernism."[61]

Bender and Miller quickly plunged into what would be several years of damage control in a series of courteous but firm exchanges with the Virginia brethren. A comment from the influential Virginia Conference leader John L. Stauffer revealed the severe degree of MC fundamentalist discontent and indicated to the church hierarchy that it had better make efforts to placate them beyond merely verbal assurances. President of Eastern Mennonite College and widely respected in Virginia, Stauffer finally asked, "Can't we cut loose in some way from Pacifists or must we break apart in the Mennonite church?" Faced with the sudden veiled threat of schism, the church leadership reacted swiftly to mollify the conservatives. The Peace Problems Committee added three new members in its American section, including bishops John E. Lapp and Amos Horst; Miller brought Gehman to Akron, Pennsylvania, to work with him in the MCC offices. Miller and Horst were dispatched to Virginia to meet with the Virginia Conference Executive Committee, where Miller stressed the NSBRO as a service board to the constituent groups, rather than a policy-making body. Most importantly in mollifying the conservatives, church leaders appointed an official "CPS Investigating Committee" that included leading critics such as Stauffer and that reported back to the conference at its 1945 session. Not surprisingly, the committee's report agreed with many of the conservative charges. It found some "socialistic and pacifistic influences" in the CPS camps, for instance; and it found dangers in NSBRO of "compromising our biblical position and being mistaken for pacifist objectors." Yet overall, the committee phrased its findings in somewhat muted tones and stopped short of demanding Mennonite Church withdrawal from NSBRO. The committee's major demands revolved around the establishment of separate CPS camps for "old" Mennonite COs. The Peace Problems Committee did set up three such camps under its own administration late in the war, but due to the gradual demobilization of CPS and disagreement with the whole idea from most Mennonite CPS men, these were minor and short-lived experiments.[62]

General Conference Mennonite Church peace leaders continued to battle an apolitical fundamentalism in their denomination, though without facing the more severe implications of MC circles. Even as Henry Fast led the delicate negotiations over the oncoming CPS system, the Peace Committee continued to receive dismal signals concerning the strength of the peace position among their young men. In September 1940, for instance, a pastor in Bluffton, Ohio, found his own young men "so unconcerned" with peace issues. Donovan Smucker wrote to Fast a month later to report on another discouraging situation in Bluffton. In that town, home to the GC Bluffton College, the son of a prominent Mennonite minister, noted Smucker, "is strutting around town in the uniform of the naval air force telling how he hit five out of five targets with a bomber." Things did not appear much better with some of the ministers. Informing Fast of his meeting with Eastern District Conference ministers that fall to discuss peace issues, Lantz noted happily that "I was quite well impressed with their attitudes." Yet one whole session, he added, was devoted to "attempting to convert" three of the ministers to "the Mennonite position. If the ministers do not know or do not believe in the principles of nonresistance how can the rank and file of the congregations believe in it?" Fast agreed, noting laconically that "some of our churches are only half awake on the issue. Those who pride themselves on their 'fundamentalism' are usually indifferent to the issues involved in military training."[63]

As the peace leadership of both Mennonite groups faced challenges from conservatives, they also began to hear dissent from other directions. A number of Mennonites beyond the fundamentalists surveyed the alternative service arrangement and found it wanting. A recognition that this dissent did not in any way negate the general Mennonite enthusiasm for CPS does not lessen its importance.

Thus Daniel Kauffman, the crusty old editor of the *Gospel Herald* and one of the most influential people in the Mennonite Church, urged Miller in 1939 to "set your foot hard against what is sometimes called 'alternative service.'" In Kauffman's mind, such service "is simply strengthening the military power of a country, something that we claim we can have no part in." In his response, Miller reviewed the many times that "old" Mennonites had agreed on the legitimacy of alternative service from the Turner statement on backward and informed him that his was the first time in his fourteen years of service with the PPC that he had heard such a perspective expressed. Alternative service was something that they had been working toward for years, he insisted, though if Kauffman disagreed, Miller would "certainly want to be corrected." So shocked was Miller at Kauffman's comments that he wondered in he should resign from the committee if his own viewpoint is "not the correct one."[64]

Obviously Kauffman's was very much a minority position, but as the war progressed, other voices rose to join his. As the outlines of the CPS program penetrated into the churches, one correspondent from Salina, Pennsylvania, wrote to ask Bender: "Why should this so-called church privilege be purchased?" Indeed, he wondered whether his church had been "*sold up the river*" by their leadership (his emphasis). Others from a conservative bent found means to question the levels of church-state cooperation in the CPS system. Shetler's *Sword and Trumpet* article listed the "chief disadvantage" of church-operated camps as "the dividing line between church and state is not as well defined as many would like to see it."[65]

Dissent also emanated from a several heretofore dependable supporters. Alarmed by plans floated late in the war for a permanent peacetime conscription and a permanent CPS, influential church leader Shem Peachey wrote to remind Bender that the original agreement had only been for a year. Now, with an open-ended commitment looming, Peachey frantically urged Bender to go to Washington and offer a million dollars to "buy" a permanent Mennonite exemption from the draft. Such an option would be preferable to Peachey "in a nation committed to permanent militarism" than the present scheme of "mortgaging our future to our government." Certainly more alarming to Bender was a short letter from an informant in

Lancaster, Pennsylvania, who reported on a speech he heard Amos Horst deliver in February 1944. The gentle, reliable leader of the Lancaster peace committee, Horst also served on the PPC and was a firm moderate ally. Yet according to Bender's informant, Horst had avowed, "I am going to state my conviction on the matter . . . I sometimes think that we should not register, and let the government take us to court and sentence our young to 5 years in the pen." The "worst part," wrote Bender's correspondent, "is that there were some who stood by him and endorsed this stand." Horst had not forgotten the church's teaching about occasions when the state's commands conflicted with those of God. Even while continuing to faithfully plug CPS, Horst informed Bender in 1945 that "we should always be prepared to make clear to government that if a civilian program . . . demands one's loyalty to the Gov. rather than to God that we would at any time withdraw from civilian service and try to live true. That we obey God rather than man, take the course with the Lord and meet the consequence with society."[66]

Faced as it was by a more serious threat from church fundamentalists, the Peace Problems Committee could afford to disregard such relatively minor dissidence. Yet while the committee calmed church conservatives and pushed the CPS program as the Mennonite solution to war, young Mennonites began to register more substantial objections to their elders' articulation of nonresistance that could not be as easily overlooked. As draft calls escalated, to their shock and dismay Mennonite peace leaders encountered wholesale defections from nonresistance in their young men's draft decisions.

Leaders became aware of this problem not long after the draft began. Reporting to the MC General Conference in the summer of 1941, Bender admitted that "a few of our young men have accepted full military service," though immediately adding that "the number is small." As the war continued, the committee began to receive indications of a worsening problem; an initial survey of congregations late in 1942 revealed about 30 percent of all OM draftees accepting military service. Bender shared these results with the larger church in February 1943 with a good deal of alarm and consternation. "Only seventy percent loyal!" he thundered. "Is this a passing grade for the Mennonite Church in God's great record book?" Later that summer in the OM general conference sessions, the committee continued its efforts to come to grips with the length and extent of the problem. A more recent census, as of August 1, 1943, revealed an even higher percentage of Mennonite men who had "become part of the military machine." In the private meetings of the OM executive committee, Bender was even more frank in his dismay, telling his fellow church leaders that "We have here in the Mennonite church seven hundred fifty members in the prime of life who didn't have the conviction to stand for this principle when it was possible in the most easy way." Moreover, he continued, he was hard pressed to put his finger on the reason why.[67]

Likewise, GC leaders began to recognize similar defections in their own ranks. The situation appeared so alarming to C. Henry Smith in 1942 that he devoted an entire article in *The Mennonite* to a discussion of "Is the General Conference Losing its Peace Testimony?" A year later, the Peace Committee conceded somewhat delicately that the many GC draftees were "confused" on the issues of military service. But by 1944–45, MCC had collected enough specific numbers revealing the extent of the breakdown of nonresistance among their young men that the general alarm took on a more focused and informed quality. In January 1945, for example, Winfield Fretz bewailed that "we are voluntarily surrendering this doctrine of our faith. The State is not taking it away." Many times when he had been out speaking on nonresistance in GC churches, he reported, the congregants had seemed offended by his "effrontery." Didn't he know, church members told him, that many members of the congregation were in the military? Didn't he know that they opposed CPS? Altogether, for a church group that had for four centuries rooted much of its identity in its pacifist nonresistance, these were ominous signs.[68]

In sum, the two Mennonite groups came through the war relatively intact and unchanged, at least in regard to their denominational structures. The same men were in charge and had begun grooming future leaders by awarding them responsible posts in CPS camp administration. In fact, ideological articulations such as Bender's Anabaptist Vision partly functioned to help legitimize the new programs and directions that he and his cohort of leaders created. Yet while they remain centrally important in twentieth-century Mennonite history, much of the story of what the war meant for the Mennonite relationship with the state is found beyond the level of church leadership and their policies. World War II would revolutionize American life in many ways, and even a group as previously isolated and inwardly focused as the Mennonites could not escape its impact. Mennonite experiences in the war would send currents of change rippling through the churches.

Bender, Hershberger and others only half realized these reverberations at the time, for they did not emanate from conferences among the bishops or theological meetings in the colleges. Instead, some of the most important changes bubbled up from below. They issued from "bull sessions" in CPS barracks late at night and from the embarrassment of hardworking farmers who, try as they might, could not quite win full approval as good citizens from their neighbors. The architects of these shifts would not be bishops, but uneasy Mennonite schoolteachers assigned to sell war stamps or frightened young COs wondering how to respond to violent mental patients with nonresistant Christian love. Both in their home communities and away at camp, Mennonite people struggled diligently to remain good Mennonites and good citizens in a nation at total war. It was hard, they discovered, to keep the two aims in balance.

CHAPTER 4

The Mennonite
People and
Total War,
1941–1945

Returning to his congregation after a six-month stint as director of a CPS camp near Marietta, Ohio, in 1941, General Conference Mennonite pastor David C. Wedel met with some confusing reactions among fellow townspeople in Halstead, Kansas. On the one hand, some people who had previously been friendly refused to speak to him anymore. They would cross the street when they saw him coming, Wedel remembered. On the other hand, other townspeople, even some "real militarists," expressed to him a grudging admiration for the young men he had worked with who had taken a stand for conscience. In other words, Wedel confronted some of the ambiguity that characterized the American response to dissent during World War II. This was a society that would work to lessen ethnic tension toward German and Italian aliens while at the same time rounding up and imprisoning without trial nearly a hundred thousand citizens of Japanese descent. As individual Mennonites labored to separate themselves in various ways from full participation in the war effort, they would likewise discover the unpredictable and paradoxical nature of wartime opposition.[1]

THE TWO FACES OF PUBLIC TOLERANCE

Mennonite COs encountered unmistakable currents of both support and sympathy for their position in the American public. CPS men stationed in Colorado Springs, Colorado, recalled H. A. Fast, soon began trickling out to different churches in the community on Sunday mornings. They were warmly welcomed by local townspeople, even as the objectors began to date some of the young women in the congregations. Assigned to this CPS camp in 1942, Harry Ratzlaff experienced no hostility from local people and testified that campers often received invitations to dinner. They managed to strike up friendly relations as well with GIs stationed at a nearby Army Air Service base. As he registered as a CO from his home in urban Los Angeles, Irvin Richert met with a good deal of support from people there. His neighbors remained friendly, and his postal worker, he recalled, "thought maybe this position was the right position to take." Richert's co-workers and boss at the county government office also fully respected his decision to follow his conscience. Similarly, returning home on furloughs from his CPS camp, Earl Loganbill never felt shunned or ashamed by non-Mennonite neighbors in rural Fortuna, Missouri; neither did Harvey Deckert, back home in Inman, Kansas on breaks from CO work.[2]

Perhaps most startling to many Mennonite COs was the attitude of warm solidarity they met with from men in uniform. Engaged in forestry work in the Sierras near North Fork, California, in 1944, one objector received a letter from a GI, a stranger, who just wanted to write to a CO about a few things. "They tell us down here," the soldier remarked, that they fought so that "all men are equal. Yet they treat you conscientious objectors as if you were Japs or something." Instead, wrote this private, "you are standing for what this country was born on." The GI admitted he would kill if he had to, but he urged this CPS man to "keep up the good work and don't lose that spirit. There are plenty of us down here that are for you 100 per cent." Similarly, as an army noncombatant stationed in Texas, Paul Springer noticed the strong currents of support for conscientious objectors among his fellow soldiers. As evidence, he clipped out and mailed home a column of letters to the editor from *Yank* magazine in which several GIs declared their admiration for the sacrificial work done by COs. Writing to a Mennonite friend back home Springer observed, "That is about how it runs in the army as far as the C. O. stand. About 4 in 5 stick up for them." Assigned to detached dairy farm service in Wisconsin in the spring of 1943, CO Robert Waltner spent some time working for a several families, the last a severely wounded ex-marine who died from his wounds shortly after Waltner left. Of all the people he had worked for, Waltner remembered, this wounded soldier was "the best of them all to me; he treated me with respect and consideration."[3]

Because of the physical isolation of most objectors, they most often encountered soldiers while traveling. In trains packed full of servicemen, Irvin Richert enjoyed "some very good conversations with soldiers." He would explain that he was dressed in civilian clothes because of his service in CPS as a conscientious objector, and "they would say, 'Well, you're doing your part, and that's all right with us.' " One of the GIs even took Richert out to dinner. When he traveled in his job as assistant director of four different CPS camps during the war, Roland Bartel would try to sit next to servicemen whenever he could, he recalled later, "because the people in the service understood us better than the civilians . . . They nearly always were sympathetic."[4]

Loris Habegger discovered the same currents of sympathy as he ventured out on the road in 1943. Director of the CPS unit at the state mental hospital in Marlboro, New Jersey, Habegger had set out for a CPS camp directors conference in Denison, Iowa. As the train left Chicago, he looked around at a blur of green uniforms and quickly realized that he was the only person in civilian clothes in the entire railway car. Inevitably, he was soon asked to explain why he lacked a uniform. "Oh, I'm in service," Habegger asserted, and went on to explain Civilian Public Service, the nature of his work, and his lack of pay and benefits. To his surprise, he encountered an ocean of sympathy among the GIs in the seats around him; the servicemen thought he was getting a "raw deal." When the train arrived in Iowa City, women from the USO moved up and down the aisle, distributing cakes and sweets to the soldiers. Habegger knew that USO volunteers had not prepared the goodies for conscientious objectors. When the GIs noticed his hesitation, they ushered him toward the feast, exclaiming, "help yourself—you're one of the boys!"[5]

Yet it was not long after Pearl Harbor that Mennonites, objectors and folks at home alike, began to confront the Janus-faced nature of American attitudes toward wartime dissent. On the other side of this genial public face loomed a less charitable one that snarled with misunderstanding and hostility. The war had barely begun when vandals splashed yellow paint across the steps and windows of the *Mennonite Weekly Review* in Newton, Kansas, and the office buzzed with phone calls warning the staff not to wash it off. Vandals also hit some of the buildings at Bethel College and the storefronts of Mennonite businessmen downtown with yellow paint. Congregants at Oak Grove Mennonite Church in Smithville, Ohio, found yellow paint daubed on the church entrance panels and another time a flag draped across the doors. Perhaps it was just a few isolated individuals who gave local Mennonites a difficult time in Kalona, Iowa. They smeared yellow paint on two Mennonite churches and threw a pipe bomb onto the bishop's front porch, where it blew out the porch light and front windows. Some time later, hooligans hung two prominent Mennonites in effigy from one of the buildings down town, where they remained for weeks until public officials took them down. In this instance, the culprits were promptly arrested, many local people sought out Mennonites to assure them of their friendship, and the state's leading newspaper, the *Des Moines Register*, published an editorial denouncing the vandalism.[6]

Perhaps such animosity partly emanated from simple public misconceptions about conscientious objection to war. At least one visitor to the CPS camp near Magnolia, Arkansas, demanded to see the barbed wire fence that he supposed would be enclosing the camp. In the summer of 1943, Amanda Ediger left Bethel College for a job working alongside of Mennonite COs at a mental hospital in Ypsilanti, Michigan. As she hitchhiked around town in her time off, conversations with drivers invariably turned to who she was and why she was there. Often local people peppered her with questions about the COs at the hospital. Did they ever get out from behind locked doors? People had the impression, Ediger realized, that the objectors were in the hospital as the mental patients.[7]

Most commonly, however, the hostility simmered at a direct and unmistakable level. As agricultural extension officials mapped out a program of sending COs into rural areas to work as dairy testers, for instance, many farmers voiced anger at the projected personnel. Said one, "I don't think I would want a C. O. to sleep at my house!" Henry Fast met with only partial success in his effort to situate the CPS camps near communities that would respond to COs, if not with complete acceptance, at least not with violent antagonism. As incoming CPS workers arrived in trucks at California's Camp Camino, local people threw tomatoes at them. Near a CPS camp run by the Friends near Coshocton, Ohio, schoolchildren regularly taunted CPS men laboring at soil conservation work. Local people in Merom, Indiana, vigorously opposed a CPS camp that opened near them in June 1941, claiming it would mean a loss of jobs under the auspices of the Works Progress Administration. Members of the local American Legion hall threatened to run the COs out of town. At Exeter, Rhode Island, doing mental hospital work, Paul Davidhizar encountered an older couple who had a son fighting in the Pacific; their anger was very vocal and nasty. Likewise, Glen Gering heard from one woman, "You don't deserve to live!"[8]

COs on the road ran into some difficult moments too. Generally Earl Loganbill met with little animosity as he traveled. But when he was pulled over for speeding in Washington, D.C., recalled Loganbill, the arresting officer treated him "like a criminal," once he discovered his CO status. "You ought to be put in a concentration camp," said the policeman. Likewise, although he encountered little tension with GIs while traveling on trains, Richert found that civilians were a different matter. "The old ladies were the hardest ones . . . They would really get after us for being slackers and not going to war." John Gaeddert had a less pleasant experience with servicemen on trains. Journeying from rural Kansas to Fresno, California, en route to CPS, Gaeddert lined up for meals with the other troops. Reading his ticket, the steward loudly announced his CO status to all within hearing and informed Gaeddert that he would eat last. Thus intimidated, Gaeddert did not take anymore meals the rest of the 52-hour trip. Once as he hitchhiked the five hundred miles back home to South Dakota from CPS, Robert Waltner was picked up by a man who said he would be happy to take him all the way to Sioux Falls. Once the driver learned of Waltner's CO position, though, he kicked him out of the car, so angry that Waltner feared he would turn violent. The same thing happened to Arthur Weaver as he hitchhiked with a group of GIs. The driver demanded that he get out immediately, despite the soldiers' pleas to "let him stay."[9]

An especially unpleasant incident happened to six Mennonite COs from McPherson County, Kansas. One hot day in August 1944, they boarded a bus full of other area young men to go to Fort Leavenworth for their preinduction physical examinations. The young men fell to talking and joking, with many of the jokes, increasingly bitter in tone, directed toward the Mennonites. The trouble began as the bus neared Emporia. One of the Mennonites offered the opinion that those heading into the military were "nothing but murderers." This comment brought him a prompt punch in the face from one of the non-Mennonites, and the hostility rapidly escalated from there. The verbal abuse intensified, with the group demanding the Mennonites recant their pacifism and heaping insults on them when they refused. Before long, groups of boys gathered around the dissenters, slapping, punching, and kicking while the bus driver egged them on. Someone procured a razor and dry shaved the three dissenters wearing beards. Similarly, when the bus stopped briefly in Emporia, another participant bought some scissors, and the group treated the Mennonites to rough haircuts as the bus rolled on. Finally, amidst their crying and praying, the young men were ordered to take off their pants and were beaten with their belts when they refused to perform homosexual acts. Officers at Fort Leavenworth took testimony about the incident, and with Kansas newspapers headlining their outrage, the perpetrators were later convicted and fined.[10]

Sequestered in isolated units, COs could rely on each other for mutual support most of the time. Wives and children, who sometimes followed them to their posts and took up jobs and residences in small towns nearby, often bore the brunt of local hostility. Harvey Deckert's wife accompanied him as he went off to camp in western Nebraska and found an apartment and a job at a grocery store in the town of North Platte. Once her employers learned why she had come to town and what her husband was, they summarily dismissed her. She found another job at a clothing store in town, and the same thing happened again. Despite their desire to live by their husbands in a nearby CPS camp, CO wives quickly departed the town of Henry, Illinois, after local toughs threatened to "go up the river" and "wipe out" the pacifists.[11]

Patriotic anger and hostility mounted to particularly intense levels in strong Mennonite communities, where enough Mennonites had gathered to seemingly pose a particular threat to local people. For example, in Newton, Kansas, the newspaper published the names and status of local draftees, and the school board would not hire graduates from the town's only institute of higher education, Bethel College. Community anger peaked, recalled Karolyn Kaufman, when the columnist Walter Winchell announced on the radio one Sunday evening that the German "Bundes Center" in the entire country was Newton, Kansas. As a young teenager and daughter of the college president, Edmund G. Kaufman, Karolyn Kaufman bore the brunt of some of the ensuing anti-Mennonite hostility. Along with her friends, she was regularly harassed while walking home from school. They could no longer could congregate at the skating rink because beating up young Mennonites emerged as a popular local pastime among many area teenagers. Junior high school became especially difficult. By refusing to join in at regular patriotic rallies and school war bond drives, Kaufman and other children of Bethel faculty stood out as special targets. Every Friday, students had to stand up and inform their teacher how many war stamps they would buy, a process Kaufman remembered as "pretty traumatic" because she would not buy any. Her parents finally pulled her out of the public schools in the eighth grade. Meanwhile, members of Newton's First Mennonite Church thought it politic to install the national flag in their sanctuary, as did congregants in nearby Tabor.[12]

The tide of popular patriotism also ran very strong in the home of the GCMC's other college in Bluffton, Ohio. Townspeople were reminded of the Mennonite and pacifist orientation of the college when its president, L. L. Ramseyer, refused to allow a local war manufacturer, the Tripplet Company, to store spare parts in an empty campus building. As a Mennonite enrolled in the public high school there, Varden Loganbill experienced a great deal of community pressure and hostility. The town had an especially active American Legion chapter that seemed to specialize in generating such feelings. One Legionnaire and draft board member delivered a speech at a school assembly that made Loganbill "awfully uncomfortable . . . just being a Mennonite . . . You felt almost to the place where you didn't like to go to town or to public functions anywhere because of the pressure that was there." When the son of the Bluffton College art professor returned home on furlough from CPS and ventured into town, local toughs beat him up.[13]

Similarly, in the village of Akron, Pennsylvania, where Orie Miller had brought MCC's headquarters to his home property, townspeople also felt threatened (especially as the MCC staff grew during the war with the added responsibility of administering CPS). When he served on the CPS staff there, Richert remembers, "We had children and high-schoolers hooting and hollering about us the whole three years I was there. We could hardly go into town, a block away, without having the name 'CO' thrown at us in a derogatory way." People were especially "mean" in the days of celebration following the victories over Germany and Japan.[14]

Sometimes this seething public anger cost Mennonites more than emotional discomfort or public humiliation; as with Mrs. Deckert, at times it cost them their livelihoods. As a primary school teacher in Reedley, California, Florence Auernheimer refused to sell war stamps to the children and subsequently lost her job. Selma Platt's ordeal in Moundridge, Kansas, a small, heavily Mennonite, wheat-farming community about twenty miles north of Newton, clearly illuminates the costs that devotion to conscience could exact in a nation with morale pumped up high for total victory.[15]

A 1924 graduate of Bethel College, Platt had taught English in the Moundridge public schools before marrying and moving elsewhere. Now, in 1941, widowed with three children, she returned to the area to resume teaching at Moundridge High School and try to pick up the pieces of her life. She had not, however, forgotten the lessons learned in her Mennonite childhood and education. "I was," she recalled later, "an outspoken pacifist at that time." As the nation veered into war, her convictions brought her what she politely labeled "difficulties." For example, when she refused to attend a school assembly where participants, in a frenzy of patriotic feeling, burned an effigy of the Japanese Emperor Hirohito, her absence upset students and other faculty.

As Platt taught an English lesson one day, the high school band began practicing the national anthem, and the notes wafted in through the windows. A few of the boys immediately stood up. Not realizing what was happening, she asked that they either sit down or leave. The boys stalked out and proceeded straightway down town to the American Legion Hall, where they breathlessly reported the outrage. Soon graffiti appeared on the windows of the downtown drugstore, saying something taunting about Mrs. Platt and Hirohito. In "a humiliating sort of experience" as she attended a high school football game, someone stuck a small note to the back of her hat, again commenting on her supposed relationship with the Japanese emperor. Unknowing, she wore the sign for hours. On another occasion, someone disconnected wires in her car and disabled it, and some "super-patriotic students" pelted her home with rocks.

The final blow came at another school assembly, where a speaker delivered a fiery recruiting speech for the military. Platt sat passively in the midst of the tumult, and people noticed. Soon afterward, members of the school board called her in for a consultation, wanting to know why she had not clapped. Platt replied that "there were a lot of things I didn't feel like I could clap about." The board warned her, she remembered later, that they would not rehire her for the next year if she did not "keep quiet about my feelings about the war." But Platt could not keep quiet. "I just felt so strongly about it. I don't feel it's right to have a conviction in that way and hide behind anything." Instead of silencing her conscience, she resigned in the middle of the school year and began searching for other work.[16]

Given the course that their leaders had mapped out so carefully, most Mennonites were able to avoid this kind of destructive confrontation. Yet there was one group of Mennonites who would have to step forward in one way or another. Writing a few days after Pearl Harbor, Walter Dyck observed to Ernest Bohn that "with the declaration of war will come the real tests to our young men." Given the pressures sweeping through their communities, these men would offer a mixed and uncertain answer.[17]

THE MENNONITE COMMUNITY AND THE DRAFT DECISION

Because the draft decisions made by thousands of individual Mennonites lie so close to the crux of the basic matter on which this study is focused, it is worthwhile to examine them more closely. Fortunately, given the importance of the question, Mennonite scholars have made careful studies along this line.[18]

Perhaps the place to begin in summarizing the census results is with an overall look at the breakdown for the two major groups (see Table 1). For

Mennonites as a whole, in the final 1947 numbers, out of a total of 9,809 draftees, 4,536 or 46.2 percent opted for conscientious objection; whereas 3,876, or 39.5 percent, accepted full military service and 1,397 or 14.2 percent chose noncombatant service.

Mennonite leaders and pastors thus had good reason for their alarm and dismay. With barely a quarter of all their drafted men adhering to the church's teaching and opting for conscientious objection, GC Mennonites had reason to question their very commitment as a "peace church," and even the conservative (by comparison) OM Mennonites had to face the reality that nearly half their young men opted for military service.

The numbers become much more revealing when cross-tabulated with considerations of occupation, education, and age. Overall, 60.8 percent of all drafted farmers chose CPS, and 56.3 percent of all teachers did so. Almost half, 47.1 percent, of all Mennonite office workers went CO, while only 31.7 percent of day laborers and factory workers did so. As late as the World War II years, the age-old Mennonite association between agrarian occupations and spiritual purity still held, at least in respect to adherence to nonresistance. The men who stayed on the farm, close to the overwhelmingly rural Mennonite community, opted for conscientious objection at a much higher rate, though they did so in proportion to the relative strength of the peace principle in their church overall. The pressures from the larger society toward military conformity exerted a much greater pull in factory and office settings than in the relative isolation of the family farm. Moreover, the larger numbers of teachers in the CPS camps undoubtedly

TABLE 1. *MC and GCMC Draft Classifications, 1947 Totals*

	MCs	GCs
1A	29.9%	57.7%
1AO*	10.6	15.6
4E	59.5	28.6
	100.0%	99.9%
Total Number	3272	3113

* The classification for noncombatant service.
Source: These numbers taken from Hershberger, *The Mennonite church in the Second World War,* 39.

reflected their employment in large numbers in rural schools and a higher percentage of college training for people in this occupation.[19]

Likewise, examinations of draft status and education testify to the relative strength of the Mennonite community as a predominant determining factor in young Mennonites' draft choices. For all Mennonite branches, 56.7 percent of those with only a grade-school education were in CPS, whereas 37.4 percent of high-school-educated men and 50.2 percent of college-educated men did so. The consideration of education underscores urban-rural differences as well as the relative impact of Mennonite teaching. Men with only a grade-school education overwhelmingly tended to come from rural environments, many of them educated in Mennonite grade schools. Similarly, the high CO percentages for college students probably reflected the marked Mennonite tendency to enroll in Mennonite schools such as Goshen, Bethel, and Bluffton Colleges, locales of a heightened Mennonite awareness and relatively strong Mennonite community. Correspondingly, the lower CO percentages for high school students mirrored the secularizing and larger societal pressures of the public high school. In a 1943 report, H. S. Bender recognized the tremendous promilitary pressure that Mennonite adolescents received from their peers in public high schools. Mennonite GIs testified to this pressure in explaining their draft decisions. Even in strong Mennonite communities such as Lancaster County, Pennsylvania, Mennonites were a pronounced minority in the high schools. Partly for this reason, by 1945 "old" Mennonites had founded five new private Mennonite high schools and seventeen new elementary schools.[20]

The relative ages of CPS and military draftees are also noteworthy. Overall, younger and older men tended to enroll in military ranks, whereas men in their early twenties preferred CPS. For Mennonites as a whole, 52.5 percent of 18-20-year-olds were in military service, whereas only 32.4 percent of the 21-23-year-olds chose this option. The later ages showed a steady increase in men choosing 1A.[21]

Clearly, for both groups the younger ages had a strong predilection toward military service, something that leaders in both groups noted at the time. Bender noted an explanation for this in 1946, explaining that they had had a "fairly strong program of peace teaching" in place in the prewar years, and "a large number of our younger people got the opportunity to develop peace convictions." But the war came along and "most of us stopped talking on the question . . . some of our brethren were afraid to speak over the pulpit and give advice, thinking it was dangerous." Consequently, Bender continued, high school boys have been growing up through four years of war with little peace training to combat the tremendous influence of "the war spirit." "When they are drafted," Bender asked, "what happens? Well, the record shows that is where we are failing."[22]

If one seeks for a single explanation of why some Mennonites elected to go to CPS while others submitted to induction into the army, the level of acculturation is a convincing explanation. The further a particular man had gotten from the Mennonite community socially and culturally, the more likely he was to enlist when faced with the draft call. The men who had left the rural community and found a social niche in the public high school, those who had settled into employment away from the farm in a factory or an office, those who had established non-Mennonite networks— these were the ones who joined the army. Of course, not all of these factors were operative for all Mennonite GIs; and certainly for many, none of them were. Yet the distance away from the rural Mennonite community must have been crucial for a large number. Altogether, S. F. Pannabecker summarized in 1943, "Under the influence of the American environment, the support which formerly came from social separation is lost. This factor, more than any other, explains the defection of Mennonite youth from the non-resistant position."[23]

A final aspect of acculturation that registered its impact on Mennonite draft decisions, a factor beyond socioeconomic considerations, was the continued effects of fundamentalism. While its influence was complex,[24] fundamentalist arguments continued to eat away at nonresistant convictions in this most crucial decision. Kreider, for instance, observed that "congregations under the spell of non-Mennonite Bible Institutes have fewer CO's." This theological influence was not confined to the General Conference Mennonite Church; it exerted a seductive effect on so many "old" Mennonites that the PPC needed to publish a separate booklet on the matter in 1943. Edward Yoder's *Can Christians Fight?* refuted, point by point, fundamentalist promilitary arguments. Still, fundamentalism wooed more than one OM draftee into military service. A Lancaster pastor, for example, testified that one of his young men enlisted because he was a "follower of national Bible preachers." And a regretful army noncombatant professed, "I was plenty misinformed by reading fundamentalist magazines before I got in the army."[25]

Exploring some individual examples of young Mennonites wrestling with the conflicting claims of God and country underscores the crucial im-

portance of acculturation and the Mennonite community in their decisions. Admittedly, for many young Mennonites, their relative distance
from their home church or the relative strength of the peace teaching in
their community seemed to make little difference in their final decision
when the draft call came. Two brothers from Salem Mennonite, in Kidron,
Ohio, for example, were enrolled far way from home at a state university
when their draft calls came. One opted for the military. The second had
been active in college peace groups where his comrades often asked him
about Mennonite pacifism, and he had "made an effort to know" so he
could answer them. When he returned to his home church, he found Salem
Mennonite teenagers largely unaware of nonresistance. This student enrolled in CPS. In 1944, members of Salem Mennonite mourned the death
of Pfc. Lester Steiner. A "regular attender" who was one of "the most active
of the younger group," Steiner was killed in action in Italy. On the other
hand, Roland Juhnke grew up in the relatively tightly bound Mennonite
community of Moundridge, Kansas, and its Eden Mennonite Church.
There his pastor, Walter Gering, carefully taught nonresistance, and
strong social and theological currents pushed the church youth toward
CPS. However, Juhnke, along with a half dozen or so other young men from
this large church, chose military service. Juhnke had made some close
friends in a local National Guard unit, and he enlisted out of a sense of duty
to them and to his country.[26]

Moreover, to attribute CO decisions solely to the "pressures of the Mennonite community" proceeds on thin historical ice, given the influence
popular patriotism exerted in many Mennonite congregations during the
war. Despite careful teaching from the top church leaders, the congregations themselves were deeply divided on the war. Lynn Leichty's pastor,
C. H. Suckau of First Mennonite Church in Berne, Indiana, for example,
cautioned young men in his church that if they opted for CPS they would
have to rely on others to fight for them; and he inaccurately described noncombatant service as "historically and traditionally the service of the Mennonite church." This church placed a display board listing all the congregation's servicemen near the front entrance, and Mennonite visitors were
sometimes shocked to see the long list of members in the military and the
comparatively few names in CPS. Likewise, as a boy in the OM Oak Grove
congregation in Wayne County, Ohio, John Smucker watched a similar list
from week to week to see which list of names would grow longer. (In this
church, the lists ended up about equal in size).[27]

Salem Mennonite Church in Ohio managed to avoid such scenes because of the pastor's close adherence to a strict course of apparent neutrality. One congregant recalled that the Rev. A. S. Rosenberger "did not influence my decision in any way"; another did not remember "him advocating any course of action from the pulpit." Instead, this minister made a deliberate attempt "to avoid conflict." Another pastor, W. F. Unruh of West Zion Mennonite Church in Moundridge, could not sit so quietly. When Unruh was installed as minister on Pearl Harbor Sunday, one of four American Legionnaires in his new congregation immediately informed him: "Now we are at war; this is no time to preach on peace." Reading of the terrible destruction of the war, Unruh eventually could contain himself no longer; and one Sunday evening, he warned of God's coming judgment because of such slaughter. A Legionnaire threatened him afterwards: "You're out now!" Undaunted, Unruh went on to preach other sermons condemning the bombings at Dresden and calling for repentance after Hiroshima.[28]

Even with these complexities, however, the weight of acculturation and the relative strength of the social and theological bonds of the Mennonite community still appear a centrally important variable in the draft decision. Over and over again, Mennonite CPS men testified to the influence of home and family that sent them that direction. Raised in Moundridge, Kansas, Rueben Krehbiel remembered, "We were pretty much removed from the outer world. We were pretty much a closed community." Like all his Mennonite high school friends and almost all the young men from Eden Church, Krehbiel enrolled in CPS. Harvey Deckert recalls opting for conscientious objection because "we just sort of grew up that way. There was no other way; it never entered my mind that I would go regular combatant." Similarly, Waldo Wedel took the CO stance because "it was taught to us in church and sort of ingrained in our belief that war was wrong." To George Nachtigall, explaining his conscientious objection to GC peace leader Albert Gaeddert in 1944, it was enough to say, "I am a Mennonite, and followed the general pattern which was established for us . . . It was the natural thing for me to do."[29]

To be sure, draftees chose CPS for more altruistic reasons as well. One CPSer, who engaged in forestry work near North Fork, California, for instance, testified that "I am in C. P. S. because I cannot harmonize the business of taking life with the teaching of the Bible." A fellow camper agreed, stating that he chose CPS "because I believe the principle of peace . . . is going one step further along the way of Christ." Waltner believed that Jesus would have chosen CPS, for "that was His will for us, that we should take a stand against the evils of war and witness to a way of peace."[30]

Yet relatively few Mennonites offered such reasoning when asked to explain their draft decisions, at least when compared with those stressing the guidance from home and church.[31] This very fact had a profound effect on the quality of the CPS experience for many. A reliance on a strong Mennonite community to steer young men into the community-sanctioned service option produced a large number of CPS boys who chose it mostly because of Mennonite expectations. Raymond Kramer expressed this problem plainly in his 1946 observation that "all too many of our C. P. S. men went to camp for reasons of 'social pressure' rather than for a deep sense of the claim of Christ upon their lives." A camp educational director held a discussion with his men on "what's wrong with our unit," and the campers listed as a prominent reason that "many of us do not know just why we are in CPS. We are here, not so much on the basis of personal conviction about a Way of Life . . . as on the basis of the desire and insistence of church and family." As a result, noted a conference of Mennonite CPS camp directors in November 1944, "There is evidence of being 'camp happy' and too much of 'sitting out the war.' "[32]

Mennonite draftees who decided differently when faced with the conflicting loyalties to God and country also cannot be neatly fit into simplified abstractions. Even so, many young Mennonite GIs also seem to have enlisted because they appeared more in tune with social networks or political analyses operative outside the boundaries of their Mennonite world. It is not hard to imagine many different scenarios of the advice of friends or parents or an influential uncle proving fundamental in a draftee's final decision. David Warkentine later recalled having little doubt in his mind that he wanted to join the navy, and why not? Living in a non-Mennonite community, he felt little pressure from that quarter; and with two older brothers already in the military, his parents did not voice any opposition. As noted above, Varden Loganbill faced a vast sea of public hostility as he considered his draft choice in Bluffton, Ohio. Not wishing to antagonize the community, his high school principal, though a Mennonite, said nothing on the topic; Loganbill's father appeared "wishy-washy" for similar reasons. As a compromise between his mother's and father's wishes, Loganbill opted for noncombatant service and spent four months in Okinawa as a stretcher bearer.[33]

In a like manner, many of these men chose military ranks because of a moral reasoning more in sympathy with the national justifications for the conflict. The most common reasons Mennonite soldiers and sailors gave for enlisting mirrored those of many other Americans and revolved around considerations of duty. Predictably, most ministers neglected to mention this in their reports to the draft census, though Charles picked it up in his report. "Such a positive acceptance of military service under the sanctions of religious duty constitutes a complete denial of the historic peace tradition of the Mennonite Church," he lamented. The servicemen, of course, saw it differently. Floyd Krehbiel reasoned that "the only way this nation is going to survive is if enough people thought highly enough of it to take up arms to protect it." This realization to Krehbiel outweighed all the "indoctrination" he had received at church.[34]

There were other considerations that led Mennonites to a promilitary draft decision. Financial reasons may have played more of a part than church leaders realized, and this factor increased in significance as the war lengthened and the government began to draft older men. As one OM pastor remarked in December of 1942, "It is coming to the bread and butter question." And Hershberger noted the increased number of Mennonites entering noncombatant service after that year. In this context, it is appropriate to briefly consider a special category of Mennonite servicemen—noncombatant soldiers. Many of these were faithful Mennonites who could not bring themselves to take life, but who also could not afford the financial blow of CPS service. MCC endeavored to provide aid to their dependents, but many men hesitated to take "handouts" from the church. Howard Buller, for instance, decided on 1AO because "I don't believe in killing . . . and at that time my folks were very poor and we couldn't see our way through going into a C. O. camp because they would have to support me." Similarly, when Levi Friesen's draft call came, his parents had just lost their grocery store, and the family had few financial options. Probed by his pastor, Friesen simply replied that he had enlisted as a noncombatant "for one reason only—I have nobody to support me." Commenting on the boys from his church who went noncombatant, one pastor testified, "It is quite evident that the financial side of the question plays an important part in their decision."[35]

Thus, the relative Mennonite resistance to the forces of acculturation played a dominant role in determining the direction of individual Mennonite draft decisions. Yet the Mennonite reevaluation of their relationships with the state on this most foundational level did not end with this decision.

Whether these young men came up with the personal wherewithal to take up alternative service or summoned the courage to enter the army, this working out of Mennonite-state relations continued as they headed off to their respective camps.

IN THE SERVICE OF THEIR COUNTRY

Several attitudinal and behavioral developments occurred among Mennonite CPS men that would register deep reverberations in the course of postwar Mennonite history.[36] One such development was that CPS camps began to function, in Sawatsky's words, as "Mennonite melting pots." Simply put, the camps threw together Mennonites from widely different theological and cultural traditions, putting them in situations where they began to live and work together and where, sometimes to their surprise, they learned to like and respect each other. Admittedly, CPS revealed the inter-Mennonite tensions too, particularly between the two opposite cultural poles of the "old" Mennonites and the General Conference Mennonites. As noted in chapter 3, the alarm among some MC youth over the apparent GC disinterest in nonconformity brought these strains into the camps, an alarm some of their elders consciously tried to foster. In turn, sometimes the more acculturated GC CPSers reacted negatively to a perceived cultural and theological rigidity of the "old" Mennonites. Responding to Bender's efforts to placate the more fundamentalist brethren by introducing a perceived conservative atmosphere into the camps, for instance, the GC minister William Stauffer wrote Fast claiming, "Our boys are dissatisfied enough. If Bender has his way we'll have more leave [CPS for military ranks]." Likewise, Roland Bartel recalled much more friction in the camps between different Mennonites than with outside groups.[37]

But such points of discontent only amounted to a few sour notes in the face of an overwhelming sense of appreciation that CPS men from different Mennonite groups began to develop for each other. To a degree, this appreciation stemmed from the inevitable breakdown of stereotypes as the men gained a new knowledge about each other. The newsletter from a CPS camp near Terry, Montana, noted, "We had intimate contacts with men from all branches of the Mennonite Church and other churches besides. We know other Mennonites as they are and not as we used to think them to be." Nor was it just the men who discovered something about their own stereotypes. On her evaluation of her work as a "CO Girl" in a state mental hospital, one Summer Service Unit veteran admitted, "I didn't realize I was such a narrow-minded Old Mennonite."[38]

FIGURE 4.1. *Conscientious objectors returning from field work, CPS Camp No. 25, Weeping Water, Nebraska, 1942–1943. Mennonite Library and Archives, Bethel College, North Newton, Kansas.*

Equally important, this sense ranged beyond the new familiarity to encompass determined new patterns of Mennonite ecumenicity. Although Mennonite-segregated camps might have made sense to conservative bishops in Virginia, large numbers of Mennonite CPS men judged them a uniformly bad idea. CPS men from a camp in the Shenandoah Valley agreed. One OM objector voiced his conviction that CPS "has resulted in more branches of the Mennonite Church working together than has ever been accomplished before," something he found "broadening." A fellow GC camper agreed, arguing "when I consider the benefits derived from the contacts made in camp, I strongly favor retaining the present set-up." In their evaluations of CPS, 67 percent of Mennonite COs thought that the results of such Mennonite intermixture were "beneficial" in their own group, whereas only 9 percent found it "harmful." Perhaps the best expression of this feeling came out in a reply to a questionnaire that the "Camp Committee" of the Lancaster Conference distributed to their CPS men. "I feel that you, our church leaders and home ministers," this camper wrote, "have overlooked the rare and excellent opportunity you have for guiding us into a richer . . . consecration to our common Lord and Master, after the government has gotten us together in a way that the church could not have done."[39]

A second and equally significant development occurred in the creation of a shared ethic of compassionate service as a hallmark of a new Mennonitism. Such an orientation found expression in a number of places even before the war. One potential CO wrote to Henry Fast in October 1940, for example, voicing his hope that objectors could engage in such activities as "reconstruction work" or "aiding suffering civilians in war-torn places . . . That is where we could let our light shine much better than in doing farm work, forestry, and things along that line."[40]

The problem, as Fast replied to the young Arnold Reimer, was that "the kind of work we will finally undertake is not, first of all, what we would like to do but what the government will permit us to do." And at least for the first several years of CPS, what the government would permit, many felt, was not too exciting or significant. Indeed, much of the reason for the concentration of COs into isolated areas lay in specific Selective Service policy. Giving the COs glamorous work might tempt the insincere to claim sudden pangs of conscience. The menial nature of much CPS work triggered a great deal of the discontent and criticism of CPS among COs as a whole. Even the generally less contentious and more satisfied Mennonites quickly perceived that the labor they found themselves engaged in was far from the people-oriented program of "constructive good" that many had envisioned. An MCC camp newsletter, for instance, carefully detailed an example of such "CPS piddling." For four days COs labored to break up a rock, although dynamite, which was nearby and available, could have accomplished this task much sooner. The foreman merely explained that if they had used dynamite, the men would have finished the task too quickly. Given the large and depressing number of similar incidents, one Mennonite CPSer wrote home to complain of "the puttery work we have here . . . I feel that my time here is a waste and a loss to the country's good work." Even Mennonite administrators were subject to this frustration; Loewen remembered feeling some "real anguish" that he was "on the shelf, and here the last cataclysm was occurring and you were off digging postholes."[41]

Accordingly, MCC worked hard to provide work more directly related to human need and suffering. Selective Service quickly ruled out COs engaging in social welfare work because of the "possibility that they might spread their philosophies and thus hamper the war effort." To many COs, the more ideal arrangement would be going into the war zone and laboring in reconstruction work as pacifists had done during World War I. There they could physically repair the devastation the war had wrought and even more visibly demonstrate their willingness to engage in sacrificial service. MCC created a number of relief training schools toward this end and had already dispatched Robert Kreider to China (under the auspices of AFSC) to begin these efforts when Congress prohibited CO work overseas in 1943. Consequently, AFSC had to call him back and orient the relief training schools for postwar efforts. Kreider was stranded in South Africa, where he worked for two months in a Zulu hospital in Durban before catching a ship for home. Altogether, the congressional prohibition in the Starnes Rider came as a grievous letdown to many objectors. As the *MCC Bulletin* admitted, "Today C. P. S. has been disappointed in its one great hope."[42]

More success came with MCC's investigation into the possibility of objectors laboring in mental hospitals. Never in high demand because of the low pay and the unpleasant nature of much of the work, positions in mental hospitals became even more difficult to fill with the onset of the draft. Understaffed and overwhelmed by their numbers of patients, hospital administrators welcomed the army of CO workers the NSBRO would send them. For their part, CO administrators pursued the idea because, in Fast's words, "it was an effort to get closer to serving people rather than just taking care of the soil and the trees. Part of the push came from the boys themselves." By September 1945, over 1,000 Mennonite COs served in twenty-six mental hospital and training school units; by the end of the war, over 1,500 Mennonite CPSers had served in mental hospitals. Similarly, MCC funneled men into public health work as well, mostly putting them to work constructing sanitary privies in a program of hookworm eradication and other public health efforts in Florida, Mississippi, and Puerto Rico.[43]

Thus, even with the restrictions imposed on them, CPS did much to stimulate among Mennonite objectors an aggressive, passionate concern for the poor; and it did even more to pull Mennonite youth out of rural isolation and plunge them into a world of unmistakable need. In this world, they encountered new areas of concern and challenges to their nonresistance that their elders had not foreseen. For instance, many Mennonite COs learned a lot about the grim realities of American race relations. Initially, the potential for this seemed limited, given MCC's decision to obediently segregate its CPS unit in Gulfport, Mississippi, in accordance with

local law. Mennonite administrators at first shrugged off the intense criticism leveled at them by many COs, explaining that an interracial camp was
impossible in Mississippi. This way, they explained, Mennonites could
minister to both races and quietly demonstrate their belief in human brotherhood. But interracial contact occurred anyway, despite administrative
pragmatism, and it imparted some lessons to sheltered Mennonite COs.
While constructing sanitary privies around Mulberry, Florida, objectors
warmly welcomed a local black farmer through the front door of the mess
hall and ate dinner with him, only slowly realizing his amazement and fear.
On staff at Mulberry, Roland Bartel shook hands with an African American
in the local post office. A local white took Bartel aside and reprimanded him
severely. Members of a camp near Orlando who had been working in a black
high school threw a party for the graduating class. Shortly afterward, the
local Ku Klux Klan warned them to "lay off."[44]

Beyond the South, too, COs received new perspectives on race. FOR
organizer and racial activist Bayard Rustin received a warm welcome from
objectors in Mennonite CPS camps in Fort Collins, Colorado, and Weeping Water, Nebraska, where he lectured on nonviolence and American racial injustice. "Rustin's visit was definitely a high spot on our camp program," reported the Weeping Water camp newsletter. Before long, several
camp papers had begun to issue forthright editorials on racial pain and the
evils of segregation; so did MCC's newsletter. Nor was racial awareness
confined to the pain of African Americans. In 1942, Gaeddert suggested to
Miller that Mennonites take interned Japanese families into their communities. On their own, COs at Camp Camino built a number of toys for the
children at a Japanese internment camp nearby. The shipment of the box
of toys from the CPS camp to the internment camp caused a stir at the train
station, remembered Walter Unrau. A railway agent opened it carefully
amidst a big crowd, thinking it was guns and ammunition.[45]

Young objectors faced innumerable challenges to their convictions in
mental hospital work. There rough supervisors often informed the COs by
word and example to handle the patients overly firmly, to "whip them, or
they will whip you." Usually COs learned how to deal with potentially violent situations with their convictions intact. At one hospital for the vio-
lently insane, orderlies had sequestered a crazed inmate in a padded cell,
but he still waved a razor blade. They called two COs to "take care of him."
The two went in the cell, carrying a mattress for protection in front of
them, and calmed the inmate down. Another CO found himself confronted
by a huge inmate (nicknamed "Evil" by the orderlies) towering above him

FIGURE 4.2. *CPS Camp No. 8, Marietta, Ohio. Buildings left to right: dormitory; dormitory; kitchen; (rear, long building) shop, recreation, visitors quarters; (foreground) coal bin; (small, white building) laundry; (far right) bath house and latrine. Mennonite Library and Archives, Bethel College, North Newton, Kansas.*

and holding aloft a heavy oaken chair. Although the usual response from an orderly thus threatened would have been to deliver a swift kick in the groin, related Fast, this CO asked the inmate, "How do you expect to sit down on that when you hold it up like that?" The inmate merely laughed, put it down, and walked away. Working as a mental hospital attendant, Bill Keeney found his commitment to nonresistance tested a number of times. Once a violent inmate escaped from his hand straps and came after Keeney "with those fists going." Keeney reminded the inmate of his friendship and refused to fight back. The inmate returned to his bed and held out his hands for the restraints. Patients who had been regularly abused by non–CO orderlies and thus had been kept restrained most of the time learned to trust Keeney and his fellow COs. Within a month, Keeney remembered, they had "gotten rid of" most other orderlies and COs ran the ward alone.[46]

Yet such happy stories were not the only kind to emanate from CPS hospital units. All too often, pacifist COs let fear, overwork, and tension get the better of them and temporarily set nonresistance on the shelf. One unit's newsletter admitted that "Some of us have been brutal . . . we have cuffed, kicked, and sworn at our charges." Similarly, another CO hospital orderly

reported to Melvin Gingerich after the war that he had repeatedly witnessed fellow COs who "struck unwilling patients and beat up noisy and
troublesome patients in order to make them behave." (He himself admitted
to striking them, but never to beating them up.) In 1946, a Virginia jury
sentenced a Mennonite objector to two years in prison on involuntary man-
slaughter charges. He had participated in the beating of a patient who had
subsequently died.[47]

Such incidents notwithstanding, a new consciousness about the biblical
mandate for human service penetrated deep into the Mennonite identity.
Mennonite CPS publications—especially the newsletters published by
each camp—testified to this new mandate repeatedly. The *Pike View Peace
News*, for instance, pointed to a whole new orientation among Mennonites
and argued, "The change is not coming about through an overthrow of the
doctrine of 'separation from the world.' It is coming about through a new
vision of what it means to 'let your light shine.' " Similarly, a writer in *High
Sierra Vistas* argued that after they are released is "when work for C. P. S.
fellows really begins. Then is when we can put into practice those principles which we have been preaching: aid to the suffering, food to the hungry,
love and kindness to the recent enemies of our country, charity, by word or
deed to the distressed." Another CPS publication that year put it more
simply, remarking, "Never before have we as a Mennonite people been so
'world conscious.' " In other words, during the war Mennonites seized on
the initiative offered by the state to manifest what Hershberger had called
their "curative mission." Instead of pressing for justice, they would quietly
deliver it, in word and deed.[48]

Nor was such a service consciousness confined only to men at camp. The
degree to which the church's laity had been infused with this rekindled
ethic was demonstrated by a parallel movement among young Mennonite
women. Proudly calling themselves "C. O. Girls," they ventured to mental
hospitals and volunteered alongside the men for jobs that nobody else
wanted. The initiative came from a Bluffton College home economics professor named Edna Ramseyer. She had labored in several Quaker work
camps in the late 1930s, and the new currents moving in her church only
further stimulated her drive for work of human service. In 1943, teaching
at the relief training school in Goshen, she recalled, "Some of us got together and asked why girls couldn't participate in some of these things as
well as fellows." By August, Ramseyer and others had drawn up a constitution, taken the name, and formulated their agenda. They would labor diligently in the hospitals, first only in the summers and then year around, in

FIGURE 4.3. *Teachers of the "Grottoes Cooking School," CPS Camp No. 4, Grottoes, Virginia. Left to right: Mary Emma Showalter, Edna Ramseyer, Ava Horst. Mennonite Library and Archives, Bethel College, North Newton, Kansas.*

order to express their convictions about peace, relieve human need, and support "the stand taken by the young men." In the summers of 1944 and 1945, Ramseyer organized a number of women's service units, consisting mostly of female students from the Mennonite colleges, who moved onto the grounds of mental hospitals in several states and plunged into work as attendants, dietitians, and the like.[49]

As historian Rachel Waltner Goossen has pointed out, this engaged group of Mennonite women also fought a subtle battle with patriarchal church leaders, who tended to view the women workers as a merely a device to boost the morale of CPS men. To this end, MCC Chairman Peter Hiebert had even suggested the women change their name, reasoning that it might offend conservative Mennonites. The women, however, insisted on viewing their work as sacrificial Christian service in its own right and kept calling themselves "CO Girls." Goshen student Doris Miller, for instance, volunteered for the work "because of my own deep convictions." Her motivation was "to support CPSers and contribute to peace." In their evaluations of their experiences at summer's end, many women voiced their com-

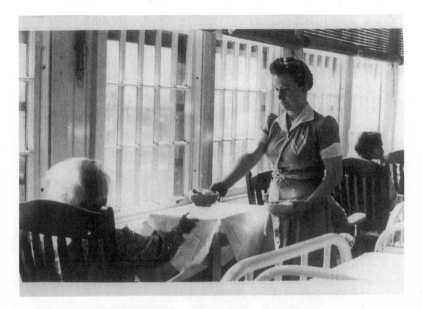

FIGURE 4.4. *"CO Girl" at work: CPS Unit No. 85, Rhode Island State Mental Hospital, Howard, Rhode Island. Mennonite Library and Archives, Bethel College, North Newton, Kansas.*

mitment to the service ethic that drew them to mental hospital corridors. Moreover, for these CO women, as in the case of so many CO men, such work could function as an expression of good citizenship in nonresistant ways. As phrased by Ramseyer later, "This was an opportunity for women to express their interest and concern about some of the same things the fellows were doing, about war, and peace, and serving; if we didn't believe in killing then we should be willing to serve constructively." The purpose was clearly evident at the time. In their notes to speakers about the new initiative, the organizing committee instructed these organizers: "Guard against being anti-patriotic. Positively prove yourself good, loyal citizens."[50]

In sum, it is difficult to underestimate the powerful effect this new service consciousness had on American Mennonites during the war years. In future years, both denominations would be deeply shaped by a number of young men who had served in important posts in camp administration. In men like Kreider, Ediger, and Loewen for the General Conference, and Atlee Beechy, Grant Stoltzfus, and John Hostetler for the Mennonite

Church, the two groups had a nucleus of future leaders who had been steeped in the service ethic. Even beyond these leaders, thousands of young Mennonites returned from CPS infused with a similar vision. "Never before has such a reservoir of talent and training been made suddenly available for the work of the church," recognized the *Gospel Herald* in 1946. Without a doubt, through their varied experiences, CPS men and women received a hands-on introduction to Christian service work, a seed that would bear significant fruit in the postwar years.[51]

Thus young Mennonites shared much of the enthusiasm for CPS that their elders displayed so readily. Even so, their own familiarity with the system furnished grounds for an informed critique of it and produced a dissent of which their elders were only vaguely aware. Indeed, it is plausible to argue that beneath the apparent triumphs of CPS for American Mennonites, down in the camps a groundswell of discontent rumbled as well. In this dissent, CPSers began piecing together a critique of Mennonite-state cooperation and of state power and authority that would emerge later in more potent forms in the postwar decades.

It necessary to discuss this incipient Mennonite radicalism in the CPS camps in light of the recognition that compared to other COs, Mennonites were truly the "good boys" of the CPS system. From their first contact with the government as it came knocking on their doors in the form of draft notices, these young men obeyed its directives quite submissively. Even more radical leaders, such as Ediger, who had labored with Quakers and fellowshipped in the "Harlem Ashram," recalled that he "never came close" to taking the nonregistration stance. The only moral struggle that a radical like Kreider experienced, he remembered, was whether or not to take the ministerial deferment.[52]

Likewise, once lodged in the camps, Mennonite CPSers engaged in few walkouts, work slowdowns, strikes, or acts of noncooperation to protest the nature of CPS as a Selective Service program. A notable exception came when one CPS crew out of Colorado Springs, consisting mostly of Amishmen, were toiling at draining an earthen dam. Gradually they realized they were working on the site of a planned army base, Camp Carson. They abruptly packed their tools and drove back to camp.[53] These were young people who had been raised to honor Romans 13 ("the powers that be are ordained of God"), who believed deeply in the two-kingdom understandings passed down by their Anabaptist ancestors. Thus, they would take a negative view of the strikes and walkouts that occurred at other CPS camps. The Grottoes camp newsletter editorialized in December 1942, for instance, that "whenever a man refuses to register . . . he casts a shadow upon all true conscientious objectors." Instead, the paper continued, we should thank God and the government for even providing alternative service at all. One non-Mennonite CO in an MCC camp recalled the "lack of social action or conviction to act on socially or politically involved situations" among Mennonite CPSers. More than once they booed him as he announced meetings of the camp FOR group at the dinner table. Similarly, in 1943 Gaeddert noted "the old breach between the so-called FOR group and the Mennonites" at Camp Camino. For their part, more radical objectors roundly criticized Mennonite docility. After all, reasoned one critic, "Jesus did not petition the Roman authorities for a law which forced others to go the second mile."[54]

Nonetheless, young Mennonites shoveling away in the CPS camps and even laboring in camp administration slowly began to develop a radicalism of their own grain that took on increasing depth as the war years ground on. In groping toward a more activist approach to society and in laying the foundation for a questioning of the state, this generation in the camps began considering issues that would take center stage as they grew into positions of church leadership in later years. The dissent emanated from a number of sources. Young radicals transformed into dutiful camp administrators did not always lose the informed, critical perspective they had developed previously. As Gingerich pointed out, in such positions these men continually faced the variety of tensions coming their way as war objectors administering a Selective Service program. While publicly they affirmed the program, privately such tensions led many to a mounting dissatisfaction with the whole arrangement. As one young CO and camp administrator wrote to Albert Gaeddert, "In our selling of the CPS 'vision' . . . we act as though CPS is a beautiful and glorious experience"; when in actuality, he admitted, they knew that it was merely "the best that could be worked out on short notice." After the war, a number of former administrators testified that they would never again be caught in such a dual role.[55]

So too did the genocidal nature of modern war induce a discomfiting sense among many Mennonites both inside and outside of the camps. In a careful description of the atom bomb and Protestant reactions to it for readers of the *Gospel Herald*, Howard Charles recognized that "we need to raise our voices in protest against this atrocity." In a statement that the peace committee of the GC Western District Conference sent to district ministers as the war wound down, they asked, "Ought not our Church send to Japan one missionary for every man from our Church who helped to rain destruction upon their land?" It was primarily because he was an American that Howard Blosser felt compelled to engage in postwar reconstruction work in Germany. In that way, he and others could "sort of undo . . . what we as a nation had done"; they might demonstrate to people that "look, not all of us are that way. We're here to try to make amends or do the service that's necessary." With equally auspicious reverberations, a dissenting Mennonite CO at the Powellsville, Maryland, conscription institute privately argued among his fellows that "modern total war demands we bear total witness against it."[56]

The main lines of questioning occurred among CPS men, the rank and file, laboring away at camp. Mennonite leaders were aware of this dissent but usually dismissed it as the product of too close an association with non-Mennonite firebrands. Writing years afterwards, Hershberger admitted that when certain radical objectors in Quaker camps took the nonregistration position, "a few of our boys were affected by this." Certainly that influence was there, and it may have struck a more responsive chord among Mennonites than Hershberger or other leaders realized at the time. Bender had assured the Virginia Conference conservatives that outside speakers had minimal access to Mennonite camps. Meanwhile, Frank Olmstead, Chair of the War Resisters' League, wrote to inform Fast that he had "thoroughly enjoyed my visits to the Mennonite camps in Colorado Springs and Nebraska, and gained every assurance that I was welcome. In fact they worked me harder than any other camp did. I have never been so besieged with questions and small groups wanting additional information as in your camps." Campers in different locales enjoyed hearing from Bayard Rustin; and objectors at the MCC camp near Marietta, Ohio, thought that a 1942 visit by Winston Dancis, also of the War Resisters League, "certainly enriched our camp experience."[57]

More significantly, Mennonite dissent in the CPS camps may have sprung from more homegrown sources. One MC camper, for example, expressed his concern that "when I see [the church] becoming involved in a church-state set-up I begin to wonder," and he queried whether perhaps the leadership should have given more thought to mass migration. Another MC CPSer agreed, pointing to the Mennonite migrations because of the threat of military service in the past, and conjectured that what Mennonites generations back had objected to they now accepted without question. Other young dissenters found different points of dispute. "I am not able to find enough grounds in the Bible to sanction the CPS program," wrote an

OM objector. "I feel that we have compromised greatly in trying to maintain and uphold the Spirit of Non-Resistance by letting ourselves being domineered by the Militarists via Government." Further, this CO wondered, "Where is the place to draw the line against war? As I see it now, it would be the first step—not registering." Similarly, a CPS man from Lancaster responded to a conference questionnaire with his measured opinion that while some benefit may accrue to the CPS man from his experience, his "testimony" would have been far greater if he had stood his ground, followed his vocation, and then gone to jail if it had come to that. "I do not believe good can come from the church cooperating with the state in forcing Christians to do things," he explained.[58]

Like many of the non-Mennonite critics, many of these young men directed their fire at the unpaid aspect of CPS labor. "Lincoln abolished slavery," declared a Mennonite CO in the California Sierras, and "today CPS is again using means of slavery and the church is sponsoring CPS." Others stopped short of these positions, but still wondered aloud about the wisdom of their church's wartime compromise with the state. Many of these doubts surfaced as MCC began to consider its response to possible postwar conscription and took special care to survey CPS opinion on the issue. Overall, the letters gave a cautious endorsement to CPS as a temporary wartime expedient but spoke strongly against any permanent arrangement along this line. Instead, many urged a completely church-run program of alternative service and underlined the dangers of further cooperation with the state. One draftee voiced his conviction that "we cannot be too careful with our compromising with the government," while another advocated that the church create its own voluntary service program and ask that the government accept it in lieu of military service. If the state should refuse, he argued, "the church should go ahead with their program and suffer the consequences, but under no condition submit to Government control to the extent of the present program." Another Mennonite CO agreed, wondering, "Are we compromising Christian ideals to avoid persecution? Certainly we do not welcome bodily persecution, but just how far do we go before we draw the line? Personally, I feel the line of demarcation is failing."[59]

In sum, perhaps the strongest single piece of evidence for an incipient Mennonite radicalism in the CPS camps is found in an undated note from Gingerich to Hershberger accompanying some of this correspondence. Gingerich wrote,

✓   These letters reflect in part the great underlying uneasy conscience of many
of our men in CPS. I am convinced that this was much more general than the
Peace Problems Committee and many others of our leaders recognized. I have
too much of a confidential nature from our own most deeply thinking boys to
pass this whole thing off as a manifestation of radicalism produced by our
contacts with pacifists.[60]

Mennonite Church leaders' convenient explanation for CPS dissent as
a mere product of too much fraternization with non-Mennonite radicals
was severely tested as the MCC leadership went out into the camps to confront some of these questioners head on. This occurred in a series of larger
CPS meetings known as "conscription institutes" conducted in the spring
of 1945. MCC gathered all its leading lights in administration and scholarship in four different CPS camps purportedly to discuss with CPS men
some of the issues the church faced in dealing with conscription, both now
and in the future. Years later, CPS administrator Ediger recalled an additional reason. MCC went through the considerable expense and trouble of
the institutes, Ediger remembered, because "we had a certain share of fellows who were debating . . . the matter of walking out of CPS and getting
imprisoned."[61]

From the perspective of MCC leaders, if the purpose of the institutes
was really to rein in some radical thinking among CPSers, the conferences
were only partially successful at best. Hershberger's and Bender's new
conceptualizing of nonresistance had apparently penetrated only so deeply
in the churches; for the discussion at these meetings revealed that some
Mennonite COs held on more tightly to the older, more prophetic implications of their Anabaptist heritage. Bender, for instance, labored hard at the
passive formulations of nonresistance, reminding those at the Powellsville,
Maryland, institute that Mennonites opposed war, not conscription, and
that much good had arisen for Mennonites from it. In this case, conscription gave birth to CPS, which had clarified the Mennonite witness
and brought about unity and a "spiritual awakening" in the church. It had
demonstrated that Mennonites could finance, administer, and lead a large-
scale program; and it had taught them, he insisted, that "government is not
a monster." Mennonites should oppose conscription, Bender affirmed, but
only in certain ways: "If by opposition we mean putting pressure to bear,
then it is outside of the Christian's duty." Likewise, at California's Camp
Camino in April, Bender told the CPS delegates that "we cannot impose
justice on a wicked social order . . . sometimes we can do nothing but pray."

Asked whether citizens do not have a remote responsibility in the acts of the state, even if they do not approve of them, the PPC chair maintained, "We do not."[62]

A shifting majority of the delegates (MCC requested two from each Mennonite CPS camp in the region) appeared at times to accept the fundamentally careful views of older men such as Bender. A wide majority at Powellsville cautioned against pressuring the state and agreed that the church could accept alternative service agreements, though preferring "less interference by government." Yet there was wide agreement on a willingness to witness to government on peace and justice issues that appeared to break new ground for most Mennonites. Bender recognized at Powellsville the hidden but prophetic qualifier articulated by Hershberger in *War, Peace, and Nonresistance* that sometimes nonresistant people had an obligation to testify to the state. "If by opposition we mean testifying against this evil [of conscription]," he avowed, "then there is no question that we should oppose it . . . We are the light and it is wrong to hide a light where it will not be seen." Mennonite CPSers only followed this line of thinking to its conclusion, which lay further than Bender was yet willing to follow. At Powellsville, delegates proposed resisting conscription "up to the extent of nonviolent direct action," and most of the delegates affirmed that "making our statement known to government was an evangelistic function and therefore the responsibility of the church."Later the delegates mulled over how to oppose conscription, and while some felt the only course involved bringing it to God in prayer, the larger group avowed that "we should act according to our best knowledge of God's will for us, and this might include considerable direct witnessing." Roland Bartel stressed at Camino that CPS was clearly an aspect of military conscription, "a part of this act of war." Even more revealing was Ediger's summary of "What we have learned from the C. P. S. program," also at Camino. Simply put, Ediger relayed that "We have learned to question government." At Medaryville, summarized the camp newspaper, many of those present stood at the point of repudiating conscription, saying "they could not [register] again, knowing that seeing their convictions thru ultimately might mean another five years of their lives—spent in jail." Needless to say, the article continued, "this undoubtedly alarmed and disquieted some of the church leaders who were present."[63]

If MCC leaders were concerned at some of the opinions expressed in the official assemblies, they would have been even more perturbed if they could have heard some of the discussion in the delegates' private sessions. These have been preserved in a remarkable document that somehow ended up in the MCC files. Written up by Daryl Frey, a delegate and an obvious participant in (in his words) these "barracks bull-sessions," the delegates "advanced many ideas they did not express at open meetings." Considered as a whole, these private statements leave little doubt of the truth of Frey's observation that "some C. O.'s have troubled consciences."[64]

A large part of the private discussions revolved around a refutation of many of Bender's teachings in the regular sessions. Bender's affirmation of the good that came out of conscription, charged one of the participants, was "expedient, short sighted, and pragmatic . . . Is the expedient thing always the wisest in the long run?" Moreover, what kind of witness did this really amount to, he wondered, when COs "are hidden away, isolated both physically and spiritually, from their fellow-men?" "What are we even doing here in a barracks?" wondered another. Instead of stressing the good that could emerge from CPS, according to Frey, delegates privately judged harshly the implications that the arrangement had for their church. During an open session, one participant informed Bender that "by working with the government now we are helping to impose conscription on ourselves and the rest of our nation." At night another delegate hotly declared that "by accepting C. P. S. they had endorsed war for everybody but themselves." Moreover, the arrangement had silenced the prophetic word that many of these troubled Mennonite objectors felt needed to be delivered to the state. "Has not the extent of our compromise jeopardized the effectiveness of our witness against war?" cried one activist. Indeed, the question bore deeply on what it meant to provide service altogether. Maybe bearing their most effective witness against war and offering their best service to the nation were identical aims, suggested a delegate. Maybe opposing the evil of war was another kind of service Mennonites needed to offer to their country.[65]

Nevertheless, as the camps shut down in 1946–47, Mennonite COs began to look back on their experience with a great amount of satisfaction. In MCC's evaluations of Civilian Public Service near the system's end, CPS men exhibited few overwhelming complaints about their years invested.[66] Nonetheless, CPS affected some deep attitudinal and behavioral changes on these men that emerged as foundational in the years ahead. A small but significant number had begun to press against the edges of the traditional Mennonite conceptions of church-state relations. In the postwar decades, these initial stirrings would result in whole new frameworks of permissible Mennonite thought and action, with implications that older leaders like Harold Bender had scarcely imagined.

MENNONITE GIS AND THE CHURCH

A discussion of Mennonites in World War II, whether or not church leaders were happy about it, must include at least a brief analysis of Mennonite
military men. For these people seemed to represent a failure for the church
and have thus fallen into a kind of Mennonite historical vacuum. We have
explored one crucial aspect of their experience: why they went into the military. It yet remains to touch on two more: their church's response, and the
sensitive process of coming home.[67]

Depending on the degree of relative toughness with which his particular
church tried to draw the line with "the world," the individual GI could
expect to receive a varying kind of chastisement for his participation in the
military. Heinz Janzen had no recollection of his minister ever discussing
the issue of his navy enlistment with him, and Howard Buller's pastor only
brought it up in a nonjudgmental way. Likewise, Galen Koehn once attended Bethel College Mennonite Church in uniform and received no negative reactions whatsoever. When he and his five brothers entered military
ranks as combatant soldiers, Fred Reichenbach escaped any reprimand
from their home congregation of St. John's Mennonite in rural Pandora,
Ohio. As it turned out, most of the young men from this church entered
military ranks. The church threatened its first few soldiers that they would
not be allowed back into membership, but after more young men opted for
the military, recalled Reichenbach, "the church backed down and accepted
what was happening."[68]

But not all General Conference churches were this easygoing. Eden
Mennonite Church in Moundridge, Kansas, for instance, placed military
members "not in good standing" and hotly debated an even more strongly
worded resolution against their errant GIs. The proposed constitution for
Alexanderwohl Mennonite, near Goessel, Kansas, refused to let noncombatant members vote or participate in church discussions and ruled that
those in regular military service or defense work had "severed their relationship with our church." Returning home to Eden Mennonite Church
on furlough from the Air Corps, Roland Juhnke found himself confronted
by some of the church's many COs, who "were quite vocal . . . and quite
negative about my stand and my attitude." Likewise, Levi Friesen, who had
recognized the necessity of Christian pacifism but enlisted as a medic for
lack of financial support, returned home from the army for good on the
Saturday night following his demobilization. Having been gone for three
years, he owned no other clothes but his uniform, and thus he wore it to
church the next morning at Bethesda Mennonite in Henderson, Nebraska.

A uniformed Mennonite in church served as a red flag to some of the congregants. After the service, remembered Friesen painfully, one member "ran me down and really chewed me out."[69]

In this discipline, these GC congregations echoed the chastisement more commonly employed in Mennonite Church congregations. In Central Mennonite Church in Fulton County, Ohio, for example, the congregation suspended the memberships of those who opted for the military; and in 1944, the reigning bishop held servicemen back from communion. Similarly, at Oak Grove, those who entered the military "came under congregational censure." Most MC churches either excommunicated the men or stopped just short of doing so. Of the total of 180 military men in the Indiana-Michigan Conference, for example, 40 were "immediately excommunicated" by their churches, while 115 others were "considered not in good standing; further action deferred."[70]

Writing from France in February 1945, a soldier had already focused his thoughts on a future problem. "There has been a question on my mind and I'd like you to be frank in answering it," he requested of Illinois Conference secretary Leland Bachman. "'What will be the . . . outcome of us boys in the army as far as the church is concerned?' I think we should know now." The Mennonite Church wrestled with the degree of discipline they should exercise toward returning veterans. At the Peace Problem Committee's August 1944 meeting, Bender appointed a special committee to study the problem and report back with a suggested procedure for receiving their veterans. The resulting procedures tried to provide grounds for bringing the men back into the churches without condoning their error. Each pastor, recommended the committee, should meet personally with each returning veteran and demonstrate that "this violation is a denial of the New Testament teachings and practices of Jesus and His disciples." However, "upon evidence of penitence" and a promise to sever their contacts with postwar military organizations, veterans should be welcomed back into fellowship again. The district conferences adopted these recommendations with varying degrees of latitude, ranging from the Virginia and Ohio districts, which followed them nearly verbatim, to the Illinois Conference, which did not.[71]

Many veterans balked at returning home from years of sacrifice and danger only to be asked to renounce the whole experience. Not surprisingly, the Mennonite Church experienced substantial losses in membership from veterans who never renewed their membership. By 1949, when the PPC made a careful study of the matter, the Ohio Conference had restored only 59 of 181 veterans to full membership; the Virginia Conference, only

12 of 68; Lancaster, 17 of 104. Because of the war, the Mennonite Church
lost approximately 900 young men, a serious blow to a denomination of
roughly only 50,000 total congregants.[72]

The General Conference Mennonites resolved the issue differently.
Their designated subcommittee recommended that churches make no distinction between veterans returning from either CPS or the military. Instead, pastors should meet with the returning man to evaluate his experience, talk about his vocation, and welcome him home. Warning against
"any pointing of fingers," the committee suggested that each congregation
should follow this up with a special service of "praise and thanksgiving, of
confession and repentance."[73]

It is impossible to know how many returning GC veterans came home to
their churches once again, or the degree to which individual congregations
were able to facilitate such a noncondemning homecoming for their men.
Tabor Mennonite Church at Tabor, Kansas, drew up a statement for veterans to sign, confessing their violation of the 1941 Souderton declaration.
Then all congregational members, led by the pastor, signed the confession,
an action that greatly united the church. After they identified themselves
as "Peace Christians," military veterans such as Frank Keller and Heinz
Janzen later rose to positions of importance and respect in the larger denomination, Keller as the minister of a prominent Kansas congregation
and Janzen as the executive secretary of the denomination in the late 1960s.
One veteran, however, even until the mid-1970s retained a wellspring of
bitterness toward fellow members of his church. For years, he maintained,
he had been the subject of "snide comments" and "subtle discrimination"
because of his military service, a hurt that ran so deep he would not allow
the tape recording of his interview for fear it would dredge much of this
back up again.[74]

One more example will suffice to illustrate the kind of experiences that
the conflicting loyalties between God and country could deliver to the conscientious young person caught between them. Consider the difficult experience of Oliver Stucky. Like so many young farm boys attending Eden
Church in Moundridge, Stucky faced the draft call early in the war and
obediently entered CPS. The decision was initially easy for him. It was "the
right thing to do at the time, and there was pressure from my parents. I was
a pacifist, I've always been a pacifist. And the church taught it." In his time
as a CO, Stucky ran the whole range of CPS experiences. In Colorado he
lined rivers with rocks, planted trees, worked a shovel on a road crew, and
lent his hand with cooking. Outside of Belton, Montana, he drove a truck

and did some timbering. Repeatedly, Stucky was struck deeply by the routine public hostility he and his fellow COs received from the general public. It was difficult for Stucky to take, because he felt his service in CPS was an demonstration of true patriotism. Along with a majority of men from his camp, he readily (but unsuccessfully) volunteered for an elite CO "smoke-jumping" unit being formed. To him, this was a perfect way of showing people that he and his fellow objectors were not just "hiding" to avoid danger. When an opportunity for mental hospital work opened up in 1942, Stucky leaped at the chance. "I felt I could be of better service to mankind in a mental hospital than doing what I was doing," he recalled.[75]

Yet mental hospital work was not enough, to Stucky, to demonstrate his intense desire to engage in public service. In 1942 he finally transferred into the army medical corps and pushed for an assignment as a "front-line medic." Though his parents were "heartbroken," Stucky transferred into the army "because I felt that I could do even more good to mankind there than I could in the hospitals." Moreover, he had another reason for the change. His time in CPS "had psyched me up as nothing else could," Stucky averred. "I was getting tired of being called an s.o.b., unpatriotic coward, and so forth. And I was going to prove once and for all that I wasn't anything like that." The best way to do this, in his mind, was to volunteer to serve as "cannon-fodder replacements for medical corpsmen on the front line," a position regarded by many of his fellow soldiers as "suicidal."

Once he arrived at the front in Europe, at times it seemed that Stucky's odds were indeed slim; he recalls that he was "absolutely certain I was going to get killed." At one point he replaced a medic who had been killed and toiled in combat until he contacted hepatitis and had to go to the rear. The medic who replaced him was killed a few days later. Stucky saw his company personnel turn over repeatedly. In one particular maneuver, out of the nine medics accompanying the attack, only Stucky was not killed or wounded. Still, "nothing was going to stop me going after those wounded guys," not even reprimands from officers for needlessly endangering himself.

When he returned home to Eden Church in Moundridge after the war, miraculously intact, Stucky found "some unpleasant attitudes" expressed toward the church's military veterans, himself included. Three years before, as a CPS man, Stucky had had to travel into town in Belton, Montana, only with groups of a half-dozen or more COs, for their mutual protection from hostile townspeople. These men were cowards, local Americans felt, and were disloyal to their country. Now, back home at Eden Mennonite Church, some fellow church people refused to speak to Stucky and other soldiers. These men were part of the military machine, local Mennonites felt, and were disloyal to their church. It seemed that Oliver Stucky had finally come full circle.[76]

"WE HAVE LEARNED TO QUESTION GOVERNMENT"

Several larger conclusions emerge from this complex welter of events and personalities making up the Mennonite experience in World War II. Viewed as a whole, the church emerged from the war years much more fractious and divided than men like Bender, Miller, or even Harshbarger had suspected. Certainly, the personal reflections of Mennonite Church peace leaders on these hectic years must have tasted somewhat bittersweet in many ways. In spite of its slightly tarnished veneer, the CPS system still appeared to them as a stunning triumph, a view that they continued to cherish throughout the postwar era. They could take less satisfaction in other experiences of the war era. Foremost among these ranked their precarious and even ugly clash with their denomination's fundamentalists, an encounter that veered at one point dangerously close to a church schism. Bending to meet this crisis, they could cock an ear in the other direction and pick up scattered cries of church dissent from the wartime compromise they had so carefully constructed with the government. Gradually increasing in volume and tenor, too, were similar cries of informed dissatisfaction from heretofore compliant and obedient young men in the CPS camps.

In yet another direction, much louder and more inescapable, came the rumble of the wholesale collapse of years of careful church teaching among a substantial portion of the church's membership. In spite of all their diligent work in the prewar years, the church leadership could now ruminate on the stunningly large numbers of young Mennonites who deserted one of the fundamental principles of the church—men who in many cases were now lost for good. The old formulations of the Mennonite cultural and behavioral worldview had never been watertight, but now the war had revealed them to be leaking like a sieve. Beyond whatever satisfaction which they could take in CPS, the Mennonite Church leadership could reflect on a number of disasters.

The General Conference Mennonite leadership, on the other hand, could look back on the war years with less sense of consternation only because they had received so many discouraging signals before the war. They must therefore have entered this era of crises with much less initial optimism. To be sure, the GCMC appeared as divided and diverse as the Mennonite Church, but given their dedication to congregational autonomy and pluralism, this certainly appeared as nothing new. In some ways the church had responded to the war magnificently, much better than Harshbarger and his colleagues had had reason to expect. Dissimilar and disagreeing congregations that heretofore had struggled to find points of common ground suddenly united themselves behind a massive church-run program for war objectors.

Yet no matter how much satisfaction this outpouring of church support for CPS could provide, General Conference Mennonites who still held to the ancient church precept of nonresistance could take limited solace in the events of the war years. Surely their very understanding of themselves as a "peace church" was in grave jeopardy when two-thirds of their young men entered military ranks once the state pointed to a crisis and came calling. For a church that had traditionally found one of its very reasons for being in a strict dedication to the commandments of God over those of country, its theological and cultural underpinnings had clearly begun to come unglued.

By no means, however, were the war years an unmitigated calamity for American Mennonites. Even while aspects of their old identity slowly came apart, new currents and energies broke forth in the war years to help construct a new one. This war, like other wars, certainly amplified the call of good citizenship for all Americans—a call that public hostility toward conscientious objectors clarified and reinforced. As the walls of separation that Mennonites had traditionally erected around their communities crumbled, they wanted more than ever to be good Americans. Civilian bonds and CPS were the most dramatic manifestations of this Mennonite desire, but there would be others. Much more than their fathers' experience in World War I, the combined forces of CPS or the military took an entire generation of Mennonite young men out of a world of rural isolation and scattered them around the nation and the globe. Not only did outside society increasingly break into the Mennonite communities, but for some years, it simply swallowed up its sons (and some of its daughters) and sent them back noticeably changed. For those opting for alternative service, this change often became manifested in a markedly more outward-looking orientation, one focused especially on the world's needs and pain. Especially for youth who chose work in public health efforts or in mental hospitals, they came face to face with a needy and hurting larger society, and they responded with compassion and tremendous energy. A former CPSer recollected later that his fellows "saw areas of opportunity for service and life occupations they had never even thought of." The seeds implanted in these war years would blossom into a variety of new undertakings in the postwar decades.[77]

CPS had wrought other foundational attitude changes as well. A church traditionally suspicious of government had spent some years cooperating intimately with it and had learned a great deal in the process. In their close work together helping to create CPS, the urbane, sophisticated Quaker leader Paul French once turned to H. A. Fast and asked him, "You Mennonites are a little bit afraid of government, aren't you?" Fast admitted that they were. "We never had a very high regard for men in government," he explained, and "our whole history was just to shy away a little bit from government relations." Yet following French's example, Fast gradually lost his fear. He began to develop more confidence in himself and in the position he represented in Washington. He found that as he did so, the big men in Washington had more respect for him. This confidence grew to encompass Mennonite leaders beyond Fast. Hence Bender repeatedly told the men at the conscription institutes, "Government is not a monster to be feared."[78]

Yet Mennonites had also become aware that neither was it a distant, unresponsive, unmovable force, something like a storm or a plague that one merely had to endure. If church leaders somehow failed to grasp the full implications of this point, their young charges in the CPS camps did not. Correspondingly, during the war years, Mennonites began to work toward a new understanding of the state and a newer Mennonite relation to it. More specifically, particularly the younger generation housed in the CPS camps began to pioneer a new way of addressing the state; they groped toward a method of *witnessing to* the state about Mennonite concerns. Ediger stated simply that "we have learned to question government." And with the budding Mennonite service orientation, their list of such concerns quickly grew ever longer.

Finally, and perhaps most significantly of all, the war had rendered it painfully clear that the ancient Mennonite reliance on social isolation would no longer suffice as a means of maintaining nonresistance. Any facile assumptions that the young people would adhere to the faith of the ancestors unaffected by the larger socioeconomic changes engulfing the Mennonite community plainly crumbled as the results from the draft censuses began to filter in. As Kreider wondered in 1942, "Does the preservation of the Mennonite heritage necessitate a return to community and cultural insularity?" Of course, Mennonites could try, in desperate campaigns for nonconformity, to preserve the older understandings in an ever-shifting world, but such programs could only offer the shakiest of foundations. Instead, they would have to cultivate, in Charles's words, new "inner spiritual resources" if they were to preserve the ethnic and cultural understandings that had shaped the Mennonite world for centuries. And with the pace of social change in postwar America, they would need to tackle this undertaking with a fair amount of urgency.[79]

CHAPTER 5

The Decline
and Revival of
the Mennonite
Community

In the middle decades of the twentieth century, the walls fell in on the Mennonite rural community. As summarized in chapter 2, for a previous half-century, Mennonites had been selectively borrowing from outside culture and had found in such innovations as revivalism, Sunday schools, and church educational and denominational institutions much that they could use to strengthen their own identity. Even in trying to say no to some of the society beyond their rural communities, Mennonites sometimes found themselves saying yes in other ways. By the 1920s, for instance, sectors of the church had begun to point to the perils of too much free borrowing. Yet in opposing further adaptations, many leaders drew upon a fundamentalist orientation that they themselves had taken in from the outside. Two decades later the forces of socioeconomic change had combined with the hammers of war to stretch the mechanisms of cultural separation to a breaking point. By the 1970s they were gone altogether, and so was the cohesive integrity of the socioeconomic milieu that had sustained the Mennonite ethos for centuries.

This central historical development would, at the very least, exercise far-reaching effects on the shape of the Mennonite peace position. In 1942, before the draft censuses began to suggest differently, Hershberger had confidently asserted that the Mennonite Church retained nonresistant principles "largely because its vigorous Christian community life has fostered the spirit of nonresistance." If that community life began to break down, he warned, not just nonresistance but all Mennonite distinctives would "suffer accordingly." Looking back on the sweeping pace of socio-economic change twenty-five years later, the Mennonite sociologist Paul Peachey posed a different kind of problem. "Now that the ethnic insularity is shattered," he wondered, "will Mennonites in fact escape the fate of a gullible and even vulgar Americanization?" It was a question that the developments of the preceding years increasingly had pushed to the forefront of the Mennonite agenda and one that the pressures of war had further accentuated.[1]

As the impinging world undermined older patterns of ethnoreligious isolation, Mennonites responded in various ways to this eradication of older conceptions of community. With the fragmentation of traditional formulations, Mennonite leaders moved to shore up the boundaries of their rural communities by instituting additional mechanisms of cultural separation and by attempting to reinforce the Mennonite commitment to agriculture. Yet these measures proved inadequate to stem the onrushing tide of a national urban culture and economy. By the 1970s, Mennonites had focused their attention on newer constructions of community that did not necessarily revolve around a shared geography or agricultural callings. And increasingly these newer renderings were anchored in bedrock notions of peace and service, retooled as key to an emerging Mennonite identity in a postagrarian world.

THE MENNONITE COMMUNITY BESIEGED

Although the Mennonite experience is unique, it also mirrors, in many ways, the historical developments shaping other religious and ethnic groups in American life. Thus Mennonites, like other Americans, began to witness the slow but steady infiltration of a national urban culture as early as the turn of the twentieth century. The cultural historian Robert Wiebe has characterized the years from 1877 to 1920 as being key to a fundamental shift in American life. In the earlier part of this period, he argued, rural, isolated "island communities"—small, internally focused localities marked by "ethical" values—dominated the nation. By the 1920s, Wiebe maintained, this world had given way to a new system, a nation dominated by the regulative, hierarchical priorities of an urban-directed life. The older island communities had vanished. Instead, rural hinterlands were linked to urban centers through rules with impersonal sanctions, formulated by a new, bureaucratic-minded middle class.[2]

Like other Americans oriented around rural island communities, Mennonites felt the tug of this new culture and witnessed its tentacles linking them ever more firmly to national life. Because Mennonites strengthened the walls of their rural communities with a religious ideology that branded such cultural incursions not only as outside influences but also as "worldly" and sinful, they resisted these changes perhaps longer than their secular neighbors. But by the midcentury years, the mechanisms of Mennonite isolation were clearly breaking down.

In 1945 the Virginia bishop John Mumaw summarized these changes for the "old" Mennonites as a group. Mumaw held little back in his rosy depiction of the time-honored Mennonite rural community: one "definitely marked with the spirit of Christian brotherhood," a group consciousness rooted in Bible teachings and "characterized further by an unmistakable simplicity of life." The bishop plainly intended his article to served as a warning bell, outlining the number of different forces eating away at this community. Among such forces, Mumaw identified materialism, the growing attraction of higher education (which "has had a tendency to lead the church into regrettable accommodations of doctrine and practice"), and urbanization with the corresponding corrosive influences of city life. In addition, he highlighted the twin impact of the spreading evil of secularization and the subsequent "enervation of religious tolerance" that weakened the Mennonite will to fight off the forces undermining their community. Likewise, Melvin Gingerich cautioned in 1942: "Our former rural security is disappearing, we are becoming secularized, our community life is breaking down, and our culture is losing its distinctive qualities." Worse, as other Mennonites realized a year later, "the present war is hastening this process."[3]

General Conference Mennonites had begun to detect the impact of the same sort of processes. Because of their scanty financial resources to purchase farms and an individualism among their elders that denied them assistance, young people were leaving the Mennonite community, noted one Mennonite in 1935. Twelve years later, surveying the increased integration of General Conference Mennonite into the mainstream of society in such aspects as modern communication and transportation networks, mounting industrialization, and "increasing totalitarianism through state and national control," Bethel College President Ed. G. Kaufman worried that "it becomes more difficult to maintain Mennonite non-conformity."[4]

As the peculiar nature of Mennonite fundamentalism indicated, at least a firm minority of Mennonites had stirred to tackle such threats in the thirties. The government's knocking on the doors of thousands of Mennonite

homes in the form of draft notices, however, signified an inescapable threat
to their quiet existence and awakened the church at large to dangers posed
by society far beyond the crisis of war mobilization. In some ways, CPS
loomed as only the tip of the iceberg. Thus, by the war years, leaders from
both denominations had begun to organize a unified response, rooted in a
reinforcement of the besieged Mennonite rural community. They would
directly confront the enticements of a national urban culture by preaching
the farm as the foundation of their religious life.

As with Mennonite adaptations of fundamentalism, the midcentury
movement to combat Mennonite cultural drift borrowed from currents in
the larger culture. Leaders of the Mennonite community movement
quickly discovered new allies in economists and Department of Agriculture officials worrying over the decline of rural American communities in
general. Alarmed by the growing data at about the time of World War II
suggesting the increasing dangers besetting the traditional family farm,
scholars such as former TVA head Arthur Morgan—who had authored a
book called *The Small Community*—and Department of Agriculture economists Walter Kollmorgen and Oliver Baker began to point to the rural
Mennonite community as a model for other Americans. With such affir-
mations, Mennonite leaders labored with increasing diligence to make
their own people, in the words of the historian Gingerich in 1942, more
"community conscious."[5]

For the "old" Mennonites, Guy F. Hershberger's writings and activities,
more than anything else, served this purpose. Certainly, the call to rural
community fit hand in glove with other aspects of his thinking by the 1940s.
As a leading light of Mennonite scholarship and the holder of a doctorate in
American history, Hershberger knew how to speak to a people increasingly
inhabiting both Mennonite and American societies. By 1938 he began to
regularly evoke the pastoral rhetoric of such people as Jefferson and Creve-
coeur, rooting the Mennonite economy in the old Jeffersonian vision of
small-scale farms and manufacturing centers. Similarly, in the foundational Mennonite "curative mission" that he laid out in *War, Peace, and
Nonresistance*, Hershberger drew upon a number of people—Morgan,
Gandhi, Adin Ballou, P. A. Sorokin—arguing for the political relevance of
rural, nonresistant communities. Following the course of other dissenting
religious groups, he argued, Mennonites must set themselves apart, like a
city on a hill, and beckon the rest of society to a purer moral order.[6]

In a series of articles and papers during the war years, Hershberger hammered away at the theme that "the Mennonite way of life can best be main-

tained in a rural environment." His reasoning stemmed in his conception of the church as a true brotherhood, a "large family," or what sociologists refer to as a "primary group." According to Hershberger, the main problem was that over the past three-quarters of a century, Mennonites had witnessed "a complete revolution in industry, in agriculture, and in transportation" that had removed much of the interaction among primary groups and promoted instead impersonal, "secondary experiences and relationships." Needless to say, these sorts of relationships characterized urban life. Thus, quite clearly, to Hershberger the Mennonite church could "best maintain her primary group intimacy . . . by keeping the church rooted in rural soil." Not just nonresistance but many other Mennonite principles hinged on it. Where Mennonites had remained primarily rural, as in Russia and the United States, he wrote in 1942, they maintained their nonresistance; where they had urbanized, as in Holland and Germany, it was gone.[7]

The young Bethel College professor J. Winfield Fretz functioned in a very similar manner to alert the General Conference Mennonite Church to the burgeoning crisis of the Mennonite community. As with Hershberger, these concerns did not spring up in Fretz out of the blue. Reared on a Pennsylvania farm, Fretz had, by 1940, completed his studies in sociology at the University of Chicago, where he had written both a master's and a doctoral dissertation on Mennonite mutual aid. At Chicago, he had absorbed the prevailing sociological wisdom of the day, affirming that under the pressures of modernization, intimate, primary group relationships would inevitably give way to anonymous, impersonal ones indicative of mass urban society. He studied in an era and a place where Tonnies' "*Gemeinschaft* to *Gesellschaft*" continuum ruled the day. All around him, it seemed to Fretz, Mennonites were sliding inexorably toward *Gesellschaft*. To rally his church to this crisis, Fretz turned at times to reasons and language almost identical to those of Hershberger for a new back-to-the-country movement. He argued in 1945, for instance, that "the city by its very nature prohibits the kind of intimate social relations that are possible in smaller rural areas." As a result, he maintained, in the city "community life has been destroyed." The editors of *The Mennonite* in the spring of 1942 awarded him a regular column to address such concerns, and in the ensuing weeks Fretz presented this general theme from a variety of angles. Other writers chimed in too. William Stauffer, for example, declared that "[we will] maintain our historic principles only as we again become rural."[8]

Nor were church leaders content merely to issue verbal statements on the problem. As scholars undertook to describe the magnitude of the crisis,

FIGURE 5.1. *Mennonite Community activist and Bethel professor J. Winfield Fretz, 1949. Mennonite Library and Archives, Bethel College, North Newton, Kansas.*

they also took more concrete steps to somehow reverse the slide. For instance, Hershberger seized the unique opportunity for internal education that the cloistered CPS camps provided. His contribution to the popular "Mennonite Heritage Series," a pamphlet entitled *Christian Relationships to the State and Community*, repeatedly pushed the virtues of the Mennonite rural community. More to the point were four special CPS camps called "Farm and Community Schools" that Hershberger and others pulled together. Hershberger even served as special lecturer at one of them. In these camps, CPS men not only learned the latest farming methodologies and technology but also absorbed the larger vision, as reported in the *Gospel Herald* in 1944, of "farming as a way of life and as a means for expressing the ideals of Christian brotherhood, so long familiar to Mennonites."[9]

Similarly, Hershberger and others managed to mobilize much of the Mennonite Church bureaucracy behind community-building efforts as well. In 1941 the church committee he headed, the Committee on Industrial Relations, prevailed upon the OM General Conference to look closely at the problem of "economic relations" and to "take steps to develop a forward looking program of community building." The conference agreed and in 1943 charged Hershberger's committee with leading these efforts. The committee's immediate work focused on study conferences. A "Conference on Mennonite Community Life," held at Goshen, Indiana, in March 1945, served at least to further educate church leaders in the problems. Another conference in 1943 produced more tangible results. Con-

cluding that the Mennonite community faced pressures from all sides, conference delegates came up with a program called "Mennonite Mutual Aid"   ✓
and garnered conference acceptance for it the following year. Eventually
the program developed into a Mennonite equivalent of life and auto insurance, but initially it gathered $600,000 to loan to 320 ex-CPS men for the
purposes of business, farming, or education.[10]

Altogether, the drive to reinforce the Mennonite rural community took
a myriad of forms. At times, like in the CPS venture, it drew upon new
patterns of Mennonite ecumenicity. In 1941 a collection of pastors, historians, sociologists and other church leaders met in Chicago, initially to address the threat of war and its impact on the Mennonite way of life. Discussion quickly grew to include the disintegrating Mennonite community. By
1942 this convocation had been organized on a biennial basis and entitled
"The Conference on Mennonite Cultural Problems." The gathering,
which existed well into the sixties, provided a forum where the Mennonite
intelligentsia could get together to dissect and discuss the course of acculturation. In the more immediate postwar years, Fretz and Hershberger created two new publications as platforms for further teaching and research
on these troubling economic indicators. For the GCMC, Fretz declared in
the first issue of *Mennonite Life* in 1946 that the very hope of all society lay
in the preservation of the rural community. Hershberger pressed similar
themes among "old" Mennonites with the founding of the Mennonite   ✓
Community Association. In the inaugural issue of its publication, *The
Mennonite Community*, in 1947, he announced that he would promote "a
community with an improved agriculture based on the sound Mennonite
traditions of the past." The first and subsequent issues featured paeans to
rural community life by the likes of Baker, Kollmorgen, and Hershberger;
ideas on mutual aid by Fretz; and reports from different farm conferences
conducted by the parent body. Meanwhile, Hershberger's Committee on
Economic and Social Relations (CESR) sponsored regular small conferences in a number of Mennonite areas, sometimes more than once a year,
well into the 1960s. In such get-togethers, Hershberger aimed at the participation not just of church leaders but also of local "practical people," and
he oriented the conferences around nuts-and-bolts issues such as small
business concerns and employer-employee relationships.[11]

In sum, by the end of the war it had become obvious to nearly every
thinking Mennonite that the old, traditional rural community was in peril.
After a Mennonite Church conference had surveyed present trends in
1945, Orie Miller could only summarize that the picture for the agrarian

community appeared "disconcerting and dreary."[12] From almost every quarter came threats to its existence: new industries entering the hinterlands; urban influence and standards penetrating into most Mennonite homes through the radio; young people obtaining rapid mobility in automobiles that could whisk them off with equal ease to urban employment, to a university far away, or to new and questionable sources of entertainment closer to home. Underlying many of these changes now was a suddenly demanding government that carried Mennonite young men away to labor camps hundreds of miles away, or even worse, to military adventures overseas. Accordingly, pragmatic and alert leaders unpacked and examined the crisis in a flurry of concentrated activity and did much to mobilize the church on behalf of its besieged communities. But nobody could forecast whether these efforts would suffice to save the rural community from the changes that would be sure to come in the postwar world.

THE MENNONITE COMMUNITY OVERRIDDEN

Not long into the 1950s, it became clear that such efforts simply would not suffice; nor could anyone come up with any other options that would. Mennonites could no more keep their people immune from the tremendous socioeconomic changes sweeping the nation than could sailors hold back the tide. The message was clear to many individuals caught in the middle of such changes. In 1953, for instance, Virginia Conference Bishop John Stauffer, decrying the "worldward" drift in the churches, declared to another assemblage of church leaders that "we are being Americanized more and more."[13] Even more disturbing to church leaders charged with somehow keeping their people together, such changes did not occur only over generations but could now could be measured in spans of mere decades or sometimes even in a matter of a few years. Considered cumulatively, these changes can be summarized by looking briefly at developments in agriculture, urbanization, occupation, education, and theology.

As scholars such as Gilbert Fite and John Shover make clear, American agriculture has been in considerable flux for at least a century and a half. Especially in the Midwest and Great Plains states, where the vast bulk of Mennonites resided, farm mechanization had proceeded rapidly by the first decades of the twentieth century. Still, observed Fite, scientists had ushered farmers only to the edge of the chemical revolution by the eve of World War II.[14]

As in so many other aspects of American life, however, it was the war that effected sweeping changes in American agriculture. With the lure of higher paying war work, the excess farm population quickly turned into a deficit

FIGURE 5.2. *Mennonite farmer N. P. Gerber and horses Polly, Bell, and Maud get in the wheat harvest, Putnam County, Ohio, late 1920s—early 1930s. Courtesy of Mennonite Historical Library, Bluffton College.*

population as an estimated five million farmers left for the military or the cities. Even with widespread farm deferments, Selective Service periodically needed to mobilize soldiers, prisoners of war, and conscientious objectors to get the crops in. Wartime scarcities shot farm prices skyward. Wholesale prices of farm products doubled from 1939 to 1945, and farm income had more than doubled by 1943. No wonder a small group such as the Mennonites could pour so much money into CPS; they clearly had much more to give. Perhaps most important for longer term agricultural trends were the technological innovations that emerged, now driven by farm labor scarcities. With only a slight increase in acreage but increased attention to technological prowess, farm production increased by 33 percent in five years of war. "The war years," averred Shover, "marked the takeoff of the mechanical revolution in American farming." Farmers had already become increasingly reliant on tractors; but between 1941 and 1945 they used half a million more along with a host of new combines, crop pickers, sprayers, and dusters, in spite of government rationing of farm machinery through November 1944. Better fertilizers and pesticides also contributed to what, in retrospect, appeared as a watershed era in American agricultural history.[15]

The results of this agricultural revolution from 1940 to 1970 assumed a

FIGURE 5.3. *Mennonite farmers harvesting soybeans, Putnam County, Ohio, late 1940s. Courtesy of Mennonite Historical Library, Bluffton College.*

paradoxical cast for American agriculture. On the one hand, farmers and other Americans could regard what Shover called "one of those quantum leaps in output that technologists love to celebrate." The forces of technological change had wrought a sea-change in farmer productivity in a matter of a few decades. In 1820 one farm worker supplied a subsistence living for four other people. By 1945 the ratio reached one to 14.6 people; and less than three decades later, by 1969, economists estimated that farmer furnished the subsistence for 45.3 other people.[16]

On the other hand, the darker picture for American tillers of the soil was that concurrent with their ability to produce so much more food on decreasing amounts of farmland, technology had increased to such a point that a rapidly decreasing number of them were required to do it. In 1945, farm labor absorbed 18.8 million man-hours; fifteen years later, even as production levels skyrocketed, this measurement of farm labor had dropped in half. In less than two decades, in other words, half the number of farmers could produce the same or a greater amount of crops. The nation lost over 1.6 million farmers in the 1950s and almost a million the following decade. In the single state of Kansas, for instance, two researchers discovered that the number of Kansas farmers declined by 52 percent in the twenty years from 1940 to 1960. Meanwhile, to most effectively utilize their agricultural technology, remaining farmers discovered that they needed to cultivate more land; and as the number of farmers tumbled precipitously, average farm sizes nearly doubled from 1940 to 1960. Younger operators trying to get established after the bounteous years of World War II found themselves in an especially tough position. Farming was increasingly becoming a difficult occupation to get started in.[17]

The reverberations from this agricultural revolution shook the Mennonite rural community to its core. In the "man power survey" that they obediently compiled for Selective Service in 1940, the Mennonite Church listed 60 percent of its members as "farmer." Thirty years later, a 1972 church member profile listed only 38 percent of that extensive sampling as having a "rural farm" place of residence. Similarly, in Leland Harder's large target group of General Conference Mennonites in the early sixties, he noted that the number of farmers in that denomination had dropped from 54.1 percent of the church membership in 1943 to 30.8 percent in 1960. Using a different sample, in 1980–81 Harder calculated these numbers as 35.1 percent of the GC membership as farmers in 1960, 23.4 percent in 1970, and 17 percent in 1980.[18]

Many Mennonite farmers, like so many other rural Americans, simply "lost their farms after years of hard labor on them," noted Gingerich in 1942. "They have been reduced to the status of renters, paying their yearly rents to insurance and loan companies for the privilege of remaining on the land they have developed." Likewise, the increased cost of farming seems to have been a principal factor in driving so many younger people to new occupations. Fretz testified similarly in 1942. While he admitted that young people left the farm for a number of reasons, including a search for adventure or to go away to college, the "majority," Fretz averred, moved on "for the simple reason that there is no place for them to earn a living for themselves and for their families on the old home place or in the local community."[19]

Bethel College economist Lloyd Spaulding's study of agricultural trends in three counties in central Kansas from 1949 to 1954 exemplified such trends underway for the GCMC. In this area, the heart of the GC Western District Conference, Spaulding documented the gradual expansion in average farm acreage and the concurrent decline in the number of farms. In addition, he highlighted the growth of commercial agriculture in the booming farms and also the shift in a large number of farmers to part-time work away from the farm. Spaulding illustrated his argument with some statistics from individual GC churches in this period. For example, in the Bethel Mennonite Church in Inman, Kansas, in 1946, 70 percent of the heads of families were engaged in agriculture as their primary occupation. Ten years later, only 34 percent were. Tabor Mennonite Church in Newton witnessed a drop in the number of their farming members from 68 to 48 percent in the same period. Another study in 1958 of Alexanderwohl Mennonite Church, a large and prominent GC congregation near the small, central Kansas community of Goessel showed that in the ten years from 1946 to 1956, the number of full-time farmers in the congregation had declined from 62 to 38 percent. The church's young people, commented the author of the study, simply lacked the financial means to get started in farming.[20]

This decline in the number of farmers added significantly to strengthened patterns of urbanization in the postwar decades, a trend deeply affecting the Mennonite community. As the *Mennonite Weekly Review* editorialized in 1957, "Everywhere there is evidence of the rapid urbanization of our people."[21] Look, for example, at Table 2.

Plainly the agricultural revolution that eliminated so many farmers reverberated among many Mennonites as well, sending them migrating to the cities to seek alternative forms of employment. As Mennonites left the farm, they still showed an overwhelming preference for homes in the rural countryside or smaller towns. In the 1972 survey, while roughly a third of the members from both groups still lived on farms, 36 percent of the MCs and 28 percent of the GC Mennonites made their homes in "rural nonfarm" settings, and 26 and 40 percent, respectively, resided in cities smaller than 25,000 people. A parallel study of five major Mennonite groups in the

TABLE 2. *General and City Membership, (Old) Mennonites, 1940–1960*

Year	OM Membership	City Membership	Percent City	Percent City Increase
1940	56,487	3,508	6.2	
1945	57,334	4,569	8.0	30.2
1950	64,591	5,618	8.7	22.9
1955	71,675	7,412	10.3	31.9
1960	73,576	8,187	11.1	10.5

Source: Paul Peachy, *The Church in the City*, Institute of Mennonite Studies no. 2 (Newton, Kans.: Faith and Life Press, 1963), 74–75.

late 1980s found 53 percent of GCs living in towns or cities of 2,500 people or more and 37 percent of MCs doing so.[22]

As they left the farm, Mennonites increasingly gravitated toward urban and especially professional occupations, a trend that continued through the 1960s. In 1971, Leland Harder provided evidence of a 12 percent decline in the percentage of GC farmers and an 8 percent rise in the percentage of professionals in that decade alone. By 1970, the GCMC membership rolls listed more professionals—especially public school teachers and nurses— than farmers. "It seems evident that when our people leave the farm," Harder concluded, "they go into the professions more frequently than any other type of gainful employment." This conclusion appears even more on target after taking into account people who left the church. Harder found the drift to the professions so acute among ex-members, especially younger ones, that he termed all varieties of the professions as "threatening" to the denomination.[23]

Mennonites were able to enter the professions in greater numbers in the postwar years because of a concurrent shift to much higher levels of participation in higher education. This tendency appeared, like so many others, partially as a result of Mennonite experiences in the war years. Responding to a poll conducted by MCC, 26 percent of CPS men indicated they were planning to continue their education after the war. The new Mennonite Mutual Aid program produced funds to enable young MC men to go to school. Likewise, the Peace Committee of the Western District Conference urged the General Conference to create an "Educational Rehabilitation Fund" for this purpose, and in 1945 the GCMC created a "Board of Mutual Aid." GC colleges made it possible for ex-CPS men to enroll without tuition for as many months as each had served in CPS, up to 27 months. Together, these programs seemed to function as sort of a Mennonite equivalent of the GI Bill. Not surprisingly, one student remembers Goshen as "inundated" with new students after the war.[24]

In a 1968 study of Mennonite Church trends toward higher education, sociologist Calvin Redekop noted that the higher the education of the parents, the greater the chances were that their children would also attend college. From 1960 to 1964, the number of GC college students rose from 2,080 to 2,514, a 21 percent increase. In the same period, MC young people increased their numbers in college from 1,981 to 3,030, an increase of 53 percent. Even more significant in positioning these young people to absorb outside cultural influences was a new trend toward attending non-

Mennonite colleges by an increased proportion of these young people. In 1960, 57.2 percent of GC youngsters attended non-Mennonite colleges, a figure that rose to 67.5 percent by 1970. In the early sixties, at least, this trend appeared for the more prosaic, nonideological reasons of lower cost and closer proximity to home of state schools. Even so, as chapter 8 will explore, through the channel of such schools, church young people ushered powerful new political and cultural currents into the Mennonite world.[25]

Finally, alongside the easing down of the traditional Mennonite cultural barriers—indeed, with the rapid integration of large numbers of Mennonites into full participation into American society and culture—came openness to new theological currents as well. In other words, one area that the war years did not change was in the continuing Mennonite receptivity to theological fundamentalism. Indeed, the increasing acculturation and intensified Mennonite desire for acceptance into larger American society may even have accentuated fundamentalism's appeal. As historians of fundamentalism such as Joel Carpenter and George Marsden have suggested, this theological current tended to attract not only Mennonites but also members of a variety of immigrant-based denominations, particularly those with northern European roots. For it appeared to be a modern and thoroughly American Christianity, to be a way, in Carpenter's words, to "sing Zion's songs in a strange land." By adopting fundamentalism, white Protestant ethnics like Mennonites could strengthen their own faith communities while simultaneously defining themselves in an acceptable way as Americans.[26]

Yet, as with so many other aspects of acculturation, the development did not bode well for adherence to Mennonite distinctives such as pacifism. Bender's 1953 deliberations on "Outside Influences on Mennonite Thought" speak clearly to this point. As he admitted, "For most of us the day of isolation is wholly past. We are increasingly in the midst of the stream of American life and religious influences." The substance of Bender's article identified outside intellectual influences penetrating into the Mennonite world through a variety of channels: neighborly contacts, tracts and periodicals, the radio, and Bible schools such as Moody and the Bible Institute of Los Angeles. Bender admitted that some of those influences had even been beneficial. In the piety, spiritual dedication, and missionary enthusiasm of many such groups, Bender thought them "nearer to original Anabaptism than we ourselves now are." Yet also because of such influences, he maintained, Mennonites had been losing key doctrines such as nonresistance. While finding a variety of reasons for the inroads that such outside currents had made into Mennonite thought, Bender concluded plainly that "Fundamentalism is currently the greatest danger."[27]

Considered cumulatively, these social and cultural changes spelled nothing less than an inescapable new reality for the church. As church ethicist J. Lawrence Burkholder recognized in 1959, after "many years of isolation," Mennonites "are no longer able to resist the forces that have made modern America what it is today." This is not to claim that Mennonites had altogether ceased farming or living in rural areas; throughout this period they continued to hold a membership that was far more rural than the U.S. population as a whole. Perhaps claiming that Mennonites became urbanized seems tenuous in light of 1972 data demonstrating that only a quarter of MC and forty percent of GC Mennonites lived in towns and cities with populations over 2,500 people. Yet enough had taken up nonfarm and town residences and obtained nonfarm educations that an isolated, rural vision could no longer function as normative for them. No longer was the tightly focused Mennonite community merely besieged; a national culture and economy had broken through its sociocultural defenses to compete for the allegiance of its people.[28]

TWO RESPONSES

As Mennonites began to realize the failure of their efforts to preserve their rural communities, the responses of church leadership fell into two basic patterns. On rejected the rural community as a desirable vision for Mennonites. The other took shape in determined exertions to keep the cultural boundaries intact in spite of urban sociocultural incursions. To this end, church leaders embarked on one last, desperate campaign to enforce Mennonite nonconformity.

Because of the wide-ranging theological and cultural understandings of the General Conference Mennonite Church, it would perhaps be erroneous to claim that few GC Mennonites had strict conceptions of nonconformity. Certainly they viewed with alarm the dissolving of their traditional cultural boundaries from the outside world. As one GC leader complained to the Mennonite World Conference in 1939, "The former separation from the world is losing ground. Conformity to the world is increasing." Yet, stemming from their relative autonomy in South Russia, GC Mennonites had traditionally displayed a greater openness to outside culture—in Juhnke's words a "positive orientation toward the sociocultural possibilities." In these isolated Russian villages, church administration had spoken to as-

FIGURE 5.4. *Sunday morning worshippers at First Mennonite Church, Bluffton, Ohio, about 1955. Courtesy of Mennonite Historical Library, Bluffton College.*

pects of existence beyond the spiritual and had ordained cultural activity as an important component of life. New leaders in America such as C. H. Wedel and Henry P. Krehbiel repeatedly stressed the church as a continuing cultural enterprise, one that could learn a good deal—missionary zeal and revivalism, for instance—from other Christians beyond their gates. GC Mennonites would root their separation not in peculiar clothing but in other Dutch-Russian ethnic aspects, such as a low-German dialect. Thus in July of 1947, the respected GC leader and scholar Ed. G. Kaufman recognized that the church "has never adopted strict regulations regarding dress."[29]

While thus avoiding much of the agony engendered in the MC struggles over nonconformity, the greater GC openness to acculturation rendered it all the harder to maintain that critical distance from society. As the president of the Eastern District Conference observed in 1942, "One of the great dangers among the General Conference Mennonites is that in attempting to proclaim our freedom from the plain garb we have become enslaved by the fashions of Hollywood and Paris."[30]

The "old" Mennonites preferred to put their weight on the plain garb. In the postwar years, these Mennonites continued to engage in such structuring against an even more rapid pace of change, but finally the apparatus of rules and regulations grew so extensive and top-heavy that it collapsed of its own weight. In the words of one Franconia bishop, "The first conference rule book in my time was only several pages. Then when the 1940 discipline came out it was a little thicker. In 1947 another rule book came out and it was even thicker. By 1959 it was still larger and that is when we went over the cliff."[31]

The whole issue of nonconformity appears as centrally important in an accounting of the Mennonite peace position. While items of clothing such as a head covering or plain coat only seemed to be archaic measurements of ethnic solidarity, to "old" Mennonites they symbolized the degree of separation from the world, a trait that nonresistance had depended on for centuries. As John Stauffer avowed in 1953, "nonresistance is in reality a phase of nonconformity to the world on the issue of violence and warfare."[32]

Once again, the problem seemed especially crystallized by the war years. Pressures to conform to the standards and values of a crusading national community appeared all the more palpable once that critical distance from outside society had begun to lessen. Observing such trends in 1942, Melvin Gingerich lamented that "Mennonites became more and more interested in proving to other that they were really not so 'queer' after all and that in the main they differed little from the society around them. Many were slow to confess that they were Mennonites." Little wonder that many Mennonite Church leaders articulated, in the words of one historian, a kind of Mennonite "domino theory" about dress regulations: once they went, all else would follow.[33]

The violations of these dress codes were many and were increasing. As noted by one MC committee, they included "the holding of life insurance, membership in labor unions, immodest and worldly attire (including hats for sisters), the wearing of jewelry (including wedding rings), attendance at movies and theaters." Moreover, the record of such wrongdoing continued to accumulate for the following two decades, with penalties of embarrassment at being denied communion and then the forfeiture of church membership for members who persisted in such errors. Off in Germany doing MCC work in 1947, Bender heard from Donovan Smucker, then a professor at the GC seminary in Chicago and a frequent Bender correspondent, that in a recent visit to Goshen College he observed that "the faculty and student body of Goshen have for all purposes abandoned plain clothing." The church held special conferences on the problem, bishops railed from the pulpit, but still the disobedience continued. At a special meeting called by the bishops in 1962, Lancaster bishops noted the continued problem of a lack of adherence to dress and other conference nonconformity standards.[34]

In trying to enforce such prohibitions, OM bishops faced two fundamental difficulties. First, while the traditional mores of the Mennonite rural community had long shaped peoples' lives, the particulars of dress and lifestyle, as has already been noted, only began to be codified ever more precisely well into the twentieth century. Hostetler outlined this process occurring in Franconia in the twenties and thirties; much the same thing happened in Lancaster. The Lancaster bishop Paul G. Landis, for example, later recalled bishops formulating written rules about dress about the same time, and even then respected members of the Lancaster Conference ignored them until a real rigidity set in by the time of the Second World War. He remembered that as a young minister, neither he nor his family donned the traditional Mennonite "plain coat" until revivals swept the district in the early 1950s, when "it became a symbol of a new commitment."[35]

A second difficulty was that church members increasingly began to subvert nonconformity rules because of the blandishments of an ever more attractive popular culture. With the lessening of Mennonite isolation, members had a hard time understanding the evils inherent in a different hairstyle or in a simple necklace or necktie. Thus the bishops began to encounter a quiet, mass resistance. According to Landis, "the only way we knew how to change in those days was by popular disobedience, and if we had enough disobedience they eventually dropped the rule . . . that was the way to change, just get enough people to gang up." Of course, this meant no end of headaches, heartaches, and painful moments for the church. Landis recalled a conflict he had as a young bishop with an older bishop who was "very legalistic." In each congregation, this bishop had a collection of teenage girls that he had refused to baptize because of their noncompliance with certain church dress requirements. After his ordination as a bishop in the late 1950s, Landis asked for comments in a meeting with some of the laity. He received "an avalanche of members of the churches saying that we have to receive these young people." Caught in the crossfire over whether to "hear the voice of the people" or to side with the senior bishop, Landis chose the former and admitted the girls into membership. Still, this incident multiplied many times over throughout the church certainly made these, in his estimation, "trying times."[36]

In the end, the church had no choice but to dismantle the extensive defensive structuring it had created. As early as 1950, articles appeared in the *Gospel Herald* questioning such extreme rulemaking. The Mennonite Church leadership rewrote the church discipline in 1964–65 to encompass a less demanding code, but this triggered a reaction from denominational conservatives who refused to agree to it. Yet while the church bureaucracy settled into a long stalemate over this issue, in the congregations the laity, in incidents like the one described above, gradually forced the issue. Congregation by congregation, district by district, the last stand of nonconformity slowly crumbled.[37]

In the end, moreover, their piecemeal removal of such rigid restrictions cost the Mennonite Church a good deal more than sweat and pain for a couple of hard decades. In many cases it cost them good, solid members. In the early 1940s, for instance, at Zion Mennonite Church, near Hubbard, Oregon, a younger, more aggressive minister bucked up against the authority of his senior minister and the district bishop by marrying a congregant with a non-church-member and not endorsing restrictive attire. Finally excommunicated in 1944, he took 66 members with him to a General Conference congregation a few miles away. Ten years later, GCMC leaders met with a group of discontented Mennonites in Idaho who had left their OM congregation and desired to form a GC church instead. Although they honored the doctrines of Mennonitism, they had approached the General Conference, wrote one GC leader investigating the situation, because "they feel the church rules as to dress and headcovering and other requirements are not necessary."[38]

The respected GC pastor Walter Neufeld had a different vantage point on the stresses in the churches that nonconformity could create. His observations anticipated an emerging newer basis for a reformulated Mennonite identity. Neufeld pastored a Wayland, Iowa, congregation in the 1960s, about sixty percent of which was comprised, in his estimation, of Mennonites who had broken with the Mennonite Church because of its nonconformity restrictions. This exodus created an interesting dynamic both within the congregation and also in the relations with the remaining OM congregation in town. One of the major topics of conversation among these excommunicated "old" Mennonites, Neufeld remembered, was "all the dumb things" that OM youths did. "The gist was," recalled Neufeld, "those kids can do anything they want, and as long as they went CO it was okay." When his congregants observed "old" Mennonite youths misbehaving badly, a prevalent comment was that "I'd rather have my kid join the army than be like that."[39]

By the early 1970s, then, few obvious cultural differences separated "old" Mennonites from outside society. As the denominational organ admitted in 1973, "We have dropped teaching on nonconformity to the point that it is a silent subject." Mennonites could reflect back on a rural heritage, and a disproportionate number still farmed, yet culturally they had come a long way from the days of rural isolation. As a Virginia Conference scholar recognized in 1973, "The Mennonite Church seems to be swiftly losing its last external vestiges of nonconformity. To a large extent we have melted into the mainstream of American cultural life."[40]

Yet as some Mennonites campaigned desperately to resist these new socioeconomic changes by retaining a viselike grip on the remaining indicators of cultural separation, others began to offer a completely opposite second response. Instead of battling the Mennonite drift off the farm and the acceptance of new occupations and lifestyles, these leaders found in such changes less cause for alarm. In fact, as the sixties wore on, some began to argue that acculturation might serve a beneficial function in renewing Mennonitism as a religious community and thus bringing them back closer to the essence of Anabaptism.

In spite of the dire wartime predictions of people like Winfield Fretz, by the late fifties sociologists were discovering that leaving the farm did not necessarily spell the collapse of Mennonite family life.[41] Concurrently, important new developments in Anabaptist historiography greatly assisted Mennonites in interpreting these changes, especially the growing Mennonite urbanization, in less threatening terms. Sparked by Bender's Anabaptist Vision, Mennonite scholars threw themselves into Anabaptist studies with renewed vigor in the postwar years. In doing so, they discovered the urban roots of their revered ancestors and began to realize that the connection Mennonites had traditionally made between spiritual purity and the agrarian life had not been delivered on stone tablets from Menno Simons or Conrad Grebel but instead had developed only as a response to severe persecution. Much of this new turn emerged in the early 1950s with the influential critique of a young group of MCC workers in Europe, published in a series of pamphlets called *Concern*. These notions also struck a particular chord among many General Conference academics. Bender's historical studies had repeatedly stressed the Swiss/South German stream as the "normative" Anabaptism-Mennonitism, an understanding that underlay much of Hershberger's work as well. Indeed, whenever the "old" Mennonites informed the world that they were "The Mennonite Church," whether or not they intended it, the implication clearly followed that other

Mennonite bodies were merely further derivations, if not deviations, from this Mennonite mother group.[42]

General Conference scholars were understandably irked. Their reply not only challenged Bender's "monogenesis" theory of the founding of Anabaptism and stressed the plurality of Mennonite roots, but it also focused on the urban origins of Anabaptism. In terms of ethnicity, such origins helped to explain the easier path to urbanization followed by many General Conference Mennonites and especially by a third group, the Mennonite Brethren. In terms of history, the emerging argument was that since Anabaptism was also born among more cosmopolitan Dutch and North-German merchants, the farm was thus not somehow written into the Mennonite charter and that the more intense persecution suffered by the Swiss/South Germans might have warped their understandings of the essence of Anabaptism. In fact, their trials might have dulled their missionary fervor and created an unhealthy devotion to agricultural isolation. Other people besides Bender could turn to Anabaptism for a usable past. The message seemed fraught with implications for Mennonite life in post-war America. In the words of sociologist and lay leader Leland Harder in 1964, "The identification of the 'Mennonite way of life' with agriculture was an historical accident; and now that persecution has ceased, we can move freely again among the masses, witnessing to our faith."[43]

Others followed along the same lines of analysis to recognize that second, long-subsumed phrasing of Anabaptist identity: the prophetic Anabaptist voice. It had emerged among the young dissenters in the CPS camps and would increasingly echo in the postwar years. At another "Study Conference on Christian Community Relations" hosted by Hershberger and his associates at a Mennonite retreat center in Pennsylvania in 1951, the "Findings Committee" articulated this newer formulation of Anabaptism. Though "the program" of their Anabaptist ancestors was "primarily evangelistic," the committee concluded, "they did have a voice on the evils of their day. They were not known as the 'quiet' until after they had lost their evangelistic zeal."[44] Perhaps remaining true to such ancestors would entail recapturing that kind of voice, some Mennonites began to suggest, a process that would no longer countenance satisfied isolation on the farm.

The analyses of such educated men as Peachey and Harder presented these themes to Mennonite intellectuals. Other writers took to the pages of the denominational press to begin a popular questioning of Mennonite ethnicity and the rural community among the laity. In the *Gospel Herald* in 1962, Roy Koch pointed to the vast predominance of Mennonite ethnic names on the church membership rolls as evidence that "we are not a successful evangelistic church." The outpouring of letters to the editor in response to Koch's opinions demonstrated that he had struck a nerve. Likewise, in the pages of *The Mennonite* two years later, Rudy Wiebe brought an analysis of the dangers that ethnicity and culture posed to Mennonite religion to the attention of GC Mennonites. Mennonites, he argued, are primarily a *people*, "a motley of groups held together by ethnic and cultural trappings. When will we repent of this and ask God's help to cut the spiritual life within our Mennonite churches free from this cultural hangman's noose?" The radical vision of free, voluntary commitment among their Anabaptist forbears had been imprisoned in a Mennonite ethnic heritage.[45]

By the late 1960s, a fair number of Mennonite scholars and leaders had followed such reasoning along to arrive at exceedingly negative interpretations of Mennonite ethnicity. In 1968, for instance, voicing a term that would get much play in Mennonite circles, the GC pastor Walter Neufeld condemned the old communities as "complacent Mennonite ghettoes" which had blinded them to a world of pain and need. Another writer declared in 1969 that while other churches were peace churches and baptized only adults, the prophetic voice was Mennonites' "unique contribution." Gary Schrag thanked heaven that the church was "in a state of radical transition." "As long as we were settled in little closed communities," he stated bluntly, "we were of no earthly good to the world." Of course, such terminology was apt to anger conservatives. The *Sword and Trumpet*, for instance, objected strongly to references to the "Mennonite ghetto," observing that "just a few years ago our Mennonite sociologists were telling us that our genius and our hope lay in the Mennonite community." As far as conservatives were concerned, it still did.[46]

Yet, like the conservatives' refusal to give in on the discipline of nonconformity, in the early 1970s such comments came merely as lonely voices crying in the wilderness. By the mid-1960s, the Mennonite community movement, as guided by people like Hershberger and Fretz, had just about played itself out. In 1954 the community magazine finally succumbed to the stresses of a shaky financial base and evolved into *Christian Living,* which was more of a conventional denominational family publication. The last community conference ran its course in 1965. While activists reestablished the Mennonite Community Association in 1972, they formulated it only as an interest group within a church of many more diverse orientations and as one designed to speak to a different kind of intentional community movement that was emerging among Mennonites and others.[47]

In sum, like their secular neighbors by the turn of the twentieth century, Mennonite "island" communities had begun to face the infiltration of an urban culture linking them more firmly into a national society. The more direct forays of the federal government into their lives in World War II had sparked a Mennonite resistance to such a process, rooted in a determination to protect the rural community from the inroads of modernization. But this campaign ultimately failed, because in spite of their leaders' warnings and injunctions, the laity simply refused to go along. A daunting number of otherwise solid congregational members simply wanted to wear their hair as they wanted or watch a ball game on TV without incurring a public reprimand from a church official.

Nevertheless, these were about as good a set of boundary maintenance mechanisms as many Mennonites could come up with. When such procedures failed and when the walls of community isolation crumbled, the Mennonite world clearly teetered on the edge of a slide into oblivion. When they had completely lost the defensive structures, both sociological and cultural, that had sustained their identity and way of life for centuries, what would prevent Mennonites from blending, without a murmur, into a mass society? With no shield between themselves and the government, the question of drawing a line of resistance on the question of war or any other matter would be moot. Given the direction of Mennonite acculturation, what would hold them together now?

A NEW MENNONITE COMMUNITY?

In 1973, J. Lawrence Burkholder, by then president of Goshen College, addressed the vast numbers of town and city Mennonites searching for community in an unfamiliar land. What they needed, Burkholder felt, was a new model that tried to preserve some of their older, rural community values, now adjusted for new considerations of urban life. Although it is hard to gauge the degree to which his comments were able to serve as such a model, at least he spoke to the urgency of the problem. With the old community gone, could Mennonites find another?[48]

As Mennonite sociologists began to work through social and cultural indicators in the 1970s and 1980s, they arrived at a number of different and sometimes conflicting findings concerning the viability of a sense of community that was no longer anchored in a tightly focused rural world.[49] Yet in the most recent updating of the extensive sociological analysis of 1972, the "church member profile" project, Kauffman and Driedger reported in 1991 that aspects of modernization in the years since the 1960s have not fundamentally destroyed Mennonite distinctives. Drawing on another vast sampling of members from five major Mennonite groups, these sociologists found that by the late 1980s, Mennonites had left the farm in increasing numbers, had further advanced in their educational achievements, and had increasingly obtained professional occupations. Larger percentages of Mennonites had moved to urban areas. Yet overall, their commitment toward Anabaptist understandings remained largely unaffected by these developments. Moreover, Kauffman and Driedger postulated, while Mennonites in the late 1980s no longer necessarily located their identity of peoplehood in rural enclaves, they did maintain a newer sense of community in social networks.[50]

It is precisely this concept of a new Mennonite community as a shared experience and ideology that requires a renewed focus on the Mennonite relation to the state. As the old separated community dissipated, Mennonites worked to construct another one based in a shared understanding and orientation toward society. Hostetler maintained that as "old" Mennonites dropped forms of cultural separation, they came up with new forms of commonality that expressed key values. "Separation from the world," she declared, "was being expressed through peace and service programs rather than in prescribed nonconformity." Acculturation did not mean Mennonites would cease being different than others; it only meant they would cease looking different. Harold Bauman, the campus pastor at Goshen College in the sixties, observed that up to the mid-1960s Mennonite students by and large shared the values that taught that to be a Mennonite was to look and act differently. After that point, he remarked, most students came to the college without viewing Mennonites as in any way different than others "except on the matter of pacifism." As Winfield Fretz, Robert Kreider, and Cornelius Krahn analyzed Mennonite altruism in 1958, they noted that patterns of benevolence reinforced a Mennonite sense of separateness. In 1971, for example, one congregant wondered "If we lose our peace principle, what reason do we have for being Mennonite? . . . It is our peace principle that gives us reason for existing."[51]

As the postwar years wore on, what it meant to be a Mennonite revolved not so much around cultural or behavioral characteristics that rendered them instantly identifiable to the outside world, but rather around a set of shared values and commitments. And more and more these newer—or perhaps rediscovered—values, ideals, and experiences emerged out of a budding dialogue and reevaluation about how to relate to the state.

CHAPTER 6

New Directions
and Forms of
Witness,
1946–1956

Albert Gaeddert faced a host of worries in September 1947. As a farmer, he scanned the skies for some rain to moisten the dry soil on his Kansas farm. As secretary of the Peace Committee of the General Conference Mennonite Church, he fretted over ways of nurturing a growth of a different sort. The recent war had indicated the stunning degree to which the church's young people had abandoned the denominational peace position. As a result, as Gaeddert wrote to a fellow committee member, "we stand in need of a rethinking of the entire issue." The problem, he went on, was that they could no longer see nonresistance as a mere doctrinal principle. Instead, "we face the larger issue of placing this truth into the whole fabric of our living and doing . . . we are dealing with the building of convictions into the lives of people." While he still felt at a loss in knowing how to do this, Gaeddert did have one idea. "The positive side of our witness, especially in times of peace, needs to be made clear to our people," he posited, "and we need to find handles by which we can take hold."[1]

Gaeddert's articulation of the task at hand and his suggestion about how to go about accomplishing it encapsulates much of the focus of Mennonite energy in the initial postwar period. In the decade after the war, Mennonites set out with increased determination to shore up the vast erosion in the adherence to their peace position that the war experience had uncovered. Not only did they clearly need to inculcate their young people in

Mennonite peace teaching, but developments during the war years quickly led them to reevaluate some of the implications of that teaching. Mennonites also moved to capitalize on the new currents of creative energy that the CPS experience had sparked among the church at large. Not only ex-COs but also thousands of Mennonites of all ages began to reevaluate their identity as an isolated, self-absorbed people and to express instead an outward-looking, service-focused orientation.

Finally, this period of reconsideration and new initiatives occurred in a climate of first cold and then hot war. The new dictates of total war so terrifyingly expanded upon in World War II found even further elaboration in the immediate postwar years. With the ready identification of a new enemy, the American state prepared to engage in a new kind of "limited" war. At the same time, it also prepared itself to possibly follow new warmaking maxims to their logical end: the complete and total annihilation of the entire enemy nation. The ensuing air of international crisis registered significant reverberations on a developing new Mennonite stance toward the state.

THE WAY OF PEACE AND THE NATIONAL SECURITY STATE

Following a short period of limited demobilization in 1946–47, the U.S. government began to construct the foundations of a new postwar military-state structure, one so completely oriented toward military pursuits that a number of analysts later termed it the "National Security State."[2] The origins of the Cold War and the National Security State are exceedingly complex and have been carefully explored elsewhere.[3] Suffice it to say that by the later 1940s, the Soviets had replaced Hitler in the American mind as the new totalitarian enemy that must be stopped at all cost.[4]

A series of foreign policy crises, indicating to Americans both in and out of politics what appeared the inescapable nature of the Soviet threat, furnished the necessary political capital for a massive American military buildup. Vast sectors of the American industrial base similarly gravitated toward defense production, creating what Dwight Eisenhower would later label as a "military industrial complex." With the Soviet explosion of an atomic device in September 1949 and the U.S. intervention in the Korean civil war, the massive new military buildup envisioned by Truman's defense review, entitled NSC-68, became a reality even more rapidly than any Pentagon official had dreamed. With the Korean crisis, the Truman administration managed to compress a planned four years of military buildup into just half that time. By the end of January 1951, Truman had received emergency powers from Congress to facilitate war mobilization, had doubled the number of air force groups to ninety-five, reintroduced selective service, and doubled the size of the army to 3.5 million men and stationed them in a string of military bases that circled the globe. Expenditures for the defense needs of the national security state were $12.9 billion in 1950, $22.3 billion in 1951, and $50.4 billion in fiscal year 1953. The warfare state that Mennonites and their leaders had begun to deal with in 1940 was not, as it turned out, a temporary aberration in American history. Instead, it would be a permanent and ever-growing reality.[5]

Moreover, the type of warfare threatened by this new National Security State made it increasingly difficult for an aware people of peace to go comfortably on with untroubled consciences. For in terms of military tactics, the warfare state of the Cold War promised to pick right back up where it had left off in World War II. This would be a national defense policy rooted in the ultimate acceptance of genocide as a legitimate means of warmaking. The momentum for establishing the atomic bomb as the cornerstone of American military policy emanated from a highly charged Air Force, flush from its central role in the military victory of World War II. Schooled in the theories of Douhet and Mitchell, air power enthusiasts followed the logic of terror bombing to view the bomb as only the best weapon in their arsenal. With strategic bombing as an accepted military practice, why not embrace the possibility of strategic atomic bombing? Moreover, the bomb promised to solve a pressing domestic political problem for the Truman administration in the immediate postwar years. Even as he began to convince his fellow citizens that their own security rested in thwarting Soviet expansionism around the globe, the president also confronted a widespread unwillingness, personified in the budget-minded Republicans controlling Congress, to match the Soviets soldier for soldier. An emphasis on air power, anchored in the threatened use of the bomb, appeared a heaven-sent solution to this thorny political dilemma. In one stroke, the bomb would neutralize the Red Army in Europe, provide a means of deterring other aggressors, and rapidly deliver American power to any corner of the world—all this on the cheap.[6]

Impelled by such considerations, beginning as early as 1946, according to historian Gregg Herken, war contingency plans placed atomic attack as an important part of any full-scale conflict with the Soviet Union. By the summer of 1949, war planners had arrived at a massive atomic attack on Soviet cities not just as a main element but as almost the sole extent of the prospective American war effort.[7]

Of course, such a buildup would not have been possible if national leaders had not been careful to also tend to the ideological arena. Demagogues like Senator Joseph McCarthy emerged to stoke the fires of anxiety and fear. As a result, as scholars such as Richard Fried and Stephen Whitfield have made clear, a popular and deep-seated anticommunist consensus came to rage through American life and politics with little restraint. Already by the spring of 1947, the diplomat George Kennan observed "the hysterical sort of anti-communism which . . . is gaining currency in our country."[8]

The climate was devastating for the any kind of renewal of the larger pacifist movement. Radical activists soon lost formerly sympathetic allies as colleges faced McCarthyite pressures, liberal church people swung over to Niebuhrian neo-orthodoxy, and labor unions purged the left from their ranks. By June 1950, the peace movement mounted only feeble protests to the Korean War and watched as former stalwart pacifists such as Norman Thomas and Dwight McDonald backed U.S. intervention. A more vigorous dissent occurred on a level beyond the merely rhetorical as a small but spirited group of pacifists, many of them former CPS men, refused to register for the draft as demanded by the new Selective Service Act of 1948. The state exhibited little patience with such a danger to national unity in this time of crisis; and by early 1949, seventy-eight of these dissenters, the bulk of them Quakers, were facing prosecution. The zeal of the prosecutors and the relatively stiff sentences meted out to these men indicated to many pacifists that the government had clearly embarked on a campaign of repression.[9]

Perhaps in days gone by, securely tucked away in their isolated rural villages, Mennonites could have remained immune from such developments. Given the inroads that acculturation had made among them by now, however, Mennonites were as prey to the winds of fear and hysteria as other Americans. "If one disagrees with prevailing opinion, you are treading on dangerous ground," wrote General Conference Peace Committee member Rufus Franz from Oregon in 1948. The price of dissent was clear to Franz. "When a society is as sick as ours is and has no clear direction to go, no real leaders to follow, feels fearful and insecure," he reasoned, "it becomes easy to make scape goats [*sic*] out of a group such as the communists, Negroes, Jews, Labor, John L. Lewis, Wall Street, perhaps Mennonites." The leadership was certainly aware of how deeply fear had penetrated the churches. At the June 1950 General Conference meeting, with war having broken out in Korea two months earlier, the Peace Committee pushed through a motion to "urge our people to hold themselves clear of the pressures and emotions of a war situation."[10]

Mennonites began to discover, as did other Americans in such a climate, that they could come under suspicion for no reason at all. One spring day in May 1963, for instance, young Danny Hostetler of Orrville, Ohio, was heading east on a train toward Philadelphia, sharing the other half of the seat with a soldier in uniform. To pass the time, Hostetler perused a book by the gentle Quaker leader Elton Trueblood, *The Company of the Committed*. After a while, the soldier got up and left, and soon afterward the conductor asked Hostetler to come with him to see a man in the rear coach, who identified himself as an FBI agent. The agent wanted to know why Hostetler was reading a communist book. After examining the work carefully, he finally determined that it had no explicit communist connection and told Hostetler he could return to his seat. The soldier returned momentarily as well, and Hostetler wanted to know why he had reported him to the FBI. A long talk about matters of faith ensued, with the soldier finally admitting that he had equated the word "committed" in the book title with "communist."[11]

Fear thus remained a factor in the Mennonite sifting of war and peace matters in these years. So too did the image of the Soviet menace. Indeed, their own recent history was such that the anticommunist message found particular receptivity among many Mennonites, especially in groups such as the General Conference, whose particular Mennonite ethnicity was predominately Russo-German. This Mennonite antipathy for communism had begun with the very rise of the Soviet state and had intensified in the interwar period. For these wealthier, German-speaking Mennonites living to themselves, appeared to be the epitome of the dangerous, antisocialist *kulaks* that the rising Soviet hierarchy found so threatening. Throughout the interwar years, stories had filtered out from Russia of the disappearances, forced separations, and liquidation of entire Mennonite settlements and of the numbers of men sent to Siberia. Not surprisingly, with Germany's invasion of the Soviet Union in 1941, these Ukrainian Mennonites greeted the Germans as liberators, and many proved to be easy recruits for the German army.

When the Germans retreated three years later, they carried back with them their ethnic German populations, including some 35,000 Ukrainian Mennonites. The retreat soon degenerated into a rout and then panic. Hundreds of Mennonite refugees died in the crossfire between the Soviet and German forces, and those that fell again into Soviet hands were quickly dispatched to slave labor camps in Siberia. At the war's end, the Soviets insisted on the repatriation, as "Soviet citizens," of the survivors remaining in Western hands. Ultimately only 12,000 Mennonites found refuge in the West, primarily in South America and Canada, through the heroic intervention of MCC representatives such as Peter and Elfreida Dyck and Robert Kreider. Meanwhile, American Mennonites could only absorb the news with shock and forward their relief monies to MCC. While few Mennonites showed any good will toward Germany, little doubt remained in many minds about who the ultimate enemy was.[12]

The Mennonite leadership could issue declarations about remaining uninvolved emotionally with the state's new militaristic crusade, but perceptive leaders also had to acknowledge that, guided by this historical legacy, the American anticommunist message effectively hit home among many of their people. As their country and Russia seemingly veered toward a collision course in the crises of spring 1948, Donovan Smucker, at a meeting of the MCC Peace Section, predicted that, in contrast to World War II, this time there would be "a different psychology" among their people because of Mennonite experiences "under Russian oppression." H. S. Bender noted in 1950 the increased difficulty many were having in trying to "withhold themselves from the military struggle" in a time when "Communism seems to be advancing."[13]

Finally, anticommunism and the military solutions it postulated appeared so alluring to many Mennonites because both came delivered in a highly attractive religious wrapping. In Cold War America, this meant the rise of Billy Graham and the movement of "New Evangelicalism" that he personified. During the war, a milder group of fundamentalists had pulled themselves together into a new religious coalition they called the National Association of Evangelicals. Holding onto fundamentalist doctrine but eschewing the bigotry, exclusivist orientation, and intolerance of the more militant fundamentalists, these "Neo" or "New" Evangelicals, as they styled themselves, thus set out to attack social liberalism and to win America, a nation they felt was "ripe for revival," for Christ. Under Graham's skilled guidance and leadership, the revival did come. Crisscrossing the country in revivals that won the endorsement of political leaders from the president on down, Graham and his New Evangelical cohorts reached America for Jesus with a message that perfectly blended the call to Christ with a patriotic anticommunism and an affirmation of the American way of life. Behind Graham, it seemed at times the whole nation chimed in to the same chord. A number of analysts have described the broad, if shallow, levels of public religiosity of America in the 1950s.[14]

Graham's message had a resounding appeal among many Mennonites. Personally, the evangelist seemed magnetic. When Graham conducted a revival at Richmond, Virginia, in 1956, for instance, eight hundred Mennonites from the Shenandoah Valley boarded thirty cars and twenty busses to travel the hundred miles to hear him. As the adults appreciated Graham, their children gravitated toward Youth for Christ. As a young man growing up in Lancaster, Pennsylvania, in the 1950s, Henry Benner regularly attended the large Youth for Christ meetings at the Lancaster YMCA. Of the five to six hundred youths attending regularly, Benner estimated that perhaps a third were Mennonites, a number also confirmed by a Youth for Christ leader.[15]

Mennonite leaders watched this development with alarm. As so many Lancaster County youth trooped to exciting Youth for Christ rallies, one local Mennonite youth leader worried about "the great influence which the fundamentalist forces are bringing to bear upon us" at such affairs. He had attended these meetings, declared Milton Lehman, and had noted how so many local Mennonite youth were attracted to them. The major problem, Lehman warned, was that "it is difficult for our young people to find their way through the flood of words and ideas which call them to fight communism in the name of God and country." The continued Mennonite drift toward a popular, nationalistic evangelicalism posed just as much danger as the older threat of militaristic fundamentalism—perhaps greater, because the earnest, inspiring Graham and his theologically conservative gospel seemed so attractive and so safe in many other ways. For an acculturating people who yearned for full acceptance as Americans, Graham's gospel offered a means to an acceptable national identity even more appealing than a combative, militant fundamentalism. Compared with the "go-getting faith" of popular evangelicalism, observed Peace Problems Committee member Ford Berg to Peachey in 1954, many Mennonites found their church's old ethic of nonresistance an outdated "faith of has-beens . . . a faith of works" with insufficient evangelical zeal.[16]

The ready Mennonite absorption of the individualistic piety, missions enthusiasm, and affirming nationalism of Graham's New Evangelicalism threatened to work a transformation in foundational Mennonite values, a transformation that could sweep away not only nonresistance but also many other Mennonite distinctives. Summarizing a study of Mennonite worship patterns, John Howard Yoder decried in 1964 that "major Mennonite emphases are wholly or largely lacking in the regular diet of Mennonite churches; that in their place there are characteristic elements of what we might call 'general American evangelicalism'" such as a greater emphasis on personal piety and a de-emphasis of church discipline, social concern, and sense of conflict with the world. It was partly to protect their own that many in the Mennonite hierarchy worked so hard to reach evangelicals such as Graham with their peace position in the postwar years. As one MCC Peace Section chief admitted in 1967, "As an increasing number of Mennonites associate with popular . . . evangelical organizations (Christian Businessmen's groups, ICL, Billy Graham, Christianity Today) it will be important that the witness of radical discipleship be heard in those circles."[17]

In sum, Mennonites faced a variety of challenges as they worked to solidify their peace testimony among themselves and aim it at others in the immediate postwar years. They needed to find a way of expressing their own sense of social responsibility as good American citizens in a time of national crisis while simultaneously expressing their primary loyalty to a Lord of peace. They faced another tough climate in trying to perform this old balancing act, a climate that would remain the reality in America for the next half-century. From 1946 to 1969, the National Security State would spend over a trillion dollars on military items and defense. In 1970 the fiscal budget plan for the Department of Defense would top out at $83 billion dollars, substantially more than the entire productive capacities of many countries.[18]

The prospects appeared rather daunting for the continued health of a Mennonite peace position. They were quite clear to MC historian Melvin Gingerich. "We are entering a period of militarization such as the world has never before witnessed," he noted in 1951, "and consequently our peace teaching will be tested as it never has before." Similarly, in July 1955, the emerging GC peace leader Elmer Neufeld traveled to Washington, D.C. for two days of lobbying against a new military reserve training bill requested by the Pentagon. He spent some time observing the parade of military brass testifying for the bill before a Senate committee. Watching this lineup, one fellow pacifist observed to Neufeld that "we are like a voice crying in the wilderness." Penning his reflections to Ediger later in the week, Neufeld could only wonder, "What ought to be our relation to a government so preponderantly militaristic? . . . What is the eventual prospect for our nonresistant views?" Moreover, Neufeld could come up with no shred of answer to such questions. "May God prepare us," he concluded, "for the time of crisis."[19]

THE POSTWAR PEACE PROGRAM

After all the exertions and sacrifices of the war years, Mennonites, like other Americans, had grown weary of turmoil by the late 1940s. In 1947, Rufus Franz observed "a sort of lethargy or 'let down' feeling in our churches in the matter of even discussing or using the topic peace." Even the Peace Problems Committee, remarked one member, needed to be shaken out of "its doldrums." A number of ministers may have deliberately downplayed talk of peace to refrain from further inflaming congregations that had divided over the question during World War II. Winfield Fretz found that in many congregations nonresistance was "such a delicate subject" that ministers avoided it, "lest discussion alienate members or even lead to church splits." The same kind of tensions also infused the atmosphere at Mennonite colleges in the postwar years, since the student body was comprised of both ex-GIs and ex-CPS men. As one MC activist fulminated, "Too many of our college presidents are pussy-footing about and are afraid to stress nonresistance, lest the ex-GI's present be offended and the enrollment thereby decreased."[20]

The task at hand seemed to once again put a premium on more and better peace education. A large part of this task concerned the preparation of new literature and making sure it got to the people. By 1954, for example, the Mennonite Church had available no less than twelve separate books and nine smaller pamphlets of relatively recent vintage bringing the nonresistant message. Similarly, the General Conference Mennonite Church issued a number of books and pamphlets over these years, including Fast's *Jesus and Human Conflict* and another work, *The Power of Love*, which were specifically designed for Sunday school use. To reach their ministers with a peace message apparently unfamiliar to many of them, the Peace Committee produced a quarterly called *The Peacemaker;* and to reach their youth, they began in 1954 another quarterly entitled *Youth and Christian Love*. In addition, in 1955 the denomination's Board of Christian Service inaugurated a series of monthly or bimonthly mailings to all youth, male or female, beginning once they reached their seventeenth birthday.[21]

Simultaneously, peace leaders moved to personally address their young people. One method was a series of intensive local study conferences on peace known as "Peace Institutes." Patterned after the old Conscription Institutes of CPS days, and held in a number of different locations from 1948 through the 1950s, the institutes brought collections of primarily younger Mennonites together for several days of lectures and discussions on peace. To illustrate the content of such institutes, at the first one, held in February 1948, in Moundridge, Kansas, attendees heard testimony from ex-CPS men and repentant former soldiers, listened to a scriptural explication from Gaeddert and a presentation of "The Christian Answer" from J. W. Fretz, and then were broken into discussion groups to mull over the material.[22]

Church leaders found an even better way to insert peace teaching onto the local level in something they called Peace Teams. These involved taking small groups of three to four young men, preferably ex-CPS men, training them extensively for a couple of weeks, and then sending them off into rural Mennonite communities around the country to conduct an ongoing series of smaller peace institutes. Since, as the war made clear, reasons for a man's defection from nonresistance could vary widely depending on his individual circumstance, the roving peace instructors would live with a local pastor for a few days, poke around in the community, conduct discussion groups and give-and-take sessions among local Mennonites, and in all other ways, in Peace Team leader John Hostetler's words, endeavor to "get into the local crux of the problem."[23]

In their tour of the local communities, the Peace Teams uncovered a number of matters for concern by the wider church. Several congregations illustrated the degree to which tensions from the war still registered marked strains. In Fisher, Illinois, reported one of the teams in 1948, local toughs warned them to lay low on their message to avoid offending several military veterans who "have just become re-adjusted." Another factor eroding nonresistance that the Peace Teams ran into time and time again was fundamentalism. More than once the teams uncovered the prevailing attitude that "salvation is the most important thing, not nonresistance. Therefore our real business as a church is to do mission work and save souls; nonresistance is a minor part of the Bible." They found such attitudes particularly places in regions such as Illinois, where the influence from Bible institutes such as Moody in Chicago had penetrated deeply. In other places, the Peace Teams found that too great an openness to an outside culture resulted in an uncongenial climate for their message. As one team member summarized, an historical approach worked well "in a community that wants to be 'Mennonite,' but not too effective in one that wants to get away from the 'old way.' "[24]

Finally, the peace leaders in the GCMC moved concurrently to solidify the peace position in their denomination by sponsoring a study conference on peace and war issues in Moundridge, Kansas, in April 1953. The unexpectedly large crush of delegates and visitors did much to help the church directly confront many of factors that had put their commitment to nonresistance in such a precarious position. The very language emanating from the conference illustrates the degree of angst with which delegates wrestled with these problems. One student participant, the young Canadian peace activist Frank Epp, declared, for example, that "the church had been more concerned with accommodating itself to the government than to the gospel."[25]

Viewed in retrospect, the gloom and doom seems misplaced—a strangely discordant note in what were otherwise years of boom and revitalization for the General Conference Mennonite Church. In the years from 1945 to 1960, for example, the church began a number of new missionary ventures overseas and greatly expanded its denominational programs at home. So much did GC church activities and structures expand that the church finally began to take on the more complete trappings of other American denominations. As late as 1940, the church had no conference headquarters, Robert Kreider remembered later; and chairpersons of different church boards kept important church files in their briefcases. Finally unleashed from the Depression, rendered financially flush by the prosperity of the war and the postwar boom, and now reinvigorated by the energies and leadership of returning CPS men, the General Conference Mennonite Church—and to a degree, the Mennonite Church as well—engaged in a burst of denominational activity at home and abroad. The GCMC established a central administrative headquarters in downtown Newton, Kansas, where from 1944 to 1963 the number of administrative staff grew from one to thirty-one.[26]

Perhaps as a partial result, by the early 1950s, the GCMC began to receive indications that their extensive postwar peace education efforts might be paying off. In a 1952 survey of Bethel College students, four-fifths upheld the "traditional peace teaching" of the church without modification; three-fourths believed the CO position to be a "practical" one; and over half of the student respondents affirmed Voluntary Service as a highly satisfactory alternative to military service. Perhaps most important of all in this time of hot war in Korea and cold war everywhere else, eighty percent of the respondents declared that Christians should not fight in case of a war with the Soviet Union.[27]

Perhaps the real nuts-and-bolts work in the reconstruction of a General Conference peace position occurred in the patient hands of committed pastors. Take, for example, First Mennonite Church in Berne, Indiana, where pastor C. H. Suckau's rigid dispensationalism had helped push the majority of the church's young men toward military service in World War II. After Suckau left in 1943 to serve as president of Grace Bible Institute, the congregation called Olin Krehbiel, a different sort of minister, to the pulpit. Calm and deliberate, Krehbiel had graduated from Bethel, pastored a church in Pennsylvania, and unlike Suckau was deeply committed both to nonresistance and to firm ties with the GCMC. Soon after taking charge, Krehbiel began to reorient the church along these lines by working closely with the church's young people.[28]

At times they seemed to lead him, rather than the other way around. Not long after the war, for example, a few young military veterans asked Krehbiel if he would meet with them to talk through, as phrased by the church's historian, the "war-involvement issue." Agreeing, Krehbiel invited what he thought would be a small group to meet in his living room one evening. Instead, the group overflowed the room and spread down the hall, while Mrs. Krehbiel held a parallel meeting with the wives of these veterans. Soon Krehbiel had harnessed this group of young people to a range of church building and growth projects, and had found in them his nucleus for church renewal. Lynn Liechty, who participated enthusiastically in the group, recalled later that Krehbiel "began to open up to us the whole matter of what it meant to be an Anabaptist Christian." Not only did the pastor chisel away with Mennonite peace teaching, bringing in speakers such as Ediger and Smucker for weekend retreats and sermons, but he also tied the effort to a wholehearted devotional orientation and revivalistic spirit. Thus safely evangelical but now with the backing of what one participant called the "young bulls," Krehbiel successfully faced down a large bloc of the congregation's unhappy dispensationalists. They were "exciting days," remembers Liechty, and one of the high points of his life: "this whole Anabaptist thing was becoming embedded in us." And in this manner a kind of Anabaptist Vision sprang up once again at Berne, which remained a nonresistant congregation closely tied to the General Conference.[29]

Indeed, not long into the war years, it had begun to become apparent to church leadership that churches far beyond Berne harbored massive new energies for peace and service work. Visions and energies had burst forth in the war that now pointed in a number of directions.

NEW INITIATIVES

Church leaders quickly realized that CPS had sparked some extensive new commitments to relief and service activities among CPS men. Early in the postwar years, it became increasingly clear to them that a new service orientation had come to grip much of the rest of the church as well. While Mennonites would later express this newfound orientation in a variety of relief projects, in the immediate postwar years it came to fruition in three separate initiatives, all stemming from their collective experience in the war.

One of two initiatives emerging directly out of CPS was the growing program of Mennonite Voluntary Service (VS). In response to pressure to participate in Civil Defense activities, a special subcommittee appointed by the OM Peace Problems Committee in 1943 had urged the establishment of "Mennonite service units for a long-range program of Christian testimony and Mennonite witness." The "CO Girls" of World War II became the first expression of this idea, and the momentum continued after the war. Repeatedly, the men and women testified that they saw no reason why the work had to end just because the war did. CPS camp newsletters regularly called for the establishment of a postwar voluntary service program.[30]

It should be clear, then, that the emerging Voluntary Service program in 1946–47 took shape as a natural outgrowth of values and patterns formed during the war. At a special meeting of the MCC membership on October 31, 1946, the agency gave official approval to a permanent service program that would function alongside the separate VS programs by individual Mennonite groups. Volunteers, mostly young people, would be sent to work for a period of a year or less in units engaged in such activities as mental hospital or public health work as in CPS, conducting summer Bible schools, working with handicapped or delinquent children, or other social welfare activities. In some cases, such as the CPS camp at Gulfport, Mississippi, VS workers—including now a number of women—merely replaced CPS men, and the work went on unhindered. Already by 1946, VSers with the MCC program had made the shift from summer programs to year-round work, a trend that separate VS programs among the Mennonite Church, the General Conference, and the Lancaster Conference (which operated its separate program) followed directly. From 1946 to 1949, the

FIGURE 6.1. *The birth of Mennonite Voluntary Service: Playground supervisors during recess at Turkey Creek (Colored) Bible School, Camp Gulfport, Mississippi, summer, 1946. Left to right: Rosella Reimer, Jeanette Richert, Lois Musselman. Courtesy of Mennonite Library and Archives, Bethel College, North Newton, Kansas.*

number of long-term volunteers in MCC VS increased from 3 to 103; it leveled out at around 130 volunteers per year through the 1950s and 1960s.[31]

Certainly, church leaders created such programs to provide opportunities for their people to express a self-sacrificing Christian love. Even so, it remained clear that VS programs served some additional functions beyond that of simple Christian altruism. Not only did VS emerge as a result of experiences in CPS, but it came to fruition out of the general war-induced drift toward acculturation. During the war, the traditional boundaries they had constructed against the outside world began to crumble, revealing human needs that Mennonites found harder to ignore. Now that it was closer, however, the outside world also appeared dangerously attractive to Mennonite youth, and VS could also function to meet this threat. The 1946 report of a special PPC subcommittee admitted that church leaders in part pushed VS because of the attraction that evangelical movements were holding for their young people. The report acknowledged that "these are days of a 'Youth for Christ' crusade in American Protestantism; there are some who feel that we need a movement of 'Youth for Christ and the Church' which will win the loyalty and response of our youth."[32]

The second service-oriented initiative to emerge from the Mennonite experience in World War II was the continuing Mennonite energies in mental health work. Altogether fifteen hundred Mennonite CPS men, about a third of their total number of COs, served in some way in mental hospital work. Like CPS men engaged in other types of activities, they saw no reason to end such efforts with the termination of CPS. At its annual meeting on January 3, 1947, MCC agreed to found "three small homes for the mentally ill and/or rest homes." A month later, a group of MCC and CPS administrators put together a governing board for what would soon be known as Mennonite Mental Health Services. From this beginning, MMHS would move forward to establish a number of facilities for the mentally ill around the country, both Mennonites and others, thereby fueling a growing Mennonite reputation for excellence in the field of mental health.[33]

The third new venture embarked upon in these initial postwar years did not grow as directly out of the war experience as did the other two, but still strong links appear. Certainly, what became known as Mennonite Disaster Service (MDS) emerged out of the growing Mennonite awareness of the world at large, triggered by the war, and out of Mennonites' increasing inability to keep their eyes only focused inward on the needs of their own communities. Numbers of CPS men had been organized into disaster relief units (though not all, to their disappointment, were called into service). As early as 1948, Gingerich wrote to Ediger to inquire whether such men could be reorganized into functioning, on-call disaster relief units, mobilized to meet disaster for the indeterminate future.[34]

Two years later, Gingerich's idea took root, beginning at a young married couples' Sunday school picnic organized by two MC congregations, Hesston and Pennsylvania, in south-central Kansas. A number of the young people, with a fair sprinkling of CPS veterans among them, began brainstorming for ways to express "the practical outworking of concern for their neighbors." This led quickly to a service unit formed in the two congregations that began to organize volunteers to pitch into flood relief efforts following unusually heavy rains in Kansas in the spring of 1951. Organizing begat organizing, and in March 1952, a large meeting came together to pull together a body to give focus and direction to spreading disaster relief efforts. Eighty men from twenty-eight separate congregations from four different Mennonite groups produced the larger umbrella structure of

MDS. Each area would assemble a team of volunteers, ready to mobilize in a short time, to wade into whatever disaster relief and cleanup work a regional or national board directed.[35]

With this structure, local Mennonite communities all over the country rapidly organized their own MDS units. Not only did the program meet the needs of locally oriented religious communities, but the rapid founding of hundreds of MDS units illustrates the degree to which otherwise ordinary church members had been seized with the desire to engage in human service. Frustrated with an image of themselves as tiresome war objectors, they wanted to demonstrate what human good they could do. A Mennonite pastor, organizing an MDS unit in a small, heavily Mennonite community in Minnesota, perhaps phrased this best: "The Mennonites are usually known above all else for what they don't do in time of war. This is one opportunity for positive witness."[36]

In sum, the experience of CPS had laid the foundation for some significant changes in the Mennonite churches. A growing service orientation, originally stimulated in the CO camps, grew to encompass large numbers of Mennonites throughout the church. Epitomized in the new programs of Voluntary Service, Mennonite Disaster Service, and Mennonite Mental Health Services, these new service commitments would supply an effective antidote to the fragmenting effects of acculturation. As the erosion of nonconformity dimmed one vision of what it meant to be a Mennonite, volunteers aiding in tornado cleanup efforts, caring for the mentally ill, and laboring at hookworm eradication would help to furnish another. The old Mennonite community of an inward-focused, isolated rural people was slowly giving way. In its place began to rise a new sense of community—community in the shared experience of service.

NONRESISTANCE IN COLD AND HOT WAR

Unlike the period following World War I, Mennonites in this second postwar era had to work at the tasks of peace education and benevolent efforts against the backdrop of continuing international crises in which their country took a leading role. As they endeavored to strengthen their own peace position, this atmosphere of continuing crisis would serve to keep the pressure on in a variety of ways and to prod them along to a new orientation to the state.

The pacifist community, like the nation at large, would enjoy only the briefest of respites from tension and turmoil in the postwar years. With the release of the last CPS men at the expiration of the Selective Service Act of

FIGURE 6.2. *Members of Mennonite Disaster Service from Lancaster, Pennsylvania, erect an implement shed for a farmer in Elkhart County, Indiana, following the Palm Sunday tornado of 1965. Mennonite Central Committee Collection, courtesy of the Archives of the Mennonite Church, Goshen, Indiana.*

1940 in March 1947, they would have just one year before international threats nudged the president to go before Congress to ask for another draft bill. As legislation reviving the draft wound its way through Congress in the spring of 1948, pacifist spokespeople, including Albert Gaeddert, duly appeared to testify against it with the usual lack of result; the president quickly signed the legislation into law. Yet pacifists did not try very hard to alter the content of the legislation, for they had received an unexpected gift. Congress had decreed that all the conscientious objectors that it certified would be completely deferred from any kind of service whatsoever, military or alternate.[37]

Yet Congress also moved at the same time to assure generals like Hershey that any objectors he might have to deal with in a future alternative service program would be less of a "troublesome problem" than they had been in World War II. At the same time that Congress deferred objectors, it markedly tightened up its definition of conscientious objection to a recognize only COs whose military objection came from a belief in a "Supreme Being." In effect, this qualification served to weed out objectors primarily motivated by moral or humanitarian concerns—precisely the type who had given Selective Service such problems during World War II. As a result, the vast majority of objectors during the entire Cold War era—until the Supreme Court broadened the definition of conscientious objector with the *Seeger* and *Welsh* rulings in 1964 and 1970—would come from the three Historic Peace Churches. Until the mid-1960s, the majority of them would be Mennonite.[38]

With the passage of the bill, MCC issued an initial statement regretting the reinstatement of the draft and its explicit recognition of conscientious objection on solely religious grounds. Along with similar expressions from the MC and GC peace committees, the statement also recommended that Mennonite young men register for the draft as required; but it urged them to volunteer instead for the Voluntary Service program. The pushing of VS, in fact, would characterize much of the Mennonite response to the draft and the international threats which continued to roil the nation. Mennonites could not countenance such military measures, but by seizing on the VS program, they could still make their own contribution to world peace. For example, the *Gospel Herald*'s editorial in response to the draft bill trumpeted Voluntary Service as their answer to charges of being "yellow slackers," of not doing their part. "We are put on our own honor and on our own initiative," read the editorial, "to send both our young men and our young women into service that our consciences can approve and that both government and populace will admit is significant and valuable." The General Conference hierarchy pushed the VS program as their answer to war in an equally energetic manner. Responding to a lessening number of volunteers in early 1951, for instance, Ediger wrote of VS as a tremendous opportunity that they must not "waste." Nearly all Mennonite groups gave prominent play to a statement from MCC in October 1950, pressing VS as the Mennonite solution "in light of the Present Emergency" on the international front. Even more to the point here is the resolution passed by the GCMC's Western District Conference at its annual convention in 1950. With the government drafting local boys and sending them into combat in Korea, the conference moved "that our Western District Conference Churches be urged to supply Voluntary Service Workers from among their boys of draft age *at least*" at the same ratio that the government drafted other local men.[39]

So much, in fact, did Mennonites desire that their developing service commitments function as their sacrificial response to world militarism that they did not greet this gift of deferment with open arms. For a group willing to sacrifice freely in nonmilitary ways as proof of their worthiness as citizens, deferment did not ask enough of them. Thus as word of a possible deferment for COs filtered down, participants at an MCC Peace Section meeting in April of 1948 discussed whether or not to "protest" it and agreed to issue a statement to, in Gaeddert's words, "clarify our willingness to do constructive service." Their resulting declaration condemned the government's restrictive definition of COs and requested "that any Selective Service act recognize the right of a conscientious objector to serve" in relief projects instead of military roles. Suggestions from an MCC Peace Section meeting in 1951 that at least some members of the group would "welcome" a draft of COs clearly indicated a continuing Mennonite unhappiness with this dismissive CO arrangement.[40]

International events gave these dissatisfied Peace Section members what they wanted soon enough. By July 1950, the tension of the Cold War had broken out into open combat as U.S. army divisions engaged the North Koreans; in November Chinese troops pouring across the Yalu river had sent U.S. forces into headlong retreat. Selective Service correspondingly began to increase monthly draft calls; and as numbers of such draftees began to return home on stretchers or in body bags, the public's tolerance of CO deferment quickly dissipated. Once again, the issue of conscientious objection had touched the sensitive public nerve of equity. Larson recounts how various local draft boards began to reclassify COs into combatant or noncombatant roles and how by the spring of 1951, Congress had started to reconsider deferment. As public resentment grew, fanned by such groups as the American Legion, it became obvious to all concerned that COs would soon be sent into some sort of alternate service.[41]

Quite early the MCC Peace Section sensed the new winds blowing and began to make preparations for the return to a conscientious objector program. At a meeting in July 1950, a special MCC meeting called to address such matters recognized the coming end of deferment and decided to approach General Hershey to sound out any Selective Service plans for such a program. With equal foresight, in January 1951, the Peace Section formulated some "Guiding Principles on Alternatives to Military Service" and circulated them around to different Mennonite groups for comment. These principles envisioned a program that would improve on the obvious deficiencies of CPS in a number of ways. Unlike the World War II program, this newer alternate service arrangement would need to include completely civilian direction, offer service of real and actual importance in the health and welfare fields, and be remunerated labor in a length of service term comparable to men in the military with the same kinds of benefits, dependency allowances, and the like.[42]

As different Mennonite groups considered these guidelines, the criticism of Mennonite church-state cooperation formulated during the war quickly reappeared to make a substantial impact on the shape of their thinking. Former CPS administrators, now risen in many cases to important positions of church leadership, remembered their uncomfortable task of administering a Selective Service program. A special joint meeting of several MC committees in March 1949 listed as a "lesson for the future" that they must not "be agents for the government." Reporting on the concurrent negotiations toward a CO service program, the Peace Problems Committee reassured the MC General Conference, meeting in 1951, that they would accept neither the financial arrangement of CPS (i.e., unpaid CO labor), nor church administration of a Selective Service program.[43]

Not only Mennonites but the entire pacifist community was determined to avoid the many mistakes of CPS; in the end, their heavy lobbying effort of 1951–52, headed principally by representatives of the National Service Board for Religious Objectors (NSBRO), achieved a much more satisfactory CO program. In brief, the passage into law of the Universal Military Training and Service Act of 1951 ended deferment for duly classified COs and directed them into "such civilian work contributing to the maintenance of the national health, safety, or interest as the local board may deem appropriate."[44]

In February 1952, President Truman signed an executive order laying out the arrangement. True to the wishes of the Historic Peace Churches, it was expressed in a relationship between the individual CO, his employer, and more faintly, the government—with church administrators nowhere in the picture. COs would be assigned to work in paid or volunteer positions in government or nonprofit organizations engaged in health, welfare, charitable (such as Mennonite Voluntary Service), educational, or scientific activities. Although they would not be permitted to remain in their home communities, the COs (or I-Ws, as they came to be called in accordance with their classification) could volunteer instead of waiting to be drafted and could exercise some choice in the type of service they entered.

While NSBRO did not get all it wanted, the new I-W program stood as a great improvement over CPS, especially in the freedom, the promise of more meaningful work, and the paid labor it awarded COs. From the state's perspective, the arrangement had promise. Selective Service would not need to handle the especially troublesome objectors since many of them no longer qualified as COs. With objectors now buried away either individually or in small groups, ideally far from their homes, quietly engaged in inconspicuous hospital jobs few other people wanted, the agency received few complaints from the public (although the American Legion continued to beat the tom-tom about government leniency with the "slackers"). Employers tended to find these young Quakers, Brethren, and Mennonites at least as satisfactory—and in many cases more so—than other employees. So satisfied with its I-W men was one hospital that it prepared a special brochure and sent copies to different Mennonite colleges, asking prospective I-Ws to consider their institution when selecting their place of service. By 1953, Selective Service chiefs had grudgingly begun to judge the program a success.[45]

After a final tinkering with the basic regulations, the program finally got underway in July 1952, as newly drafted I-W men trickled off to their jobs in different locations all over the country. By 1955, a total of 4,500 men labored away in this program, over two-thirds of them Mennonite. For a small number this entailed overseas relief positions with MCC or a new overseas counterpart to Voluntary Service called PAX. Their tasks ranged from scrubbing floors in a Palestinian hospital in Jordan to maintaining vehicles with a road-building crew in Peru. For most of the I-Ws, however,

FIGURE 6.3. *I-W man serving at a children's hospital in Iowa City, Iowa, 1955. Mennonite Central Committee Collection, courtesy of the Archives of the Mennonite Church, Goshen, Indiana.*

their work meant low-level, low-paying hospital work in the United States. A 1955 survey of Mennonite I-Ws found that about two-thirds of them served in mental or general hospitals of some sort working as attendants, nurses' aides, or orderlies. Some had more specialized work, such as operating room technicians or medical records keepers; while less highly educated COs often took positions as drivers or laundrymen.[46]

As with CPS, the I-W program registered significant reverberations in the life and history of the Mennonite churches. As the draft became in all respects permanent, I-W service rapidly became the normative experience for Mennonite young men and counterpart to other manifestations of the church's growing service ethic. Longer term implications of this CO program will be considered later (see chapter 7). For now it is simply necessary to note aspects that began to register a more immediate impact.

First, as did CPS, taking thousands of young men from predominantly rural communities and scattering them individually or in small groups around the nation did much to introduce these men to an outside society and culture in an immediate and inescapable manner. For a majority of them, the experience inserted them into an urban culture as well. J. S. Schultz's 1955 study of Mennonite I-Ws found three-fifths of his sample of 1,794 COs living and working in cities with populations over 50,000. For vast numbers of I-Ws, the city would no longer remain a strange and forbidding place. At the very least, nearly all COs faced a new and different style of life. Declaring that he and his fellow COs were "making the greatest and most radical occupational changes of our lives," for instance, a I-W man working in a Staten Island hospital testified that "Nearly all of us here . . . are farm boys who suddenly, and almost unexpectedly were ushered into an entirely new way of livelihood."[47]

Secondly, given the problems that later enveloped the program, it is equally important to highlight the enthusiasm with which Mennonites greeted the new alternate service arrangement. Like Voluntary Service, Mennonite Disaster Service, and other ventures, the sacrificial service of I-W men, whether or not they received remuneration, appeared to wholly fit in with the developing Mennonite self-perception as a servant church. The men themselves found the program more than satisfactory as a means of Christian expression. One hospital laboratory technician, for example, saw his work "infinitely more beneficial to the growth of God's kingdom than participation in a military program." Considered as a whole, four-fifths of Schultz's respondents judged I-W service "a good opportunity for Christian witness."[48]

The larger church shared these sentiments as denominational magazines repeatedly praised the program during these years. At least some of the satisfaction church leaders found in the new program emanated from its potential for reinforcing a Mennonite service ethic and for stamping the new basis of Mennonite identity in a whole generation of young men. At a time when the church faced the corroding effects of acculturation, such an experience might prove a way to refasten the church's hold on its young people. By repeatedly reminding these men that they carried the torch of the church into new areas and that they should let their conduct reflect well on their church, leaders expressed more than missionary and service concern for others. Leaders seized on the draft machinery to work some lessons into their youth in order to, in the words of one I-W program supervisor, "keep them Mennonite." Others beyond church ranks perceived this process occurring. Hershey's aide Colonel Kosch observed that "Mennonites tend to use Selective Service as a means of converting their young men." Altogether, as with CPS a decade before, Mennonites optimistically found in this new alternate service arrangement a source of a dozen new blessings.[49]

However attractive the program, many young men did not find the draft decision an easy one; and they faced the same sorts of community pressures, in kind if not always in degree, that their elders had in World War II. Delegates to the important Peace Section Study Conference at Winona Lake, Indiana, in November 1950, recognized that their young men still gravitated toward the noncombatant position "because of social pressure. They want to be like others in the community, who go into the army." Especially the first wave of draftees, heading off either to deferments or to hospital work instead of to combat in Korea, felt the influence of their two communities, one national and one Mennonite, and faced the same old difficult decision between the two. "All of us at some time or another are called 'yellow,'" stated a I-W man, who wondered about the real reason he and his fellows faced such accusation. Was it because "we would break mother's heart if we would enter military service?" Or "would we take up arms if we knew we would not be socially ostracized by our home folks?" Communities also found ways of manifesting their unhappiness after the decision had been made. Citizens in McPherson, Kansas, once again exhibited the special venom that some of them seemed to have for the Mennonite pacifists in their midst. More than fifteen objectors had lost their jobs by December of 1950, and the American Legion was working to persuade local businesses to fire all the rest of the COs in town. Moreover, they had begun to spread their campaign to nearby Hutchinson through letters to the newspaper.[50]

The community pressures Mennonites felt are also revealed by their sensitivity to the public's need for what appeared as equitable treatment. One ex-CPS man wrote to MCC from Montana, for instance, cautioning in 1951 that "if we want the general public to look favorably upon us to some extent at least, we must do something besides staying at home enjoying ourselves." Administrators assigned to I-W matters with MCC devoted much of one issue of their bi-weekly publication for I-W men, the *One-W Mirror*, to the sticky issue of taking trips home. Victor Olsen of Selective Service had relayed complaints he had received from congressional representatives who heard from their constituents when the objectors appeared at home too often. Representatives in Congress had created the system, one I-W man reminded his fellows, and they could easily repeal it. Beyond self-interest, many of the men took the issue of equity to heart simply as good Americans. "Your service is a 'living sacrifice,'" urged one CO, "make it such. The boys at the front are in danger of death."[51]

Nonetheless, Mennonites were generally satisfied with the new CO pro-

gram. These levels of approval could only have been accentuated by results
of a new draft census in 1954 (see Table 3).

Quite clearly, something was happening among the General Conference
churches to push their CO percentages substantially higher than they had
reached a few short years before. Even the heavily acculturated Eastern
District had a fourth of their young men opting for I-W instead of military
service, and the Western and Northern Districts had resisted this sort of
military acculturation to the degree that they now had solid majorities of
their young men choosing alternate service.

Since no censuses were conducted before the beginning of the I-W program, it is impossible to know how many men chose military service over
deferment. At a meeting of district peace committees in 1955, church leaders at least came up with some of their own reasons for their higher CO
percentages in the early 1950s. Certainly the more attractive CO program
was a large factor in many men's thinking. In contrast to CPS, I-W service
offered them paid labor that held less threat of financial hardship for their
families; moreover, they had the choice of a variety of more directly service-
oriented work. Leaders also suspected that the influence of ex-CPS men in
the churches, along with some of the "negative experience of many who had
served in the army" had registered an impact. Yet perhaps the fundamental
factor concerned their listing of "peace rather than wartime." While pacifists and Selective Service had begun to cobble the program together in
1951, by the time I-Ws first headed off to work, the shooting in Korea had

TABLE 3. *Draft Classification of GCMC Draft Registrants, 1944 and 1954*

| | Totals (number/percentage) | |
Classification	1944	1954
1A	1435/55	717/42
1AO*	474/18	194/11
IO**	711/27	819/47

* The classification for noncombatant service.
** The classification for conscientious objectors. After men received their work
assignment they entered the category of I-W.
Source: General Secretary's Annual Report to the Board, 1954 Board of Christian
Service Report, November 24, 1954, Bound Volumnes MLA.

about stopped. Community pressures that had mounted when COs were merely deferred and that had exercised a political clout that resulted in the I-W system had greatly abated once the casualty lists shortened. These young men made their military decisions in a much less warlike atmosphere than their elders had in 1942–45. For a church struggling with heavy pressures toward acculturation, the degree of pressure from outside society remained critical.[52]

These same conclusions appear even more applicable to the MC men, whose greater degree of resistance to acculturation even in the early 1950s helped to account for much higher CO percentages than church leaders probably dreamed possible. As finally tabulated, the percentages of MC COs in the 1954 census ranged from 73 percent in Illinois to 96 percent in larger districts such as Lancaster and Franconia, with 100 percent of their draftees opting for I-W service in smaller conferences such as the Washington-Franklin Conference in Maryland.[53]

By the mid 1950s, Mennonite leaders could therefore reflect with some satisfaction on the apparent triumph of nonresistance. The vast majority of their young men were obediently entering a government-approved CO program, and large numbers of other Mennonites, both male and female, were devoting themselves to a similarly positive expression of Christian love and service beyond a mere no to the state's military calling. Yet just when the requirements of nonresistance appeared clear and the line with the state unmistakably drawn in a manner agreeable to both sides, the parameters of discussion suddenly shifted again. Members of a touring Peace Team in 1949 heard the concern summarized by a Michigan congregation that asked repeatedly about the problem of "voicing ourselves before the gov't, and the content of such an expression."[54] As Mennonites integrated new values of service into their fundamental identity, they began to find the older, strict demarcations of the two-kingdom theology inadequate. Propelled by a new sense of responsibility in a needy and unjust world, some Mennonites began to reason that the time had come to lay a Mennonite claim to small parts of what they had always considered the state's exclusive sphere. In other words, it was time to take a quiet, nonresistant offensive and begin to witness to the state.

ADDRESSING THE GOVERNMENT

Mennonites reached a rare unanimity on this new direction when they came together in a churchwide study conference on nonresistance called by the MCC Peace Section at a conference grounds at Winona Lake, Indiana, in November 1950. The conference discussions mulled over a variety of questions having to do with the state and the social order—definitions of the state; loyalty to different types of states; types of permissible service to society. Guy Hershberger articulated what Mennonites were increasingly beginning to recognize: that they faced a very different kind of state than had their Anabaptist ancestors, not just a warfare state but also now a welfare state. This state performed a good many functions beyond just bearing the sword, some of them useful and admirable service projects that invited Mennonite participation. The old divide between the church and the world should no longer be so simplistically applied, he argued.[55]

Equally as noteworthy, discussions also revolved around the variety of linkages participants found between the call to service and the call to citizenship. Once again, Mennonites wrestled with the stinging charge of pacifist social irresponsibility leveled by Niebuhr, particularly his aside about Mennonite parasitism. Much of the growing Mennonite demand for "positive service" alongside conscientious objection had stemmed from a reaction to this characterization. Now the delegates at Winona Lake searched to find a means of expressing an acceptable citizenship that would unite Mennonites of all persuasions but that would not also somehow blur the traditional lines between the two kingdoms. Though many agreed that because of measures of coercion involved in politics they could "find only a limited expression through political channels," through "non-political channels of service and evangelism" they could "contribute significantly to the welfare of the state. We need not be, therefore, 'parasites of the state.'"[56]

In his address, Hershberger reminded participants of his distinction in *War, Peace, and Nonresistance* between doing and demanding justice, a concept that many had rallied around. Yet he also turned to the rebuke issued by Niebuhr ally John C. Bennett, who had described Mennonites as offering merely a "strategy of withdrawal." He admitted that he did not think Christians should assume full responsibility for the social order, but he hastened to add that this refusal did not amount to a strategy of withdrawal. Instead, Christians should strive to develop an "enlightened social conscience," Hershberger asserted, which would readily speak to the state about social evils such as war and push forward "an aggressive program of love and action" that would "set a standard for Christendom and for the state."[57]

Some of the speeches delivered appeared to similarly solidify emerging stances or even to break new ground. Robert Kreider's address, for example, proclaimed that "Christ has given us a prophetic Gospel which must be preached to all men." Pointing out how Mennonites have unhesitatingly gone to government to obtain special CO privileges, he asked whether they felt similarly impelled "to speak to men in high places" on behalf of interests other than their own. "Ought we not to voice the Christian conscience where other groups of men—men not of our brotherhood—experience injustice and misery?" Kreider queried. While Kreider admitted having articulated "a more aggressive, out-going approach to community responsibility than has characterized our Mennonite tradition," this would not long remain a minority position. As always, J. Winfield Fretz proved especially articulate about the acculturation process that had caught up the church, a process that fueled these new prescriptions to the social order. Urging Mennonites to "once again capture their evangelical Anabaptist zeal," he argued that "we have had our nonresistant doctrine vacuum packed, as it were, within the confines of the Mennonite cultural walls. This seal has been broken during these thirty years of world wide relief activities with the Mennonite Central Committee. We must therefore go on. We cannot retreat into the shell of an isolated group existence."[58]

Altogether, the sessions at Winona Lake assumed critical importance both because of the forthright nature of the discussions among a widely representative group of leading Mennonites and because of the influence that these discussions exerted on the churches. The discussions and the influence were summarized in the statement that emerged from it, "A Declaration of Christian Faith and Commitment." Because the statement obtained the signatures of representatives of a large number of different Mennonite groups, it achieved a wide distribution. In fact, one analyst later called it "the only extensive inter-Mennonite theological document ever produced."[59]

It had much of importance to say. Articulating a wide range of social service values and commitments rooted in basic Christian understandings, the delegates acknowledged the Mennonite "obligation to witness to the powers that be of the righteousness which God requires of all men." Here was the hidden, prophetic qualifier that Hershberger had articulated in *War, Peace, and Nonresistance*, now widely affirmed as basic to emerging Mennonite peace theology. Delegates to Winona Lake offered a new rationale for such a prophetic witness to the state: it emanated out of an growing willingness to include the state as subject to, in a new and lasting phrase, the "Lordship of Christ." Part of the heritage of nonresistance, they agreed, required testimony to the state. Moreover, they did not stop there. These Mennonites also stressed that the testimony should be issued not only on their own behalf but also for others. In this, they added a further rationale: that the "social order, including our own segment of it, must be constantly brought under the judgement of Christ." In time, such a recognition would go a long way toward bridging the gap between the two kingdoms. Not long after the conference, the larger bodies of both the Mennonite Church and the General Conference issued new conference peace declarations that reinforced these service commitments and incorporated a sense of this obligation to witness to the state about issues of social justice.[60]

The first major issue that surfaced in these years to build on this growing determination to speak to the state was the ongoing postwar specter of Universal Military Training (UMT). This was a proposal, formulated and urged in the late 1940s and early 1950s by various military-minded public lobbying groups, to create a national military reserve corps. Each American male would serve an initial six months in military training, and then be placed in these military reserves for the following seven and a half years. Pacifist groups—and many significant nonpacifist ones—saw this scheme as a heavy step toward the complete military regimentation of the country. In spite of the influence of UMT proponents like Eisenhower and Truman, through rallying every possible resource, a broad-based opposition movement defeated UMT in several close battles in Congress.[61]

Given the fact that even the most extreme UMT proposals clearly excluded traditional objecting groups such as the Historic Peace Churches, adherence to a strict two-kingdom posture would have quickly defined the issue as the state's concern and none of Mennonites' business. Thus the lengthy and vocal Mennonite anti-UMT campaign assumes some significance. For throughout the church, the series of UMT proposals evoked an immediate, heated, and lasting outcry.

As Mennonites first began to focus their attention on the issue at an MCC meeting in October 1947, already one leader recognized, "We need to take a stand against such legislation." Take a stand Mennonites did, in a flurry of congressional visits and mailings, testimony and protest that defies simple condensation here. Certainly the leaders did their part, sending a representative to serve at the NSBRO office in Washington to track the legislation and stalking the halls of Congress themselves at times to solicit legislators. At times they evinced surprisingly advanced political techniques; for instance, as Donovan Smucker testified to Congress against the proposal in 1948, several hundred Mennonites, many in plain dress, packed the hearing room to silently demonstrate their solidarity.[62]

These and other anti-UMT exertions together assumed an importance beyond an ultimately successful effort to defeat an especially militaristic development. They demonstrated that Mennonites were losing some of their traditional squeamishness about participating directly in the hard corridors of the political arena. While MC Mennonites held themselves back a little from this process, GC and MCC leaders (and MC people such as Miller and Bender, in their positions of leadership in MCC) freely engaged in what can only be described as plain political lobbying—this, and against a proposal that betokened no direct harm to Mennonites whatsoever. Changes were indeed in the wind. When he testified before congressional committees against the proposal in 1951 and again in 1955, for example, Harold S. Bender declared that UMT was a faulty and mistaken course not just for Mennonites but for all Americans—on whose behalf, he claimed, he spoke.[63]

Clearly, a considerable ferment had begun to occur in Mennonite peace theology, born out of the social changes engulfing the traditional Mennonite rural community. Established leaders sifted through the emerging issues and ably channeled this rethinking through established forums such as peace conferences and publications in the denominational press. The men (a term that is used literally and deliberately here) in the denominational hierarchies studied and discussed the breaking issues and decided how the new developments would be phrased to the laity in the conference statements. They did not, however, always have the last word. Again in the fifties, as in the CPS camps a decade earlier, changes began to seep upward from articulate lay people. A few younger GC men began to call into question the basis of the entire relationship Mennonites had constructed with their government in the era during and following World War II. Once the leadership had respectfully voiced their objections and concerns about new policies, Mennonites had complacently complied with whatever directives Selective Service saw fit to issue, and why not? Recently that arm of the state, historically so dangerous to Mennonites, had seen fit to treat them quite benignly. Other young men had been summarily drafted and sent into overseas combat, but the state had constructed a special category, specifically designed to include quiet, malleable dissenters like the Mennonites, that first deferred them and then directed their young men into tolerable, sometimes rewarding, paid service at home. Of course Mennonites would cooperate with such treatment. But now a few GC men called that concurrence into question at its most vulnerable point. They wondered whether Mennonites should register for the new draft act.[64]

Gordon Kaufman (son of Bethel College president Edmund G. Kaufman), then an ex-CPS man in graduate school at Northwestern University, provided the initial salvo in June 1948. Though few if any Mennonites had walked out of CPS, he recognized in the pages of *The Mennonite*, "quite a few" Mennonite CPSers "began to wonder if they should cooperate" in the event of a future draft. "Perhaps the time has come," wrote Kaufman, "for some of the younger pacifists within the Mennonite Church to call attention to some of the factors which have been influencing them in their re-thinking of the whole question of conscription." Kaufman explored the nature of mobilization for modern war, a mobilization that seemed to him to be readily underway. Conscription was the "last and biggest step" the government took to announce its readiness to conduct another war, he cried. If Mennonites "are really working for peace," he wondered, then wouldn't a true "positive contribution" mean their refusal to cooperate with such measures?[65]

As a small collection of others had begun to do in the larger pacifist community, at least a few young Mennonites stepped forward and acted on what Kaufman had theorized. One of these was Dwight Platt. As a boy and a young teenager during World War II, he had watched the trials endured by his mother, Selma Platt Johnson, who had struggled hard to retain her pacifism in Moundridge, a small Kansas town fully engaged in the wartime ideological crusade. As he neared his eighteenth birthday in August 1949, Platt needed to come to grips with how much cooperation he would extend to the government's latest military requirements. It would be, he decided, less than his church was willing to provide. Accordingly, he penned a letter to the president to state his belief that "war is immoral and evil" and that "I cannot cooperate with this system." He would not register, he told Truman, on his birthday. Two years later, Platt was sentenced to a year and a day in a federal penitentiary.[66]

Another young dissident was Bethel College student Austin Regier. Like other young Mennonite radicals, Regier had come to his civil disobedience in part out of his experience in CPS, where numbers of Mennonite COs had begun to recover the message of prophetic confrontation contained in their Anabaptist heritage. In his statement to the judge before sentencing, Regier testified that his struggling with the legitimacy of draft registration began shortly after entering CPS. Transferring from soil conservation to mental hospital work because of its "greater significance," he began to question "the compromising nature of my position." After the war, he gradually realized that he should "take a clearer position against war than I could do by allowing myself to be drafted." Regier thus had come around to a position embraced by a number of Mennonite CPSers, and one that they explored deeply at the conscription institute meetings in 1945. When the draft call came around again in 1948, he had little doubt about what he should do. In 1949 he received a year's jail sentence for refusing to register for the draft.[67]

Moreover, Regier persuasively articulated to the wider church the kinds of conclusions about alternate and voluntary service that he and his fellow activists in CPS had been moving toward during the war. In their barracks bull sessions at the meeting at Powellsville, Maryland, COs had deeply dissented from the Mennonite-state cooperation that had created Civilian Public Service. While embracing the new service ethic, they had also denounced the air of state sanction that surrounded and corrupted it. In the pages of *The Mennonite*, Regier carried these arguments into the postwar years. Certainly Christians should throw themselves into service and relief work, Regier argued, "but without reference to conscription or the threat of it." Such a threat made him "skeptical," admitted Regier, of a Voluntary Service program that quickly expanded with the arrival of the draft. In his mind, he said, "as an alternative to war service, it is a violation of integrity."[68]

Of course such an argument—at this point very much a Mennonite minority position just now coming above ground—generated a good deal of criticism. One Mennonite pastor replied that nonregistration reflected "a defiant uncooperative spirit" smacking of humanism. The Mennonite NSBRO representative, Paul Goering, concentrated on the dubious political effects of nonregistration in comparison with the "reconciling role" of alternate service. Others likewise disagreed with nonregistration because it did not adequately express the Mennonite desire to display positive service instead of endless objections.[69]

Among themselves, General Conference peace leaders demonstrated less unanimity on the question; Regier's challenge had hit a sensitive spot. Ediger chose to write Regier privately as he faced trial. While extending his warm personal support and admiration, Ediger once again referred to the principle of the second mile and concluded that "the way you have chosen is not the way of Christian love." Others were not so sure. Esko Loewen wrote to Ediger to recommend that the church reconsider the whole matter of draft registration. In his mind, nonregistration was a viable option. Likewise, to Rufus Franz, the stand taken by nonregistrants was perhaps "even more consistent than the one . . . we officially favor. These young men are showing real conviction and leadership. I am proud of them." Minutes for the Peace Committee meeting in February 1949, reveal "considerable discussion on this question," centering on whether or not the church could affirm draft nonregistration. In the end, the committee tried to straddle the issue, moving that "we do not encourage non-registration," but expressing their concern that "fellowship with nonregistrants not be broken." The following year, the conference body would succeed in tabling a conference resolution brought by Regier extending General Conference support for draft nonregistration.[70]

"IS NOT THE FACT OF TOLERATION ITSELF A SIGN OF SICKNESS?"

Even so, throughout these immediate postwar years, Mennonites began to move steadily and perceptibly toward a heightened involvement with the needs and pain of outside society and to an enhanced willingness to speak to the state about these matters. Emerging from their isolated communities, they began to ask, as did Orie Miller in 1948, whether their traditional "emphasis on quietism, non-activism in politics, group exclusiveness, [has] stifled among those whom God might use in a prophetic role to government and peoples today?"[71]

A number of factors had come together to continue to push at a Mennonite reevaluation of their old, stricter conceptions of the church-state duality. Their experience in the war, especially in CPS, had made substantial contributions to this process. The dissenting voices to otherwise general churchwide satisfaction with CPS had continued to reverberate in the church, and in this case it had registered enough impact that the church refused to accept a similar arrangement in the next alternate service program. Moreover, these currents of dissent continued to push against the boundaries of what passed for legitimate Mennonite public discussion in regard to what one could say to the state. In CPS, Mennonite COs had "learned to question government"; now they were extending this lesson to ✓ larger sectors of the church.

Secondly, in sparking a number of new relief and aid programs, the CPS experience similarly reshaped the contours of Mennonite life and identity in these immediate postwar years. As with the new voices of dissent, new values and commitments devoted to human service jostled at the traditional edges of the Mennonite-state lines of demarcation. A growing sense of responsibility for pain and injustice beyond that affecting the Mennonite community led Mennonites to begin to speak to the state about them. Government, they had learned during the war, was "not a monster." Having grown comfortable in addressing it about Mennonite concerns, it would not be hard to speak to it about these newer areas of responsibility.

Thousands of church workers toiling in mental hospitals or disaster reconstruction contributed to Mennonite confidence in another way, too. When the state posited military solutions to meet its many crises, Mennonites could point to their work as evidence of some different but equally viable answers. No longer did they have to accept the state's reliance on military might as the only possible solution. Mennonite representatives accordingly began to suggest to Congress that security could also come through the practice of justice, something they themselves were just beginning to take up.

Thirdly, beyond the war, in much the same manner the crumbling of Mennonite isolation and the process of acculturation served to reinforce these service commitments and the concurrent Mennonite ability to speak to the state about them. Paul Peachey summarized this point succinctly in 1954. He recognized that the "profound social and cultural revolution" occurring among them "is effecting a subtle change in attitude toward church-world relations." No more could Mennonites adopt, as did the preceding generation, an "oversimplified" scheme of "black and white distinctions between the world and the church" which had marked off "certain areas of society as lying outside our concern as Christians." Instead, he declared, "we shall have to face the question of civic and political responsibility," a task that involves a "prophetic mission in this world."[72]

Finally, in this period too, a few church leaders put forth arguments that would take on increasing currency in Mennonite circles as the postwar years wore on. The discussion over nonregistration, serving as a precursor to similar discussions in the 1960s (but with different results), appears as a plain example of this. So did the questions from Orie Miller's son John in 1954. As the I-W program settled down into a smooth-running operation to both the church's and the government's great satisfaction, Miller pointed out that COs were no longer considered "dangerous," a public acceptance that posed a danger in itself to the church. He focused his alarm on two specific questions. First, he wondered, "Can we survive this new tolerance?" With CO service so "comfortable" and requiring such little actual sacrifice from young men, no longer did the option contribute to fostering a sense of costly discipleship. Secondly, he asked, "Is not the fact of toleration itself a sign of sickness?" Jesus, after all, had warned his disciples to expect continued persecution. And their Anabaptist ancestors had lived in such a way as to receive it. If Mennonites were settling comfortably into a respected place in the religious and political landscape, then something was seriously wrong, Miller warned, with their whole conception of the church. His was very much a lone voice in 1954. But as Mennonites more and more began to press against the older lines of demarcation with the state, such radical arguments would no longer hold sway only on the fringes.[73]

CHAPTER 7

Speaking
to the State,
1957–1965

By the late 1950s, the Mennonite stance toward outside society hovered on the very brink of a thorough transformation. For decades, the forces of socioeconomic change had ushered Mennonites ever more directly into society. So, too, an active and engaged Mennonite conscience kept pushing a sense of Mennonite responsibility to this impinging world.

At the dawn of the new decade, a host of issues had come together to further fuel this process. A burgeoning crisis in the I-W program communicated unmistakably the danger of confining the church's word against war to a comparably young and narrow segment of its membership. A breakthrough in theological understandings would do much to lessen the gap between Mennonites' preaching on witnessing to government and their actual practice. Finally, for perhaps the first time, given the much reduced distance between fragmenting Mennonite communities and outside society, a national movement of social protest would sharpen the content and tone of the Mennonite voices speaking to the state. This newfound Mennonite receptivity to social protest would do much to prepare the soil for an even greater Mennonite response to wartime protest later in the 1960s.

THE CRISIS IN CONSCIENTIOUS OBJECTION

According to Paul Landis, Lancaster Conference bishop and leader in the conference VS and I-W programs, church leaders had initially feared I-W service because it promised to draw young Mennonite men irretrievably into the big cities and because the program appeared "too easy—we will lose our convictions." In response, they formulated a follow-up program for their I-W men that would both "keep them Mennonite and keep them out of trouble." By the late fifties, however, it had become apparent to nearly everybody concerned that any kind of I-W program they came up with would accomplish neither of these two objectives. Instead, as reports of misbehavior began to filter back from concentrations of I-W men, a widening circle of church leaders and pastors faced an inescapable crisis in their conscientious objector program.[1]

To a degree, the problems with I-W can be traced to the nature of the program itself and to the conformist pressures of the Mennonite community. In pressing for a new alternative service program that solved the problems of CPS, the contending parties came up with a new arrangement that was satisfactory in many ways. But as time went on, a glaring deficiency of its own began to emerge. As the General Conference Peace Committee reported as early as 1953, "the program does not ask enough from the men." This observation echoed in the Mennonite literature of these years like a never-ending refrain. For example, fifteen months after the program began, I-W men were already reporting back to an MC administrator in Elkhart, Indiana that "such work is hardly sacrificial enough to be the moral equivalent of service in the armed forces."[2]

This perceived lack of sacrifice in I-W service loomed as a serious problem for a number of reasons. On the more lofty level, engaging in service to the needy had increasingly begun to speak directly to what it meant to be a Mennonite. As people willing to labor diligently in nonmilitary ways to demonstrate their worthiness of citizenship, they abhorred any perceived lack of sacrifice in their designated alternative-to-military service that detracted from this larger goal. On a more prosaic level, the acute Mennonite sensitivity for the public's need for equity in CO matters certainly came into play here.

As the shooting stopped in Korea and the larger popular demand for equitable sacrifice eased, another nuts-and-bolts concern about I-W increasingly emerged in Mennonite discussion. "The present I-W program in many situations does not call for a strong Christian peace position because the pressures of war do not exist," noted a presenter at a "I-W Workshop" in Hillsboro, Kansas, in 1957. With nobody being called to fight and die and with levels of public tolerance high, it cost the young Mennonite draftee little to take his stand. Given this lack of sacrifice, a number of young men were wondering whether alternative service was even necessary. One pastor penned Gaeddert, for example, that "in this time of peace with the relaxation of world tensions" many of the young men from his congregation had concluded that "it really doesn't make a great deal of difference" whether they went into I-W or military service. Even if such men ended up in I-W work, they would certainly enter into it without the ideological enthusiasm trumpeted by their elders. Another minister wrote to say that he would have more of his young men opting for conscientious objection had there been a war, because "since there is no apparent danger, they just register as non-combatants."[3]

In an unintended way, too, the pressures from the Mennonite community, so long an effective mechanism influencing young Mennonites' draft decisions, now began to work strange effects in the quality of Mennonite I-W service. In the legislation creating the program, Congress considerably tightened its definition of conscientious objector to exclude nearly everybody except applicants from the Historic Peace Churches. Particularly in an era without a shooting war, draft boards generally proved extremely lenient to men from those churches, approving CO status without much questioning of an applicant's convictions. As a result, Mennonites repeatedly began to discover that, in Edgar Metzler's words, "it is too easy to believe nothing and be a I-W," that one could achieve CO status quite easily on the basis of one's Mennonite pedigree by itself. The constraints of the closed sociological community had begun to backfire. The results now revealed themselves in the indifference of many I-W men. Touring among collections of I-W men in the summer of 1956, Peace Problems Committee secretary Paul Peachey found "a very disturbing lack of sense of mission and of direction."[4]

By itself, this disappointing lack of conviction among many I-W men ought not to have occasioned any great emergency. After all, observers had noted the same thing among substantial numbers of CPS men, yet the church still pointed to that program as a stunning triumph. In contrast to CPS, however, I-W service allowed such young men a great deal of independence; and therein lay a complex of interrelated problems. Part of it was that these were *young* men. Ignoring their church's repeated urging to go to college first or otherwise wait until drafted, the vast majority of I-W's enlisted at eighteen or nineteen out of a desire on the part of many to "get it over with." In the program's early years, 85 percent of Mennonite I-Ws had enlisted, with the average age of beginning service at nineteen-and-a-half years, compared with twenty-two or twenty-three in the military. In

the eyes of church leaders, it was particularly these younger, more immature men who were less likely to volunteer because of their desire to serve
and more likely to do so as a means of escaping the constraints of home.[5]

Secondly, these were young men who had been raised, to a great degree,
in tightly controlled ethnoreligious communities. In the case of MC men,
rigid standards of nonconformity in dress and behavior had governed their
daily behavior. Now, suddenly, at age eighteen, they found themselves in a
new and exciting urban world, where the only source of authority existed
on the job and touched only their working life. One MC I-W administrator
estimated that half of their COs were "obviously using I-W as a time to get
away from home at best and some to actually run from the church." For
men so inclined, the program functioned as a wonderful means of getting
"set free" from the strict community back home. No one but themselves
decided what they wore, where they lived, who they dated, what they would
do with their leisure time and money, or when and if they went to church.
As a result, as an MC committee discerned in 1958, for too many young
Mennonites, "I-W service becomes a 'wild-oats' period. The restraints of
the home community are left behind."[6]

Not only did many I-Ws quickly discover, in the words of one devout
objector, that "there are too many worldly things to distract us from God
and from doing His will," but a number of men began to find such worldy
things tremendously enjoyable. Before long, home churches began to hear
reports of I-Ws smoking, drinking, and going to movies; of I-Ws dating
non-Mennonite girls; even of Mennonite COs fighting each other and having run-ins with the law. In a few cases, I-W behavior went beyond the level
of teenage rebellion. In one city, several COs spent their off hours breaking
into houses; in another, summarized one church bureaucrat, a group of I-
Ws "succumbed to the forwardness of a thirteen-year-old truant girl" and
soon found themselves serving two months in prison for statutory rape.
Whispered among administrators, such reports were disturbing; but if
they found their way into conversations among regular church members,
the results could be disastrous. As early as 1954, Gaeddert felt the need to
relate some positive stories of I-W contributions in the pages of *The Mennonite* to balance out the negative stories circulating in the churches. More
ominously, in 1956, reported an Oklahoma pastor, parents in his church
were discouraging conscientious objection by their sons because of the
poor reputation of I-W men.[7]

Perhaps even worse, the church leadership increasingly perceived their
inability to do much to pull such men into line. In negotiating for an ex-

tremely tolerant CO program that sent the objector off to gainful employment, responsible only to his employer and, more vaguely, to the government, the church had effectively cut itself right out of the picture. As
Gaeddert noted, "There is absent [in the program] that which binds a man
to his church." In spite of the fact that the I-W program came into being
as a result of careful church-state negotiation and expressed perfectly the
Mennonite refusal to once again administer a Selective Service program, a
realization of the church's lack of influence in I-W came as a shock to many.
At a 1957 peace rally in the Western District Conference, for instance,
many found it an unpleasant "revelation" that "the church actually plays a
minor and unimportant role in I-W administration."[8]

Thus, the church bureaucracy in both Mennonite groups and also in
MCC embarked on a variety of different mechanisms to try to insert the
church somehow into I-W's relationship with the Selective Service. Administrators soon discovered, however, that there was no mechanism in
their programs to force refractory I-Ws to pay attention to them.[9] Hence,
they would have to come up with a program and structure for their conscientious objectors with a little more teeth in it. At a meeting of the MC
Mennonite Relief and Service Committee in 1959, for instance, administrators called for more structure in the placement of COs, both in orientation (only a small number of I-Ws elected to participate in the number of
different orientation session that different conferences at times offered),
and in supervision of the men in their off-work hours. Yet to impose such
structures on many I-W men who repeatedly demonstrated little use for it,
the church would have to rely on the only source of coercion in the entire
I-W program. They would have to turn to Selective Service.[10]

The problem came to a head most acutely in Denver. Due to the city's
large number of hospitals, its relatively high wages, and the recreational
possibilities nearby in the Rocky Mountains, Denver had always attracted
a large number of I-W men. By the late 1950s, they totaled several hundred.
Unfortunately for local churches, by this time, Denver had come to serve
as a mecca for young Mennonite COs anxious to experience a freer and
more boisterous lifestyle. Approximately thirty percent of the Denver I-
Ws had begun drinking alcoholic beverages, calculated one administrator,
with drunkenness not uncommon and smoking no longer considered an
irregularity. The reputation of Denver I-Ws was spreading in the
churches, so much so that I-Ws viewing their work primarily as Christian
service preferred to go elsewhere. Accordingly, in September 1958, the local Denver I-W advisory board, in conjunction with MC administrators,

formulated a plan to govern the supply and types of I-W men coming to work in the city. To receive permission to do his CO service there, a prospective Denver I-W would need to obtain the permission of both his home pastor and his own denomination's I-W advisory board, and he would also have to attend four orientation sessions. Any I-W who refused to go along with this program would be shipped elsewhere. The local Denver advisory board secured the cooperation of area hospitals in this endeavor, along with a promise from the Colorado state Selective Service director to release problem cases to them for transfer. With the backing of the state, I-W administrators finally had a mechanism to forcefully apply their COs to the task of Christian service, whether or not the men themselves shared this motivation.[11]

Fifteen years before, Mennonites had administered a Selective Service program, and many had ended the experience saying "never again." Thus, within two weeks of its formulation, the creators of the "Denver Plan" had begun to receive word that the church would not countenance it. As one Denver I-W put it, the plan "clearly puts the church in the saddle again." In its official words of disapproval, MCC declared that using Selective Service to enforce the church's discipline "would create an unacceptable relationship between church and state." Having denied themselves the one source of authority at their disposal to forcibly alter the program more to their liking, church officials had no other recourse but self-castigation.[12]

As both Mennonite groups found less and less use for "earning" I-W service altogether, they began to accept as a given the radical disjuncture between truly voluntary and state-forced service that CPS dissidents such as Austin Regier had articulated years before. Dissatisfaction came to a head for the General Conference Mennonite Church in 1962. The report of the Voluntary Service and I-W Committee to the Board of Christian Service that year called for a completely new alternative service program, arguing that the present program demanded little sacrifice or commitment. It was not "Second-Mile Service"; it "is not Christian, sometimes not even basically humanitarian; it is a government military alternative." The program they suggested instead revolved around a completely voluntary program like VS, though they recognized that more men would correspondingly enter the military. By 1967, the GCMC completely withdrew its support from I-W earning service, instead committing its monies and administrative energies into VS as the church's recognized alternative service program. The Mennonite Church never totally disassociated itself from earning I-W service; but, like the GCMC, the church began to place greater emphasis on the VS program. While around two-thirds of both MC and GC young men continued to opt for earning as opposed to voluntary I-W service, they did so with much less encouragement from their church.[13]

In this policy, the Mennonite hierarchies and the state began to move in opposite directions in their appreciation of alternative service. Indeed, from the perspective of Selective Service, the I-W arrangement grew perhaps even more satisfactory than it ever had before. By the early 1960s, alternative service could easily function as part of the solution to a major problem the agency had begun to face. The problem stemmed, once again, from satisfying the public's ever-present demand for the fundamental appearance of equity when the state drafted its young people. As outlined above, for a variety of reasons, equity assumes critical importance when democracies resort to conscription. Much of Selective Service policy during World War II had operated in accordance with this maxim, and the agency had been careful to tend to such considerations in the years since World War II. The notion of the draft as a universal obligation had become endangered, however, not by any foreign foe or peace movement, but by the simple force of demographics: the vast post–World War II population surge popularly known as the "baby boom." In other words, by the early 1960s the conscription system had a pool of available draftees much bigger than it needed. Given the steady stream of men volunteering for the military throughout the fifties and early sixties—in most years volunteers outnumbered draftees—Selective Service had to find an acceptable way of dismissing increasing numbers of them from the universal obligation of service without the larger public questioning whether there still was such a universal obligation.[14]

Fortunately, the agency had a ready solution at hand that it had already drawn upon repeatedly: the policy of deferring from service anyone whose skills or civilian employment it deemed critical to the national interest. In the immediate post–World War II years, widespread concern emerged that America had, in World War II, duplicated Britain's mistake in World War I and sent its most talented young men to die in combat. The new Selective Service Law of 1948 thus authorized the president to defer any category of persons he felt were essential to the national interest. Increasingly this came to mean college students. By 1951, three-quarters of the nation's college and graduate students were deferred or exempted from the draft, and they were soon joined by men in a host of occupational deferments that interest groups had wheedled out of Washington. With the demographic explosion of the immediate postwar years, however, the draft system still had more available men than it could use, and Selective Service came up with more loopholes—for married men and fathers, for example—to ease some of the pressure.[15]

In 1965 the agency issued an official rationale justifying such deferments officially called "channeling." This was a genuine opportunity, afforded by the rare but happy circumstance of a modern warfare state possessing a pool of potential conscripts even larger than its immediate military needs. In such a situation, conscription or the threat of it could become a handy instrument of national personnel planning. The threat of the draft could be used to direct the nation's young men either into the military or into a number of other state-approved military endeavors that similarly contributed to "the national health, safety, or interest." Selective Service phrased it this way: "From the individual's viewpoint, he is standing in a room that has been made uncomfortably warm. Several doors are open, but they all lead to various forms of recognized, patriotic service to the Nation. Some accept the alternatives gladly—some with reluctance. The consequence is approximately the same." People other than the Mennonites could creatively utilize the call to fight a moral equivalent of war. By directing men into either military pursuits or other more broadly defined expressions of "alternative" service, Selective Service could assure that all served in some way the needs of the modern warfare state.[16]

Even as Selective Service phrased this policy, changes were afoot that would soon work to wreck it. By late 1965 the escalation of the Vietnam War and the vast increase in monthly draft calls worked a rapid sea change in both draft policy and American attitudes toward it. The escalation quickly absorbed the excess in the manpower pool, thus solving the most immediate problem facing Selective Service. But as increasing numbers of draftees began to die in combat, the public awoke to the widespread inequities in the draft, sparking a massive and ultimately successful protest movement against the system altogether.

Half a dozen years before this movement ignited, a few perceptive Mennonites had begun to realize how effectively the state had coopted their traditional dissent against war. At a I-W planning conference in 1957, for example, one administrator stated that he had often heard Mennonites complain that I-W program was "an ideal set-up" to "smother" the Mennonite peace testimony. Peachey was even more direct in 1961. As he asserted to a collection of influential Mennonites gathered for a study conference in Washington D. C., "Selective Service sees in alternative service an

FIGURE 7.1. *Making friends in high places: Selective Service head Lewis B. Hershey with Historic Peace Church leaders, NSBRO board meeting, November 22, 1960. Left to right: Methodist peace leader Charles F. Boss, Brethren peace activist M. R. Zigler, Hershey, Orie O. Miller, J. S. Noffsinger, and Quaker leader E. Raymond Wilson. Mennonite Central Committee Collection, Archives of the Mennonite Church, Goshen, Indiana.*

arrangement to respect a minority without arousing public disfavor while on the other hand pulling the fangs from the pacifist witness."[17]

The most public and important articulation of such sentiments came from Edgar Metzler, an MC pastor in Ontario and an activist who would replace Elmer Neufeld in 1962 as chair of the MCC Peace Section. In two important and far-reaching articles in the *Gospel Herald* in 1959 and 1962, Metzler argued that I-W service, both earning and voluntary, far from any kind of witness against war, was "part and parcel with the compulsory system of conscription." Instead of persecuting its dissenters against warmaking, the state merely gave them what they asked for, shunted them off to a quiet corner, and ignored them. As a result, cried Metzler, "CO's in the United States can pursue a course that respects their conscience but costs them nothing and effectively silences their protest against the preparations for mass murder." Yet a crucial difference appeared between Metzler's arguments here and those by other church leaders ten years before complaining that deferment from the draft did not cost them enough. While like them, Metzler found the level of sacrifice in the present program inadequate, he did not do so because it failed to provide Mennonites the chance to prove their worthiness of citizenship. Instead, people of peace needed to search anew to extricate themselves from the machinery of a warfare state, he argued, in order to demonstrate Christian sacrifice and to find "a way to speak prophetically." Metzler offered them such a way: he called for non-registration with the draft. Instead of allowing themselves to be quietly "channelled" into occupations deemed suitable by the state, by their non-registration pacifists would present an unmistakable witness against war.[18]

Metzler's analysis drew a heavy volume of responses from Mennonites in the letters to the *Gospel Herald*, ranging from affirmation of it as "vital prophecy" to other more negative responses. The most weighty and particularly public response came from Harold Bender, whose alarmed language plainly indicated a firm attempt to nip such thinking in the bud. Conscription, intoned Bender, was "merely the command of the state to do work," and the Christian had no right to refuse it unless the state demanded that he "perform wrong acts." Registration was only a civil, not a military, edict; those who thought otherwise were guilty, in Bender's thinking, not just of an "error in judgment" but of "sin." It was for precisely for this reason, Bender reminded *Gospel Herald* readers, that the Mennonite Church had not legitimated nonregistration for its members. Besides, even with the problems inherent in I-W service, a far better course was available: "Shall we not take a positive attitude as Christians toward the requirements of the state which are acceptable, and cooperate cheerfully?"[19]

The debate, however, had just begun. Growing unhappiness with I-W service would quietly but increasingly pull Metzler's arguments more into Mennonite discussion. Most significantly, it was not long before a collection of younger Mennonites, sons and daughters of the CPS generation, took analyses such as Metzler's to heart in a most direct way and upset the entire Mennonite relationship with the state that their parents' service had so vividly expressed.

THEOLOGICAL BREAKTHROUGH

Not long into the postwar years, Mennonites had demonstrated such a willingness to act on behalf of an enlarged field of social responsibilities that it appeared that Mennonite practice in their witness to the state had begun to run substantially ahead of Mennonite preaching. In their condemnations of conscription because it threatened democratic institutions, for example, Mennonites expressed to Congress sentiments that their the-

ology, still officially wedded in varying degrees to two-kingdom understandings, could not entirely justify. By the late 1950s, however, Mennonites began to make corresponding adjustments in their theology that
solidified their new stance in regard to the state and pushed the Mennonite
witness into new areas of concern. Before long, such adjustments led to a
sweeping theological breakthrough that dramatically changed the content
and rationale for Mennonite prescriptions to the state.[20]

An MCC study conference on "The Christian Responsibility to the
State" in 1957 served to again focus Mennonite thinking on the central
issues and to lay some of the theological groundwork for the new shift. The
slate of fifty-nine delegates, comprised of the church's top scholars, pastors, and administrators, came together in Chicago to hear a number of
different papers and work through the pressing matter once again. The
conference discussions at least served to illustrate the diversity of Mennonite opinions on how to relate to government. As always, the delegates
differed on now-predictable lines of cleavage. Mennonite Church leaders
such as Bender held fast to church-state separation, while General Conference leaders such as Fretz, Loewen, and Harley Stuckey articulated the
greater openness to outside society that their group had displayed for several hundred years, arguing for more heightened levels of Mennonite participation in government.[21]

More significantly, these divergences occurred in debates over a theological conception that was coming to assume increasing prominence in Mennonite dialogue: the meaning and consequences of the Lordship of Christ.
While stopping short of the kinds of conclusions arrived at by Winfield
Fretz, MC theologian John Howard Yoder's address began to affirm the
need to testify to the state about its conduct in a variety of areas. Yoder
emphasized his sectarian, leavening conception of the church's influence
in society, in which the church spoke to the human condition and registered
a deep impact on the social order primarily "just by being herself." But
given Christ's lordship over all the world, the church also "has a word for
the state," Yoder reasoned. "The faithful Church knows how the State
comes into God's plan, and can tell the Statesman so, even in terms of the
relative choices of everyday statesmanship." Christians know, Yoder declared, what God's norms for it are, and hence they are more capable "than
the state itself to evaluate its compromises."[22]

Finally, amid the diversity, the GC activist and scholar Elmer Neufeld
presented a paper that provided some common theological ground on
which nearly all the participants could stand. Conservatives could take

FIGURE 7.2. *General Conference Mennonite peace leader and Peace Section Executive Secretary Elmer Neufeld, 1959. Mennonite Central Committee Collection, Archives of the Mennonite Church, Goshen, Indiana.*

heart in what he called "a deep cleavage between church and the state," his fundamental affirmation of the two-kingdom doctrine. Activists could resonate with everything else in the address, for Neufeld was really one of their own. He had entered the ranks of Mennonite leadership through a familiar kind of path, and he began his remarks by summarizing that trajectory. Reared in a sheltered rural Mennonite community, Neufeld had done a CPS stint in his late teens, graduated from Bethel College, and then served as the Mennonite representative to NSBRO. While in Washington working closely with draft officials, Neufeld had received, he told the conference delegates, a not-uncommon tribute from a Selective Service official, an army colonel who had always found Mennonites easier to work with than other pacifist groups. Neufeld was not so sure that Mennonites should take it as a compliment; in fact, he said, the colonel's words were "still ringing in my ears."

"You Mennonites are fine folk to get along with," the officer had remarked. "We like you. It would be nice if there were more people like you. But . . . you do nothing about sin, about social wrong, about corruption in government, about international tensions, etc." In other words, here again echoed the old patronizing derision, another expression of the Niebuhrian critique that slammed home among Mennonites with increasing force and vigor. Here was the charge that, combined with patterns of Mennonite acculturation into outside society, propelled an increased Mennonite willingness to speak to the state about a new set of concerns. Neufeld followed up this motivating anecdote with more powerful words, wondering whether "perhaps after all in practice we have used a legitimate and important teaching (separation from the world) to escape responsibilities that are clearly ours within the gospel of Christ." In the rest of his paper, he called repeatedly for recapturing these responsibilities, for articulating a "ministry of reconciliation" that occupied itself with evangelism but also with acts of compassion, and even for "proclaiming the righteousness of God" to those in power.[23]

Thus Neufeld managed to simultaneously mollify conservatives and speak to the activists while underscoring the Mennonites' growing image of themselves as a servant church. Moreover, he provided a platform for speaking to the state that could unite the different theological strands behind it. Stated succinctly, he pled that "when we are thoroughly motivated by the love of Christ of the cross—when we actually take our neighbor's interests as seriously as our own—our concerns will appropriately find expression in actions that do have political relevance." To serve the poor and needy entailed an inescapable political dimension; as Mennonites built an identity around one, they would have to accept the other.[24]

The sudden reality that these kinds of positions could receive widespread Mennonite affirmation could only have lasting and far-reaching reverberations. The ripples seemed to reach first, and go the farthest, in the peace thinking among MC Mennonites, especially those serving on the Peace Problems Committee (PPC). At a meeting in October 1959, Hershberger (now chair) and several other members argued strongly for Mennonites to "speak with a prophetic voice" because of the recognition that "God has only one standard of moral righteousness." The discussion concluded by recognizing that "we seem to be moving into new territory" and calling for a thorough reexamination of their theology of peace witness. To begin this reevaluation, they appointed a subcommittee consisting of Hershberger, Metzler, and Albert Meyer to prepare a revised statement.[25]

The specific theological step forward came in the subcommittee's conceptualization of a new understanding of the "Lordship of Christ." The idea had been slowly germinating in Mennonite thinking throughout the postwar era. Years later, Metzler thought Hershberger had effected the group's theological shift only by employing a crafty bit of genius. As the subcommittee of three met in a basement of Plains Mennonite Meetinghouse near Lansdale, Pennsylvania, Hershberger suggested that they anchor the new denominational peace position in what seemed to Metzler an obscure phrasing found in the previous peace statement passed a decade earlier, something about the Mennonite "obligation to witness to the powers-that-be." Instead of articulating a totally new statement, they would mask their breakthrough in older, acceptable language, rendering it less vulnerable to criticism. While this may have been true, Hershberger did not suddenly hatch such thinking out of his own fertile imagination. In *War, Peace, and Nonresistance*, he had rankled fundamentalists with his articulation of a "single moral law" to which all were responsible. And the Winona Lake Declaration of 1950 had also acknowledged the Lordship of Christ over governments and the obligation to witness to the "righteousness" that God required of all people, even those in government.

Increasingly important in this theological progression were influences again seeping in from outside. Beyond Mennonite ranks, similar discussions over the "Lordship of Christ" emerged from ecumenical discussions in Europe occurring between the Historic Peace Churches and scholars from mainline denominations in 1955 to 1962. These were called the "Puidoux Conferences" after the first meeting place in Switzerland. Mennonites such as John Howard Yoder, William Keeney, and Albert Meyer participated quite prominently in the discussions. Returning home with this new theological understanding, these men assumed key roles in the church's absorption of this thinking.[26]

Traditional two-kingdom theology had posited two completely separate ethics for the kingdom of God (i.e., the church) and that of the world, governed by the state, which God had endowed for this purpose. But now the PPC subcommittee argued that the conception of the Lordship of Christ, far from applying only to the saved, actually was meant for the whole world. God only had one standard of moral righteousness. Thus, God had expectations for the state's behavior as well, and God had bestowed upon the church the task of communicating to the state God's standards for its behavior. As the subcommittee argued, at any particular point between total order and total chaos, "the church can speak, asking that the state in question be more orderly and just, and confident that that request can be an expression of God's claim on that state." Pacifists certainly *did* have responsibility to help meet the needs of society and could certainly speak to the state about its conduct of such affairs, even if that at times meant the state might employ a means that Christians could not participate in.[27]

It was, altogether, quite an earthshaking new concept, but one that the service commitments and theologizing of the postwar years had rendered even conservative MC Mennonites ripe to accept. Not that the shift came without serious consideration. In their June 1960 meeting, members of the PPC mulled it over for two full days in discussions that at times must have been intense. Members acknowledged that the Lordship of Christ paradigm here embarked on very different directions from the way Mennonites had usually used the term. Previously, Mennonites had reasoned that Christ was Lord only over the church, the saved. Some of the participants thought the entire shift too radical, expressing concern that the new paradigm would "'baptize' the social order" and erase the traditional Mennonite distinction between the two kingdoms. In fact, a leading dissenter to the breakthrough was the most influential Mennonite Church leader of his generation, Harold S. Bender. Metzler later recalled him "reluctantly dragging his feet" on the Lordship of Christ language during the discussions until he was prodded by two old reliable conservative allies. John E. Lapp and Lancaster bishop Amos Horst pitched their appeal in the ultimate legitimation for theological reshaping, the standard of biblical authority. "Bro. Bender, the young men have brought us Biblical teaching," they pled, "and we want to be Biblical, don't we?"[28]

After two days of wrangling, the entire committee endorsed the new theological paradigm with a good deal of gusto. They agreed that it had "not blurred the line between the two kingdoms," but rather that they had attempted "to sharpen the line and add meaning and strength to the concept of Lordship." In addition, they declared that the report "had opened a new area of witness for nonresistant Christians; and that the new territory should be surveyed and occupied." Having decided on the shift, the PPC moved to communicate these understandings to the church at large. They decided to prepare a new statement of policy on the Christian witness to government.[29]

The resulting statement, "The Christian Witness to the State," received ready acceptance by the Mennonite Church General Conference delegates assembled at Johnstown, Pennsylvania, in August 1961. Under Hershberger's specific pretense of more broadly explicating the section on witnessing to government in the 1951 declaration, the PPC's statement recognized the foundation of their two-kingdom theology but then went on argue for an enhanced testimony to the state along the lines explored above. Three specific points deserve special mention here. First, rooted in this extension of Christ's Lordship to the sphere of government, the church now claimed the right to challenge rulers "to find the highest possible values within their own relative frames of reference. In doing so, the Christian may and can rightfully speak to decisions which the Christian ethic will not permit him carry out." In other words, no longer could church conservatives object to speaking to the state in matters of waging war or executing justice, claiming this was none of the church's business.[30]

Secondly, the statement articulated a number of broadly stated conceptions of the means of witness. Echoing Neufeld and finding this witness in "works of mercy" and a "ministry of reconciliation," the statement still exhibited considerable uncertainty about which specific types of witness would be acceptable. Third, though the statement appeared to radically challenge the stricter adherence to more traditional two-kingdom understandings still prevalent in places such as Lancaster and Virginia, Hershberger related later that the conference delegates accepted the 1961 declaration with little opposition whatsoever. With this apparent mandate from their constituency, the PPC could go on to formulate a much less hesitant and withdrawn message to those in power, confidently proclaiming God's will not only for the church but for the state as well.[31]

Altogether, the paradigm shift was energizing, even exhilarating, for MC peace activists. Reporting to the 1963 MC General Conference meeting, for example, Hershberger used a terminology that had not often appeared in the measured tones of bureaucratic church reports. After reviewing the extensive course of Mennonite acculturation since 1939, he announced that the church stood, in Kennedy-esque fashion, on a "New Frontier." "This is a call for a forward march," he proclaimed, for an "offensive thrust . . . a time that calls for decisive action, a time for the prophetic voice." So oriented, denominational activists labored hard throughout the early 1960s to find ways of speaking to the state out of their older tradition and newer concerns. In 1961, for instance, the MC General Conference meeting passed a resolution expressing concern to President Kennedy on a variety of peace and disarmament related issues, and in 1963 they wrote Kennedy to express specific support for the 1963 civil rights bill and the nuclear test-ban treaty. Under Hershberger's leadership, the MC Committee on Economic and Social Relations rose to new levels of activism in pushing such issues as civil rights and anti-capital-punishment positions. So much did the related areas of social and peace issues begin to intermingle now in MC thought and practice that in 1965 the two committees (PPC and CESR) merged as the Committee on Peace and Social Concerns (CPSC).[32]

They would have to work through this host of new issues without the input of one of the leading voices in the Mennonite Church, for after a brief illness, Harold Bender died of a stroke in September of 1962. Innovator in his youth, by the end of his life, Bender played more of the role of the cautious elder, often attempting to put the brakes on the new variations in Mennonite peace theology forwarded by younger activists. In the end, however, he had gone along and approved the new initiatives, thus awarding them an enormous stamp of legitimacy in the churches. As the dominant authority on peace issues in his Mennonite group, and as a man who had for half a century effectively mobilized his people around a central vision and set of achievable goals, Bender had not only held a particularly fractious set of people together, but he had helped to usher them through fifty years of extensive socioeconomic changes. As the national crises of the sixties swept up the Mennonite churches, he would be missed.[33]

In general, the General Conference Mennonite Church had an easier time arriving at an enlarged witness to the state. Arguments urging full Christian participation in politics that appeared as the left-wing fringe in the 1957 MCC conference formed mainstream discussion among many GC peace leaders and pastors.[34] Because GC congregational polity detracted somewhat from the formation of a tightly focused two-kingdom theology, the church experienced a theological breakthrough perhaps not quite as dramatically as their fellow MC Mennonites. Still, the new theological currents percolating among the MCs spilled over into the General Conference as well, and were given a particularly GC stamp by an influential study conference in 1961.

The conference came together in Chicago that autumn to explore "What is our Christian responsibility to society beyond evangelism?" Yet the central consultation only occurred after regional study groups had first worked through in detail a comprehensive slate of issues, one assigned to each area, ranging from labor relations through urbanization and agricultural problems to race relations and politics. Thus, the conference afforded the church the opportunity to sort through a variety of thorny problems. The church and state study group arrived at many of the same conclusions that the MC Mennonites were presently struggling toward. In short, they reasoned that "although there is a basic duality between the church and the kingdoms of this world, the actions of the state must not be judged by some entirely separate standard of morality . . . the state is also under the Lordship of Christ." The "Biblical-Theological Statement" issued by the conference built on such assumptions to articulate a third way between an exclusive concern with salvation or with social action, arguing that true discipleship should not include one without the other.[35]

NEW ISSUES

Recharged by such new theological understandings, by the turn of the decade Mennonites began to wrestle directly with their ability and willingness to say both yes and no to the state in a number of different areas. Perhaps the most unavoidable confrontation concerned the issue of civil defense. For a state prepared to wage total war with an ultimate reliance on nuclear war as a ready possibility, the construction of underground shelters for its population made perfect sense, particularly now as it faced an adversary armed to the teeth and apparently willing to wage nuclear war in return. By preparing people to try to survive nuclear attack, thus presumably strengthening the nation's deterrent capabilities, civil defense served strategic needs as well. With the Cold War crises of the early 1960s such as the Berlin and the Cuban Missile affairs, President Kennedy had begun to stress civil defense preparations with increasing vigor.[36]

Before long, Mennonites found themselves getting increasingly entangled in civil defense preparations with profoundly militaristic overtones. They had already faced such subtle incursions before; for example, under the guise of tornado watching in 1956, local Civil Defense offices in the Midwest had obtained the help of Mennonite Disaster Service volunteers in what in reality was an airplane spotting program. Now in 1962, officials had begun to approach rural churches to designate them as fallout shelters. On the one hand, with its emphasis on saving human life in the face of human disaster, civil defense could appear as a worthy undertaking to many Mennonites, especially to those involved in similar efforts such as MDS. On the other hand, in preparing the population to withstand nuclear attack, civil defense could not be separated from its military function, a fact underscored by the 1961 transfer of the Office of Civil Defense to the Department of Defense. While wanting to aid the injured and homeless, summarized Metzler, "Christians . . . do not want to contribute to the illusion that nuclear war can be a valid instrument of national policy."[37]

To provide some guidance in this dilemma, the MCC Peace Section and Mennonite Disaster Service met in a series of consultations in 1961–62 and came up with two separate statements that reiterated the Mennonite desire to save life and relieve suffering, but to do so completely separate from military-related activities. Echoing MCC's 1956 guiding principles in this regard, the 1961–62 statements expressed "grave reservations" about participating in the fallout shelter program. As Mennonite congregations regularly began to return their fallout shelter permits, these reservations certainly seemed to echo in the churches. After some discussion in May 1962, for example, the Mennonite congregation in Beatrice, Nebraska, voted to inform local civil defense officials that in case of emergency or disaster their doors would be open to the community. Yet "since Mennonites are historically a Peace church," they continued, "and since fallout shelters are a part of preparation for war . . . we are returning unsigned the license which proposes the possible use of our church building as a fallout shelter."[38]

As Hershberger noted in 1966, church pronouncements were all well and good in the abstract; it was only in their application to specific instances that they ran into trouble. For both Mennonite groups, efforts to witness to the state on capital punishment serve as a perfect example of this observation. The General Conference moved first. By the late 1950s, with growing conference enthusiasm for race relations and anti-nuclear work, the activists on the Peace and Social Concerns Committee felt the GCMC would easily endorse an anti-capital-punishment resolution as well. Without much prior effort at churchwide education on the issue, they submitted such a motion to the assembled delegates at the 1959 triennial conference meeting—and quickly ran into a buzz saw. To their considerable surprise, a groundswell of opposition to the statement rose from the conference floor, to which Peace and Social Concerns Committee leaders replied with considerable vigor. Quite quickly two clear sides formed on the issue, and debate hardened to the point that the conference tabled the motion and sent it back to the committee for "further study." It took another six years of intensive theological discussion about the demands of Christ's Lordship before the wider church was willing to endorse a resolution against capital punishment.[39]

Having watched the GC experience with capital punishment, the MC's Committee on Peace and Social Concerns (CPSC) proceeded much more slowly in nudging their group toward a similar stance, carefully introducing articles on the topic in the denominational press and identifying segments of the church that might object to this type of prescription to government. Alongside these careful measures, four of the district conferences had moved against capital punishment by 1965, and thus the CPSC felt confident of an easy passage of its resolution at the churchwide conference meeting in Kidron, Ohio, that summer. Yet in spite of their careful preparation, like the GCMC's peace committee, the peace activists received an unpleasant surprise in conference discussion. Right before the conference, the

Sword and Trumpet, the voice of Virginia Conference fundamentalists, had issued a sweeping editorial condemnation of the motion as "an affair of the state." As the conservatives defined the Mennonite position, they declared that "we have no position" on the death penalty, "we have no right to deny to the state the right to the use of capital punishment as civic order and the common welfare might demand." Now wielding such strict two-kingdom understandings, these dissenters loudly attacked the resolution from the conference floor and succeeded in persuading enough delegates to table it. Arguing that the church should not instruct the state and that Christ's Lordship was not "binding on the government," they suddenly uncovered a fountain of dissent to the MC leadership's new theological break-throughs. To salvage the situation, the CPSC introduced a substitute reso-lution that bypassed the theological basis and simply asked governments to discontinue the death penalty because of the sanctity of human life. Drop-ping their objections to this statement because, in the words of the *Sword and Trumpet*, it "stopped short of denying to the state the actual or ultimate right to the use of capital punishment," the delegates then voted their approval.[40]

Clearly, the dispute at the conference meeting exemplified the deeper trouble brewing in the growing dissent by MC conservatives. At the very least, the debate indicated that within the confines of the church there rum-bled a good deal of opposition to the Johnstown statement that had previ-ously lain unfocused and unstated. Since the church had accepted this statement so readily four years before, church peace leaders had charged ahead in articulating a new witness to the state on this and other issues. Suddenly in 1965, they had to look around and try to discern whether the rest of the church was following.[41]

Another issue that registered significant discussion in Mennonite circles stemmed from the renewed vigor of pacifism in the larger American soci-ety. Buoyed by the nonviolent struggle of African Americans against segre-gation in Montgomery, Alabama, in 1956, by the late 1950s, pacifists had begun to move against nuclear weapons in several concurrent campaigns. In June 1957, a group of about thirty people, led by such pacifist crusaders as A. J. Muste and Bayard Rustin, formed the ad hoc "Non-Violent Action Against Nuclear Weapons" and immediately began to practice this tech-nique at a number of nuclear installations throughout the country. Pacifists courted arrest at an ICBM base near Omaha in the summer of 1959; an-other group began a long-term, silent vigil at Ft. Detrick, near Frederick,

Maryland, to protest germ warfare research there. Such dramatic activities made good press and garnered a good deal of attention. All across the country, long dormant peace activists began to stir themselves once again.[42]

Such open confrontations with the nation's nuclear-defense apparatus sparked a good deal of interest and discussion among peace leaders in Mennonite bureaucracies. Several of the more activist-oriented scholars and pastors had carefully observed these protests at Omaha and Ft. Detrick, and a few had even participated. Before long, these activists began to urge the participation of their church in this pacifist protest movement, even urging an acceptance of the Gandhian technique of civil disobedience. In a 1960 paper on "Radical Pacifism" that achieved significant circulation among members of the church bureaucracy, Mennonite ethicist J. Richard Burkholder argued passionately that the church seriously consider such direct action as a "necessary part of its evangelistic and prophetic peace testimony." Two decades or so after the state accepted genocide as a legitimate resort in the event of total war, Mennonites finally began to seriously consider how to best dissent from such plans. Esko Loewen surely spoke for a large number of Mennonites beyond his own General Conference group when he noted in 1958 that "woefully little is being said by our church concerning the bomb which is not as it should be."[43]

Of course, the actions and arguments of advocates such as Burkholder provoked a good deal of discussion in Mennonite circles. Peace Section secretary Neufeld wondered if, even while acknowledging the state's right to employ violent means to defend itself, the church did not have an obligation to communicate divine judgment over its actions nonetheless. If Christ was also Lord over the state, then Mennonites were entitled to offer it some moral direction. Further, he observed that "this is a live issue in various parts of our brotherhood." Nor was it just the younger radicals who found themselves agreeing with Burkholder's analysis; Orie Miller privately noted his very favorable reaction, writing to Hershberger that "there might be place for the quiet vigil witness."[44]

It was difficult to know, of course, just how deeply such sentiments penetrated among the Mennonite laity. Yet when the specter of nuclear weapons came closer to home, the churches quickly found a voice. Early in 1959, the U.S. Air Force proposed building an ICBM missile base near Goessel, Kansas, a heavily GC Mennonite region in south-central Kansas barely ten miles north of Bethel College. With the issue no longer purely theoretical, local Mennonites suddenly found the resources to act and to do so rapidly. The Western District Conference Peace Committee rallied local churches to the crisis, and pastors began holding individual meetings with their congregations to discuss an appropriate Mennonite response. If they could not come to a complete accord on the propriety of suggesting that the state do away with such weapons altogether, they at least agreed that the government should not install them in Mennonite backyards. An estimated six hundred people from the area wrote letters to the president protesting this possible development before the Air Force moved the planned base further away near Salina.[45]

Against the backdrop of this uneasy development, delegates to the 1959 GC triennial conference also found the wherewithal to pass a resolution against nuclear weaponry. The statement began by summarizing the policy of obliteration bombing practiced in World War II and reasoning that "in such a time of urgency, the Christian church cannot be silent." The specter of the Goessel incident clearly hung over the resolution; the meeting participants found "most shocking to the Christian conscience are the fantastic military installations in the very heart of the nation." Overall, the delegates renewed their dedication to peace and Christian faith, denounced both war and atomic bomb tests as sin, and called on the government to pass a permanent ban on bomb testing.[46]

In a development suggestive of later trends, students at Mennonite colleges also began to resonate with the new political winds blowing on other college campuses in the early 1960s. In November 1961, reported Loewen, now dean of students at Bethel College, a "very spontaneous" movement against atmospheric nuclear testing arose among Bethel students. Actually, this was less spontaneous than he first thought; in their protest, these students joined a larger movement occurring throughout a number of liberal arts colleges that fall. Their particular impetus originated with an invitation from students at the other GC college, Bluffton, who had journeyed to Washington for a three-day fast and protest themselves. At Bethel, nearly one hundred out of a student body of five hundred fasted and vigiled for a nuclear test-ban treaty, and some went on to take their message to local business leaders and to area churches. Still others, a smaller group of eleven, journeyed to Washington to picket the White House for three days. While the incident appeared somewhat isolated, at a meeting of the "Inter-Collegiate Peace Fellowship" in 1962, James Juhnke detected a "general agreement" among these peace-minded students from all the Mennonite colleges that their respective church groups should involve themselves much more heavily in such direct action projects. Altogether, the incidents demonstrated that their elders' articulation of a strengthened Mennonite witness to the state about a variety of newer concerns struck a particularly responsive chord among Mennonite youth. Later in the decade this chord would rise to a crescendo.[47]

Propelled by new theological understandings that had come forth to accompany their enlarging social consciousness, Mennonites in these years had begun to consider a number of new issues that would extend their sense of social responsibility even further. In focusing their attention on matters pertaining to civil defense, capital punishment, and nuclear weapons, they had uncovered a number of areas beyond conscientious objection about which they felt impelled to speak to the state. Even in the more weighty reverberations of the Mennonite debate over the death penalty, however, these discussions took on an abstract and antiseptic quality that did not appear to register many ripples in the churches beyond the leadership of the peace and social concerns committees. As a national movement of social protest swept the country in the early 1960s, however, Mennonites began to consider a fourth issue that quickly overshadowed all the others. Whether or not it penetrated more deeply into the churches, at least the Mennonite reaction to the civil rights movement showed signs of taking their theorizing about social action out of its ivory tower.

MENNONITES AND THE CIVIL RIGHTS MOVEMENT

Throughout the 1940s and early 1950s, the leadership in both Mennonite groups displayed what might be labeled as a "quietly progressive" attitude on race relations. An irregular stream of articles on the topic in the denominational presses condemned racism and instructed people in the ways of racial tolerance and acceptance.[48] In the meantime, Mennonites struggled a bit with a quiet racism of their own. In 1941, for instance, the Virginia Conference ruled against racial mixing in the feet-washing service and also recommended segregated communion cups for black members. This expression of racism proceeded in place until 1955, when the conference rescinded it as unchristian. Similarly, in 1945 the conference refused to admit an African American student to its Eastern Mennonite College, though it reversed this decision three years later and became the first interracial college in Virginia. Nor was racism confined to Mennonites living in the American South. In a 1943 editorial in the *Gospel Herald*, for example, editor Daniel Kauffman denounced birth control as "race suicide," and warned that if "Christian people" persist in it, "the white race will become overwhelmed by the hordes of colored (and renegade white) races." Because church leadership recognized such expressions as more extreme

FIGURE 7.3. *Goshen professors Willard Smith and Guy F. Hershberger with Martin Luther King, Jr., at Goshen College, March 10, 1960. Courtesy of The Elkhart Truth*, Elkhart, Indiana.

manifestations of a festering racial insensitivity among their people, at the 1955 MC conference meeting, Hershberger pushed through a lengthy statement on race relations. This declaration built on a mountain of scriptural injunctions condemning racism and went on to both confess their shortcomings in this regard and to pledge a renewed Mennonite commitment to racial harmony.[49]

To a degree, the Mennonite leadership, at least, had displayed some kind of consciousness about race relations in the initial postwar years. Even so, the vast expansion of Mennonite concern over race relations concurrent with the explosion of the American racial crisis must be seen as evidence once again of the extent of Mennonite acculturation and their acceptance of newer responsibilities beyond their own communities. For by the late 1950s, the church leadership had riveted their attention on the burgeoning civil rights movement as an issue that held great significance for their common commitment as Christians. In the next few years, they endeavored to drive this message home to their congregations in a number of ways.

As early as December 1956, for example, MCC had agreed to incorporate "a mission of good will, fellowship and inquiry" to Americans "involved in current race relations problems." By 1957, Mennonite leaders and seminary students had begun to tour the South and send back firsthand reports of the injustices there. Elmer Neufeld, for example, traveled through the South one summer with several African American friends he had met at Woodlawn Mennonite Church, a biracial GC congregation serving the Mennonite seminary community in Chicago. They made a point of attempting to eat together in segregated restaurants, but they often ended up all eating outside, for they had made a pact not to eat where they could not all eat together. On such excursions, Mennonites like Neufeld, Vincent Harding, and others began to forge links with the movement demanding civil rights. For the more progressive-minded in the peace committees, the deeply Christian, reconciling nature of Martin Luther King's program of nonviolence contained a number of attractive aspects, despite what appeared as elements of coercion in his nonviolence and his liberal theology. People like Hershberger and Peachey expressed particularly deep admiration, and Hershberger was influential in arranging for King to speak at Goshen College in 1960.[50]

Occurring as it did against the backdrop of the Mennonite reorientation toward the state, the impact of this protest movement served to solidify some new stances recently arrived at and to push Mennonites to new, heretofore unthinkable ones. For example, here appeared the perfect occasion to put into motion what Metzler called "the growing conviction in recent years that if we witness when our own rights are involved in conscientious objector matters, we should also witness for the rights of others." In this instance, that conviction meant a willingness to reconsider what people like Bender and Hershberger had easily dismissed for Mennonites in the years before World War II: the techniques and possibilities of Gandhian nonviolence, now translated into American idiom by King.

The courage and dignity that infused the struggle in Montgomery made a lasting impression; developments there, Hershberger jotted to Metzler, "have given all of us occasion to take a fresh look at the whole matter" of nonviolence. Mennonite leaders studied it carefully. Metzler reported back from an FOR training conference in nonviolence he attended in 1959 that while Mennonites could teach the FOR something about relating nonviolence more closely to Christian love, they stood to learn a lot as well. At a similar conference later that year in Atlanta sponsored by the FOR, Southern Christian Leadership Conference (SCLC), and Congress of Racial Equality, Hershberger and Neufeld arrived at the same kind of conclusions. The phrasing of nonviolence there seemed more secular in orientation, they noted, and many participants seemed only to view it as a tactic.

All the same, the two men urged that Mennonites cooperate closely with the SCLC and "continue the development of an aggressive Mennonite program of work in the area of race relations."[51]

As joint secretary of the two Mennonite Church committees charged with overseeing peace and social concerns, Hershberger threw himself into the heart of his church's racial struggle. In a host of speeches and articles, he worked tirelessly to raise Mennonite consciences on the issue, and he discovered that here too the prophetic Anabaptist identity could be creatively applied. In a major address to a Mennonite Conference on Race Relations in Atlanta in 1964, he presented Anabaptist ancestors as virtual forerunners of the civil rights movement. With such a heritage, he wondered, how could Mennonites easily conform to the practices of a racist society? Anabaptists refused to let human laws deter them from doing God's will. In using this model, Hershberger and others found more legitimation for quiet, respectful civil disobedience. Challenging segregation in business establishments, he cried in 1960, was a "proper thing for a Christian to do," even if it defied discriminatory statutes. "We must guard against confusing nonresistance with obedience to all laws," he reasoned.[52]

Hershberger even provided an example of acceptable Mennonite behavior on this matter. While attending the 1959 nonviolence conference, Hershberger and Neufeld walked into an Atlanta restaurant with several African American officials from CORE, among them Wyatt Tee Walker. There they deliberately broke a segregation law and ate together in defiance of it. "At that time," Neufeld remembered later, "it was obviously an act of civil disobedience." Similarly, journeying home from a Florida vacation in 1964, Mennonite professor J. L. Burkholder stopped off in St. Augustine to visit students involved in the civil rights struggle there. Caught up in the emotional fervor of the movement, within hours he had broken a desegregation law in a hotel restaurant, and he spent the next three days in jail.[53]

Mennonites had spoken and written much in the 1950s about manifesting a "ministry of reconciliation" in response to war and injustice; here suddenly appeared a perfect opportunity to turn the rhetoric into reality. In 1961, MCC established a VS unit in Atlanta with the aim of doing just that. The new unit would "witness to the Christian way of love and self-sacrifice" not only in race relations but "in all aspects of life." Moreover, recognized the Peace Section, "Christian obedience may at times lead to violation of government laws and regulations." Anabaptist theology had always stressed their higher calling to obey divine rather human laws when the two conflicted. Now their descendants were stretching this calling to fit

FIGURE 7.4. *Vincent Harding and Delton Franz, co-pastors at Woodlawn
Mennonite Church in Chicago, late 1950s. Courtesy of The Mennonite.*

new circumstances.[54] In Rosemarie and Vincent Harding, the Mennonite
leadership had stumbled across people who could actually transmit these
lofty words into reality. Finding himself tremendously excited by the radical Anabaptist heritage, Vincent had joined the GC congregation on
Woodlawn Street in Chicago and risen to the associate pastorate of that
church, all the while pursuing a Ph.D. in history from the University of
Chicago. As a highly educated, articulate Mennonite pastor and an African
American, Harding quickly became the Mennonites' premier counsel on
race relations (in Hershberger's words, "the expert, Vincent Harding").[55]

Established as head of the special Atlanta Voluntary Service unit in 1961
with the express purpose of fleshing out a Mennonite ministry in racial
turmoil, the Hardings immediately began to carry out their mission with
verve, skill, and enthusiasm. By the spring of 1962, they had expanded their
focus of activities to include the simmering confrontation in Albany, Georgia. There they befriended a number of hardened local segregationists, and
Vincent spent three days in jail following his arrest for praying at the city
hall. Likewise, as the focus of the civil rights movement shifted to Birmingham, Alabama, a year later, the Hardings moved too. There they exercised their unusual ability to establish trusting relations with angry whites.

Meanwhile, they sent up-to-date dispatches back to the Mennonite press, describing the movement's struggles in vivid detail.[56]

Perhaps, given the reactions to Harding's work by some of the Mennonite leadership, it would have been better to have left the fine words on paper. Not only did Mennonite leaders face the continuing possibility of a conservative backlash to this type of activism, but the Hardings' recovery of a kind of Anabaptist Vision in the field of race relations left even some of the MCC hierarchy a little nervous. At an "informal consultation" with Harding following his arrest in Albany, MCC chiefs pressed him rather hard on his work in general and his jailing in particular. MCC executive secretary William Snyder wanted to know, for example, whether his jail stint "strengthen[ed] or hinder[ed] our role as reconcilers in the South?" Unable to attend the meeting, the director of MCC Voluntary Service urged that they communicate to Harding that "he could 'cut off his water' if he doesn't change his approach . . . Vince tends to begin from the assumption that everyone is prejudiced. This rankles people." Further, urged Edgar Stoesz, they needed to exercise a good deal of care in releasing word of such experiences, the jailing in particular, to the Mennonite press. Harding closed the session by recognizing that a number of Mennonites had "serious questions about my witness and work."[57]

Indeed, the leadership had begun to digest the not entirely comfortable knowledge that having inaugurated a prophet in their midst, they could not always contain the direction of his fire. For Harding also functioned in an equally energetic capacity in calling the church to activity in the racial struggle and in puncturing inflated Mennonite estimations of their own moral purity. As a Mennonite convert, he had some hard words for the church. "This still prevalent idea of a culturally chosen Mennonite people has been as deeply prejudicial and divisive in our lives as any racial segregation," he thundered at a special MCC conference on the race crisis in 1959. "We must confess that we have too often allowed non-resistance to become synonymous with sitting on our hands and closing our eyes and turning our backs on injustice and hatred among men."[58]

When Mennonites stated that they saw the racial crisis as something happening a long way from their communities, Harding would simply remind them that this was no guarantor of freedom from prejudice. For Hershberger, Harding and others uncovered a fair amount of evidence that Mennonite acculturation had also led to acceptance of many of the racial attitudes prevalent in America in the early 1960s. Visiting the Virginia

Conference in 1962, for example, Harding uncovered evidence of a "frightening moral insensitivity" to racial problems among Mennonites there. Deeper in the South, Hershberger ran into more blatant prejudices. Touring the scattered MC churches in Mississippi and Louisiana in the summer of 1964, he more than once encountered the question "Do you want to bring 'niggers' into our church? Is this what you are trying to do?" Nor was such racism only confined to the South. Visiting Pennsylvania churches, John A. Lapp "was again reminded of the deep seated prejudices there. Respectable ministers are still spouting the myth of Noah's curse on Ham."[59]

Thus, church committees hammering away on the themes of racial brotherhood and legislation had their hands full. The program they came up with had two major thrusts. First, church leaders articulated a witness to the state on behalf of civil rights laws unmatched in the GCMC since its exertions in the anti-UMT campaign, and for the Mennonite Church, nearly unparalleled in its history. For the GCs, the Peace and Social Concerns Committee made a major effort to mobilize their people on behalf of the 1963 civil rights bill, an effort reinforced in many local district conferences. The Western District Conference, for example, passed an extensive race statement in 1963 endorsing this legislation and urged people to write to their congressional representatives on the issue. Similarly, for the MC Mennonites in 1963, Hershberger's Committee on Economic and Social Relations sent each senator and representative a letter supporting the civil rights legislation; and the entire MC General Conference endorsed a telegram to Kennedy on its behalf. Scarcely ten years before, MC Mennonites had had trouble supporting any kind of advocacy to government officials outside of conscientious objector matters. Now the leadership spared little energy in rousing their people to present such an witness on a completely unrelated matter. These appeals wrought some success. The congressman from the Elkhart-Goshen area, reported Hershberger, received more mail supporting the 1964 civil rights bill from Mennonites than from any other religious group.[60]

Secondly, realizing that the "fundamental challenge" facing them involved dealing with the racism in their own communities, Mennonite leaders embarked on what one called "a massive effort of education" to enlighten their people on racial issues. To this end, the denominational organs rolled off a steady stream of articles on racial injustice and on the proper Mennonite response to it, voicing a softly stated support for most of the more significant efforts of the civil rights movement (though the *Gospel*

Herald usually expressed its disapproval of civil disobedience). Between 1957 and 1969, for examples, the *Gospel Herald* published some 114 articles on race relations, with the number peaking at 24 in 1965. Both Mennonite groups produced a number of different official pronouncements on the racial crisis, and district conferences regularly echoed such statements. MCC convened two larger conferences on the Mennonite response to the racial crisis, including one in Atlanta to focus on the matter in southern Mennonite churches in particular. The MC Mennonites similarly convoked a series of regional meetings in 1964–65, and both groups employed several traveling special "race secretaries" to bring the message to individual churches.[61]

In comparison to the exertions and sacrifices made on behalf of civil rights by other Americans and even by other church groups, the Mennonite contribution was rather minimal. They had written some letters and contributed some supplies, and a few of them had been jailed. The impact of the movement on the church, however, took on more substantial dimensions. By the early 1960s, two decades of a growing Mennonite service orientation toward an ever more pressing society outside the disintegrating spatial boundaries of the Mennonite community had considerably enlarged the Mennonite field of responsibility. As a significant movement of social protest swept the country, Mennonites could no longer define it as none of their affair. Instead, evincing a ready willingness to witness to the state on concerns beyond their own, they extended this newfound commitment to racial harmony into an active campaign in their churches. Change was indeed in the wind.

HOW DEEP THE CHANGES?

In 1964 MCC launched a series of regional study groups, each tackling a different issue and coming back together in 1965 to share their findings in an extensive "Church–State Study Conference" that October. So much did the creators of the conference feel that Mennonites as a group had decided the question of witnessing to government that they agreed that the conference would bypass this question. Instead, it would focus on the "formulation of some guiding principles for church–state relations" as its central goal. In their explication of "Why Are We Here?" the conference delegates not only summarized many of the changes that had come to shape the church in the postwar years, but they also underscored a new one.[62]

As they had recognized at Winona Lake fifteen years before, not only was the church changing but so was the state. In their ancestors' day, the state

had functioned primarily to "bear the sword" in its suppression of evil;
but it had also showed a marked proclivity to wield that sword against the
Anabaptists. This resulted in the strict Anabaptist insistence on a wide separation between the two kingdoms, which they bequeathed to their Mennonite descendants. Now, however, the state did more than maintain order.
It had embarked on a wide number of social welfare programs that sometimes mirrored in quality efforts Mennonites themselves had made along
these lines. The evil state had become the Welfare State. As the nature of
the state had changed, so had the role of God's people living in its boundaries. No longer were they timid subjects, cowering submissively before a
wrathful king that God had established on the throne. Instead, these medieval subjects had become modern citizens, called upon to participate in
democratic affairs as full and accepted members of the body politic.[63]

Minutes from several of the regional study groups highlight the scope to
which the participants, at least, had begun to take for granted their collective mandate to witness to the state on a wide variety of matters. For instance, in the March 1965 meeting of the church-state study group, drawing on the energies of Mennonites in eastern Pennsylvania, they discussed
whether they could "tell the state how to wage war." Recognizing that they
could not expect the state "to give up force," the group did feel "we can ask
it to observe restraint . . . .it can respond to a degree to the Lordship of
Christ." While they could not decide how much they could ask of the
state—"Do we request the state to adopt completely our point of view or
only to come part way?"—the transformation was stunning. The participants agreed that government was engaged in a "dirty business." For generations, Mennonites had turned to this recognition as a basis both to excuse themselves from this dirty business and to refuse to speak to the state
about its conduct of such affairs. Now, however, this collection of Pennsylvania Mennonites from a number of different groups affirmed that "the
church cannot turn its back on any issue." The study group on "the State
and Public Morality" provided additional confirmation of this sentiment,
deciding that the church should speak to the government on a wide number
of morality issues, ranging from divorce and marriage laws to those related
to highway safety and business ethics. In outlining new areas for church-
state cooperation and building further on the theological foundation that
endorsed this expanded witness to government, the 1965 conference demonstrated again that Mennonites had substantially reevaluated their traditional stance.[64]

But had they? Or rather, which Mennonites had engaged in such a reevaluation, and which ones had not? Throughout these years, this question had resounded uneasily beneath the surface of the work of the peace and the social concerns committees and gnawed away at the labors of the theological study groups and conferences. Witness, for example, the quiet resistance to much of the race relations work. Activist pastors like Delton Franz and Lynford Hershey repeatedly heard angry opposition from people in their churches. In a 1965 "for discussion" article in the *Gospel Herald*, the MC fundamentalist Sanford Shetler opined that such activist efforts "discredit the church." Instead, Shetler lauded the racial program embarked upon by the archsegregationist governor of Alabama, George Wallace. Shortly thereafter, the *Gospel Herald* received a large number of letters strongly supportive of Shetler's analysis. Since the toilsome years of World War II some twenty years before, the MC traditionalists had remained remarkably quiescent, focusing their fire on such issues as lapses in nonconformity. Somewhat belatedly, by 1965 they had suddenly awakened to the vast social and theological changes occurring in the church and had gathered themselves to resist.[65]

Particularly worrisome to many church leaders was the spreading realization by the early 1960s that the influence of right-wing, nationalist preachers such as Carl McIntire had begun to spread more deeply through many of their churches. They took a number of immediate steps to combat it. Hershberger saw fit to publish an article in the *Gospel Herald* condemning the anti-Catholic hysteria sweeping through conservative Protestantism during the election of 1960. More generally, the Peace Problems Committee prepared a statement warning against the type of extreme anticommunism voiced by men like McIntire. Both the MC and GC conference meetings officially adopted the statement "Communism and Anti-Communism." Still, in 1964, "realizing that many of our people were influenced by Right-Wing extremism," the PPC-CESR published another article in the denominational organ asking their readers to remember the church's statements on civil rights and the nuclear test-ban treaty when deciding who to vote for in the presidential election that year. The literal flood of angry letters in response demonstrated to Hershberger and other leaders that "many of our Mennonite people are politically minded more than we knew."[66]

The next seven years would increase rather than lessen the tension between a progressive Mennonite leadership and less activist members in the churches. For by the mid-1960s, another national protest movement brewed—one that congregations would have even a harder time remaining immune from. Witness the tensions then displayed by the chair of the Peace and Service Committee of the Western District Conference. In the fall of 1965, the committee had been asked by Bethel College students to join them that month in a protest march in Washington. Wondering if they could instead find a means for a "more positive witness," the chair wrote that "some of us have scrupulous feelings as to how far we as peace loving christians should go in participating in the various demonstrations which are being staged in our day." But means of positive witness would remain more elusive in this instance. For now their students marched, not on behalf of civil rights or a test ban treaty, but against a war their government waged with increasing ferocity in Indochina.[67]

CHAPTER 8

Draft Resistance,
Nonresistance,
and Vietnam,
1965–1973

Vietnam exemplified many different things for American Mennonites. Like other wars, this conflict forced a generation of young
men to explore the depths of their fidelity to one of their church's fundamental teachings. For mission and relief workers in Vietnam, the war
offered a crucial testing ground for a Mennonite mission of reconciliation
in a site of violence and pain. Meanwhile, for the church at home, Vietnam
furnished the point of friction for another heated struggle within the
church leadership as Mennonite activists and conservatives articulated
competing conceptions of the proper Mennonite relationship with the
state. As a result, a church already fractured by a process of acculturation
emerged from the war years in many ways even more fragmented. Similarly, the forces of political and cultural assimilation of the 1960s carried
the domestic turmoil engendered by the war into the churches, with the
Mennonite laity mirroring the political polarization occurring nationally
over the combat in Indochina.

Above all perhaps, the conflict in Vietnam symbolized for the church at
large a fundamental test of loyalties. For forty years American Mennonites
had fashioned a delicate arrangement with their government that had allowed them to remain both good citizens and good Christians. Excused
from military service, Mennonites had testified to their patriotism by engaging in a number of different forms of "positive" service, work that simultaneously fueled their growing self-definition as a people of service. In

the national turmoil over the war in Vietnam, however, they found it increasingly difficult to maintain this balance. As Vincent Harding phrased the Mennonite dilemma in 1966, "We have a choice to make. It is now thrust before us with every bomb that falls in Vietnam, with every patriotic speech that rings out in our communities . . . Christ's or Caesar's—whose people are we?"[1] In particular, such questions came to be pushed most loudly by younger people. As had Mennonite churches, Mennonite college campuses had grown increasingly open to outside society. Accordingly, Mennonite college students found elements of an antiwar popular culture reinforcing prophetic strains in their own tradition. Thus motivated, many of these young people began to argue with force and reason that the paths toward good citizenship and faithful discipleship had begun to diverge.

About twenty-five years before, in the conscription institutes, many of the church's future leaders had "learned to question government." In the intervening years, their fellow congregants had undergone a tremendous transformation. The process of acculturation had broken down the walls of their cloistered communities and integrated most Mennonites into national society. In the process, returning CPS men had taken up positions of leadership in their churches and had placed on the Mennonite agenda a new set of social concerns that familiarity with outside society had rendered them no longer able to ignore. Moreover, they had constructed a theologically acceptable means of speaking to the state about this growing list of concerns. Now these arguments from their young people would strike a sudden and responsive chord. For they would be articulated against a backdrop of a nation once again waging modern war. Yet this war would ignite a protest movement that would shake the nation to its core.

TOTAL WAR AND DOMESTIC AMERICA IN THE 1960S

The course of American involvement in Vietnam proceeded differently from other American wars in this century. Instead of serving as the necessary concomitant to the war effort as in World War II, in the Vietnam War the ideological commitment both preceded and propelled the military one. In other words, the reflexive response of the anticommunist consensus guided American involvement in Vietnam. As Dean Rusk, later John Kennedy's secretary of state, put it in 1950, "This is a civil war that has been in effect captured by the [Soviet] Politburo . . . So this isn't a civil war in the usual sense. It is part of an international war."[2]

Impelled by such rationales, the drive to establish a noncommunist government in Vietnam was carried forward in a bipartisan manner by the next four successive presidents. Following the collapse of French rule in Vietnam, Eisenhower's men ignored the international settlement of the war at Geneva and instead created a new noncommunist nation of South Vietnam. They installed a hand-picked dictator, Ngo Dinh Diem, at the helm of this creation and propped up his unpopular rule with massive American military aid. An equally ardent cold warrior, Kennedy guarded this inheritance with matching vigor, funneling millions more in weaponry and aircraft into the country. Yet even this gushing pipeline of aid, which by the early 1970s had transformed the tiny country of South Vietnam into the world's fourth largest military power, proved inadequate to prevent a communist victory in Vietnam.[3]

Lyndon Johnson quickly built on these previous commitments to fully launch America's next major land war in Asia. The force of advisors bequeathed from Kennedy was augmented by a million more GIs who were sent out into the jungles and rice paddies as combat troops. Almost sixty thousand of them ultimately died there. American planes furrowed the skies over Vietnam, engaging in the most devastating bombing campaign in human history. Already by 1967, American planes had made over one hundred thousand separate sorties in bombing runs that had pummeled the enemy nation.[4]

The air war only increased in intensity and destructiveness under Richard Nixon. Indeed, under his policy of "Vietnamization," bombing promised to perform the same kind of satisfying functions it had initially held out to Johnson. Faced with a massive demand from the American public to bring the troops home but aware that South Vietnamese troops could not stave off the communists by themselves, Nixon compensated for the gradual withdrawal of American ground troops by pushing the throttle of the American air war forward even further. With few strictly military targets left by the late 1960s, Nixon's crew aimed their bombing at enemy morale. Through this vehicle, the new team would search, as aide Henry Kissinger phrased it, for Hanoi's "breaking point." So Nixon bombed—secretly in Cambodia and Laos, wreaking untold devastation, and openly in North and South Vietnam, with the B-52s taking off daily to drop their loads. Already by 1970, more bombs had been dropped on the small nation of Vietnam than on all targets throughout the previous course of human history.[5]

With every escalation of the war orchestrated by the Pentagon, the ranks of the peace movement swelled with a matching intensification. Activists cobbled together increasingly massive demonstrations against the war. In

October 1967, for instance, perhaps as many as a hundred thousand Americans rallied against the war in fifty different cities; and in the huge "Vietnam Moratorium" of October 1969, around 15 million demonstrated in large and small ways in localities across the country. A month later, close to a million people gathered to peacefully denounce the war in Washington. Following Nixon's announcement of the invasion of Cambodia in 1970 and the deaths of protesting students at Jackson and Kent State Universities, the nation witnessed what one historian called the "greatest single campus uprising in American history." Demonstrations rocked two-thirds of American college and university campuses, and nearly five hundred of them temporarily shut down in response to the protests.[6]

Meanwhile, thousands of young men resisted the war and the draft in more personal and costly ways. The number of men declaring themselves conscientious objectors soared. For the first time in modern era, Mennonites were suddenly a pronounced minority among conscientious objectors. In the five years between 1965 and 1970, over 170,000 registrants obtained CO classifications, so overwhelming the selective service system that it was not able to arrange alternative service jobs for up to half of these objectors. In 1972, the year before the draft ended, more registrants were classified as conscientious objectors than were inducted into the military. Beyond those opting for conscientious objection, large numbers of men refused to register for the draft or in other ways cooperate with the selective service system. In 1965 a small group of pacifists gathered to openly burn their draft cards. They were soon joined by compatriots across the nation who destroyed or returned their draft cards or deserted the military and who consequently faced years in jail or the permanent loss of U.S. citizenship in exile in Canada. In response, other Americans rallied behind the war and the president, denouncing antiwar activists as "hippies" and "traitors." The chasms of personal and political polarization between families and communities ran deep. Hundreds of cities exploded with racial violence, indicating that there were chasms between the races as well. In many ways, the very fabric of the nation seemed to be unraveling.[7]

These protests reverberated through the hallways of American churches. Even former cold war ideologues like Reinhold Niebuhr and John C. Bennett came to add their voices to the dissent. Yet the polarization wrought nationally by the war also deeply divided the churches. The sociologist Robert Wuthnow has described how the war, along with the preceding currents of religious political activism in the civil rights struggle, triggered a restructuring of American Protestantism between religious conservatives and liberals that extended and deepened in succeeding decades. One group of church people, styled by Wuthnow as "liberals," came to be associated not only with opposition to the war but also with direct action against it. "Conservatives"—in Wuthnow's terms, "evangelicals"—gravitated toward more hawkish stances on the war and argued, moreover, that the way to effect change was by changing the individual's conscience and thus behavior. Engaging in direct action, they believed, was not the place of the church; instead Christians interested in social change should focus their effort on personal salvation, evangelism, and prayer. As Wuthnow summarized, "These two orientations—evangelism and social justice—in fact became the polar positions around which religious conservatives and religious liberals increasingly identified themselves." This split was soon manifested in the many church schisms and dissenting splinter groups that began to fragment nearly all major Protestant denominations.[8]

Here, then, was the larger climate in which Mennonites framed their dissent against war in the 1960s. As the state followed the anticommunist imperative and the dictates of modern war to their logical end in Vietnam, the nation shook with protests demanding peace and social justice. It was a favorable climate for an ethnoreligious group that had increasingly come to take peace and justice issues to the heart of their redefined identity. For two decades, Mennonites had been attuning themselves ever more carefully to national concerns. Now they suddenly found themselves oriented to act vigorously. In Vietnam, in fact, Mennonites could speak to an international issue with which they had some personal familiarity.

THE MENNONITE MOVEMENT AGAINST THE WAR

Because of the work of MCC and the mission programs of individual Mennonite groups there throughout the 1950s, Vietnam was not altogether a strange and foreign concern. Although deeply influenced by the larger antiwar movement, Mennonite protest against the war thus emanated, fundamentally, from the same kind of impetus that drove Mennonite Disaster Service, MCC, and other church service organizations. Mennonites had been exposed to human need and injustice now in a new locale, and they refused to keep quiet about the larger ramifications involved in meeting this crisis.

For instance, first-hand reports were filtering back to Lancaster County Mennonites from their mission workers at the front. In 1957 the Lancaster Mennonite Conference had sent its own missionary couple to labor in Vietnam; and since that time, it had dispatched several other young mission workers to assist there in a combination of evangelism and social welfare work. Among them was James Metzler. The son of Lancaster missionaries, Metzler was no wild-eyed radical. Yet as early as 1964, he had begun to send back accounts to the conference missions publication suggesting that this was not the clear-cut struggle against communism that the U.S. government portrayed. That December, for instance, Metzler began to write of American as well as Vietcong atrocities, warning his readers that "a 'free press' is not necessarily free from propaganda," and confessing his growing inability to "condemn one side as guilty and the other as just." In graphic depictions of violence the following October, he relayed the American indifference to the deaths of Vietnamese peasants; and by May 1966, he urged Lancaster Mennonites to take a prophetic stance in regards to the war. "Silence can only mean consent," Metzler warned, "where there is opportunity to speak."[9]

Altogether nearly one hundred Mennonite mission workers spent time in Vietnam, many of them similarly radicalized by their experience.[10] Their service in Vietnam with MCC focused a host of questions about how to witness for peace and reconciliation in a war setting in which they were continually identified as part of the U.S. military by the peasants they worked amongst and also manipulated in subtle ways by an omnipresent military machine engaged in a death-struggle with communism. Like James Metzler, these mission workers increasingly began to direct their questions—and their dissent—homeward to their churches. In the face of such a situation, many Mennonites wondered, how could they continue to minister to human suffering in Vietnam without also speaking to one of the actors that they perceived caused so much of the suffering?

Given its responsibilities for the bulk of Mennonite work in Vietnam, MCC began to consider addressing the state about its warmaking there as the Johnson administration escalated the war effort in 1964–65. As early as the spring of 1964, the Peace Section executive secretary reported an increasing number of expressions of concern about the war from members of the constituency. The volume of these communications had increased to a point a year later that the agency had to consider some kind of a statement on the war. As the secretary wondered, "Do we have nothing to say when so much is at stake?" Accordingly, the Peace Section passed a statement on the war in July of 1965, pledging "to promote discussion of the moral issues raised by the war throughout the brotherhood," a discussion that it hoped would enable members of the churches to resist pressure to accept the war and also "to communicate intelligently their protest to the government."

FIGURE 8.1. *Mennonite peace leaders (left to right): Guy F. Hershberger, MCC Peace Section executive secretary Edgar Metzler, Peace Section chair William Keeney, and Paul Peachey. At the MCC Peace Section meeting in January 1965, in Chicago. Mennonite Central Committee Collection, Archives of the Mennonite Church, Goshen, Indiana.*

The Peace Section itself endeavored to render such a protest, sending a special MCC delegation to the White House in July 1966 with a letter condemning the war. The letter carefully described the extent and nature of Mennonite relief efforts in Vietnam and then outlined the contradiction the agency had come to feel in "trying to help the people on one hand while at the same time our government was engaged in an escalating war that was devastating the countryside and creating enormous and tragic suffering for the civilian population." "The time has come," MCC's letter continued, "when we can no longer maintain faith with the homeless, the hungry, the orphaned and the wounded to whom we minister unless we speak out as clearly as we can against the savage war in which our country is engaged." As MCC had led Mennonites into the crusade for civil rights, they now plunged into advocacy on an issue that because of Mennonite relief work seemed somewhat closer to home.[11]

Having spent much of the previous eight years redefining the parameters of Mennonite theology and tradition so as to admit such a witness to the government, the peace committees of both major Mennonite groups quickly seized on Vietnam as an issue very much within their enlarged field of responsibilities. Thirty years before, many Mennonites had regarded the state's waging of war as an unfortunate manifestation of maintaining order in a wicked world. Now the church leadership judged their government's latest war as a wicked and immoral affair that, far from lying outside their scope of concerns, demanded active Mennonite attention and dissent.

For such was the thrust of the antiwar statements that both church bodies delivered at their general conference meetings in the summer of 1965. Admitting that the suffering in Vietnam stemmed from a variety of sources, the Mennonite Church's message to member district conferences still found that it is "the brutal warfare waged by the forces of our own country that cause our primary distress." The statement went on to roundly condemn the government's justifications for the war and to urge government leaders to enter into sincere negotiation to end the war. Declaring that they a spoke from a "love for our nation," the statement closed by exhorting MC congregations "to give themselves to serious study, conversation, and prayer concerning this crisis." In addition, they recognized, "It is incumbent upon us as the People of God to set the pace in sacrificial service" to the war's victims and "to those who live in poverty and need." Again, the church would need to balance its criticism with "positive" action.[12]

Similarly, the delegates at the General Conference Mennonite Church's triennial conference, held that summer in Estes Park, Colorado, saw fit to deliver several prescriptions to the government on the war. Calling for a halt in the bombing of civilians and the torture of prisoners, the statement urged United Nations involvement in producing a settlement of the war as well as economic development in Vietnam "to demonstrate our sincere desire and good faith to end the conflict." Like the MC statement, the GC statement went on to urge member congregations to study and discuss the war and "to communicate our spiritual and moral concern for Vietnam to the public."[13]

Peace leaders in both denominations quickly moved to formulate a Mennonite antiwar position throughout the later 1960s. They pushed their efforts along two lines: expressing protest to the state on one hand, and motivating their people toward dissent on the other. The MC Mennonites repeatedly attempted to root their advocacy in the careful lines of theological and political argument they had mapped out earlier in the decade. First, they offered a steady stream of articles in the denominational press that served both to educate their people on the crisis and to nudge them to appropriate forms of action. The weekly publications of both Mennonite groups put out a joint issue devoted to the war, an issue that hammered against the war from a number of perspectives. In a series of articles in 1966, Committee on Peace and Social Concerns (CPSC) chairman Lapp outlined reasons to speak to the state and ways of witnessing to government. Edgar Metzler offered his reasons for opposing the war, combining the language of patriotism with that of evangelical religion; while Vietnam missionary Donald Sensenig wrote of the harm the war wrought in the church's mission efforts there.[14]

The second thrust of CPSC work in these years found its most notable expression in the words of Orie Miller. Now an elderly man, Miller commanded tremendous respect from Mennonites of all political and cultural persuasions, and his words from the floor of a special MCC inter-Mennonite consultation in Minneapolis in 1966 registered significant reverberations. Obtaining recognition from the chair, Miller stood up to voice his conviction that Mennonites needed to create for themselves some new and appropriate ways of protesting the evils that now seemed so rampant around them in society. Once again, the prophetic stances of Mennonite ancestors could be harnessed for present political needs. After all, cried Miller, "the Anabaptist movement . . . was born in a radical protest against evils that had come to be taken for granted." With their descendants "having forgotten how to protest through long disuse of that facility," Miller stated flatly, they had to rediscover "a Mennonite or a Christian way of performing this ministry."[15]

Thirdly, as they had begun in 1965, the CPSC persisted in its efforts to speak to the state about the war. In spite of the number of opposing voices raised from Lancaster and Virginia Conference delegates, the CPSC convinced the 1967 general conference meeting to endorse another respectful but firm letter to the president condemning the war. Lapp appeared before the House Armed Services Committee in 1967 to condemn the draft in particular on behalf of all Americans. "We question the validity of conscription as a permanent feature of national life," he testified, not only for Mennonites, but for all kinds of "selective" objectors to unjust wars. A decade and a half before, the MC hierarchy had called for their peoples' opposition to UMT only hesitatingly, still unsure of the degree they could speak to the state. Now, following the Cambodia invasion, one writer called on Mennonites to flood Congress with letters, telegrams, and personal visits in protest. Even the larger church hierarchy felt impelled to speak in a like manner at particularly horrible junctures in the war. Following the saturation bombing of North Vietnam over the Christmas holidays of 1972, the

MC Board of Congregational Ministries sent an emergency letter to each pastor. Arguing that "It is imperative that we find some way to be prophetic," the letter called on congregations to mobilize their protest in these and other ways. Meanwhile, John E. Lapp joined John Howard Yoder and 56 other denominational leaders around the country in an open letter to the White House condemning the bombing as immoral.[16]

The corresponding General Conference committee found itself able to take this kind of activism much further and embarked on an explicitly antiwar agenda in the mid-1960s. The multitude of educational efforts and activities conducted against the war by the church in general and the Peace and Social Concerns Committee (PSCC) in particular are so varied and extensive that they resist easy condensation here. For example, Maynard Shelly, the editor of *The Mennonite* from 1961 to 1971, took on the role of an antiwar crusader, publishing an average of fifty articles a year on some facet or another of the war through the latter 1960s. By the relatively early date of October 1966, the PSCC had distributed filmstrips on the war to every congregation, mailed nine separate pieces of antiwar material to pastors, and made other material available for distribution; they had participated in visitations to Washington to express their opposition; and they had sent out "what to do" suggestions along with their 1966 regular "Peace Sunday" mailing.[17]

Moreover, not only denominational peace activists but also other GC leaders had gone beyond these educational efforts to advocate a number of overtly political measures expressing their opposition. The clearest and perhaps most dramatic instance of this came in a special message formulated by the GCMC Council of Boards in December 1967 and forwarded to church councils. In it, the church hierarchy called not only for congregational study of the war and letters of protest to Washington but also for a number of other measures carrying this dissent to heights that would have been the province only of a few radicals on the GC fringe twenty years before. For example, the statement called for congregations to consider resisting the special "telephone tax" levied by the government to pay for the war, for financial support to those resisting at higher levels, for "witness" at facilities producing bombs and other war materials, and for sending medical aid to war victims in North Vietnam in clear violation of the law. Throughout much of the twentieth century, the GCMC had endorsed the larger Mennonite compromises with the government in several different CO programs, all the while formulating the means of addressing the state on a number of different issues. Now one of those issues had brought them to the edge of an open break from this carefully constructed arrangement.[18]

In these protests, the church moved to find ways to express the cherished concept of positive service, although the methods they used in the Vietnam context seemed to break sharply with the older, concurrent goal of offering such service as a means of reinforcing Mennonite citizenship. In particular, the idea of forwarding medical aid to North as well as South Vietnam presented new possibilities in this regard. MCC, along with other groups such as the Quakers, had begun probing early in the war to find means to do this; and the church made a major effort along these lines in the "Vietnam Christmas" program of 1971. In the PSCC's rough polling of congregations on this topic in 1966, a number of churches found the notion appealing. One church commented that "this is positive witnessing"; another held that "this would demonstrate that love is not determined by the flag flying over us but the love of Christ in us." Still, this was a sort of witnessing that communicated a new message; as PSCC Secretary Stanley Bohn hoped, "This kind of action toward North Vietnam could be a way Mennonites could communicate to others that Christ is bigger than the United States." Enough Mennonites from a range of different groups agreed with this analysis that contributions for medical aid for North Vietnam totaled $26,000 in 1971, a response that MCC thought "much greater than anticipated."[19]

Before long, the antiwar analysis coming from their church leaders (a message now reinforced by many similar messages in the surrounding society) had moved a number of individual Mennonites from both major groups to action. In the spring of 1967, students at Eastern Mennonite College held a silent weekly vigil against the war outside the county courthouse in downtown Harrisonburg, Virginia. Mennonite activists in Elkhart, Indiana, published an antiwar statement in Elkhart and Goshen newspapers, hoping to stimulate local discussion on the war. In addition, they vigiled silently in front of the post office in Elkhart, amid jeers and a few firecrackers tossed by passersby. In December 1967, Goshen College students held a campus rally that raised almost five thousand dollars in medical aid for North Vietnam. Local veterans groups sponsored two newspaper ads in response, one suggesting that the college be investigated by the House Un-American Activities Committee. Mennonite activists, both young and old, mounted silent vigils in Oklahoma City, Denver, Chicago, and Wichita. Following the invasion of Cambodia and the deaths of four protesting students at Kent State in May 1970, Mennonite antiwar activity sprang to new heights. The president of Eastern Mennonite College, in the heart of the Virginia Conference, wrote to the president to demand U.S. withdrawal from the war. A special convocation of students at Goshen College brainstormed ways to express their further opposition, and at a similar gathering at Bethel College, history professor James Juhnke declared his candidacy for Congress on an antiwar platform. At the MCC headquarters in tiny Akron, Pennsylvania, a group of Mennonite housewives went door to door to solicit support for the McGovern-Hatfield amendment, which promised to deny funds for the war.[20]

Yet just as the national antiwar movement provoked a countermovement in reaction, so too did Mennonite ranks begin to divide. As the leadership had discovered earlier in the decade in their efforts at condemning capital punishment, many Mennonites who readily accepted theological arguments advocating an enlarged testimony to government began to object vehemently when peace committee members began to apply these words to specific circumstances. The debate over these earlier issues, in fact, paled in comparison to the uproar arising among the church's theological and political conservatives as the Mennonite hierarchy endeavored to speak to the state about Vietnam.

MOUNTING CONSERVATIVE RESISTANCE

Already up in arms over developments earlier in the decade, MC conservatives in Lancaster and especially in Virginia greeted the CPSC's antiwar efforts with immediate and well-kindled alarm. By the spring of 1966, Virginia Conference chiefs were delivering regular broadsides to the CPSC leadership, especially to committee secretary Paul Peachey. As the conference moderator, J. Otis Yoder assailed Peachey in February: "The CPSC has assumed a mandate has been handed to them," an assumption Yoder vehemently disavowed. "The grass-roots as I sample them do not favor White House visits," he maintained. That May, he asserted to Peachey that "the CPSC is going in the wrong direction because they start from the wrong theological base." If this remained unchanged, Yoder warned, "Biblical non-resistance will be lost to the beatnik pacifists." After meeting with some of the dissidents that March, Peachey summarized their complaints for committee members. The CPSC, they charged, had deviated from "the Anabaptist view on church-state relations" and, having "overstepped its mandate," had embarked on a course of "social and political actionism."

As a result, they felt that "the churches are being sold a bill of goods which they can no longer accept."[21]

Beneath these accusations of betrayal and deviation lay a conservatism that appeared as a curious mixture of adherence to traditional, unvarnished two-kingdom theology and—at least for some—sympathy to the arguments of right-wing nationalism. Points of theological dispute peppered all of the traditionalists' arguments. The state and the church each had their own particular spheres of power and influence, they held, and neither kingdom should impinge on the turf of the other. Thus J. Otis Yoder sent a message to all Virginia Conference pastors in 1966, claiming that the special *Gospel Herald* issue on Vietnam was "overstepping the proper bounds in the appeals made to government." Similarly, a *Sword and Trumpet* editorial "On Vietnam" questioned "the obligation, or even the competency, of the church, as such, to pronounce upon matters of international policy." The new theological breakthroughs achieved by the CPSC had appeared to push beyond such polarities, and these had been accepted without a murmur by the church. It seemed clear in 1966, however, that the dissent had only been deferred. As Peachey listened to conservative objections, he found them saying that the new thinking on the Lordship of Christ "was really forced on the church." As he wrote to Lapp, "the one morality concept is still a bone that sticks in many a throat."[22]

Moreover, this feeling that the denominational peace committee had "overstepped its mandate" in its appeals to the state was accentuated by a revival of the traditionalists' fear, expressed so often during the World War II years, of the kind of liberal pacifist company it appeared people like Peachey were keeping. Joining fifty mainline church and Jewish leaders in an antiwar protest delegation to the White House and to Congress as Hershberger and Lapp had done in 1965 did not sit well among many conservative Mennonites. They were "deeply concerned that the Biblical position be clearly distinguished from the popular pacifism," asserted J. Otis Yoder to Peachey in 1966. "How can people like your committee not see that the way you have identified with the F. O.R, the N. C. C. and the like can only lead to classification with them?"[23]

For at least some of the MC dissidents, this theological conservatism came with currents of nationalism as well. While fighting hard against a perceived Mennonite political and cultural drift, a sector of the traditionalists themselves displayed a willingness to accept outside analyses as well—only it was from the far right, instead of the left, of the national American political spectrum. Indeed, just as the larger church reinforced peace and justice issues as a basis for a new Mennonite identity, conservatives may have seized right-wing politics to bolster their own identity while dress codes and other nonconformity measures crumbled. Writing from Eastern Mennonite College in Virginia, John A. Lapp posited in 1966 that "the embattled hierarchy here is turning to the political sphere on which to preserve their identity. Since the traditional Mennonite forms are fast disappearing this will be a new line to separate the sheep from the goats."[24]

Hence conservative leader Sanford Shetler expressed abundant sympathy for the racial program of Alabama Governor George Wallace in 1966 and wondered scornfully, "Just how much is any Anabaptist going to become excited about the fact that negroes can or cannot vote?" Perhaps, to be fair to Shetler, such comments emanated at least in part from a traditional Mennonite antipathy to voting rather than to blatant racial insensitivity, but Shetler's foreign policy concerns also demonstrated an absorption of American nationalist influences. He took a strange position for someone so committed to pure biblical nonresistance, railing in his publication *Guidelines for Today* against a perceived U.S. imbalance in nuclear missiles and warning that antiwar activists were joining with a "fifth column of leftists and communists" to "disarm" the Unites States both militarily and spiritually.[25]

Accordingly, MC leadership moved here, as they had done in World War II, to set up some kind of a dialogue with their dissidents and to somehow placate their fears. Most importantly, the CPSC named a number of the most prominent antagonists to a "Preparatory Commission for the Study of Church–State Relations" and had them sit down for a series of meetings in 1968–70. The discussion took place almost totally on issues of theology and ethics, with the commission arriving at a number of points of agreement and dispute. After much wrangling, they could agree that "there is but one standard of morality and righteousness to which all men are called" and that Christians might sometimes communicate their concerns to those in government. More problematic for the group remained differences in such issues as the proper functions of government, the relationship of the Christian to nationalism and patriotism, and the old sticking point, "What is the extent of the Lordship of Christ?" J. R. Burkholder, a major participant in these extensive debates, remembered later that the discussion went "round and round on the kingdom of God and the lordship of Christ." Still, while disagreement remained, the consultation did much to ease the tensions.[26]

Neither could the MCC Peace Section remain immune from the growing dissent to Mennonite antiwar advocacy, a development that became apparent relatively early. By the fall of 1966, Peace Section members had received enough indication of this dissatisfaction that before they could go on with further public statements, they agreed, they had to attempt to work through some of the differences in the constituency. To that end, the Peace Section Executive Committee agreed to call together a consultation with representatives from different Mennonite groups. At the consultation that December in Minneapolis, the Peace Section leadership quickly found any kind of consensus on the war very difficult to achieve. Given the presence of delegates such as J. Otis Yoder and Sanford Shetler, along with a number of both MC and GC activists, not surprisingly the consultation could arrive at little agreement on several different doctrinal issues. As *The Mennonite* reported, they found general affirmation that the church should testify to government but differed on how and on what issues the church should speak.[27]

The initial findings statement developed at the conference emphasized the idea of one morality and the call to witness to government and did not include the traditional word *nonresistance* once. Yet when it was released in January 1967 to constituent peace committees, the refigured statement mentioned the concept of nonresistance five times and stated that "any witness to the secular order should be modest and selective." The January statement also admitted that the Peace Section needed to "develop better means for listening to the voice of the brotherhood," and to obtain "more regular and systematic communication" between the agency and the constituency. Clearly MCC chiefs themselves had listened carefully to the more conservative district peace committees.[28]

Another arena of conflict for the agency was the activities of the Peace Section's new Washington Office. Headed by GC pastor Delton Franz and functioning as MCC's "listening post" in Washington, the office began operations in August 1968 with three directed purposes: to function as an observer of legislation, to equip constituent groups to speak to the state, and to serve as a "source of knowledge and expertise on peace and social issues related to government." Stated by themselves, these appeared somewhat innocuous and worthy goals; and, as the Peace Section continually reminded its constituency, "The Washington Office is not an office for lobbying." Franz plunged into the task energetically and soon was reporting back on the status of legislation affecting a large number of arguably "Mennonite" concerns: nuclear weapons, Vietnam, antipoverty and civil rights

bills, and the like. He even offered charts "rating" congressional representatives from Mennonite areas on their relative support or opposition to
such concerns.[29]

Depending on one's perspective, Franz and the Washington Office were
either fulfilling the mandate for which the office had been established or
were "telling the government what to do" in a manner completely out of
bounds with traditional Mennonite church-state separation. Conservatives held to the latter interpretation. In a blistering letter to Franz, for instance, Emmet Lehman pointed out how large numbers of Mennonites did
not support the type of positions he advocated or agree with the statements
of opinion passed by Mennonite leaders and conferences upon which
Franz based those opinions. Instead, in the past decade he found "a tremendous gap between the positions and pronouncements of the leadership
of the Mennonite Church and the lay members." Moreover, Lehman
wrote, if the function of the office was to advocate policy or represent principally "the political actionist elements of our constituency," then the new
Washington Office had become "a first class fraud . . . whose result will be
to further divide our constituency along the line of our political positions."[30]

The grassroots constituency was indeed divided. The same lines of fracture that generated so much heat among the Mennonite leadership perco-
lated down to effect similar cleavages among the laity. As with disgruntled
pastors and church officers, the resistance to Mennonite antiwar advocacy
in the churches stemmed from two sometimes overlapping, sometimes diverging sources of dissent. First, there were a number of Mennonites who,
like Virginia and Lancaster conservatives, still took their bearings from the
old, unmodified, two-kingdom theology. As one progressive scholar wrote
to Lapp in 1972, "Unless we start with the assumption that Bender's thinking is still intact in the minds of many people in our circle we are simply not
realistic." Church peace committees ran into evidence time and again that,
as Grant Stoltzfus had suggested, many Mennonites were "still in the
Bender past. It was safe and predictable." Asking their people to write to
Congress as part of the "Peace Sunday" program in 1968, for example,
the CPSC heard from one pastor who regretfully informed them that "we
cannot fully endorse your recommendations to Congress as nonresistant
Christians seeking to maintain the separation of church and state." Despite
MCC executive secretary William Snyder's observation that "Harold
Bender was not regarded as canonical except in his own group," many GC
churches rooted their opposition in the older theology as well. As the

church council of Salem Mennonite in Freeman, South Dakota, informed the PSCC, "We do not feel it to be a function of the church to dictate to the United States or other government what course of action they should take."[31]

Secondly, with the easing of social boundaries that they had constructed between themselves and outside society, many Mennonites began to adopt the political perspectives of other rural and small-town white Protestants. In other words, like many of their neighbors, they evinced a good deal of affinity for the patriotic, "God and country" sentiments that served as the backbone of the national support for the war. The leadership realized this quite early. For example, Lapp recognized in 1965 that his fellow Mennonites were "really becoming more and better supporters of the war" because of the general prosperity of the times and also because of "the subtle and cunning ways" that the administration presented its program. Likewise an MC pastor in Kansas testified that "many of our people have absorbed much of the Johnson propaganda and stand with him."[32]

Many Mennonite teenagers also cast off enough of the blandishments of an antiwar popular culture to stand with their national leaders on the war. A I-W administrator testified to the "tremendous amount of respect" I-W men manifested for government militarism, something they had been taught "very strongly in their homes and churches." After spending an evening at a Mennonite youth meeting in 1968, one MC administrator discovered that the youths there evinced little interest in the denominational peace teaching. One young man informed him that three quarters of his Mennonite fellows "would go into the army if it weren't for their parents."[33]

Many older GC Mennonites testified to their devotion to their country in its global battle with communism and repeatedly communicated their disapproval of their church's antiwar advocacy. Here again the experiences that they or their near ancestors had endured under communism in Russia probably played a role. As he pastored the heavily Russian Alexanderwohl congregation near Goessel, Kansas, Ronald Krehbiel found that his congregants had "deep feelings against communism." While most congregants were pacifists and three quarters of his youth opted for conscientious objection, many of them nonetheless seemed to Krehbiel to be happy that "American troops were fighting in Vietnam and stopping communism." The antiwar articles Shelly published in *The Mennonite* evoked a large number of angry responses from such Mennonites. One reader cried that Mennonite participation in antiwar marches "is giving aid and comfort to the communists"; another found in such protests evidence of "the work of Satan" in the church. Not only GC leaders but also other denominational peace activists heard from these patriotic dissenters. Young antiwar radicals with the Bethel College Peace Club received a letter from one Kansas woman, for instance, who suggested, "Use your influence to get our government to resume bombing on targets that count and force North Vietnam to a settlement." One man wrote to say that the club's activities "makes me regret I graduated from Bethel" and that he hoped his son "will answer his draft call like a man."[34]

Finally, it is important to note here the continuing influence of an extremist fundamentalism on a fair proportion of Mennonites. As Lapp observed in 1967, "There are a large number of people who listen to McIntyre [*sic*] in his 'holy war against communism.'" Young Mennonite radicals, observing McIntire's "March for Victory" in Washington in October 1970, were surprised and distressed to discover a fair sprinkling of older Mennonites marching in McIntire's ranks.[35]

In sum, as the war in Vietnam effectively polarized much of larger American society, on a smaller scale it registered much the same effect on American Mennonites. Both church activists and conservatives could claim grassroots support for their programs and opinions because the grassroots itself was bitterly divided. In time these cleavages not only existed among individuals but also pervaded congregations. One student of this matter found a large number of churches holding to the view that "politics should not be preached over the pulpit." Much of the conservative critique reflected this calling. The way to reach society, it was thought, was through individual regeneration, which would happen through prayer, repentance, and salvation. As CPSC secretary Peachey observed in 1967, "We are being pulled in sometimes opposing directions by influence around us: groups stressing personal conversion, on the one hand, and groups stressing social action on the other." In other words, Mennonite polarization during the 1960s was in itself a reflection of the degree of Mennonite acculturation. For it reflected much of the same patterns and divisions that, as Wuthnow demonstrated, divided a wide number of Protestant denominations in these tumultuous years.[36]

At times the church polarization seemed palpable, omnipresent, and bitter to those it touched. At a Mennonite missions conference in 1970, "the polarities became almost more than the convention could tolerate," observed John A. Lapp. "One crowd cheered criticism of Washington, another cheered 'our great country.' Something has to give."[37]

FERMENT AMONG THE YOUTH

Though serious, such fragmentation was at least nothing new in a group as historically contentious and divided as American Mennonites. Two decades before, Mennonites had emerged from another period of war as fractious as they appeared at any point in the 1960s but had still maintained and even strengthened the foundational consensus that allowed them to pursue simultaneously the goals of good citizenship and faithful discipleship. The issue that would finally lead to the breakup of the quiet compromise they had fashioned with the state, in fact, did not concern the theological bickering, acceptance of nationalist sentiment, or other such immediately apparent causes of Mennonite fragmentation. Instead, the fundamental issue devolved from the bedrock Mennonite concept of conscientious objection, and it would be fashioned not as much by Mennonite leadership as by Mennonite youth.[38]

The leadership certainly remained aware of the growing inadequacy of the I-W arrangement. Harding stated the issue quite plainly in 1966. "Safe and sound I-W service is almost, if not totally sinful," he wrote to Bohn, "when a generation of young men are increasingly being fed into the fires." At a joint CPSC-PSCC meeting in 1967, members wrestled with signals of draft resistance among their young people; and while they could support it themselves, they could come to "no clarity" on what they could "call the churches to do" on the matter. Meeting separately, the PSCC did ask Bohn to write to churches to ask them to receive draft cards that members might turn in, although the evidence remains scanty whether any GC churches did so.[39]

Still, when conscientious objection appeared threatened, once again the Mennonite leadership sprang to its defense. In May 1967, in one of Congress's periodic renewals of the draft, the House Armed Services Committee recommended a new draft bill that proposed, among other measures, to draft all COs into the military and then furlough them to civilian work. In contrast to their befuddled paralysis in the crisis of World War I and their heavy reliance on more sophisticated Quaker allies in the early days of World War II, this time Mennonite peace leaders descended on Washington to lobby with skill and effectiveness. The MCC Peace Section immediately sprang into action. John E. Lapp ambled over to see his neighbor and good friend from Lansdale, Pennsylvania, Congressman Richard Schweiker, who sat on the committee. Lapp patiently explained Mennonite concerns to him. The Peace Section airmailed a special letter on this development to its members, and within a few days Lapp, Hershberger, and other leaders had hustled down to Washington to engage in a full-scale lobbying effort with other Historic Peace Church representatives. It was all a mistake, admitted one representative; the bill was never aimed at "legitimate" COs such as the Mennonites, but rather at "phonies," the young men who were insincerely declaring themselves as COs in order to oppose the Vietnam War. Within a week, with Schweiker quoting extensively from an MCC statement in congressional debate, Congress returned to the established language on conscientious objection. Of course, in their humble testimony, Mennonite leaders carried the veiled fist of massive Mennonite civil disobedience if the provisions remained unchanged, and they pointedly alluded to the Mennonite experience in World War I as a reminder. Even so, Mennonite participants in the affair received some warm congressional kudos; several congressmen were effusive in their praise of gentle John Lapp and his "very touching plea for peace."[40]

Mennonite leaders and young radicals found very different lessons in the affair. To the peace bureaucrats, the entire episode testified dramatically to the need for a Mennonite "listening post" in Washington so that they would never again be caught by such a surprise. They established MCC's Washington Office shortly thereafter as a direct result of the experience. Young Mennonite radicals, agonizing over the bloody war in Vietnam and the threat the draft posed to so many young men, saw it differently. Uncomfortable with the easy way out of the draft dilemma furnished by their Mennonite pedigree, such dissidents viewed the incident as a classic case of Mennonite defense of their own special position. Thus it remained for Mennonite young people to refocus the issue of draft registration in a development that once again took shape in the potent intermixture of Mennonite tradition and the inroads of acculturation.[41]

Like other young people of their generation, Mennonite college students reacted with energy and passion to the dissent that leaders they respected articulated against the government's war in Vietnam. Indeed, before long these young people had begun to respond with more energy than some of their elders found comfortable. For instance, the Bethel College Peace Club carried out a "Repentance Walk and Mail" in the fall of 1966. The initial impetus for the march came originally from the college administration, which had asked the club to sponsor a college convocation on November 11. After meetings that fall with PSCC Secretary Bohn and with Atlee Beechy, former director of Mennonite relief activities in Vietnam, the club decided to include in this campus meeting a three-mile march to

FIGURE 8.2. *The "Repentance Walk and Mail" against the war in Vietnam, Bethel College, fall 1966. Courtesy of The Mennonite.*

the main post office in downtown Newton, where they would mail letters to congressmen to express their opposition to the war. Given faculty and wider Mennonite support and the quiet, respectful demeanor of the student organizers, the administration also initially supported the march, holding that much of the reason for the existence of the college lay behind what the Peace Club was trying to do.[42]

In other times of war, however, Mennonites had found it politic to stifle their dissent; and as the college administration soon discovered, wartime opposition had its risks even in the 1960s. Vernon Neufeld, the college president, and three college board members living in and closely associated with the Newton business community began receiving hundreds of telephone calls from citizens opposing the march. Outraged by a protest march on Veterans Day, the local American Legion and VFW posts quickly organized a parade to tour through Newton later on the same day. One former student came to campus to warn darkly of local toughs buying yellow paint and baseball bats with which to attack the marchers. Given the polarization over the war that had come to pervade Mennonite ranks, even more disturbing opposition came from sources closer to home. The campus paper, along with the nearby *Mennonite Weekly Review*, vehemently opposed the activity. Several students threatened to intervene physically in the march and hung an effigy of a peace activist from the administration building. In response to such pressure, declaring that "great and irreparable harm" had already come to the college because of the plans and that "greater harm" would follow, Neufeld asked the students to call off the march. The young activists compromised, deciding to proceed instead to a neighboring post office on the outskirts of town and thereby avert any confrontations. Dressed conservatively in accordance with a discipline the students circulated—jackets and ties for the men, skirts for the women—nearly a hundred students, faculty, and even some local Mennonite ministers held a service of repentance for their nation's course in Vietnam and then marched the few blocks in silent protest.[43]

The lines of acculturation, as administrators at a number of Mennonite colleges discovered, could cut a number of different ways. While the lowering of cultural boundaries had rendered some Mennonites more receptive to patriotic perspectives, for many Mennonite college students this openness to outside society and culture had an opposite effect. Like fellow students at secular colleges and universities—where increasing numbers of these Mennonite students enrolled—they began to march to the beat of an antiwar popular culture.

The student-based antiwar movement plainly exerted considerable influence on the political analyses and activities of young Mennonite dissidents. As some 525 Mennonite students and young Voluntary Service workers descended on Washington for the massive peace march of November 1969, the Washington Office found this a clear indication "that something is 'blowin' in the wind' across the Mennonite college landscape." Not only did such students regularly begin to participate in this and other national marches, but they also organized a number of similar activities on their own campuses in accordance with patterns of national student dissent. Students at Bethel, Goshen, and other Mennonite schools organized antiwar "teach-ins." Such an event at Goshen College in October 1969, for example, featured talks by Doug Hostetter, recently returned from MCC service in Vietnam, and a Mennonite veteran who relayed "a GI's view of militarism and the war in Vietnam." The activists followed these talks with a time for letter-writing to Congress and a silent memorial in the campus plaza. Students at Bluffton College organized an antiwar letter-writing session at the student union and marched solemnly to the post office downtown to mail their pleas to Congress. At the town's Memorial Day parade in 1969, traditionally dominated by patriotic groups, Bluffton students entered an antiwar float and pulled it down Main Street to the accompaniment of a mixture of cheers and boos.[44]

Some of the activists forged even more explicit links to national protest movements and leaders. Students from the Indiana University chapter of SDS traveled to Goshen for a two-day conference in March 1966, highlighted by an address by national SDS chair Clark Kissinger. Goshen students and SDS members found their worldviews sometimes converging and sometimes conflicting, but relations proceeded amicably nevertheless. Writing later to thank the Goshen activists for the "stimulating and educational confrontation of views you made possible," the Indiana University SDS chair said that "probably no other meeting with a student group has reminded us so forcefully of the values that must underlie our politics within SDS."[45]

Activists at Bethel began to push even harder against both the war and the inherited modes of Mennonite political passivity. They were led by a cohort of energetic new students, including Kirsten Zerger, whose mother, Karolyn Kaufman, had borne the brunt of such ugly hostility as a teenager in Newton during World War II. The Bethel activists soon formulated more exact ties with the national movement in their antiwar protests. Fresh from Vietnam teach-ins and fasts the previous year, the Bethel College Peace Club found seventy-two students, about a sixth of the student body, at its first meeting in the fall of 1969. The Bethel Peace Club quickly decided to orient its activities around the national efforts of the "Vietnam Moratorium Committee," which had called for a national day of protest that October 15. They began corresponding with the committee's national office in Washington and sent out speakers into a number of local churches and civic groups to explain their protests. For the "Vietnam Moratorium" day, Bethel activists held a rally and four-day vigil on campus, ringing an old bell once for every once of the 40,000 American casualties in Vietnam. Then, brushing off administrative objections and considerable friction and resistance from much of the student body, the protesters marched to downtown Newton to mail antiwar letters and continued marching twenty miles south to Wichita. The event generated national publicity, with a picture of the bell-ringing on the front page of the *New York Times* and the Kansas students featured prominently in national television news coverage. Even the plans of the march elated national "Vietnam Moratorium" organizers. "Bethel College made my whole day," wrote one of them from Washington that September. "Everyone in the office thought I was out of my mind as I ran around in ecstatic glee talking about the Mennonites and their bell."[46]

Nor did Vietnam serve as the only focus of students' political expression. As in the move for "student power" at larger campuses, students at Mennonite schools mounted protests against more prosaic grievances as dorm

FIGURE 8.3. *Ringing the bell at Bethel College, Vietnam Moratorium demonstrations, October 1969. Courtesy of The Mennonite.*

rules, dress codes, and compulsory chapel attendance. Underground newspapers sprang up at Bethel as well as at Goshen, where administrators found an issue of "The Menno-Pause" particularly offensive and expelled its four student instigators. "You can definitely see a growing radicalism among the students," commented Bethel's student body president in 1969. One college administrator saw it differently. Noting that his students had attended "the urban high school and associated with the modern American kids," he characterized some of them as caught up in an "anti-Mennonite rebellion." At Bluffton College in the late 1960s, recalled a former student, "spontaneous demonstrations" often burst forth at night, expressing no viewpoint in particular but accompanied by loud rock music and dancing. A few times such gatherings brought the county sheriffs onto campus.[47]

The impact of the national protests not only involved a political acculturation to the antiwar movement, but for many radicalizing young Mennonites, it also involved a cultural borrowing as well. A generation before, many of their parents had blazed the trail in adopting the clothing and hairstyles of larger society. Now these Mennonite young people did the same, going barefoot, wearing blue jeans and colorful clothing, the men growing beards and long hair, the women foregoing makeup and hairpins. To their elders, many of whom had just come to terms themselves with the styles of modern life, this new turn would pose a tremendous problem. As *Gospel Herald* editor Paul Erb admitted, viewing the countercultural appearance of draft resisters at the 1969 MC general conference meeting, this "modern style of nonconformity" was "not in our tradition," and it "gave a great deal of offense."[48]

Of course, the young radicals had their own analyses of their elders' discomfort with their attire. Draft resister Doug Baker viewed this displeasure as potent evidence of the degree to which the older generation had accepted the styles and values of larger American society. Recognizing that "we were immediately identified as 'hippies'" at the 1969 MC general conference meeting, Baker maintained that "Mennonites had succeeded so well in getting rid of their ethnic hang-ups and prejudices, that they felt definitely threatened by those who challenged the society they now identified with." Indeed, in a situation in which so many had so recently acculturated, claims that certain styles were not in the Mennonite "tradition" seemed on shaky ground. Responding to the intense criticism of the resisters' appearance at the 1969 meeting, Goshen campus pastor Harold Bauman reminded his ✓ fellow delegates of a time twenty years before when "you were almost ostracized from the church for having a crew cut." Even more to the point was a young Virginia Conference scholar's observation in 1970: "While the parents of my generation were still trying to keep the neckties off their sons, and long hair on them," he pointed out, "the parents of a generation only ten years younger are struggling to keep the neckties on and the long hair *Conrad* off."[49] *Brunk*

Finally, as young Mennonites began to follow the antiwar analyses they found in larger society to an open disobedience of their government, they did so in ways greatly influenced by the national protests of the times. ∟ Twenty years before, nonregistration would have functioned to reinforce Mennonite distinctiveness in a society seeped in militaristic fervor. By the time that growing numbers of young Mennonites began to reconsider their church's and their own cooperation with the draft in the late 1960s, however, draft resistance had become, as historian and activist James Juhnke recognized in 1969, "a thoroughly American phenomenon."[50]

Even so, it is inaccurate to wholly characterize the protest of young Mennonites as merely and wholly a product of antiwar dissent on the nation's college campuses. In spite of the levels of Mennonite acculturation, these remained young people who had been raised in a very conservative religious world, one different enough that most could not resonate fully with an angry and somewhat hedonistic antiwar popular culture. Mennonite theologian John Howard Yoder pointed this out quite perceptively in 1970, arguing that campus peace activism "leaves many young Mennonites emotionally stranded. They tend to sympathize with the antiwar goals, yet to feel estranged by the ideological character and nastiness and irreverence of the style of activists." Thus it was that throughout this era, young Mennonites formulated their resistance deeply rooted in their Mennonite world. As the PSCC secretary observed after meeting with some Mennonite draft resisters, "Persons such as these are taking their historic Mennonite tradition very seriously, the tradition that has been taught them by their elders in the church."[51]

Like their elders, Mennonite young people increasingly began to highlight the inadequacy of safe, government-approved I-W service as any kind of dissent to injustice and war. "Much alive on our campuses is now the feeling that I-W is not enough of an answer to the draft," relayed a pastor in the fall of 1965. As these youth worked toward resisting the draft, the inadequacy of I-W loomed prominent in their reasoning. Arguing that CO status "makes us easy to handle and it gets us out of the government's hair," a budding radical studying at Harvard wondered "whether some Mennonite men ought to sever their connections with Selective Service." Explaining his noncooperation, David Rensberger explained that "allowing oneself to be quietly sent off to hospitals and farms too often silences and renders impotent the peace witness." Sometimes the finger came back, pointed quite directly at an older generation that had so carefully carved out a protected space for Mennonites in the American warfare state. "Mennonites stopped fighting the battle against militarism when we were granted a nice easy way out, two years of alternative service," wrote an angry Bluffton College student to *The Mennonite*. Unable to decide whether or not to register for the draft, Nathan Habegger blamed his elders, crying, "You've allowed the military to take over our lives in this country, and now I am faced with allowing this to happen to me."[52]

As the basis for this analysis and many others, young Mennonite dissidents followed the course mapped out by other creative dissenters in recent Mennonite history. Like some of their elders, they discovered in Anabaptism a rich basis for group identification and legitimation for their dissent. In particular, the younger radicals brought out into the open and forcibly wove into mainstream Mennonite thought the second, subsumed basis for Mennonite identity that had long functioned as a quiet underground alternative to the Quiet-in-the-Land pose. CPS radicals had pushed its edges;

civil rights activists had breathed it further into being. Now the antidraft dissidents of the 1960s would complete the reemergence of a radical, prophetic Anabaptist vision.

In the hands of these radicals, this new Anabaptist vision would look a lot like the New Left. Young draft resisters found in their radical Anabaptist ancestors a perfect model for resisting the state out of a higher obedience to God. In the early 1970s, Bethel Bible professor Alvin Beachy noticed a sharp upturn in enrollment in his class on Anabaptism. Plainly many of his students found in Anabaptism some rich resources for constructing a usable past, much as some of their elders had decades earlier. Bethel College peace activist David Janzen, for instance, rooted a 1972 analysis of "prophetic lifestyles" in a lengthy description of Anabaptist life and practice, pointing out how their ancestors "had no interest in preserving the state, as they were self-disciplining citizens of God's kingdom." One young radical complained that their parent's "assimilation . . . into the world" had "hidden the purpose and the reality of the Anabaptist vision from the eyes of their children, thus denying them the only true way of Christian living." Goshen seminary student Wesley Mast returned his draft card to President Nixon, explaining that he did so out of a higher obedience to Christ. In this action, Mast continued, "I stand within the history of the early church who refused to take the oath to Ceasor [sic] (very similar to carrying a draft card)." Having "caught a whiff of the radical Anabaptist vision," Michael Friedman also found it necessary to return his draft card. Yet he viewed many fellow Mennonites as "still too intoxicated with the satisfactions of having finally achieved first-class citizenship in America" to "identify with the resistance movement." "We have become 'respectable citizens,'" Friedman lamented. "We have become thoroughly acculturated."[53]

In these comments, Friedman framed the fundamental issue perfectly and unmistakably. These young people had been moved to action by the suffering in Vietnam but had found the traditional Mennonite answer to such suffering inadequate. Positive service, manifested in a government-approved alternative service arrangement, would no longer suffice. For many of these young radicals, it had come down to a choice between pursuing the demands of good citizenship or remaining faithful to an underground, prophetic stream in Mennonite teaching and history. These resisters had, moreover, arrived at this juncture through a potent combination of initiatives and influences. They had inherited years of their church's learning to speak to the state, a voice that was now undergirded and reformulated by currents in the outside society and culture. Having come to this choice between conflicting loyalties, the young radicals gathered themselves, in the summer and fall of 1969, to thrust it upon the church at large.

"CHRIST IS BIGGER THAN THE UNITED STATES"

Just as many young people had arrived at this juncture out of a mixing of their Mennonite tradition with larger movements in society, so too had the two larger Mennonite bodies been perfectly positioned to confront this choice through their interaction with the process of acculturation. There were new winds blowing in the church. At bottom, these new commitments had come to be shaped by new historical models articulated by church leaders and activists, usable pasts that legitimated such changes for a great mass of the laity. Bender's Anabaptist Vision had been followed by other visions that had increasingly emphasized the prophetic nature of the Christian calling. Now the accumulated weight of these Anabaptist visions would bring the Mennonite churches to one of those periodic turning points in which they, like their Anabaptist ancestors, would be called upon to decide to whom their ultimate loyalty belonged.

Thus it was that when a collection of Mennonite draft resisters arrived at the churchwide MC general conference meeting in Turner, Oregon, in August 1969, to try to obtain church endorsement for their actions, they received a much warmer welcome than they had expected. In successive meetings with church hierarchy, while hearing the uneasiness and doubts from some delegates, the resisters discovered a number of MC leaders surprisingly receptive to their message. Earlier that month, CPSC secretary Hackman had written to the church's executive secretary to say that he had found "these young men . . . quite responsible in their approach to this issue" and recommending that, if need be, the CPSC scrap its entire agenda at the conference to deal with their concerns. In its allotted time before the conference delegates, the CPSC did just that. Lapp led off with a lengthy introduction outlining the recent history of the Mennonite relation with the state, showing how their respect for government and the respect Mennonite quiet service and humble behavior had earned from government had placed them in a dangerous position. "If we are not careful," Lapp declared, "we may lose our spiritual life." The CPSC chairman then turned to two resisters, Doug Baker and Jon Lind, for their statements and testimony.[54]

Baker carefully rooted his argument in Mennonite history and theology. Calling for a "dynamic tension" between church and state, he referred to

FIGURE 8.4. *Mennonite draft resisters Tim Beachy and Jon Lind talk with a delegate at the Mennonite Church's conference at Turner, Oregon, in 1969. Courtesy of Hope Lind and Oregon Mennonite Historical and Genealogical Society.*

the church's 1937 statement on nonresistance and claimed that the resisters reaffirmed the position of noncooperation outlined in this statement. Reminding delegates of their Anabaptist heritage and quoting prophetic passages in the book of Amos, he argued that "changing times and changing situations demand that as Christians we reinterpret our relationship with the world." The resisters' statement attempted just such a reinterpretation. "By cooperating with [Selective Service], we, in effect," the statement read, "are sanctioning its actions." Therefore, they pledged, they would no longer cooperate, not out of an "attempt to willfully rebel against the state, but out of our first loyalty and obedience to God."[55]

Baker was followed to the podium by Jonathan Lind, who relayed some of his experiences as an MCC relief worker in Vietnam and explained how his decision to destroy his draft card grew out of such experiences. Lapp then introduced ten CPSC resolutions in line with the resisters' arguments. These resolutions reaffirmed the church's 1937 and 1951 statements and also its commitment to the legitimacy of alternative service, counseling MC Mennonites to "respect civil authority." Yet the resolutions also recognized "the validity of noncooperation as a legitimate witness" and pledged "the offices of our brotherhood to minister to young men in any eventuality they incur costly discipleship."[56]

Given the political polarities that had come to rend the churches, the CPSC's unusual report occasioned a good deal of predictable controversy. One delegate, a pastor from Denver, endorsed the resisters' position as "a possibly more legitimate form of peace witness for Mennonite young men than the present alternative service program." Another delegate agreed, placing the decision for noncooperation alongside of those made by Conrad Grebel and other Anabaptist heroes. Conservatives focused their objections on what they saw as an "immature and premature" resolution, with J. Otis Yoder urging delegates to table the issue for further study. In the end, however, the refusal of the delegates to do this and their endorsement of the CPSC's statement affirming noncooperation with only minor modifications testified above all else to the changes that had taken root in the church. Not only young progressive ministers but also older church stalwarts such as Orie Miller supported the move. To the great surprise of the young dissidents, so did the leader of the traditionalist forces in Virginia, evangelist George Brunk. Initially leery of the statement and its countercultural presenters, Brunk testified publicly that after talking with them he came away "impressed with their spirits." The support of trusted conservatives like Brunk did much to assuage the anxieties of others of like mind. Such conversions, both at the meeting and in the years of speaking to the state before it, led to the conference's final passage of the resolutions with only a few dissenting votes.[57]

For the General Conference Mennonite Church, the real battle over affirming noncooperation took place at the Western District Conference meeting in October 1969. There members of the Bethel Peace Club and local VS workers brought two resolutions to the conference for adoption. One pledged the conference's active support to the club's Vietnam Moratorium activities, a motion that delegates, motivated in part by their objections to the young people's appearance, narrowly voted down. The other motion, which Shelly called "perhaps the most radical document of all," fared better. By a vote of 180 to 146, the delegates declared, "We recognize total noncooperation with Selective Service as a meaningful witness of one's beliefs and as a witness compatible within the historical traditions of the Mennonite church." This resolution did not pass, of course, without a good deal of conservative unhappiness both inside and outside of the conference meeting. Yet delegates at the Western District's conference the next year voted down a motion brought by dissenting delegates to rescind this support for noncooperation. Admitting that the church's endorsement of draft resistance had effected "a considerable amount of controversy and discussion," the Western District Conference Peace and Social Concerns Committee still argued for its maintenance, pointing out that "the Anabaptist movement was inherently one of civil disobedience."[58]

With less discord, both the larger GCMC and the MCC Peace Section subsequently moved to pledge their support to Mennonite draft resisters. Dominated by young radicals, the Peace Section's November 1969 assembly rather easily arrived at a similarly worded statement. Likewise, while the topic of draft resistance brought "vigorous dialogue and some disagreement, as one would expect," reported a participant at the GCMC's 1971 triennial conference, delegates approved a new peace statement, entitled "The Way of Peace," by a 73 percent majority vote. Not only did the statement recognize both noncooperation and tax refusal as a "valid witness," but went on for some pages to reaffirm the preeminent importance of the commands of Christian discipleship over those of citizenship. Reiterating their obligation to obey the government and declaring their support for alternative service arrangements, the statement pounded away with the message that "a Christian owes ultimate allegiance to Jesus Christ." If a young man felt this higher loyalty mandated his noncooperation with the draft, then the church would support him in this decision.[59]

True to their words, the leadership of both groups went on to manifest this support for their draft resisters in a number of ways. Soon after the conference sessions, for instance, the CPSC moved to provide financial, counseling, and other types of support to MC noncooperators. Perceptive observers discerned some support for the young men in the churches. A member of a Peace Team, itinerating through Indiana and Michigan churches in 1971, found that "by and large draft resistance was accepted as a viable Christian alternative." Even in the more conservative areas, church leaders stuck by young men who chose to follow this more costly draft alternative. Given the disproportionate number of Lancaster County youth who resisted the draft, the peace committee there repeatedly discussed ways of providing support to these young men, even though they acknowledged that "many of our brotherhood" disagreed with draft noncooperation. For instance, in 1972 they contributed three hundred dollars to a special fund to assist draft noncooperators.[60]

Throughout much of this century, both major Mennonite groups had found it possible to remain good Mennonites and good Christians through simultaneously pursuing alternatives that would render them good citizens as well. Now they had come to an unmistakable fork in the road. The supporters of the churches' affirmation of noncooperation often argued that this move was perfectly in line with the contours of Mennonite history, an argument that admittedly carried some weight. Mennonites had always emphasized the demands of the Christian conscience as preeminent over any particular directives from the state, they pointed out. Moreover, both church groups continued to acknowledge the legitimacy of alternative service as they had traditionally done. At their churchwide conferences in 1969–71, delegates had only taken the additional step of recognizing the validity of noncooperation with the draft for young men whose consciences did not allow them to go along.

Yet given the shape of postwar Mennonite-state relations, this additional step assumed an immense significance. If church leaders and peace activists failed to concede this point, their conservative opposition saw the decision more accurately as a clear break with the past. Had this move, worried one Mennonite, "put into jeopardy the work of the last fifty years done by our sincere leaders and granted us by a sympathetic government?" Virginia Conference dissident J. Ward Shank interpreted the events with equal clarity. "I believe that the action of this conference represents a new turn in our 'peace' position," he avowed. "We are now on another watershed."[61]

The deeper implications of this decision ran along several related lines. First, it indicated that, as Juhnke suggested in 1969, the "great compromise" that Mennonites had established with the federal government had come to an end. After the debacle of World War I, both the Mennonites and the government worked hard to come up with some kind of formula that would save the government from the trouble, and the church from the horror, of having to imprison quiet, obedient citizens for reasons of conscience. The bargain they struck revolved around the state-endowed privilege of alternative service. In return for this special position, created in part through Mennonite-state negotiation and designed for religious groups like themselves, the government desired only ready Mennonite cooperation. In addition, as the state assumed the military commitments accompanying its newfound role as a world policeman, it needed groups such as the Mennonites to stifle any larger dissent to this arrangement that might arise out of an underground, prophetic stream in their own tradition.[62]

As Juhnke observed, church leaders accepted this deal happily and nearly completely. Accenting a two-kingdom ethic that defined the state's affairs as none of their concern, some leaders could easily fit the pact into certain stresses in their theology. Even better, the benefits they received from the arrangement were bounteous.[63] Safe from a persecuting government, the church could launch new missions programs, educational organizations, and relief efforts. Moreover, as this study has demonstrated, in an era in which this ethnoreligious group faced dramatic social and economic changes, this compromise came endowed with even more crucial advantages. In exchange for merely their cooperation and their silence—tendencies their history and outlook had rendered them ripe for anyway—Mennonites received by far the better end of the bargain. They received space from the state to enter modern America together, as Mennonites. This compromise allowed the church as an organized entity room to successfully negotiate the pressures of acculturation and to bring their people safely and intact into some kind of accommodation with national society.

Perhaps the only problem with the arrangement is that it went too far. In their glad acceptance of these liberal provisions, church leaders had grown inattentive to the prophetic undercurrents in their tradition, passed down from ancestors whom the state had burned at the stake. As young draft resisters confronted the church in 1969, John E. Lapp wondered "whether we are not where we are today because we have joined hands closer with Selective Service than we intended." And as Mennonite young people applied their tradition to some of the larger dissenting currents moving in their society, many arrived at the point at which they could uphold this compromise no longer. After all, "burning at the stake is a tradition no one revives with enthusiasm," conceded *The Mennonite* in 1969, "but it still may be the most Mennonite tradition of all."[64]

One observer at the 1969 Peace Section assembly noted that "noncooperation with Selective Service has our Mennonite people scared white."[65] The young people had forced them to finally confront a decision that this compromise had helped them avoid for four decades, a decision that drew a solid line between the allure of good citizenship and the demands of their faith. Through their service and relief efforts, Mennonites had conveniently found it possible to pursue both simultaneously. In fact, for nearly two decades, the closest Mennonites had come to officially protesting the compromise they had arranged with the state occurred when the government had temporarily excused them from it.

Now Mennonites found themselves forced by their youth to choose between these two alternatives, a choice that their entrance into national society had made all the more disconcerting. As a minister told a member of a Peace Team trying to get across to congregations the new currents in Mennonite peace teaching in 1971, "These people have worked hard to be accepted as good community citizens. They don't want to hear about peace issues you are raising, even if it is part of the faith they claim. It makes them different." Mennonites had emerged from their insulated communities to take on roles as productive, respected citizens and had found these roles a source of tremendous satisfaction. No longer were they queer members of an isolated religious sect. Through their voluntary service to the poor and needy in a hundred different projects, they demonstrated that they were neither "slackers" nor parasites willing to accept the goods of a wealthy society but unwilling to sacrifice on its behalf. Confronted by youth in "hippie" dress, demanding their opposition to a society they had worked so hard to get into, it is little wonder that so many Mennonites reacted so vehemently. For example, when considering the Bethel Peace Club's anti-war resolution, more than one delegate at the 1969 Western District Conference session argued that "a public resolution such as this may be harmful to our public image." Even more to the point was Harding's question about the Mennonite response to Vietnam in 1965. "Are we prepared to seek alternatives to our nation's present path," he asked, "alternatives that may carry us out of the mainstream of American life—just at a time when we thought we were being accepted?" The answer, at least as decided at the church conferences, would be yes—but very, very painfully so.[66]

Finally, it is necessary to realize that the number of actual Mennonite draft resisters, like the number of war tax refusers, remained very small. Peace Section executive secretary Walt Hackman discerned in 1972 that the previous two years marked the apex of Mennonite noncooperation. Two later students of the issue estimate that no more than fifty young Mennonites took this stance out of the thousands who opted for alternative service in the Vietnam war years. Beyond this small number of open nonconformists, the strains manifested by these conflicting calls of loyalty continued to polarize the churches. Given the large number of individual Mennonites and churches who preferred to hold more tightly to traditional two-kingdom theology or to fashion their stance with the state more in accord with a popular patriotism, the Mennonite decision to affirm the validity of noncooperation took on a symbolic significance as much as it did an actual one.[67]

Yet recognizing the symbolic importance of this move does not lessen its significance. For Mennonites have always shown a marked penchant to deal in the world of representations; throughout their history they have endowed symbols with tremendous evocative importance and power. Anabaptists practiced adult baptism to demonstrate their opposition to the prevailing church's identification with the state. Much later, their descendants mandated the head covering and the plain coat to portray their separation from an encroaching outside society. Motivated by different concerns, at the same time Mennonites pointed to their young volunteers in soil conservation, flood relief, or mental hospital work as evidence of their determination to contribute positively to their country. Now Mennonites would turn to the civil disobedience being practiced by a small number of their young people as a symbol of their obedience to a higher calling than that of the state. Though in doing so they broke decisively with the recent contours of Mennonite-state relations, they did remain faithful to an older tradition.

Sometimes it took outsiders to encapsulate these images best. Judge Wesley Brown of the Federal District Court in Wichita, Kansas, for instance, spent some days in April 1971, presiding over the trial of Bethel College student Dennis Koehn, charged with refusing to register for the draft. Brown had grown up among the Mennonites in Kansas and had known and respected them for years. In many respects, Brown admitted during the trial, he thought Mennonites were "a very beautiful people . . . I just hope they eventually become American citizens."[68]

Yet Judge Brown suspected that Koehn's resistance had been encouraged by his church, and this greatly dismayed and angered him. For if the church could be found to have done this, he warned, it would bring them "to another whole phase of the legal consequences." So, over the objections of Koehn's lawyer, who claimed he was putting the Mennonite churches "on trial," Brown closely questioned the witnesses brought in to testify, including Koehn's pastor, Esko Loewen, and William Keeney, academic dean at Bethel. Under the judge's persistent inquiries, Keeney laid out a short history of Mennonite nonresistance from the years of the Anabaptists through World War II. The judge admitted a number of church statements as evidence, including the Winona Lake Declaration and the Turner and Western District Conference Statements of 1969 and probed Keeney for their meaning. "Do you mean to state," he quizzed Keeney, "that the church approves and recommends the disobedience of the law of the land in respect to registering for the draft?" Keeney explained that the church remained obedient to state authority but also recognized that an individual's ultimate obedience was to God and thus would support someone acting in response to this higher calling.[69]

Altogether, Judge Brown could not conclusively determine that Koehn's church had directed him to disobey the law; the Mennonite leaders he met in the trial "did a great job of avoiding a direct answer." Yet the symbolism of Koehn's case was inescapable to him as well. "If things of this kind can be done in the name of religion," the judge cried, "what other deprivations to our society can be done in the name of religion?" In the end, having found Koehn guilty and sentenced him to an indeterminate time in prison, Brown grew strangely reflective. "Young man, you are a tragedy of our time," he concluded, "or maybe a light in the darkness for some."[70]

CHAPTER 9

Transformed Landscape, Transformed Voices

In the late 1920s and early 1930s, Orie Miller and his denomination's peace committee saw fit to deliver a variety of prescriptions to the national government. Among other issues, they communicated their concerns to the state on behalf of disarmament, foreign relations with Mexico and Nicaragua, and spreading military training programs on the nation's college campuses. Thirty-some years later, other Mennonite peace leaders relayed similar concerns to the state. In a number of different expressions, they asked the government to withdraw from armed conflict abroad, to pass strengthened civil rights legislation, and to work toward another disarmament treaty. In both instances, as Hershberger noted later, church leaders heard "a certain amount of dissent" from church members unhappy with such communications to the state, though this dissent represented a "minority view." What happened in Mennonite-state relations in the 1930s occurred again in the 1960s. So what had changed?[1]

What had, in fact, changed was the entire Mennonite landscape. As a younger man, Miller had articulated a witness to government on behalf of a people still primarily located in close-knit, isolated rural communities. For centuries his people had secured both a comfortable living and a way of life from the soil, an arrangement so satisfactory that they had rooted their entire religious identity in it. By the 1966 MCC consultation in Minneapolis, however, Miller could look around at people whose everyday environment had undergone a profound transformation in the span of his life.

These were a people not only of farms, but of cities and suburban tract homes, of apartment complexes and college dormitories. These Mennonites devoted their workday energies to a myriad of tasks in a wide variety of settings, laboring in universities and factories, offices and shopping centers. While a faithful minority still wrung a living from the soil, they did so in larger expanses of land and with complex and expensive equipment. From a glance around the conference floor, moreover, it quickly became apparent that many of these Mennonites had not only accepted the residences and occupations of their non–Mennonite neighbors, but had adopted their tastes in dress and appearance as well.

As the Mennonite world had changed, so too had the content of the Mennonite message to the state. For several centuries of their life in America, Mennonites had asked little from government except to let them alone to pursue their God in their own quiet way. Even as Miller worked with his peace committee in the late 1920s, he could not go far beyond its platform of merely "keeping government informed of our peace position" and meekly encouraging state officials "whenever possible in a wider application of the policy of goodwill." As Miller stood up in the 1966 meeting to suggest that his people articulate a Christian protest to the state, however, it was clear that the substance of such an expression would need to differ markedly from that of thirty years before.

For with their expanded landscape, Mennonites had taken on a newer self-conception as a people of peace and service, an identity that was accompanied by a wide array of new concerns and responsibilities. These new commitments had thoroughly affected the shape of Mennonite-state relations. Mennonites had begun to speak to the state about concerns that appeared to affect themselves little if at all. Two years later, the church hierarchy would set up a Mennonite office in Washington, which would function to regularly testify to the state on such matters. The reigning two-kingdom theology of Miller's youth had undergone a profound reworking; and now, under the banner of extending the Lordship of Christ to the affairs of the state, Mennonites had on hand a ready theological rationale for such political activity. Moreover, within three years, this new openness to a broadened landscape would lead directly to the breakup of the careful Mennonite arrangement with the state that Miller and others had spent many years meticulously tending. And in the next decade or two, Mennonites would, on the official level at least, give their sanction to nonviolent direct action as a legitimate means of achieving peace and justice—a strategy that had appeared an anathema to many church leaders three decades before.

Mennonite interaction with the process of acculturation in general, and the initiatives of the state in particular, had shaped and molded every step in this array of changes. More immediately, as the turbulence over Vietnam eased both in the nation at large and in the church, this interaction continued to exert a substantial influence.

ACCULTURATION AND THE LINES OF LOYALTY

As Mennonites entered the more placid waters of the 1970s, they continued to move along with the political and cultural currents of larger society. As with the nation at large, they quickly turned their attention from the war to other, more subjective concerns. With the political decisions to end the draft and withdraw American troops from Indochina, as the MCC Peace Section summarized in 1974, "the United States, and to some extent Mennonites as well, breathed a sigh of relief and tried to put peace and war issues out of their minds." Similarly, Lancaster Peace Committee secretary Ray Geigly recognized the same year that with the end of the draft there was "a noticeable decline in the interest of peace and social concern issues within our constituency."[2]

Perceptive observers noted a similar trend on Mennonite college campuses. An Eastern Mennonite College senior, for instance, noticed in 1972 "a shift in student mood from one of crusading for social reform to a more introspective passivism." A reporter on the matter for *The Mennonite* found "the look inward" prevalent at other Mennonite schools, accompanied by an apolitical evangelical enthusiasm, particularly among the younger students. Bethel's president, in fact, located a real "generation gap" between students who had arrived at college "before Kent State and Cambodia" and those who came after. The dwindling number of young radicals, of course, greeted this development with some dismay. Calling for a "radical Menno gathering" in 1972, David Janzen, for instance, grieved over "how many of the Mennos" he had known in the peace movement who had "already slipped into degrees, nuclear families, buying houses and generally dying to anything beyond themselves."[3]

This is not to claim that Mennonites reverted to patterns of an earlier political quietism; those days had vanished with the plain coat. Yet in the 1970s, as in the previous decade, Mennonites continued to take their political cues from a national society that could no longer be described as "outside" the boundaries of their world. For example, as a movement for "Women's Liberation," swept the nation, so too did Mennonites began to devote energy and attention to women's issues. The Peace Section created a special "Task Force on Women and Society," which quickly began to address itself to brass-tacks issues such as MCC employment practices and the low number of women in high-level MCC administration posts. In addition, the task force began publishing a regular monthly newsletter called *Women's Concerns Report*. The Peace Section devoted its 1973 general assembly to "the interdependence of men and women." A study guide entitled "Women in the Church" explored some of these issues for MC Mennonites. At their 1973 churchwide conference, the study session on "Women's Role in the Church" drew the largest attendance of the entire sessions. In discussion that was "almost dramatic," delegates loudly applauded a statement that Mennonite men had "sinned against the women of the church in the past" and owed them an apology.[4]

Likewise for the General Conference Mennonite Church, a special consultation on the role of women came up with a variety of recommendations in the same year. Highlighting the wide differential in pay and responsibilities awarded to male and female church employees, the consultation recommended, among other measures, new Sunday school curricula on women, the inclusion of women speakers and leaders in conference activities, and the restructuring of church boards to include more women in positions of authority in the church.[5]

Indeed, so much did Mennonites follow along in political and cultural patterns emanating from larger society that the question of a new identity began to resound in Mennonite circles with ever increasing vigor. "The Mennonite Church is facing a crisis in identity," suggested a perceptive MC pastor in 1973. With "external symbols of dress, hair or other practices which gave security and group acceptance" nearly gone, he called upon the church to root its sense of identity instead in Anabaptist religious understandings, reinforced and strengthened for the times. Another Mennonite analyst called upon his church to "admit the slow destruction of the old community" and called for a religious revival to pave the way into a new one. Likewise, recognizing "a good deal of self-consciousness about the Mennonite identity," a mission leader articulated a similar path to recovering a sense of peoplehood beyond their sense of "ethnic shame." It lay, argued Menno Wiebe, in rejecting a personal, privatized evangelicalism "which has made and continues to make deep inroads into the Mennonite community," and in "discovering an up-to-date Anabaptist theology."[6]

While these cries for a new Mennonite identity would continue to echo through the coming years,[7] the extensive socioeconomic changes of the postwar years had rendered the matter particularly pressing by the early 1970s. For the immediate process of acculturation had fragmented the churches, and many of the specific developments of the 1960s appeared to reinforce these lines of separation in groups beyond the ranks of the Mennonites. As noted in chapter 8, Princeton sociologist Robert Wuthnow has argued persuasively that the twin issues first of the civil rights movement and then of the war in Vietnam triggered a deep political and behavioral fragmentation in the ranks of American religion. Wuthnow moved beyond these "movement-specific" descriptions to locate reasons for this "restructuring of American religion" in the socioeconomic changes of the era, especially in the growth in technology and higher education. As educational levels rose in the nation, Wuthnow argued, the more highly educated left the churches in large numbers, and a sharp move to the left occurred among those who stayed. Correspondingly, outside the "mainline" churches, resurgent evangelicals led a mirroring movement in the other direction. Less highly educated and thus less attracted to this pattern of religious and cultural liberalization, these evangelicals greeted the social upheaval of the 1960s with a sharp turn to the right. In response to the civil rights and antiwar crusades and to the deeper social changes of the postwar years, the American religious environment has been polarized into two separate and almost hostile camps.[8]

As with larger American society, so it was with Mennonites. The deep fragmentation of the Mennonite churches between social action on the one hand, and a gravitation toward issues of personal salvation and evangelicalism on the other, appeared even more palpable and alarming to church progressives by the early 1970s. Saying that "we have drifted far with American evangelical Christianity," which has greatly privatized Christian faith, Franconia Conference peace leader James Longacre maintained in 1973, for example, that "a vast gap exists between the biblical and theological assumptions of our seminary and college teachers and the people in the churches." While the former often took their bearings from "Anabaptist-Mennonite principles," the laity turned instead to a pietistic popular evangelicalism and interpreted church-state separation as "the isolation of Christianity to private matters."[9]

Sufficiently concerned over the ambiguity of Mennonite identity and concerned about what they perceived as "the impact of modernization" on Mennonites, some of the church's premier sociologists—J. Howard

Kauffman and Leland Harder in 1972, and Kauffman and former GC peace committee head Leo Driedger in 1989—undertook extensive surveying of a large sample of Mennonites. Gathering the opinions, socioeconomic data, and religious practices of over three thousand Mennonites from five major groups, these sociologists uncovered in both major surveys a good deal of evidence suggesting that Mennonites who had been more influenced by the acculturating processes of higher levels of education, urbanization, and a rise in socioeconomic class tended to be more supportive of the church leadership's newer sociopolitical stances. In other words, the patterns Wuthnow had found in his examination of the wider church held true to a large degree for Mennonites. A number of correlations between their respondents' opinions on church-state separation with socioeconomic indicators convinced the sociologists that the shift to higher education, urbanization and rising socioeconomic status among church members positively influenced their views on a number of issues. Such Mennonites evinced much less racial prejudice and more interest in women's rights and pacifism; they tended to strongly affirm Mennonite participation both in politics and in peaceable demonstrations to obtain social justice.[10]

In contrast, these Mennonite sociologists found that a number of other Mennonites followed the drift rightward that Wuthnow described, and they did so heavily influenced by an acculturation of their own. "Many homes are being bombarded daily by fundamentalistic preaching via Christian radio that is quite far from nonresistant," discerned one Lancaster County Mennonite in 1970. Rural and less-educated Mennonites have had their political views shaped by influences from their environment, a fact seen most vividly in their acceptance of fundamentalism. Harder and Kauffman found that their socioeconomic class scale was more strongly related to fundamentalism than to any other variable. In other words, lower class, less educated, and rural Mennonites tended heavily toward fundamentalistic theological understandings, which in turn markedly influenced other attitudes. As Harold Bender had feared in the 1950s, these sociologists uncovered among many Mennonites decades later a heavy fundamentalism that significantly undermined pacifist commitments, racial tolerance, support for the work of MCC, and other expressions of Christian social concerns. Even with the methodological difficulties that render some conclusions a bit tenuous,[11] it remains clear that the polarization in Mennonite ranks in the 1960s had much to do with the fractures wrought by the process of acculturation.[12]

Yet, while an understanding of acculturation is crucial in any account of recent Mennonite history, this study has also shown that Mennonites did not absorb these changes as passive objects, blown this way and that by the winds of social transformation. Indeed, church leaders had continually and repeatedly incorporated aspects of the acculturation process in general— and the initiatives and encroachments of the state in particular—as a means of reinforcing the call and the bonds of the church. Faced with the inescapable evidence of Mennonite political and theological fragmentation, church leaders would move again to shore up Mennonite fragmentation wrought by socioeconomic change and to strengthen a central, common ground.

Advising a former student, Guy Hershberger articulated a central conception that he and his fellow church leaders were trying to manifest. "What we are interested in is not Fundamentalism (with Capital F)," he told John Oyer in 1953, "neither liberal social gospel—but rather good old fashioned Anabaptism which is New Testament Christianity." A dozen years later, John E. Lapp struck the same chord. In the spring of 1967, he prepared and delivered to the CPSC and also to his denomination's general council a thoughtful analysis of the Mennonite predicament. The CPSC chair outlined the strong attraction that many MC Mennonites demonstrated for the growing movement of neo-evangelicalism, represented in such persons as Billy Graham and organizations such as the National Association of Evangelicals (NAE). Moreover, he underscored the affinity some Mennonites had for groups such as McIntire's American Council of Churches even further on the right. On the other side, Lapp pointed to a growing number of Mennonite people attracted to the religious left because of its advocacy of peace issues.[13]

In these conflicting currents, Lapp posed the central problem: "Since the Mennonite Church is an evangelical body of believers who do believe in the evangelical gospel . . . but are also a peace church, it creates a dilemma for us." The one side so attractive to many Mennonites offered an evangelicalism that had heavily imbibed American militarism and nationalism, while the other side expressed social concerns but lacked an evangelical emphasis. As a result, Mennonites found themselves caught in the middle, with members gravitating to either pole. The solution Lapp offered was to somehow "chart a third path" between the two, combining an evangelical concern for the soul with a liberal concern for peace and justice. As Lapp recognized, the church had already embarked upon this path; in this plea he outlined much of the Mennonite calling in the postwar years. Yet the polarities of the time, Lapp made clear, demanded Mennonites to be much more conscious and directed with their program. The way between the two poles was to somehow deepen a Mennonite understanding of themselves as an "evangelical peace church."[14]

Throughout the postwar years, while simultaneously developing their voice of protest to the state, Mennonite leaders had carefully tended their theological and organizational ties with the new evangelical movement. Both MC and GC Mennonites repeatedly sent observers to evangelical conventions, who usually reported back with careful evaluations of the lack of commitment to social concerns expressed there. At times Mennonite lay people moved from observation to participation in different evangelical events and conferences. For instance, more than one hundred and fifty Mennonites took part in a "U.S. Congress on Evangelism," held in Minneapolis in the fall of 1969. While angered and offended by certain parts of the program, many found it a positive experience as well. "As I listened I became involved as the Holy Spirit searched and spoke to my heart regarding my own neglect in sharing Christ with those outside the church," reflected a Lancaster bishop. Similarly, in 1968 and 1970, around five hundred Mennonite college students attended the huge missions conferences at Urbana, Illinois, sponsored by Inter-Varsity Christian Fellowship. While many of these young people did not accept the evangelical line uncritically, noting the missions thrusts that did not promise to minister to the body as well as the soul, they found such conferences worthwhile all the same. Evangelicals themselves certainly facilitated this Mennonite participation as they began to wrestle more consciously with the social demands of the gospel in the late 1960s.[15]

By the early 1970s, church leaders had moved even more explicitly to reinforce Mennonite missions and evangelism efforts, even joining in some of the larger, pandenominational evangelical thrusts of these years. Representatives from a number of different Mennonite groups, for example, joined forces in April 1972, for a special all-Mennonite consultation on evangelism entitled "Probe '72." More than 2,100 Mennonites gathered in Minneapolis to dialogue and strategize about different methods to convert others to Christianity. Likewise, more than two thousand Mennonites came together a month later at Goshen for a special "Festival of the Holy Spirit," while another two thousand convened in July for another huge missions conference at Eastern Mennonite College. By 1973, this evangelical fervor among Mennonites already appeared to be in full swing. In the words of *Gospel Herald* editor John Drescher in 1972, "Today there is a growth of evangelistic concern at the grass roots of the church."[16]

In this renewal of Mennonite energies for evangelism, however, the church hierarchy did not neglect or downplay the peace and social concerns commitments that developments in the postwar years had pushed to the forefront of Mennonite consciousness. Indeed, in their evangelistic efforts, Mennonites showed a marked ability to combine this missions fervor with the peace and activist causes that had triggered such deep lines of fracture in many American church groups. At the Probe '72 conference, for instance, one pastor led a workshop on "Peace as Evangelism," arguing that "a true evangelist cannot be silent about war." Dramatizing the Mennonite mandate to engage in "service evangelism," other participants staged a mock trial of the church at large, charging the church with, among other crimes, refusing to speak out against social evils, such as race hatred and discrimination against women, and willful negligence of the poor and hungry. Delegates overwhelmingly voted themselves a verdict of guilty for these crimes. While Billy Graham may have chosen at his rallies to thoroughly amalgamate the gospel he preached with American patriotism, at the Mennonites' Probe '72, participants pondered the bombing of Haiphong in North Vietnam and held a prayer of penitence for the war and for the church's complicity in it. As Mennonites prepared for participation in the larger evangelical push of "Key 73," MCC issued a booklet entitled "Evangelism: Good News or Bad News," which pointed out that for many of the world's nonwhite people, the arrival of evangelical missionaries truly meant bad news, bringing with them racism, colonialism, and imperialism. Contributors to the booklet emphasized that a commitment to Jesus also entailed a commitment to peace, justice, and service. Canadian Mennonite leader Frank Epp argued, for example, that "The lamb is a lamb, not a wolf. His spirit is a dove, not a hawk—and not an eagle!" One Mennonite congregation in 1972 expressed its evangelistic inclinations in operating a draft counseling center, while another "communicated the Good News" by constructing nonprofit housing for low-income people.[17]

Thus, Mennonites showed themselves as remarkably able to move into the breach between politically quiescent evangelicals and cause-minded mainline liberals as outlined by Wuthnow. Mindful of the fragmentation that had penetrated their own ranks, church leaders moved consciously to heal this polarization. Moreover, this movement into a Mennonite middle ground did not occur only among church leaders and denominational elites. The extensive polling data done in the early 1970s and late 1980s suggested that a fair number of lay people followed them into this twin affirmation of both evangelism and social concerns, though still exhibiting some hesitancy over their church's reformulated witness to the state.

On the one hand, these sociologists concluded that Mennonites remained a very conservative group on a theological charting. Mennonite scores on two larger, denominational "doctrinal orthodoxy scales," these sociologists noted, placed them next to the Southern Baptists on the most orthodox end of a liberal-orthodox continuum, with nearly 90 percent of the respondents in 1972 opting for the most conservative response. Vast majorities of their respondents in both surveys could point to a personal conversion experience and testified to the importance of Bible study, prayer, and a personal relationship with God in their lives. Yet these conservative white evangelicals, Harder and Kauffman uncovered, also pledged their commitment to a number of sociopolitical stances more often located at the other end of any kind of pietistic or doctrinal scale. In 1972, 87 percent of the MCs and 66 percent of the GCs, for instance, still agreed that the Christian should not take part in war or any war-promoting activities. By 1989, these numbers were at 78 and 65 percent, respectively. Beyond this basic Mennonite position, the arguments of church leaders that Mennonites needed to speak to the state about their social concerns appeared to have found some widespread acceptance. In 1972, for example, less than a third of the MCs and only 14 percent of the GCs definitely agreed with the statement "It is not the business of the church to try to influence the actions of government in regard to such issues as war and peace, race relations, poverty, etc." At the same time, an increased percentage of Mennonites in 1989 agreed that they should "actively promote" their peace position and attempt to win others to it.[18]

Perhaps most important for a church trying to hold to a middle course between a conservative evangelicalism on one hand, and a social activism devoid of missions concern on the other, was what appeared, by the late 1980s, as a fundamental commitment among many Mennonites to an "Anabaptist" conception that nurtured both expressions. Through their answers to questions on a variety of issues, the sample of Mennonites in Kauffman and Driedger's survey registered their relative commitments on several scales the sociologists had constructed. One tested the sample's dedication to Anabaptist concepts (for example, infant versus adult baptism, commitment to nonparticipation in warfare), and another reflected their commitment to fundamentalist understandings (for example, biblical inerrancy, hell as a punishment for earthly sins). Somewhat surprisingly, the sociologists found that Mennonites holding to Anabaptist beliefs also demonstrated a much higher commitment to other measures of religiosity than the fundamentalists, including church participation levels, personal devotional behavior, and personal religious experience. Equally important, while both Mennonite fundamentalists and Anabaptists manifested a concern for evangelism, only the Anabaptists combined that concern with a high commitment to peacemaking and service. In addition, those scoring high on the Anabaptism scale also demonstrated a high amount of racial tolerance and interest in welfare for the poor. In other words, the Mennonites holding Anabaptist principles demonstrated an ability to move into the breach that Wuthnow theorized and that had opened in Mennonite ranks in the 1960s. They displayed an ability to combine an evangelical impetus with a concern for peace and justice. In contrast, in addition to their lack of interest in racial justice, gender justice, and governmental aid to the needy, Mennonite fundamentalists demonstrated little interest in peace, service to the poor, or any other matters beyond the realm of the strictly spiritual. Finally, most significant in a church group that has increasing numbers of its members gravitating toward urban environments, higher education, and higher socioeconomic status, the data uncovered in the late 1980s suggested that Anabaptist conceptions especially appealed to such people. If this holds, then it would portend continued strength for an Anabaptist position in the Mennonite churches in the future.[19]

In the past several decades, Mennonites in both major groups have continued to build on the trajectories they established in the years between 1935 and 1975. They have reinforced their willingness to speak to the state about a wide range of social justice issues. They have reaffirmed their legitimation of draft nonregistration, solidly declaring their personal, spiritual, and financial support for noncooperators. In 1983, GC Mennonites went as far as to affirm the church's refusal to withhold tax monies from church employees engaged in war tax resistance. In effect, this committed the church to civil disobedience. And in these years, the general conference bodies of both major Mennonite groups have embraced nonviolent direct action as a legitimate and sometimes necessary course for people of peace. As a joint MC-GC statement declared in 1983, "If a structure does not profess values which can be engaged for urging it toward greater justice, a more radical witness, including non-violent protest, may be in order." By the late 1980s, Mennonites had joined with Friends and Brethren to create "Christian Peacemaker Teams," which dispatched trained nonviolent activists to international trouble spots such as Iraq, Haiti, and Palestine in order to flesh out a nonviolent response to injustice.[20]

Altogether, when compared to the timid and reserved Mennonite voices raised against injustice and war a half-century ago, Mennonites seemed to have come a long way. Aside from a few archtraditionalists, Mennonites obedient to the new church teaching could no longer rationalize their own inactivity in the face of evil as something required under a quietistic, simplistic doctrine of the two kingdoms. Instead, reformulated understandings of Mennonite identity called church members to meet human needs through sacrificial service. Equally important, the new Mennonite stance—which they increasingly came to characterize as "Anabaptist"—deemed it an inadequate and irresponsible Christian response to see injustice, poverty, and war and refuse to speak to the state about them. Being a modern-day Anabaptist has come to demand that one take up the prophetic voice in a manner that would countenance, even demand, nonviolent initiatives on behalf of peace and justice.

In the end, this story seems to point to at least two principle areas of conclusion. One concerns the implications that the modern warfare state, in both its foreign and domestic exertions, continues to hold for people of peace. The second emanates from what a survey of recent Mennonite history might indicate about the elastic and mediating ability of religious ideology in the workings of social change.

PACIFISM AND THE MODERN WARFARE STATE

As this account highlights, the pressing and inescapable challenge for modern pacifists entails coming to grips with the modern warfare state. This is a state whose embrace of the means and methods of total war has brought inescapable and dangerous changes in wartime for civilians both at home and in the enemy nation. Both areas of emphasis inexorably confront modern pacifists.

First, modern total war is a combat logically and systematically directed at enemy civilians. Civilians may have had a difficult time remaining immune from the ravages of war in premodern conflicts, but in the modern era they have been transformed into direct, deliberate targets of attack and annihilation. This development has not occurred because national leaders have been innately evil, or because the people are extraordinarily callous or bloodthirsty. As part of the rationale for the construction and use (or threatened use) of incendiary bombs or nuclear warheads, there is no reason to do other than to accept the intentions voiced by governmental leaders at their face value. These warmaking systems may well have been constructed by well-meaning people sincerely trying to avert further injustice, brutality, or a wider war.[21]

Nonetheless, in practice, the mechanisms of total war have been and are aimed at civilians, even children; the very nature of modern war entails the destruction of people formerly designated as "noncombatants." Such a course is not necessarily a cause for celebration by the modern warfare state; indeed, as Reinhold Niebuhr urged, in its best moments it may even kill enemy noncombatants as a "tragic necessity," with proper heaviness of heart. For a modern state at war, incinerating enemy civilians is merely functional. When warfare has come to mean total economic and social mobilization of a society, with large numbers of civilians fully integrated into war production, the massive destruction of enemy civilians is entailed—indeed, in the minds of war planners, even required. Of course, such practices also stand in violation of nearly every ethical principle that the church has maintained for two millennia.[22] If pacifism is to have any modern meaning, it plainly needs to exert itself ever more completely and unreservedly against the plans or practices of modern, total war.[23]

At the same time, the orientation of modern warfare that pacifists need to most vigorously oppose has in its very nature rendered them increasingly irrelevant and isolated. A state engaged in modern war, for whom the difference between total victory or devastating defeat rests to a large degree upon its ability to marshal all of its socioeconomic resources, cannot afford widespread dissent. It cannot allow large sectors of its population to remain uninvolved in the war effort. It must manage dissent very carefully. As this account has illustrated, in twentieth-century America the warfare state has developed new innovations in its dealings with wartime opposition. Instead of crushing it—and thus making a mockery of the very values for which its soldiers purportedly fought—since World War I, the American state has worked to carefully manage and effectively isolate dissent in its programs of alternative service. A state agency like Selective Service may still not be entirely happy with alternative service arrangements, but viewed in historical perspective, such programs have worked beautifully in accordance with its agenda. In the guise of broad liberality, these programs have isolated and largely rendered irrelevant a vast sector of the potential opposition to the state's practice of total war. The challenge for pacifists remains somehow to reassert that opposition in a meaningful and effective way. Indeed, as the modern warfare state sinks its tentacles further into the bones and sinews of civilian society, assimilating all stripes of people, economic arrangements, and institutions into the encompassing purposes of total war, pacifists will be challenged on a deeper level than merely expressing wartime opposition. They will be hard pressed to personally disentangle themselves in a meaningful manner from the ways of war altogether.

Mennonite have been only relatively recent participants in the larger pacifist community. As such, their story in recent American history might be taken as only marginally relevant to this larger struggle. On the contrary, however, recent Mennonite history clearly illustrates the reaches of the new warfare state. So all-embracing was its grasp that even a newly emergent group such as the Mennonites had to deal with its presence. It is precisely because Mennonites have taken their own commitments as a people of peace seriously, interweaving them into the heart of their postwar identity, that the Mennonite story in the past half-century has taken many of the twists and turns that it has.

The decision by Mennonites to confront more forcefully the warmaking of the modern state appears all the more remarkable in light of the several escape routes open to them that might have relieved them of such a course. They have had at least two ways out. First, Mennonites might have opted for an easy way out of any serious confrontation with the state by resting content in communities isolated by spiritual separation, if physical distance no longer remained possible. True to one reading of their heritage, they might have devoted themselves merely to preserving the ethic of "absolute love" in quiet, nonthreatening service to those around them. This option appeared to dovetail nicely with some ways of reading their two-kingdom theology. It required merely that Mennonites adjust their two kingdoms in a way that their primacy to God's kingdom did not require any interaction with the violence and injustice of the secular one, outside of a few periodic suggestions, meekly voiced to those in power, to leave them out of it. Moreover, this option was urged on them most powerfully by some of their country's most profound religious leaders: Reinhold Niebuhr, John C. Bennett, and more recently, more briefly, Martin Marty.[24] And it promised to garner them some good press, win some public admiration and national acceptance so alluring to an ethnoreligious people traditionally on the margins of society and suffering from a case of "ethnic shame."

Secondly, less within their tradition but like other Christians marching to the beat of a conservative, orthodox, evangelical theology,[25] Mennonites might have read their dual allegiance differently. Like many other evangelicals, they might have established an equality of obligation to their two king-doms. By declaring that God's commands about peace apply to only the heavenly realm, they could thus participate fully in the practice of state-directed violence in this world.

At least on the official level, Mennonites have refused to take either of these options. Propelled by their willingness to embrace the causes of com-passion, peace, and justice for others besides themselves, and articulating these concerns out of a recovered heritage of prophetic Anabaptism, Men-nonites did not accept the patronizing dismissals offered by people like Niebuhr.[26] Except for a few archtraditionalists hanging on desperately to apolitical nonresistance, Mennonites have not as a group huddled toward this escape hatch out of church-state confrontation. An unavoidable pro-cess of social transformation broke through the walls of their cloistered ru-ral communities and brought them face to face with social needs and politi-cal choices they could no longer easily ignore. On the level of church doctrine and on the more prosaic level of individual action and protest, an increasing number of Mennonites accepted these problems as their own. For Mennonites, as for other pacifist groups, asserting their own relevance as dissenters in the climate of the modern warfare state has entailed com-bining a cry for peace with an acceptance of responsibility to speak for jus-tice. As members of a larger society still saturated in the ways of violence, however, and where justice still seems in short supply, Mennonite pacifists, like all others, need to ponder anew where to go from here.

Yet it is perhaps the second way out of serious confrontation with the modern warfare state that continues to tempt Mennonites most enticingly. As this study has demonstrated, a thread that has run through much of twentieth-century Mennonite history has been the appeal of a separatist fundamentalism and, perhaps more powerfully, the pull of a conservative evangelical movement. To many of the Mennonite laity, evangelical leaders have appeared magnetic and articulate, their theology safe and attractive, their worship style alluring. At the same time, and perhaps less noticeable to many Mennonite congregants, many such conservative evangelicals have also established cozy relationships with American nationalism and milita-rism and have spiritualized into irrelevance ethical issues other than those of personal morality. In fundamentalist/conservative evangelical hands, the call to salvation for oneself and others could become so blinding that all other social issues fade by comparison. In the late 1960s, Mennonites came to a choice between competing sources of obligation, God *or* country, a choice that seems to crop up periodically in their history. In dealing with the appeal of a nationalistic evangelicalism, they may be facing another such defining moment.

Mennonites do have, however, some particularly rich and powerful resources by which to further root their faith and identity. In the twentieth century, these resources have served them very well.

SOCIAL CHANGE, RELIGIOUS MEDIATION

"If religion has been restructured," theorized Robert Wuthow, "this restructuring has been possible because religious organizations have had the resources with which to respond to the challenges set before them." The fundamental change reshaping American religion in the postwar years, he argued, developed out of the reaction of religious organizations to the undercurrents of social change. In Wuthnow's words, "The ways in which American religion has been restructured . . . have been conditioned by the cultural, social, and political environment in which it functioned and the internal resources with which it was able to adapt to these challenges."[27]

In sum, Wuthnow's conception of religious organizations adapting to the process of social change in a fashion that sustained their own viability in American life does much to encapsulate the series of transformations that has characterized the Mennonite story in the twentieth century. The larger forces of acculturation in general and the state in particular introduced the church to a number of socioeconomic changes that rapidly ate away at the traditional Mennonite community. Having functioned for centuries as the cohesive center of this community, the church was profoundly threatened by such forces; for these changes thus threatened to greatly reduce, if not altogether eliminate, the church's hegemony and role in the life of the Mennonite people.

Yet the church did not respond passively to these forces, acquiescing without a murmur to the fragmenting and scattering of its people and to the obliteration of the bonds that had preserved them as Mennonites. Instead, the church effectively and repeatedly mediated this process of social change, responding with a variety of institutional and ideological initiatives to keep Mennonites intact as a separate and identifiable people in modern America. In this process, Mennonites have had rich resources to draw on, namely an Anabaptist conception adhered to by many church members that combines the spiritual impetus with the social one. Moreover, in pursuing this new basis of Mennonite identity, both Mennonites and their

leaders have continued adjusting and readjusting the process of drawing
the line in their respective obligations to God and country on behalf of a
religious group that took this question very seriously.

Of course, given the contours of Mennonite history for the past half-
century, this conception of the church as brokering the process of acculturation should not appear as particularly dramatic or new. A number of Mennonite scholars have analyzed Mennonite history and sociology through
the lens of acculturation. One scholar found the GCMC's "readiness to
acculturate" part of the denomination's "genius." John Howard Yoder
painted this process in much darker hues in 1969 when he characterized
much of the Mennonite story of the entire past century as "a series of bor-
rowings from the surrounding Protestantism in an effort to renew the
Mennonite reality." "Each stage of the creative adjustment was a response
to a threat from the outside," Yoder continued, "by accepting and integrat-
ing that which threatened." Thus when Mennonite youth wanted to go off
to college, the church created its own colleges; when Mennonites found
themselves threatened by conscription, they created service agencies as an
alternative. Because he found such adjustments as compromises of an original "Anabaptist Vision," Yoder interpreted them much more negatively.
Yet in the service not just of Yoder's vision but of a larger Anabaptist whole,
it seems clear that step by step, the church has taken these outside threats
and reworked them to serve as a source of strength and renewal for an ever-
elastic Mennonite tradition and life.[28]

While this conception should come as no striking innovation to Mennonite scholars, students of wider religious and social change might well take
note of it. For the Mennonite relationship with the state detailed in these
pages offers seemingly abundant reason for social historians to pay more
attention to the impact of religion and religious ideology, particularly for
so-called "white ethnic" groups. Historian Timothy Smith has claimed
that scholars have long analyzed the ethnoreligious systems of racial
minorities as doing much to sustain these groups' "emerging social and
political systems." Conversely, however, they have treated the religious ideologies and institutions of "white ethnics" as "backward-looking, dysfunc-
tional, or arcane." Scholars such as Smith have found that religion often
helped to define and sustain these groups' ethnic identities. Eugene Genovese has portrayed a slave religion which continually served as a source of
meaning and identity in a system that threatened to dehumanize its prac-
titioners.[29] While the impact of the state's initiatives and postwar social

change presented nowhere nearly as dire personal consequences to American Mennonites, these developments did result in the destruction of their traditional world and threaten to preclude the possible creation of another.

Instead, Mennonites repeatedly translated these incursions into institutional and ideological forms that they could use to moderate their church's transition into national society. And in this process, their inherited ideology of church-state relations, something they once characterized as "nonresistance," proved crucial. Indeed, if this study has demonstrated nothing else, it has outlined how the Mennonites' continual reevaluation of their relationship with the state has functioned centrally in the reformulation of their life and identity in a time of great economic and social transformation. Certainly if religious ideology can assist in such a task, then it ought to warrant more careful treatment from social historians in the future.

Moreover, the particular Mennonite story portrayed here might cause theorists of modernization to somewhat temper their interpretations of recent American life. While the Mennonite church ceased to be oriented around a close-knit, rural, ethnoreligious community, it did not cease to function as centrally important in Mennonite life. In a variety of institutional and ideological endeavors, the church continually reestablished itself as an intermediate solidarity between Mennonites and their government. In a time when the state repeatedly sought to ordain itself as the focal point for all civil loyalties, the church reminded Mennonites of their fealty to a higher source of authority. Neither did the church in this instance fall victim to the sort of "compartmentalization" that modernization theorists have often posited as a fundamental characterization of contemporary religion. The refusal of Mennonite leaders to confine themselves either to social activism or to private matters of morality underscored their firm intention to speak to all spheres of life. Indeed, as time went on, they even began to include in their purview ground they had traditionally conceded to the state.

Finally, beyond the world of scholars and academics, the Mennonite wrestling with where to draw the line between obligations to church and state in the years from World War II through Vietnam could function as a valuable point of orientation for American churches. Particularly in times of war, when the state's list of its citizens' obligations grew ever more intense and all-encompassing, adherence to theological understandings that pointed in a different direction could sometimes be an unpopular and even dangerous affair. As American church history will testify, it is very hard to draw the line with the state. Against such a backdrop, the Mennonite attempt to do so stands out in bold and remarkable relief.

Sifting through these conflicting obligations drew some of the best energies of Mennonite church leaders and agencies for a considerable length of time. Yet arguably the most common and most disconcerting decisions occurred on the individual rather than the church level. In this vein, as this study began with a short vignette, perhaps it is best to end with one.

By the spring of 1970, the citizens of Hesston, Kansas, had discovered that not even a small farm town like theirs would be able to escape the anger and confrontations engendered nationally by the conflict in Vietnam. The previous October, in days of a national student moratorium against the war, students from the previously apolitical Hesston College had organized a protest walk from the campus to the town's post office to mail protest letters against the war. Several town hotheads threatened violence, but the event had proceeded without incident. Not long afterward, a few students from the small Mennonite college raised an improvised Vietcong flag on the campus flagpole to commemorate Ho Chi Minh's birthday. Outrage swept the Hesston community, and a number of student-community discussions did little to ease the strains.[30]

Accordingly, local civic leaders attempted to draw the community together again in a common ritual that might, they felt, defuse the tensions. The Lions Club had donated a new flagpole for the city building. The dedication ceremony could bring some healing to the town. To this end, the planners were careful to include the town's traditional wartime dissenters, the Mennonites. They invited the town's most prominent Mennonite pastor, Peter Wiebe, to give the main address at the ceremony.

The dedication ceremony initially proceeded without a hitch. The high school band played patriotic tunes, and the VFW color guard proudly brought forth the flag. The two-hundred odd citizens in attendance removed their hats, and a sergeant from nearby McConnell Air Force Base reminded them that America was "God's gift to mankind." For the town's patriotic faithful, Pastor Wiebe started off well. "The American flag is to be a symbol of the best for which the American people stand," Wiebe agreed. Referring to a low-cost housing project city officials had advocated, Wiebe declared that the flag itself demanded its construction, for "if we do less than this for our underprivileged, then it is a sham, a farce, and it ought to be torn down." He was proud to see the flag fly, Wiebe went on, but "not on a military base in another country. I have a feeling that we do not belong there, and history in Vietnam and elsewhere is proving how badly mistaken we have been in our military efforts." In his conclusion, the pastor asked his somewhat stunned audience to join him in "the army of the Lord," under the "Commander in Chief . . . the Man of Sorrows, the Prince of Peace." The audience moved somewhat reflexively into a recitation of the pledge of allegiance. Wiebe instead remained silent, folding his hands behind his back and bowing his head as if in prayer.

List of
Abbreviations

AFSC   American Friends Service Committee

AMC   Archives of the Mennonite Church, Goshen College, Goshen, Indiana

CESR   Committee on Economic and Social Relations (MC)

CO(s)   Conscientious Objector(s)

CPS   Civilian Public Service

CPSC   Committee on Peace and Social Concerns (MC)

FOR   Fellowship of Reconciliation

GCMC   General Conference Mennonite Church

GC(s)   General Conference Mennonite(s)

HPC(s)   Historic Peace Church(es)

I-W(s)   Conscientious objector(s) in the Korean and Vietnam War draft (1951–1973) who had received a service assignment

LMHS   Lancaster Mennonite Historical Society, Lancaster, Pennsylvania

MC   Mennonite Church

MCC   Mennonite Central Committee

MDS   Mennonite Disaster Service

MHLB   Mennonite Historical Library, Bluffton College, Bluffton, Ohio

MHLG   Mennonite Historical Library, Goshen College, Goshen, Indiana

MLA   Mennonite Library and Archives, Bethel College,
        North Newton, Kansas

MMHS   Mennonite Mental Health Services

MQR   *Mennonite Quarterly Review*

MSHL   Menno Simons Historical Library, Eastern Mennonite College,
        Harrisonburg, Virginia

NAE   National Association of Evangelicals

NSBRO   National Service Board for Religious Objectors

OM(s)   "Old" Mennonite(s)

PC   Peace Committee (GCMC)

PPC   Peace Problems Committee (MC)

PSCC   Peace and Social Concerns Committee (GCMC)

UMT   Universal Military Training

VS   Voluntary Service

Notes

1. Liechty's story has been constructed here from an oral interview, Keith Sprunger with Lynn D. Liechty, March 4, 1988, Schowalter Oral History Collection, Mennonite Library and Archives, North Newton, Kansas (hereafter abbreviated as MLA). See also Naomi Lehman, *Pilgrimage of a Congregation*, 370–73.

2. Quoted in Albert Keim, "Service or Resistance? The Mennonite Resistance to Conscription in World War II," *Mennonite Quarterly Review* (hereafter abbreviated as *MQR*) 15 (1978): 155. I am also indebted to Professor Keim for pointing out the appropriateness of the quotation.

3. Mennonites also referred to the principles of nonresistance when confronting sources of economic power, such as labor unions.

4. John R. Mumaw, *Nonresistance and Pacifism*, 20.

5. For a useful summary of two-kingdom theology, see Thomas G. Sanders, *Protestant Concepts of Church and State*, 6–8.

6. Ibid., 7, 24–67, 225–31. On Lutheran theology on this point, see H. Richard Niebuhr, *Christ and Culture*, 170–79. A brief summary of Calvinism and Neo-Calvinism can be found in Nicholas Wolterstorff, *Until Justice and Peace Embrace* (Grand Rapids, Mich.: Eerdmans, 1983), 54–67.

7. Sanders, *Protestant Concepts of Church and State*, 84–85; Hans Hillerbrand, "The Anabaptist View of the State," *MQR* 32 (1958): 84–92.

8. Guy F. Hershberger, *War, Peace, and Nonresistance*, 160. Mumaw, *Nonresistance and Pacifism*, 12. Mennonite bishop quoted in Leo Driedger and Donald B. Kraybill, *Mennonite Peacemaking*, 57. For concise summaries of Mennonite two-kingdom theology, see Sanders, *Protestant Concepts of Church and State*, 75–82; and Mulford Sibley and Philip Jacob, *Conscription of Conscience*, 19–21.

9. There have been several exceptions to this general rule. Two Mennonites, for

example, served in Midwestern state legislatures in the early twentieth century. One, Peter Janzen, was offered the nomination for governor of Nebraska but turned it down on the grounds that he could not serve as the commander-in-chief of the state militia. See Hershberger, *War, Peace, and Nonresistance*, 163–64; John Redekop, "Politics," in *Mennonite Encyclopedia*, Vol. 5, ed. Cornelius Dyck and Dennis P. Martin (Scottdale, Pa: Herald Press, 1990), 711–14.

10. Hershberger, *War, Peace, and Nonresistance*, 160; Mumaw, *Nonresistance and Pacifism*, 12. Admittedly, by offering definitions of nonresistance formulated by such OM writers as Hershberger and Mumaw, I am presenting a conception heavily weighed toward their understandings—and with Mumaw's inclusion, a conservative OM formulation at that. Yet it would be erroneous to claim that the members of the more liberal GCMC were not shaped by two-kingdom understandings as well, though most GC Mennonites would countenance a less strict degree of obedience to government than Mumaw would demand. Notwithstanding the ethnic and cultural differences that have historically characterized the two groups, and the GCMC's greater openness to outside society, the GC scholar Rodney Sawatsky recognizes that for much of the postwar era, OM understandings have been largely normative for the GCMC as well (*Authority and Identity: the Dynamics of the General Conference Mennonite Church*, 5, 38–39). The volume and tenor of angry, dissenting letters to the editor of *The Mennonite*, objecting to GCMC dissent to the Vietnam War, testify as well to the influence of the two-kingdom ethic among GC Mennonites.

11. Guy F. Hershberger, "Biblical Nonresistance and Modern Pacifism," *MQR* 17 (July 1943): 127; Don E. Smucker, "A Mennonite Critique of the Pacifist Movement," *MQR* 20 (January 1946): 80–88.

12. Niebuhr's classic denunciation of modern liberal pacifism is found in his polemic "Why the Christian Church is not Pacifist," in *Christianity and Power Politics* (New York: Charles Scribner's Sons, 1940), 1–32; see especially pp. 4–5 for his treatment of Mennonites. For a general sketch of traditional Mennonite hostility toward liberal pacifism of the pre–World War II years, see Sanders, *Protestant Concepts of Church and State*, 102–104. For lay Mennonite political party preferences in 1972, see J. Howard Kauffman and Leland Harder, *Anabaptists Four Centuries Later*, 164. For a summary of Mennonite postwar political activity, see Redekop, "Politics," in *Mennonite Encyclopedia*, 5:713.

13. Roland R. Goering, "Die Stillen im Lande," *Mennonite Life* 14 (January, 1959): 31.

14. Paul Toews, "Mennonites in American Society: Modernity and the Persistence of Religious Community," *MQR* 68 (July, 1989): 239–43; Toews, "The Long Weekend or the Short Week: Mennonite Peace Theology, 1925–1944," *MQR* 60 (January, 1986): 56–57.

15. "Conscription and Militarism," Mennonite General Conference Statement, Turner, Oregon, August 18, 1969, Mennonite General Conference, "Minutes and Reports," n.p., 1969, 20, Archives of the Mennonite Church, Goshen College, Goshen, Indiana (hereafter abbreviated as AMC).

16. Hershberger, *War, Peace, and Nonresistance*, 165.

17. James Juhnke recognizes the parallel symbolism here, writing that by the

twentieth century, the issue of military service "more and more replaced rebaptism as the point of greatest tension with worldly authorities" (*Vision, Doctrine, War,* 32).

18. Goering, "Can we be still . . . " from "Die Stillen im Lande," 29; Vincent Harding, "To My Fellow Christians," *The Mennonite* 73 (September 30, 1958): 597.

19. See, for instance, Leland Harder, "Mennonite Mobility and the Christian Calling," *Mennonite Life* 19 (January 1964): 7–12; Harder, "Urbanization in the Mennonite Church," *The Mennonite* 74 (February 10, 1958); "More people, more students," *The Mennonite* 76 (April 11, 1961); Kauffman and Harder, *Anabaptists Four Centuries Later,* 51–64.

20. Milton Gordon, *Assimilation in American Life* (New York: Oxford University Press, 1964).

21. On this point, see James Juhnke, "Conflicts and Compromises of Mennonites and the Draft: An Interpretive Essay," in *Conscience and Conscription: Papers from the 1969 Assembly, Sponsored by the MCC Peace Section* (Akron, Pa.: MCC Peace Section, 1969), 31.

22. For the 1972 numbers, see Kauffman and Harder, *Anabaptists Four Centuries Later,* 21.

23. Ekkehart Krippendorff, "The State as a Focus for Peace Research," in Peace Research Society, *Papers* 16 (The Rome Conference, 1970): 51–52. This development of the state's military capacity reflects its growth in a variety of other areas. Philip Resnick, for instance, noted the state's rapidly expanding economic functions, while John Boli-Bennet showed how state constitutional authority has increased correspondingly with the rapid growth in state power. See Resnick, "The Functions of the Modern State: in Search of a Theory," in Ali Kazancigil, ed., *The State in Global Perspective* (New York: UNESCO, 1986), 176; and Boli-Bennet, "The Ideology of Expanding State Authority in National Constitutions," in John W. Meyer and Michael T. Hannan, eds., *National Development and the World System* (Chicago: University of Chicago Press, 1979), 224.

24. Samuel Finer, "State and Nation-Building in Europe: The Role of the Military," in Charles Tilly, ed., *The Formation of National States in Western Europe* (Princeton: Princeton University Press, 1975), 156–60; Russell Weigley, *The American Way of War* (New York: Macmillan, 1973), 194–96.

25. Weigley, *The American Way of War,* 146; Finer, "State and Nation-Building in Europe," 161–62. Also see Edgar Kingston-McLoughry, *Global Strategy* (New York: Frederick Praeger, 1957), 23; Geoffery Perrett, *Days of Sadness, Years of Triumph: The American People, 1939–1945* (New York: Coward, McCann & Geohegan, 1973), 67. Paul Kennedy, *The Rise and Fall of the Great Powers: Economic Change and Military Conflict from 1500 to 2000* (New York: Vintage Books, 1987), also traces the crucial factor of economic strength in modern and early modern warfare; see especially pp. 191–93, 256–74. On the deliberate targeting of civilians in World War II, see Michael S. Sherry, *The Rise of American Air Power: The Creation of Armageddon* (New Haven: Yale University Press, 1987), LeMay quoted at 287; and Ronald Schaffer, *Wings of Judgment: American Bombing in World War II* (New York: Oxford University Press, 1985).

26. Finer, "State and Nation-Building in Europe," 96–97, 161–62; Kingston-

McLoughry, *Global Strategy*, 18–23. Also see David Kaiser, *Politics and War: European Conflict from Philip II to Hitler* (Cambridge: Harvard University Press, 1990), 280–82.

27. On the emergence of military service as the supreme embodiment of proper citizenship, see Mitchell Lee Robinson, "Civilian Public Service during the Second World War: The Dilemmas of Conscience and Conscription in a Free Society" (Ph.D. diss., Cornell University, 1990), 20–24; Morris Janowitz quoted at 20.

28. World War I quotes from James Juhnke, *Vision, Doctrine, War*, 241. For farm deferments in World War II, see George Q. Flynn, *The Mess in Washington*, 130–45. "The Christian and the War," *Christian Century* 59 (January 28, 1942) is quoted in Richard Polenburg, ed., *America at War: The Home Front, 1941–1945* (Englewood Cliffs, N.J.: Prentice Hall, 1968), 119.

29. For the impact of World War I on American civil liberties, and mob violence as an offshoot, see David Kennedy, *Over Here: The First World War and American Society*, (New York: Oxford University Press, 1980), 75–90. The ideological intensity of this conflict appears somewhat incongruous with economic needs in spite of the connection implied above, for because of its late entry into the conflict, this was not total economic war for the United States. Even by the time of the armistice, this country was only investing about a fourth of its gross national product in the military (ibid., 250). This is only to caution, as does Kennedy, that we need to recognize the economic mandates of the rise of total war without engaging in any kind of crude economic determinism.

30. William James, *The Varieties of Religious Experience* (1902; reprint, New York: Mentor Books, 1958), 284.

31. Anatol Rapoport, "Changing Conceptions of War in the United States," in Ken Booth and Moorhead Wright, eds., *American Thinking about Peace and War* (New York: Barnes & Noble, 1978), 68–69. On egalitarianism, military service, and American culture, see Elliot Cohen, *Citizens and Soldiers*, 124. Cohen offers a careful argument that universal conscription seems particularly suited for modern democratic states precisely because of the demand for egalitarianism in democratic political cultures; see 34–35, 145–51. Also on this point, see Gary Walmsley, *Selective Service and a Changing America* (Columbus, Ohio: Charles Merrill, 1969), 15–16.

32. On the treatment of COs in the Constitution, see Leon Friedman, "Conscription and the Constitution: The Original Understanding," *Michigan Law Review* 67 (June, 1969): 1493–552; and R. R. Russell, "Development of Conscientious Objector Recognition in the United States," *George Washington Law Review* 20 (March, 1952): 409–48. Hershey is quoted in George Q. Flynn, *Lewis B. Hershey: Mr. Selective Service*, 131. On COs in World War I, see Kennedy, *Over Here*, 163–65; and Juhnke, *Vision, Doctrine, War*, 229–41.

33. Neal Wherry, *Conscientious Objection*, 1:1–2. George Q. Flynn, "Lewis Hershey and the Conscientious Objector: The World War II Experience," *Military Affairs* 47 (February 1983): 2–3. Hershey is quoted in Flynn, *Lewis B. Hershey*, 132.

34. Even these three groups differed markedly in their ability to say no to the military. The Church of the Brethren (COB) began to refine its pacifist commitments as late as the early twentieth century. While COB leadership worked hard in

teaching the peace position to the laity, Brethren response to the draft suggests their efforts were only partially successful. Of the 24,228 Brethren men drafted in World War II, a full 88 percent (21,481) entered regular military service, while over half of the 2,700 remaining draftees joined noncombatant ranks. This left only 1,300 men, barely 5 percent, who remained obedient to the church's instruction and entered CPS.

The Friends, too, though inheritors of a long and courageous tradition of war-time dissent and conscientious objection, were less able than Mennonites to translate this tradition into pacifism among individual Quaker draftees, at least before the 1960s. (Both groups' peace positions fared better in the nationwide antiwar sentiment of the Vietnam years.) Roughly 75 percent of drafted Friends in World War II entered military ranks.

The Friends and the Brethren experienced similar difficulties with their draftees throughout the fifties and early sixties. According to a 1967 Selective Service report, of the 17,576 participants in the I-W program from 1952 to 1967, only 14.4 percent of the total were Brethren and 3.8 percent Friends.

In contrast, 67.2 percent (11,576) of the I-W men to that point had been Mennonites. Though their rate of conscientious objection was not nearly as high in World War as in post–World War II years (a fact that occasioned Mennonite leaders no small amount of alarm), Mennonites made up the bulk of conscientious objectors in that conflict as well. Over half of Mennonite World War II draftees entered the military in either combatant or noncombatant roles. Still, 46 percent served in the CPS camps. Mennonites thus accounted for 38 percent of all the men assigned to CPS, more than any other religious group.

See Wherry, *Conscientious Objection*, 321–22; for Quaker figures, see William Darwin Swanson Witte, "Quaker Pacifism in the United States, with Special Reference to Its Isolationism and Internationalism" (Ph.D. diss., Columbia University, 1954), 49; "Mennonites Lead List of Conscientious Objectors," *The Mennonite* 82 (February 21, 1967): 122.

35. Lawrence Wittner, *Rebels Against War*, 62–95; Edgar Metzler, "Is Alternative Service a Witness for Peace?," *Gospel Herald* 55 (December 11, 1962): 1060.

36. Calvin Redekop, *Mennonite Society*, 4; Harold S. Bender, "The Anabaptist Vision," *MQR* 18 (April 1944): 79–86. For a masterful historiographical overview of the massive amount of literature on Anabaptism, see John Oyer, "Historiography, Anabaptist," in *Mennonite Encyclopedia* 5:378–382.

37. Redekop, *Mennonite Society*, 10; Bender, "The Anabaptist Vision," 69, 71; Hershberger, *War, Peace, and Nonresistance*, 84–85.

38. Leo Driedger and J. Howard Kauffman, "Urbanization of Mennonites: Canadian and American Comparisons," *MQR* 56 (July, 1982): 270–73; James C. Juhnke, "Mennonite History and Self-understanding: North American Mennonitism as a Bipolar Mosaic," in Calvin Redekop and Samuel Steiner, eds., *Mennonite Identity: Historical and Contemporary Perspectives* (Lanham, Md.: University Press of America, 1988), 88–94. On the impact of persecution on the Anabaptists, see also Rodney Sawatsky, "The Impact of Fundamentalism on Mennonite Nonresistance" (master's thesis, University of Minnesota, 1973), 18, 23–24.

39. Juhnke, "Mennonite History and Self-Understanding," 84, 89; Juhnke's

entire chapter, pp. 83–99, is required reading here. Also see Rodney Sawatsky's response, "Beyond the Social History of the Mennonites," in *Mennonite Identity*, 101–8. Also see Juhnke, *Vision, Doctrine, War*, 38–40.

40. Cornelius J. Dyck, *Introduction to Mennonite History*, 181; Harder and Kauffman, *Anabaptists Four Centuries Later*, 21. Because the Amish and Mennonites practice adult baptism, with most baptisms occurring in late adolescence, these numbers necessarily exclude children and youth in their early teens.

41. The nomenclature itself presents a bit of a problem. The official name for this group is The Mennonite Church; since the 1940s it has been the preferred name by Mennonites of this group. Many are offended by the use of their older, informal name of "old" Mennonites. There ought not to be a problem in simply referring to them as the Mennonite Church, or "MC" Mennonites, except that the use of that name is offensive to many members of other Mennonite groups. To other Mennonites, calling one group "the Mennonite Church" implies a certain level of marginality and subordination to the other denominations. Since the exclusive use of one term over the other seems bound to offend some readers, I have decided to refer to these Mennonites synonymously as the Mennonite Church and the "old" Mennonites throughout the course of this study.

For the preferences of OM/MC Mennonites, see Daniel Kauffman, Editorial, "Our Official Name," *Gospel Herald* 37 (October 6, 1944): 523.

42. Kauffman and Harder, *Anabaptists Four Centuries Later*, 21, 34; Dyck, *Mennonite History*, 164; Driedger and Kauffman, "Urbanization of Mennonites," 270–71. Mennonite schisms, Juhnke writes, "always centered on the extent of change and accommodation to the American environment" (*Vision, Doctrine, War*, 110). On the Mennonite Church as presenting a kind of "normative Mennonitism" with other groups as diverging from it, see Juhnke, "Mennonite History and Self-Understanding," 86–88.

43. Harold S. Bender, "Outside Influences on Mennonite Thought," Papers from the Conference on Mennonite Cultural and Educational Problems (Scottdale, Pa., 1953), 38; Dyck, *Mennonite History*, 168–69; Bender, "Mennonite Church," in *Mennonite Encyclopedia* (Hillsboro, Kans.: Mennonite Brethren Publishing House, 1959), 3:614; Juhnke, "Mennonite History and Self-Understanding," 91.

44. Sawatsky, *Authority and Identity*, 23, 3; Harder and Kauffman, *Anabaptists Four Centuries Later*, 35–36. Nor was this congregational polity rooted only in ideology and theology. In the Great Plains states, with GC Mennonite farmers living on isolated farms some distance from each other, the congregation began to assume many of the central community functions that the village social structure had previously served for many of them in Russia; the church, instead of the village, became the locus not only for worship but also for discipline, recruitment of leaders, courting—in short, for GC identity itself. See Juhnke, *Vision, Doctrine, War*, 86.

45. Other Mennonites would also flee from Russia. In the 1920s, disliking the developments of the Russian Revolution, 25,000 fled, 21,000 to Canada and 4,000 to settlements in Central and South America. An additional 12,000 managed to escape in the wake of the German army in World War II, the bulk of them also settling in Canada, making the GCMC the largest group of Canadian Mennonites.

The remainder of Russian Mennonites, still many thousands strong, would be swallowed up in Stalin's Russia; uncounted thousands perished in the Gulags. See Dyck, *Mennonite History*, 142–43, 146–47.

46. Ibid., 154–56, 199. On greater GC openness to outside society and culture, see Lauren Freisen, "Type 2: Culturally Engaged Pacifism," in John Richard Burkholder and Barbara Nelson Gingerich, eds., *Mennonite Peace Theology: A Panorama of Types* (Akron, Pa.: Mennonite Central Committee, 1991): 15–24; and Juhnke, "Mennonite History and Self-Understanding," 93–94.

CHAPTER 2:
CHALLENGES TO MENNONITE PEACEMAKING, 1914–1939

1. Harshbarger to Neuenschwander, December 27, 1937, Peace Committee Papers, MLA-I-4B, Box 7, File 109.

2. Juhnke, *Vision, Doctrine, War*, 86–95; Krehbiel of *Kansas Volksblatt* quoted p. 90.

3. For the different ways in which the OM and GC Mennonites dealt with the coming of World War I, see Juhnke, *Vision, Doctrine, War*, 210–12; and *People of Two Kingdoms*, 98–99.

4. For persecution of WWI COs in general, see Gerlof Homan, *American Mennonites and the Great War, 1914–1918*, 109–22; Juhnke, *Vision, Doctrine, War*, 234–35. On the empty promises by government officials, see Teichroew, "Mennonites and the Conscription Trap," *Mennonite Life* 30 (September 1975): 12–13. On the ultimate release of these men and the farm furlough system, see Homan, *American Mennonites and the Great War*, 135–38, 150–51; Juhnke, *Vision, Doctrine, War*, 238; Neal Wherry, *Conscientious Objection* (Washington, D.C.: Selective Service System Special Monograph No. 11, 1950) 1:56–62; Albert Keim and Grant Stoltzfus, *The Politics of Conscience*, 46–55. To a degree, Wilson and Baker were successful in their ultimate goal of inducing COs to take up combatant or noncombatant roles. Though the numbers remain elusive, the percentages of Kansas draftees were probably indicative of the larger trends. Of the 315 Kansas Mennonite draftees (from all Mennonite groups), 141 (45%) remained true to nonresistant principles and refused military service of any sort. About an equal number, 151 (48%) accepted noncombatant service, and 23 (7%) entered regular, combatant, military ranks. See Juhnke, *People of Two Kingdoms*, 102–3.

5. Homan, *American Mennonites and the Great War*, 63–80; Juhnke, *Vision, Doctrine, War*, 218–24. Juhnke, *People of Two Kingdoms*, 104–6, 108–9.

Not all Mennonites, out of either fear or conviction, chose to oppose the war. Historian Gerloff Homan also uncovered numerous instances of active Mennonite war support: enthusiastic public statements for the cause in Mennonite newspapers and at Mennonite colleges, voluntary war bond purchases and contributions to Red Cross drives, and the like (ibid., 60–63). In such support, Mennonites during World War I furnished another historical precedent for Mennonite activity in later twentieth-century conflicts.

6. James Juhnke, "Mennonite Benevolence and Revitalization in the Wake of World War I," *MQR* 60 (January 1986): 17–18.

7. Ibid., 17–18.

8. Ibid., 18–19, 21–22.

9. Ibid., 21–23; John Unruh, *In the Name of Christ*, 11–31, 35–37. Also see Cornelius Krahn, J. Winfield Fretz, and Robert Kreider, "Altruism in Mennonite Life," in Pitirim A. Sorokin, ed., *Forms and Techniques of Altruism and Spiritual Growth* (Boston: Beacon Press, 1954), 320–23.

10. Juhnke, "Mennonite Benevolence and Revitalization," 18, 26, 29, 17; Hiebert quoted p. 26. Also see James Juhnke, "Mennonite Benevolence and Civic Identity: The Post-war Compromise," *Mennonite Life* 25 (January 1970): 34–37.

11. On this point, see Charles Chatfield, *For Peace and Justice*, 50–55.

12. Quotes taken from Juhnke, "Mennonite Benevolence and Revitalization," 29.

13. Paul Toews, "The Long Weekend or the Short Week: Mennonite Peace Theology, 1925–1944," *MQR* 60 (January 1986): 41; Edward Yoder, "The Christian's Relation to the State in Time of War. I. The Christian's Attitude Toward Participation in War Activities," *MQR* 9 (January 1935): 19.

14. I have borrowed this summary of Marsden from Paul Toews, "Fundamentalist Conflict in Mennonite Colleges: A Response to Cultural Transitions?" *MQR* 57 (July 1983): 242–3.

15. In particular, the battles centered on the two denominations' colleges. At the OM Goshen College, important administrators identified with modernism finally resigned under pressure and moved to a rival GC institution in Ohio, Bluffton College. There they remained targets of conservative attacks. In 1924 John Horsch, one of the leading OM antimodernist crusaders, published an explosive polemic, *Mennonite Church and Modernism*, that denounced these men as "traitors." Meanwhile, the conservatives closed Goshen College in 1923 to purify it from any remaining modernist taint. At the GC Bethel College, conservatives also maneuvered into control of the board of trustees and forced the resignations of several faculty and one president who did not appear sufficiently orthodox. See Toews, "Fundamentalist Conflict in Mennonite Colleges," 242–52.

16. James Juhnke, "Mennonite Church Theological and Social Boundaries, 1920–1930—Loyalists, Liberals and Laxitarians," *Mennonite Life* 38 (June 1983): 18–24.

17. Toews, "Fundamentalist Conflict in Mennonite Colleges," 246–48; Juhnke, "Mennonite Church Theological and Social Boundaries," 22–23, and Juhnke, *Vision, Doctrine, War*, 112–119. On the paradoxical nature of this borrowing, see especially Theron F. Schlabach, "Paradoxes of Mennonite Separatism," *Pennsylvania Mennonite Heritage* 2 (January 1979): 12–17. For increasing Mennonite efforts to separate themselves from wider society, see Beulah Stauffer Hostetler, *American Mennonites and Protestant Movements*, 245–70.

Theron Schlabach has offered a thoughtful and detailed argument that the new aggressive Mennonite gospel that emerged out of the extensive borrowing from Protestant revivalism differed dramatically from the older traditional Mennonite understandings. This new gospel had a "two-track" understanding that separated salvation from ethics, he argues; once one was saved, then one could think about issues of discipleship. The older traditional Mennonite gospel did not draw such distinctions (see *Gospel Versus Gospel: Mission and the Mennonite Church, 1863–1944*).

18. Guy F. Hershberger, "Harold S. Bender and his Times," and J. C. Wenger, "Harold S. Bender: A Brief Biography," both in *MQR* 38 (April 1964): 85–91, 113–16. This entire issue was a memorial to Bender. Also see Juhnke, *Vision, Doctrine, War,* 276–78. Though too late for this study, the first scholarly biography of H. S. Bender by Professor Albert Keim of Eastern Mennonite University will soon be forthcoming.

19. On the creation of the *Mennonite Quarterly Review* as Bender's expression of a revitalizing vision, see Sawatsky, *History and Ideology,* 189–205; Bender is quoted pp. 191, 202; Juhnke, *Vision, Doctrine, War,* 279–80; Hershberger, "Bender and his Time" 89–93; Toews, "Mennonites and Modernity," 240–41.

20. For the closing of Goshen College, see note 15 above. Theron F. Schlabach, "To Focus a Mennonite Vision," in John Richard Burkholder and Calvin Redekop, eds., *Kingdom, Cross and Community: Essays on Mennonite Themes in Honor of Guy F. Hershberger* (Scottdale, Pa.: Herald Press, 1976), 17–19, 24.

21. Schlabach, "To Focus A Mennonite Vision," 21–25; Sawatsky, "History and Ideology," 221–22.

22. The lot was a mechanism among "old" Mennonites whereby a slip of paper was placed in one Bible out of a number distributed to minister aspirants. The man who found the paper in his Bible was the one whom God had chosen. Paul Erb, *Orie O. Miller: The Story of a Man and an Era,* 17–30.

23. Miller quoted in the *Sugar Creek Budget,* p. 204 in Erb, *Orie O. Miller.* Also see Juhnke, *Vision, Doctrine, War,* 276–77.

24. Erb, *Orie O. Miller,* 141–48; Juhnke, *Vision, Doctrine, War,* 282.

25. On the postwar fatigue of the peace committee, see Oral Interview, Keith Sprunger, David Haury, and David Kaufman with Henry Fast, March 21, 1973, transcript p. 33, Schowalter Oral History Collection, MLA. On the committee's reorganization, see Erb, *Orie O. Miller,* 203–7, Miller quoted p. 203; and Guy F. Hershberger, *The Mennonite Church in the Second World War,* 5.

26. Toews, "Mennonite Peace Theology," 44–45, Miller quoted p. 44; for the 1927 PPC report, see Guy F. Hershberger, "The Committee on Peace and Social Concerns, Dissent: Past and Present," November, 1966, Committee on Peace and Social Concerns Files, I-3–5.12, Box 67, AMC (Hereafter referred to as Hershberger, "CPSC Dissent"), p. 4.

27. Summary and quotes from Hershberger, "CPSC Dissent," 4–8.

28. The designation of PPC leaders as "progressives" is my word and certainly not theirs; in using it I am not implying any connection between these politically and culturally conservative people and the followers of Robert LaFollette or Henry Wallace. I have chosen to call these people "progressive" to express the wide contrast between their articulation of a soft-spoken, careful Mennonite peace activism and the apolitical, quietistic variation of nonresistance urged on them by their more fundamentalist brethren.

29. Juhnke, *Vision, Doctrine, War,* 282–85, Mosemann quoted p. 283; Toews, "Mennonite Peace Theology," 44.

30. Mosemann quoted in Toews, "Mennonite Peace Theology," 45; also see

Mosemann to O. O. Miller, September 10, 1926, Miller PPC Papers, I-3–5.3, Box 9, AMC; Hershberger, "CPSC Dissent," 10.

31. Mosemann to Miller, August 16, 1926; Miller to Mosemann, August 27, 1926; Mosemann to Miller, September 10, 1926; all in Miller PPC Papers, I-3–5.3, Box 9, AMC.

32. On Bender, see Juhnke, "Mennonite Church Theological and Social Boundaries," 19–22; on Hershberger, see Hershberger, "Biblical Nonresistance and Modern Pacifism," 122–26. Also see Hershberger, "The Modern Social Gospel and the Way of the Cross," *MQR* 30 (April 1956): 83–103; and Hershberger, "CPSC Dissent," 13.

33. Sawatsky particularly stressed this interpretation in his master's thesis; see Rodney Sawatsky, "The Influence of Fundamentalism on Mennonite Nonresistance" (master's thesis, University of Minnesota, 1973), 158–61, 173–79. Miller quoted in Sawatsky, "History and Ideology," 225–26; Hershberger quoted in Sawatsky, "Influence of Fundamentalism," 160. In my reading, these qualifications are more indicative of moderate peace leaders attempting to carve out a third way between fundamentalism and liberalism.

34. This exchange between Miller and Mosemann is described in Juhnke, *Vision, Doctrine, War*, 283–84; and Toews, "The Long Weekend," 46–7.

35. Guy F. Hershberger, "The Christian Relation to the State in Time of War. 2. Is Alternative Service Desirable and Possible?" *MQR* 9 (January 1935): 30–31. On the importance of this piece, see Paul Toews, "'Will a New Day Dawn from This?': Mennonite Pacifist People and the Good War," *Mennonite Life* 45 (December 1990): 17. Also see Schlabach, "To Focus a Mennonite Vision," 25.

36. Harold S. Bender, "Our Peace Testimony to the World—Goals and Methods," in *Report of the Mennonite Conference on War and Peace*, Goshen College, Goshen, Indiana, February 15–17, 1935, pp. 33–35, MSHL.

37. Peace Problems Committee, "A Statement of Our Position on Peace, War and Military Service," adopted by the Mennonite General Conference at Turner, Oregon, August, 1937, included in the Committee's "Report to the 1937 Mennonite General Conference," 123–24, AMC; Sawatsky, "History and Ideology," 230–31; Wenger, "Bender: A Biography," 119.

38. Peace Problems Committee, "Statement of Our Position on Peace, War, and Military Service," 1937, 124–26.

39. "Resolutions Adopting the 1937 General Conference Statement on War, Peace and Military Service," Virginia Conference Minutes, August 4–5, 1938, p. 225–26, n.p., MSHL. "A Statement of the Position of the General Conference of the Mennonite Church of North America on Peace, War, Military Service and Patriotism, as approved by the General Conference, Souderton, Pennsylvania, August 17–22, 1941," General Conference Minutes and Reports, 1941, pp. 163–166, n.p., MLA.

40. Toews, "Mennonite Peace Theology," 50–51; Sawatsky, "History and Ideology," 237–39; Robert Kreider, "The Historic Peace Churches Meeting of 1935," *Mennonite Life* 31 (June 1976): 22–23.

41. Toews, "Mennonite Peace Theology," 53–54; student memories cited in Roger Juhnke, "One War—Three Fronts: Kansas General Conference Mennonite

Response to World War II," Bethel College student paper, MLA, 1975, 32–33. Also see Mark Unruh, "E. L. Harshbarger: Mennonite Activist," Bethel College student paper, MLA, 1982.

42. Ernest J. Bohn, *Christian Peace: New Testament Peace Teachings Outside the Gospels*, pamphlet published by the Peace Committee of the General Conference Mennonite Church, Newton, Kansas, 1938, 34–35, MLA. Richard Gregg's book, *The Power of Nonviolence* (Philadelphia: J. B. Lippincott, 1934), was the work that above all others popularized Gandhian nonviolence among liberal pacifists in the 1930s; on this point, see Chatfield, *For Peace and Justice*, 204–12.

43. "The Mennonite Peace Society," *The Mennonite* 51 (February 4, 1936): 4. For an example of the sort of antiwar prescriptions the Mennonite Peace Society would direct at the state, see Carl Landes, "Statement to the Naval Affairs Committee," *The Mennonite* 53 (March 8, 1938): 3.

44. For Moody influences, see Willard Smith, *Mennonites in Illinois*, 312–13, 333–34; Henry Fast to Donovan Smucker, September 21, 1940, Fast Papers, MLA-MS-49, Box 1, File 5; Fast to Russell Lantz, August 26, 1940, Fast Papers, MLA-MS-49, Box 1, File 5; Bohn to Luke Horsch, March 12, 1940, Peace Committee Papers, MLA-I-4B, Box 7, File 110.

45. On this salvation-mindedness in the GCMC overall, see R. Juhnke, "One War—Three Fronts," 17–30; Sawatsky, "History and Ideology," 237; Harshbarger to Landes, January 14, 1936, Harshbarger Papers, MLA-MS-34, Box 1, File 4. On the pervasiveness of this attitude in wider interwar Protestantism, see Robert Moats Miller, *American Protestantism and Social Issues, 1919–1939*, 126.

46. Quoted in William Juhnke Jr., "A World Gone Mad: Mennonites View the Coming of War, 1938–1939," Bethel College student paper, 1966, MLA, 2–3. By 1939, however, Mennonite pro–German sentiment began to ebb as word came of Hitler's increased anti–Semitic persecutions, beginning now to extend to Christians as well. As William Juhnke has noted, Thierstein's exhortations of German righteousness must have been sparking some opposition, for he complained early in 1939 that "it is impossible to say anything without stepping on somebody's toes." Somewhat discouraged, the editor admitted that "American Mennonites pretty generally share the intolerant American attitude against Germany." Instead, by the late 1930s, American GC Mennonites had adopted, if their publications are any indication, the popular isolationism of the American Midwest. See W. Juhnke, "A World Gone Mad," 9, 11; "If War, Will U.S. Be in It?" *The Mennonite* 54 (May 2, 1939): 2; William H. Stauffer, "Neutral Also in Thought," *The Mennonite* 54 (October 24, 1939): 4.

47. James Juhnke, "Gerald Winrod and the Kansas Mennonites," *MQR* 43 (October 1969): 296–98.

48. For a more detailed treatment of these activities, see Perry Bush, "Drawing the Line: American Mennonites, the State, and Social Change, 1935–1973," (Ph.D. diss., Carnegie-Mellon University, 1990): 62–66. "Report of the Peace Committee," Peace Committee Papers, MLA-I-4B, Box 37, File 110.

49. "Henry A. Fast, Record Since Graduation from Bethel, 1917," Addendum to Fast Papers, MLA-MS-49, Box 1; "Report of the Peace Committee to the 49th Western District Conference," October 24–24, 1940, Newton, Kans., MLA, 235.

On the WWI draftee experience as a "death knell" for future church leadership, see Juhnke, *Vision, Doctrine, War*, 276.

50. Robert Kreider et al. to Harshbarger, March 9, 1939, Peace Committee Papers, MLA-I-4B, Box 7, File 109. The letter's signers reads now like a virtual "who's who" of GCMC leadership of the postwar decades; they included Kreider, Esko Loewen, Erwin Goering, Elmer Ediger, and Arthur Friesen. Harshbarger to Landes, April 20, 1936, Harshbarger papers, MLA-MS-34, Box 1, Folder 4. Also see Landes to Harshbarger, January 22, 1936, Harshbarger Papers, MLA-MS-34, Box 1, File 4.

51. See Oral Interview, Roger Juhnke with Elmer Ediger, October 9, 1978, Schowalter Oral History Collection, MLA; Elmer Ediger to Harry and Olga (Martens), July 15, 1941, Elmer Ediger Papers, MLA (these papers were unprocessed); Oral Interview, Keith Sprunger with Esko Loewen, Oct. 9, 1973, Schowalter Oral History Collection, MLA.

52. Oral interview, Keith Sprunger with Robert Kreider, September 7 and November 24, 1987, Schowalter Oral History Collection, transcript pp. 2–3, MLA; Ediger Interview. Roger Juhnke, "One War—Three Fronts," 24; Terence Goering, "A History of the Bethel College Peace Club," Bethel College student paper, 1975, MLA, 3–6.

So influential and important was this peace emphasis among GC youth in the 1930s that the real story of the endurance of GC peace commitments in the interwar period may lie with it, rather than with the denomination's Peace Committee. Kreider recalled later that as a young man growing up in the church, he was "scarcely aware" of the committee. Instead, his lifelong commitment to Mennonite pacifism was nurtured in church youth retreats and in GC Mennonite youth group meetings. Seen in this light, Harshbarger's larger importance in GCMC peace understandings may have been in his role as a Bethel professor rather than as PC head. Similarly, it is important to at least recognize here the influence that Bethel College President Edmund G. Kaufman had on the peace positions of many Bethel College students. I have come to this understanding from personal correspondence, Robert Kreider with author, March 24, 1994; and from James Juhnke, *Creative Crusader: Edmund G. Kaufman and Mennonite Community*, 203–9, 213–19, 228–29.

53. Asked to respond, Harshbarger could only point out the existence of the Peace Committee and admit that it "has been tremendously handicapped because of lack of funds." Accordingly, Harshbarger suggested to this pastor that he "and men who share your view write strong articles for our church papers showing the poverty of our committee and demanding action from the constituency. We college leaders are still view[ed] with suspicious eyes if we are always urging action." See C. E. Krehbiel to Harshbarger, April 14, 1939, Harshbarger Papers, MLA-MS-34, Box 2, File 12; Harshbarger to Richert, May 2, 1939, Harshbarger papers, MLA-MS-34, Box 2, File 13.

54. Irwin Richert to Fast, July 16, 1940, Fast Papers, MLA-MS-49, Box 1, File 4. Fast's response is quite interesting in itself. Though Fast quite firmly held that alternative service was the best solution—as witnessed by his subsequent position as MCC's administrator of CPS—he also believed that this ought to be a personal

decision that one's conscience would lead him to. Thus, he refused to tell young Richert what to do, instead laying out a number of options for him, ranging from noncombatant service to absolute refusal to register. See Fast to Richert, July 23, 1940, Fast Papers, MLA-MS-49, Box 1, File 4.

55. Reynolds Weinbrenner to Fast, July 8, 1940, Fast Papers, MLA-MS-49, Box 1, File 4; Ellis Graber to Harshbarger, October 22, 1940, Harshbarger Papers, MLA-MS-34, Box 2, File 21.

56. Paul Johnson, *The Rise and Fall of the Great Powers*, 330–33. On the development of air war doctrine in the interwar years, see Ronald Schaffer, *Wings of Judgement*, 20–34; Michael Sherry, *The Rise of American Air Power*, 23–32, 116–17; and Russell Weigley, *The American Way of War*, 223–41. Conversely, the historian Conrad Crane has downplayed the degree to which Douhet was taught or absorbed by students in the Air Corps Tactical School in the 1930s; according to Crane, American leaders did not more consciously adopt Douhetian tactics until late in World War II. See Conrad C. Crane, *Bombs, Cities and Civilians*, 15–18, 131–36.

57. Guy F. Hershberger, "The Christian's Relation to the State in Time of War: II. Is Alternative Service Desirable and Possible?" *MQR* 9 (January 1935): 31–34; Toews, "The Long Weekend," 40–41 (Smith citation); Harold S. Bender, "Church and State in Mennonite History," *MQR* 13 (April 1939): 103.

CHAPTER 3:
THE MENNONITE LEADERSHIP AND A LINE OF LEAST RESISTANCE

1. Ernest Bohn to "Dear Brother," January 29, 1941, Peace Committee Papers, MLA-I-4B, Box 7, File 112. On the importance of World War II in the larger histories of other groups, see Richard A. Dalfiume, "The 'Forgotten Years' of the Negro Revolution," *Journal of American History*, 55 (June 1968): 91–106; Carl Degler, *At Odds: Women and the Family from the Revolution to the Present*, (New York: Oxford University Press, 1980), 419–22, 426.

2. Alan S. Milward, *War, Economy, and Society, 1939–1945*, 53. For a few comparative statistics of the two world wars, see Paul Fussell, *Wartime: Understanding and Behavior in the Second World War*, 70, 4. Roosevelt quoted in Mitchell Robinson, "Civilian Public Service During World War II: the Dilemmas of Conscience and Conscription in a Free Society" (Ph.D. diss., Cornell University, 1990), 8.

3. Richard Polenberg, *War and Society*, 8, 21–22; Richard Lingeman, *Don't You Know There's a War On?* 136; William Manchester, *The Glory and The Dream*, 354; Geoffrey Perrett, *Days of Sadness, Years of Triumph*, 255–59, 150–52, 316–18.

4. Stimson quoted in Polenberg, *War and Society*, 2. For polling data, see Richard W. Steele, "American Popular Opinion and the War Against Germany: The Issue of Negotiated Peace, 1942," *Journal of American History* 45 (December 1978): 706.

5. On war propaganda and censorship, see Michael C. C. Adams, *The Best War Ever: America and World War II* (Baltimore: Johns Hopkins University Press, 1994), 9–10; Polenberg, *War and Society*, 51–54; Fussell, *Wartime*, 143–64; Steele, "American Popular Opinion and the War Against Germany," 721–22.

6. Richard Polenberg, *One Nation Divisible: Class, Race, and Ethnicity in the*

United States Since 1938, 53–61. Also on this point see Polenberg, *War and Society*, 40–43. Surveys noted in Robinson, "Civilian Public Service During World War II," 302.

7. On the curbs placed on dissent in World War II, see Perrett, *Days of Sadness*, 91–92; song quoted p. 241. For the trials undergone by Jehovah's Witnesses, see Perrett, 225–27 and Cynthia Hastas Morris, "Arkansas's Reaction to the Men who Said 'No' to World War II," *Arkansas Historical Quarterly* 43 (Summer 1984): 157–62.

8. Milward, *War, Economy, and Society*, 297–302; Ronald Schaffer, *Wings of Judgement: American Bombing in World War II*, 35–38, 66–70, 80–106; Conrad C. Crane, *Bombs, Cities and Civilians*, 42–47; Michael Sherry, *The Rise of American Air Power*, 116–17, 147–66.

9. Schaffer, *Wings of Judgement*, 107–10, 127–48; Sherry, *The Rise of American Air Power*, 170–311; Crane, *Bombs, Cities and Civilians*, 120–42. While insisting on the operational viability of precision bombing as practiced by the American air forces in the European theater, Crane admitted that the Army Air Corps eagerly embraced mass firebombing when it turned to focus its attention on Japan in 1945; see Crane, 112–13, 133, 159–60. Polling data quoted in Paul Boyer, *By the Bomb's Early Light*, 183. *Time* quoted in Boyer, 213.

10. Lawrence Wittner, *Rebels Against War*, 34.

11. Ibid., 16–43; Morrison quoted, p. 42. Also see Charles Chatfield, *For Peace and Justice*, 221–328. On the decline of pacifism in liberal, mainline churches, see also W. Edward Orser, "World War II and the Pacifist Controversy in the Major Protestant Churches," *American Studies* 14 (Fall 1973): 5–10.

12. Paul Carter, *The Decline and Revival of the Social Gospel*, 160–62. For the central guiding role of Niebuhr's realism in the thinking of a American liberals, see the laudatory comments of Arthur Schlesinger Jr. (a preeminent political liberal of the postwar years) in Schlesinger, "Reinhold Niebuhr's Role in American Political Thought and Life," in Charles W. Kegley and Robert W. Bretall, eds., *Reinhold Niebuhr: His Religious, Social, and Political Thought* (New York: Macmillan, 1956), 125–50; and Schlesinger, *The Vital Center: The Politics of Freedom*, (Boston: Houghton Mifflin, 1949; reprint, 1962), 147, 165–66.

13. Niebuhr, "Why the Christian Church Is Not Pacifist," in *Christianity and Power Politics* (New York: Charles Scribner's Sons, 1940), 1–32, Niebuhr quoted pp. 22, 9–10. For a concise summary of Niebuhr's critique of pacifism, see James F. Childress, "Reinhold Niebuhr's Critique of Pacifism," *Review of Politics* 36 (October 1974): 475–76.

14. Niebuhr quoted in Niebuhr, "Why the Christian Church Is Not Pacifist," 4–5; also see p. 31; and Niebuhr, "Christian Politics and Communist Religion," in John Lewis, Karl Polanyi, and Donald B. Kitchin, eds., *Christianity and the Social Revolution* (New York: Charles Scribner's Sons, 1936), 457. Also see Childress, "Reinhold Niebuhr's Critique of Pacifism," 474.

15. Niebuhr, "Japan and the Christian Conscience," *Christian Century* 54 (November 10, 1937): 1391.

16. Albert Keim, "The Anabaptist Vision: Reassurance and Rallying Point for the Church," *Gospel Herald* 87 (April 19, 1994): 2–3. Harold S. Bender, "The Ana-

baptist Vision," *MQR* 18 (April, 1944): 67–88; Bender quoted on pp. 85, 88. Also see Paul Toews, "The Concern Movement: Its Origins and Early History," *Conrad Grebel Review* 8 (Spring 1990): 115–116.

17. For instance, claims of this "Goshen school" that the origins of Anabaptism lay in Zurich in 1525 and that these were the "original" and "genuine" Anabaptists have drawn particular fire as a "mythology of pure origins." See Sawatsky, "History and Ideology," 280–90; and John Oyer, "Historiography, Anabaptist," in Dyck and Martin, eds., *Mennonite Encyclopedia*, Vol. 5, 378–482.

18. Paul Toews, "Mennonites in American Society: Modernity and the Persistence of Religious Community," *MQR* 63 (July 1983): 240–41; Rodney Sawatsky, "History and Ideology: American Mennonite Definition Through History (Ph.D. diss., Princeton University, 1977), 290–93. While this rereading of Anabaptism emerged out of Goshen College and received its primary reworking at the hands of MC scholars, Sawatsky is careful to point out how the Anabaptist vision functioned as normative for GC Mennonites as well, with only slight qualification. See "History and Ideology," 279–80; and Sawatsky, *Authority and Identity,* 39–40. Primarily, the GC dissent would be focused on Bender's location of true Anabaptism in primarily the South German/Swiss ethnic milieu, in effect excluding the North German/Dutch/Russian background and thus much of the General Conference Mennonite Church; this point will be explored more carefully in chapter 5.

19. Toews, "Mennonites in American Society," 242, 239–56 passim.

20. See the Foreword by Bender and the Author's Preface in Guy F. Hershberger, *War, Peace and Nonresistance*, vii–x; Toews, "The Long Weekend," 49, 56; Theron Schlabach, "To Focus a Mennonite Vision," in John R. Burkholder and Calvin Redekop, eds., *Kingdom, Cross and Community: Essays on Mennonite Themes in Honor of Guy F. Hershberger* (Scottdale, Pa.: Herald Press, 1969), 27–28.

21. Hershberger, *War, Peace, and Nonresistance*, ix.

22. Ibid., 49–53, 194–97; quoted pp. 49.

23. Ibid., 210–24, 197–200, 295–97; quotations from pp. 214, 199, 295.

24. Ibid., 199–200.

25. Ibid., 199–200; also see pp. 298–301. On Hershberger's suggestion of a single moral law applicable to both kingdoms, see Leo Driedger and Donald B. Kraybill, *Mennonite Peacemaking: From Quietism to Activism,* 75, 78–79.

26. Schlabach, "To Focus a Mennonite Vision," 27–28; Donovan E. Smucker, "A Review of War, Peace, and Nonresistance," *The Mennonite* 59 (December 12, 1944): 1–2, 10, 11. Also see Sawatsky, "The Impact of Fundamentalism on Mennonite Nonresistance," 177–79.

27. Enough grumbling emanated from those with a more activist bent to indicate that Hershberger's delicate attempt to unite activists and conservatives around a single Mennonite social ethic had not entirely worked. Periodic expressions of unhappiness from the activists continued to echo in the postwar years. In 1948, for example, MC scholar Melvin Gingerich informed Miller that "a considerable number of General Conference Mennonites have talked to me about Hershberger's book and our peace literature in general. They are not satisfied with it and they talk of a book to be a counterpart to Hershberger's . . . They feel the book is weak in the area of our responsibility to society, that we do not state sufficiently the day to day

application of our principle in our communities and in American society. We are still so exclusive and so unaware of the problems of society around us that we have failed to see these evils and injustices." Likewise, Carl Landes denounced Hershberger's book along the same lines in *The Mennonite*. See Melvin Gingerich to Orie Miller, May 27, 1948, Committee on Economic and Social Relations Papers, I-3–7, Box 2, AMC. Landes's denunciation came in a letter to the editor in response to Smucker's glowing review; see Carl Landes, "The Reader Says," *The Mennonite* 60 (January 23, 1945): 6. Landes's name is misprinted as "Carol."

28. Robert Kreider quoted in Driedger and Kraybill, *Mennonite Peacemaking*, 78; Oral Interview, Keith Sprunger with Esko Loewen, October 9, 1973, Schowalter Oral History Collection, MLA.

29. "Report of a Conference of Mennonite Peace Groups," March 10, 1939, in Chicago, MCC Peace Section Minutes and Reports, IX-7–8, Box 1, AMC; Hershberger to Miller, August 13, 1940, and September 4, 1940, O. O. Miller PPC Papers, I-3–5.3, Box 16, AMC.

30. "Meeting of the Mennonite Central Peace Committee," MCC Peace Section Minutes and Reports, IX-7–8, Box 1; "Plan of Action for Mennonites in Case of War," September 30, 1939, H. S. Bender Papers, PPC Files, 1–3-5.10, Box 53, AMC; Melvin Gingerich, *Service for Peace: A History of Mennonite Civilian Public Service*, 34–35. Also see generally John Unruh, *In the Name of Christ*, 274–76. There was little questioning in 1940 that registration was the proper step. As Fast wrote that September, "there is pretty general agreement" on this, though their young men "should state right then and there their conscientious objection to participation in military training." See Fast to William T. Snyder, September 7, 1940, Fast Papers, MLA-MS-49, Box 1, File 5.

31. See, for instance, Milford Sibley and Philip Jacob, *Conscription of Conscience*, 140–47; and Albert Keim and Grant Stoltzfus, *The Politics of Conscience*, 5.

32. Keim and Stoltzfus, *The Politics of Conscience*, 101–11. Also on these negotiations, see Sibley and Jacob, *Conscription of Conscience*, 116–17.

33. Gingerich, *Service for Peace*, 52–55.

34. On the functional reality of the CPS system, see Gingerich, *Service for Peace*, 58, 396; Sibley and Jacob, *Conscription of Conscience*, 117–123; Keim and Stoltzfus, *The Politics of Conscience*, 112–15. Brunk and Miller quoted in Albert Keim, "Service or Resistance? The Mennonite Response to Conscription in World War II," *MQR* 15 (April 2, 1978): 154.

35. Gingerich, *Service for Peace*, 74, 84–85, 36–38.

36. George Q. Flynn, "Lewis Hershey and the Conscientious Objector: The World War II Experience," *Military Affairs* 47 (February 1983): 1–3; Flynn, *Lewis B. Hershey: Mr. Selective Service*, 131; Hershey quoted in Sibley and Jacob, *Conscription of Conscience*, p. 123; Oral Interview, Grant Stoltzfus with Joseph Weaver, May 25, 1972, Schowalter Oral History Collection, MLA, transcript pp. 17–18; Robinson, "Civilian Public Service During World War II," 205–6, 253–54.

37. Polenberg, *War and Society*, 57–58; Sibley and Jacob, *Conscription of Conscience*, 308, 121–22.

38. Robinson, "Civilian Public Service During World War II," 516–17; Her-

shey quoted pp. 252, 312. I am especially indebted to Professor Robinson for this analysis.

39. Robinson, "Civilian Public Service During World War II," 310, 515–17, 248–49; Sibley and Jacob, *Conscription of Conscience*, 217; Flynn, "Lewis Hershey and the Conscientious Objector," 3.

40. Robinson, "Civilian Public Service During World War II," 310–23; Hershey quoted pp. 188 and 312. Also on the importance of the appearance of equitable treatment between GIs and COs, see Flynn, "Lewis Hershey and the Conscientious Objector," 4; and Sibley and Jacob, *Conscription of Conscience*, 209–18.

41. Sibley and Jacob, *Conscription of Conscience*, 120–23, 323–25; Olmstead quoted p. 121.

42. Robinson, "Civilian Public Service During World War II," 239–48; Dick Hunter to Gaeddert, October 1, 1943, Gaeddert Papers, MLA-MS-50, Box 2, File 12; Wittner, *Rebels Against War*, 72–85; Guy Hershberger, *The Mennonite Church in the Second World War*, 62.

43. On Mennonite expression of satisfaction with CPS, see Keim, "Service or Resistance?" 147–49; Gingerich, *Service For Peace*, 395–97; "Letters, To Selective Service," Mennonite General Conference to Lewis B. Hershey, *Gospel Herald* 34 (November 13, 1941): 707. On MCC's decision to continue in camp administration in 1945, see Theodore G. Grimsrud, "An Ethical Analysis of Conscientious Objection to World War II" (Ph.D. diss., Graduate Theological Union, 1988), 75.

44. Keim, "Service or Resistance," 141, 155; Fast, "Mennonites and the Civilian Service Program," *The Mennonite* 56 (January 7, 1941): 3.

45. Keim, "Service or Resistance?" 143; CPSer Melvin Kauffman quoted in Kauffman, "CPS Past, Present and Future: What Do You Think?" *High Sierra Vistas* 1 (December, 1942): 9, IX-13-1, CPS Camp Newsletters, AMC; Henry Fast, "CPS Camps," *Gospel Herald* 34 (March 26, 1942): 1107.

46. Oral Interview, Elmer Ediger, Henry Fast, and James Juhnke with Orie Miller, November 11, 1969, Schowalter Oral History Collection, MLA, transcript p. 10; Bender to Bohn, October 14, 1941, Peace Committee Papers, MLA-I-4B, Box 7, File 112.

47. Gingerich, *Service for Peace*, 297–317; Schlabach, "To Focus a Mennonite Vision," 27. Also on the CPS system as a vast mechanism for educating young Mennonites in the new Hershberger/Bender articulation of nonresistance, see Sawatsky, "History and Ideology," 256–57.

48. Hershberger, *War, Peace, and Nonresistance*, 235; Leo Kanagy, *Gospel Herald* (August 19, 1937), quoted in David Peterson, "Ready for War: Oregon Mennonites from Versailles to Pearl Harbor," *MQR* 64 (July 1990): 219. Walter Dyck, "What if They Say"? *The Mennonite* 57 (January 27, 1942): 1, quoted in Roger Juhnke, "One War—Three Fronts: Kansas General Conference Mennonite Response to World War II," Bethel College student paper, MLA, 1975, 43. Orie Miller to Paul French, August 25, 1941, MCC Correspondence, IX-6-3, "CPS and other correspondence, 1940–1945, NSBRO Executive Secretary, 1941," AMC.

49. Don E. Smucker, "What I Saw in CPS," *Gospel Herald* 38 (June 2, 1944): 156; Bender, "Forward into the Postwar World with our Peace Testimony," *Chris-*

tian Missions, a supplement to the *Gospel Herald* 39 (June 1946): 214. MCC, *CPS Newsletter* I (March 19, 1943): 1, AMC. For another helpful summary of second-mile philosophy, see Editorial, "The Christian in an Evil World," *Gospel Herald* 38 (April 6, 1945): 3.

50. Roosevelt quoted in Robinson, "Civilian Public Service During World War II," 288, 289–90.

51. Editorial, "Defense Drives," *Gospel Herald* 34 (July 10, 1941): 1; H. S. Bender, "A Message to Nonresistant Christians," *Gospel Herald* 34 (January 15, 1942): 898; "Notes on Conscription Institute," Powellsville, Maryland, February 24–25, 1945, p. 4, Hershberger PPC papers, I-3–5.7, Box 36, File 38, AMC. CPSer in North Fork, California, quoted in "CPS Present and Future: What Do You Think," *High Sierra Vistas* I, (December 1942): 9, IX-13–1, AMC

52. Benevolent contributions noted in Gingerich, *Service for Peace,* 342, 358; Donovan Smucker, "What I Saw in CPS," 156; J. N. Weaver, "The Open Door in CPS," *Christian Missions,* a supplement to the *Gospel Herald* 37 (October 6, 1944): 541. Canned goods total taken from Paul Toews, *Mennonites in American Society,* 160.

53. Keim, "Service or Resistance?" 155.

54. On the census of Mennonite workers delivered to the government, see Keim and Stoltzfus, *The Politics of Conscience,* 80–81; and "Meeting of the Executive Committee of the M. C. P.C.," June 17, 1940, MCC Peace Section Minutes and Reports, IX-7–8, Box 1, AMC. For the issue of paying taxes in World War II, see Hershberger, *War, Peace, and Nonresistance,* 369; Walter Dyck, "What if They Say?" *The Mennonite* 57 (January 27, 1942): 2; and R. L. Hartzler, "Do It Now," *The Mennonite* 56 (April 22, 1941): 3.

55. On the condemnation of war bonds, see Hershberger, *War, Peace and Nonresistance,* 369. On the anxiety local Mennonites expressed over the opportunity to purchase civilian bonds, see R. Juhnke, "One War—Three Fronts," 50; and O. O. Miller to Henry Morgenthau, May 18, 1942, Hist. Mss I-278, H. S. Bender Papers, Box 52, File 24, "MCC Correspondence, 1939–1947, Miller, O. O.," AMC. For a concise summary of the civilian bond issue, see Hershberger, *The Mennonite Church in the Second World War,* 138–47, PPC quoted p. 146; Harold Bender, "The War Bond Campaign," *Gospel Herald* 36 (September 23, 1943): 538; John M. Snyder, "On the Civilian Bond Question," *Gospel Herald* 36 (September 23, 1943): 538–541; Gingerich, *Service For Peace,* 355–359.

56. Gingerich, *Service for Peace,* 358. On the tallying of civilian bonds in local war bond quotas, see Hershberger, *The Mennonite Church in the Second World War,* 145–46; and R. Juhnke, "One War—Three Fronts," 50. Perceptive Mennonites realized the weaknesses and inherent accommodations of the arrangement. Stationed at MCC headquarters in Akron, Pennsylvania, late in the war, Robert Kreider "heard a lot of complaints about the flimsiness of this enterprise" (personal correspondence, Robert Kreider to author, March 24, 1994).

Meanwhile, the pressure of nationalism was sufficiently intense that an indeterminate but still fair number of Mennonites went ahead and bought war bonds anyway; some even led bond drives in their communities. The Kansas-based *Mennonite Weekly Review* regularly accepted ads for war bonds and made few adjustments in these ads for sensitive Mennonite readers. One such ad, for instance, pictured a machine gun and told readers that "YOUR $18.75 WAR BOND coming out of the end of a machine gun, means a total of 933 shots, 187 'bursts' or approximately a minute and half of firing. Trust the guy who pulls the trigger to see that the bursts go home." Another ad presented a sketch of a bomb and entreated readers to "Put your name on this BLOCKBUSTER." See R. Juhnke, "One War—Three Fronts," 53, 55. Also see Robert Kreider, "Do We Take a Stand on Nonresistance?" *The Mennonite* 60 (May 8, 1945): 6.

57. "Report of the Peace Problems Committee" to the 1941 Mennonite General Conference, Wellman, Iowa, p. 21, n.p., AMC; H. S. Bender for the Peace Problems Committee, "Can Conscientious Objectors Work in War Industry?," *Gospel Herald* 35 (June 25, 1942): 282.

58. Oral Interview, Trent Shipley with Galen R. Koehn, October 17, 1988, Schowalter Oral History Collection, MLA. For Darvin Luginbuhl's CPS experiences, see Oral Interview, Melissa Bratt with Darvin Luginbuhl, February 7, 1995, deposited with Mennonite Historical Library, Bluffton College (hereafter abbreviated MHLB).

59. For one presentation of Jehovah's witnesses in World War II, see sources in note 7.

60. Oral Interview, John Theissen with Menno Schrag, March 1979, Schowalter Oral History Collection, MLA. On war employment in the Ohio and Eastern Amish Mennonite Conference, see Hershberger, *The Mennonite Church in the Second World War*, 127; for Lancaster, see "The Christian's Attitude in War Time," *Pastoral Messenger* 11 (October 1, 1942): 3–4; and "Lancaster Mennonite Conference Minutes of Bishop's Board Meeting," April 12–16, 1943, Rohrerstown, Pa., n.p., LMHS. On the incident in Shanesville, Ohio, see response from Million B. Hostetler, Kolb and Longenecker Congregation, Shanesville, Ohio, in "Census of Drafted Men," Mennonite Research Foundation Papers, "State of Men in Military Service," V-7–20, Box 7, AMC.

61. Ernest Gehman, "Regarding Our Unequal Yoke with Popular Pacifism," Undated Letter to Virginia Conference Ministers, H. S. Bender PPC Papers, 1–3-5.10, Box 55, AMC; Sanford G. Shetler, "The Civilian Public Service Program," *Sword and Trumpet* 11 (December, 1943): 6–7.

To his credit, GC leader Henry Fast did not let such digs get under his skin. Writing in August 1943, he admitted that "most people in our conference are not aware of serious difficulties which men like Bender, Miller and others have to deal with within their own conference group in any cooperative venture such as MCC. Some of their reactionary group have caused them a lot of trouble and they are trying to keep their ranks in tact." In fact, Fast saw the OM efforts to mollify church conservatives as something that "one could probably approve and welcome." Fast to William Stauffer, August 27, 1943, Fast Papers, MLA-MS-49, Box 3, File 22.

62. Stauffer quoted in Sawatsky, "History and Ideology," 235; PPC's responses noted in Hershberger, *The Mennonite Church in the Second World War*, 253–55, 261–64. Also see "Report of the Civilian Service Investigating Committee," to the 1943 Mennonite General Conference, n.p., AMC, 45–49.

63. H. T. Unruh to Bohn, September 27, 1940, Peace Committee Papers,

MLA-I-4B, Box 7, File 110; Donovan Smucker to Fast, October 2, 1940, Fast Papers, MLA-MS-49, Box 1, File 6; Russell Lantz to Fast, undated but found in correspondence file labeled "October-December, 1940," Fast Papers, MLA-MS-49, Box 1, File 6. Langenwalter to Fast, March 14, 1941, Fast Papers, MLA-MS-49, Box 2, File 9; Fast to Langenwalter, March 17, 1941, Fast Papers, MLA-MS-49, Box 2, File 9.

64. Daniel Kauffman to Orie Miller, September 14, 1939, Bender PPC Papers, 1–3-5.10, Box 51, AMC; Miller to Kauffman, September 19, 1939, Bender PPC Papers, 1–3-5.10, Box 51, AMC. On Kauffman's influence in the church, see Theron Schlabach, "Paradoxes of Mennonite Separatism," *Pennsylvania Mennonite Heritage* 2 (January 1979): 14.

65. Paul T. Huddle to Bender, October 17, 1941, Bender PPC Papers, 1–3-5.10, Box 51, AMC; Shetler, "The Civilian Public Service Program," 2.

66. Peachey to Bender, March 22, 1944, Miller PPC Papers, I-3–5.3, Box 17, AMC. For the report on Horst's speech in Lancaster, see Jacob Brubaker to Bender, March 4, 1944, Miller PPC Papers, 1–3-5.3, Box 17, AMC. Equally revealing was Bender's notation on top of the letter reading "For O. O. M. personal. Throw in waste basket. HSB." Horst to Bender, June 8, 1945, Horst Papers, "CPS," LMHS.

67. "Report of the Peace Problems Committee," 1941, p. 18; H. S. Bender, "In the Midst of War—Thoughts for Nonresistants. III. Mennonite Men in the Army?" *Gospel Herald* 25 (February 11, 1943): 986. Report of the Peace Problems Committee," 1943, p. 38; Executive Committee, Stenographic Report, August 1943 Session, I-2–1, pp. 5–6, "Executive Committee Reports," Box 3, AMC

68. "Betrayed conscience" quote in J. D. Goering, "Don't Betray your Conscience," *The Mennonite* 56 (April 22, 1941): 9; Bohn, "Our Peace Objectives," 3; J. Winfield Fretz, "Mennonites and Rural Life: Conscientious Objectors and the Farm," *The Mennonite* 57 (May 26, 1942): 3; Smith, "Is the General Conference Losing its Peace Testimony?," *The Mennonite* 57 (July 28, 1942): 1; Peace Committee Meeting Minutes, 1943, 4; J. W. Fretz, "Meditations on the Mennonites: Isn't It Strange?" *The Mennonite* 60 (January 9, 1945): 14.

CHAPTER 4:
THE MENNONITE PEOPLE AND TOTAL WAR, 1941–1945

1. Oral Interview, Frederic Fransen with David C. Wedel, March 24, 1988, Schowalter Oral History Collection, MLA.

2. Oral Interview, Roger Juhnke with Henry Fast, October 19, 1978; Oral Interview, Tom Penner with Harry Ratzlaff, November 26, 1989; Oral Interview, Keith Sprunger with Irvin Richert, September 29, 1979, transcript pp. 6–7; Oral Interview, David Graber with Earl Loganbill, October 24, 1988; Oral Interview, Kurt Goering with Harvey Deckert, November 4, 1975, transcript pp. 4–5; all in Schowalter Oral History Collection, MLA.

3. On the letter to a California CO, see "G. I. Letter," *High Sierra Vistas* 2 (March 1944): 8, CPS Camp Newsletters, IX-13–1, AMC; for Springer's comment, see Paul Springer to Arthur Nafziger, July 25, 1944, Hist. Mss. I-272, Arthur Nafziger Correspondence, Box 1, File 9, AMC. The letters to the editor accompanying Springer's letter appeared in *Yank: The Army Weekly,* July 21, 1944. For

Waltner anecdote, see Oral Interview, David Graber with Robert Waltner, December 30, 1987, Schowalter Oral History Collection, MLA. In his fine analysis of American attitudes and behavior in World War II (a study rooted in his own experiences as a GI in that conflict), Paul Fussell noted this solidarity clearly. "One might think that the most vigorous soldierly contempt might be directed at conscientious objectors," he wrote. "But no: since most of them were set to hard labor in camps, they were regarded as virtual members, if a bit disgraced, of the armed services" (*Wartime: Understanding and Behavior in the Second World War*, 116).

4. Interview, Sprunger with Richert, MLA, transcript, pp. 25–26; Oral Interview, Joy Linscheid with Roland Bartel, February 17, 1991, Schowalter Oral History Collection, MLA, interview notes, p. 8.

5. Oral Interview, Perry Bush with Loris Habegger, June 10, 1994, deposited with Schowalter Oral History Collection, MLA.

6. On the hostility in Newton, see Oral Interview, John Theissen with Menno Schrag, March 1979, Schowalter Oral History Collection, MLA. Hostility at Oak Grove in James O. Lehman, *Creative Congregationalism*, 258. On Kalona, Iowa, see Oral Interview, Roger Juhnke with John J. Miller, November 22, 1978, Schowalter Oral History Collection, MLA; and Guy Hershberger, *The Mennonite Church in the Second World War*, 136–37.

7. On the reaction to CPS camp in Arkansas, see Cynthia Hastas Morris, "Arkansas's Reaction to the Men Who Said 'No' to World War II," *Arkansas Historical Quarterly* 43 (Summer, 1984): 167. For Ediger's experience at Ypsilanti, see Oral Interview, Kurt Goering with Amanda Ediger Bartel, May 10, 1976, Schowalter Oral History Collection, MLA, transcript pp. 18–19.

8. Farmer quoted in "Dairy Testing," J. Wilmer Heisey to Melvin Gingerich, November 29, 1947, Hershberger PPC papers, I-3–5.7, Box 36, AMC. Fast recollections in Interview, Juhnke with Fast, MLA, transcript p. 7. Incidents in Ohio and Indiana noted in Rachel Waltner Goossen, "Conscientious Objection and Gender: Women in Civilian Public Service During the Second World War" (Ph.D. diss., University of Kansas, 1994), 42. Incident at Camp Camino in Oral Interview, Mark Kroeker with Walter Unrau, October 27, 1989, Schowalter Oral History Collection, MLA, notes p. 2. For hostility experienced by Davidhizar and Gering, see Oral Interview, Trent Shipley with Paul Davidhizar, June 6, 1988, notes p. 2; and Oral Interview, David Graber with Glen Gering, December 28, 1988; both in Schowalter Oral History Collection, MLA.

9. Interview, Graber with Loganbill, October 24, 1988, MLA; Interview, Sprunger with Richert, MLA, transcript p. 15; Interview, Shipley with Gaeddert, May 14, 1988, MLA; Interview, Graber with Waltner, December 30, 1987, MLA; Interview, James Juhnke with Arthur Weaver, August 21, 1990, Schowalter Oral History Collection, MLA, interview notes.

10. Incident recounted in Roger Juhnke, "The Perils of Conscientious Objection," *Mennonite Life* 34 (September 1979): 4–9.

11. Oral Interview, Kurt Goering with Harvey Deckert, November 4, 1975, Schowalter Oral History Collection, MLA, transcript, p. 16. Incident at Henry, Illinois, taken from Goossen, "Conscientious Objection and Gender," 134, 131.

12. For hostility in Newton, see Oral Interviews, Mark Kroeker with Rupert

Hohmann, April 17, 1990, notes p. 2; and Daagya Dick with Karolyn Kaufman Zerger, October 7, 1989; both in Schowalter Oral History Collection, MLA. On First Mennonite Church in Newton, see John Theissen, *Prussian Roots, Kansas Branches: A History of First Mennonite Church of Newton* (Newton: Historical Committee of First Mennonite Church, 1986), 73–74; on Tabor, see Ruby Funk, ed., *Peace, Progress, Promise: A 75th Anniversary History of Tabor Mennonite Church*, 97.

13. On the tensions in Bluffton, see Oral Interview, Bill Barberee with Delbert Gratz, February 13, 1995, interview notes, p. 2, deposited with Mennonite Historical Library, Bluffton College; and Oral Interview, Roger Juhnke with Varden Loganbill, November 1, 1978, Schowalter Oral History Collection, MLA.

14. Interview, Sprunger with Richert, MLA, transcript, p. 26.

15. Auernheimer anecdote in Melvin Gingerich, "The Mennonite Church in World War II: A Review and Evaluation," *MQR* 25 (July 1951): 199; for Platt's trials, see Oral Interview, James Juhnke with Selma Platt Johnson, January 25, 1975, Schowalter Oral History Collection, MLA.

16. Interview, Juhnke with Platt, January 25, 1975, MLA.

17. Walter Dick to Ernest Bohn, December 9, 1941, Peace Committee Papers, MLA-I-4B, Box 7, File 112.

18. The final tallies were reported in Howard Charles, "A Presentation and Evaluation of MCC Draft Census," *Proceedings of the Fourth Conference on Mennonite Cultural Problems*, Bluffton, Ohio, August 24–25, 1945 (North Newton, Kans., 1945), (hereafter cited as "Charles Report"). For a more recent and detailed consideration of the Mennonite draft census of World War II, see Perry Bush, "Military Service, Religious Faith and Acculturation: Mennonite GIs and their Church, 1941–1945," *MQR* 67 (July 1993): 262–68.

19. Hershberger, *The Mennonite Church in the Second World War*, 44–45.

20. Hershberger, *The Mennonite Church in the Second World War*, 42–44, 187; Charles Report, 89–90; Bender cited in Executive Committee minutes, stenographic report, August, 1943, I-2-1, Box 3, AMC.

21. Numbers taken from Charles Report, 93.

22. "Report of the Peace Problems Committee," to the 1943 Mennonite General Conference, n.p., p. 38, AMC; H. S. Bender, "Forward into the Postwar World with our Peace Testimony," *Christian Missions*, a supplement to the *Gospel Herald* 39, (June 1946): 220.

23. Robert Kreider, "Environmental Influences Affecting the Decisions of Mennonite Boys of Draft Age," *MQR* 16 (October 1942): 253–57; S. Floyd Pannabecker, "Environmental Factors Influencing Mennonites," *Proceedings of the Second Annual Conference on Mennonite Cultural Problems*, (North Newton, Kans.: Bethel College Press, 1943), 92. More recently, in a study of "old" Mennonites in Oregon in the interwar years, David Peterson has reinforced this same theme, rooting nonresistance in these Mennonites' adherence to the doctrine of nonconformity. According to Peterson, "During World War II . . . conservative leaders removed the question of nonresistance from the realm of individual conscience and placed it instead in the context of a tightly knit Mennonite community." See David

Peterson, "Ready for War: Oregon Mennonites from Versailles to Pearl Harbor," *MQR* 64 (July 1990): 226–27.

24. Peterson, for instance, argued that in the conservative MC congregations he examined, fundamentalism functioned as a means of strengthening rather than weakening their adherence to the distinctive Mennonite doctrines of nonconformity and nonresistance ("Ready for War," 226–28).

25. On the impact of fundamentalism on GC peace convictions during the war, see C. Henry Smith, "Is the General Conference Losing its Peace Testimony?" *The Mennonite* 57 (July 28, 1942): 1–2; and Kreider, "Environmental Influences," 250. On Yoder's book and fundamentalism among (Old) Mennonites, see Edward Yoder, *Must Christians Fight: A Scriptural Inquiry* (Akron, Pa.: Mennonite Central Committee, 1943) and "Report of the Peace Problems Committee," to General Conference, Goshen, Ind., 1943, 35; "Information Regarding Mennonite Drafted Men who Accepted Military Service: Draft Census, December 1944" MCC Draft Census Files, PPC Papers, I-3–5.9, Box 49, AMC. Regretful army noncombatant quoted in Editorial, "Noncombatant Service," *Gospel Herald* 37 (June 30, 1944): 243.

26. Data and quotes on Salem Mennonite cited in James O. Lehman, *Salem's First Century*, 157; Oral Interview, Roger Juhnke with Roland Juhnke, January 6, 1979, Schowalter Oral History Collection, MLA. For something of the social pressures at Eden Mennonite, see also Oral Interview, Tim Schrag with Richard Schrag, October 20, 1974, Schowalter Collection, MLA.

27. On Suckau's counsel, see letter to "Dear Friend in the Service," November 18, 1942, Hershberger PPC Papers, I-3–5.7, Box 36, AMC; see also the response by Carl Lehman, "Dear Dr. S," MCC Data Files, IX-12, "Civilian Public Service," AMC. Also on the Berne church, see Naomi Lehman, *Pilgrimage of a Congregation*, 374. On Oak Grove, see J. Lehman, *Creative Congregationalism*, 257.

28. On Salem Mennonite, see J. Lehman, *Salem's First Century*, 156. The experiences of W. F. Unruh in West Zion Mennonite Church relayed in Daryl Dean Schmidt, "War Is Sin? Mennonite Preaching on War, 1940–1945," Bethel College student paper, 1966, pp. 7–8, MLA.

29. Oral Interviews, Mark Kroeker with Reuben Krehbiel, October 1, 1989; Goering with Deckert, November 4, 1975; Linscheid with Waldo Wedel, March 19, 1988; all in Schowalter Oral History Collection, MLA. George F. Nachtigall to Albert Gaeddert, October 26, 1944, MCC Correspondence, "Campers' Attitudes Toward Conscription," IX-6–3, AMC. Also on this point see Theodore Grimsrud, "An Ethical Analysis of Conscientious Objection to World War II," (Ph.D. diss., Graduate Theological Union, 1988), 175–76.

30. Campers quoted in "Take Time To Think," *High Sierra Vistas* I (March 1943): 8–9, IX-13–1, AMC; Interview, Graber with Waltner, December 30, 1987, MLA.

31. The historian Gordon Zahn has provided additional evidence for this point. Before the National Archives arbitrarily closed them off to future researchers in the early 1950s, Zahn had obtained access to the Selective Service forms that CO applicants filled out in order to substantiate their claims for CO status. In contrast

to the highly intellectualized, very personal arguments against war commonly articulated by Friends, the Mennonite statements tended to be briefer and to the point, many times limited to scriptural citations. Many of the statements were so similar as to appear as "form answers," prepared in advance and made available to church draftees. In their statements, numerous Mennonite applicants testified to the help they had received in preparing their answers from their pastors or other church officials. Their answers, in other words, emerged from the close bonds of their home communities. Zahn data quoted in Grimsrud, "An Ethical Analysis of Conscientious Objection to World War II," 198–99.

32. Statement of Raymond L. Kramer in folder dated December 9, 1946, PPC Papers, I-3–5.7, Box 36, File 80, AMC; camp educational director Frank L. Wright, "An Analysis of Reasons for Lack of Participation on the Part of Average Men in Mennonite Civilian Public Service," undated report, MCC Peace Section Data Files, IX-12, "Civilian Public Service," AMC; "Notes of Denison Camp Directors Conference, November 12–15, 1944," Vertical File "MCC-CPS," MSHL.

33. Oral Interviews, Mark Kroeker with David Warkentine, January 28, 1989; Juhnke with Loganbill, November 1, 1978; both at Schowalter Collection, MLA.

34. Charles quoted in Charles Report, 101; Oral Interview, Timothy Schrag with Floyd Krehbiel, January 12, 1974, Schowalter Oral History Collection, MLA.

35. "Bread and butter" quote in J. W. Boyer to "My Dear Brother Harold [Bender]," December 3, 1942, "Draft Census, December 1944," PPC Papers, I-3–5.9, Box 49, AMC; Hershberger, *The Mennonite Church in the Second World War*, 38; Oral Interviews, Mark Kroeker with Howard Buller, December 6, 1988; Patrick Preheim with Levi Friesen, December 20, 1990; both in Schowalter Oral History Collection, MLA. For the comment on why some of his young men opted for noncombatant service, see the statement of D. S. Oyer in "Information Regarding Mennonite Drafted Men Who Accepted Military Service," PPC Papers, I-3–5.9, Box 49, AMC. Likewise, visiting Mennonites employed in a mental hospital in Farnhurst, Delaware, in 1943, John E. Lapp reported that many of the young men had begun to consider noncombatant work to a large degree because "there are a number who are hard pressed financially and they will not ask anyone to help them" (see Lapp to Peace Problems Committee, March 31, 1943, Miller PPC papers, I-3–5.3, Box 17, AMC).

36. For the Mennonite CPS experience, see Melvin Gingerich, *Service for Peace*; for Church of the Brethren COs, see Leslie Easing, *Pathways of Peace* (Elgin, Ill.: Brethren Publishing House, 1948).

37. "Mennonite melting pots" quote in Rodney Sawatsky, "History and Ideology: American Mennonite Definition Through History" (Ph.D. diss., Princeton University, 1977), 255–6. Stauffer and Bartel quotes in Stauffer to Fast, August 26, 1943, Fast Papers, MLA-MS-49, Box 3, File 22; Interview, Linscheid with Bartel, transcript p. 8, MLA.

38. Quote from camp newsletter in Montana in "Future Church Leaders," *Yellowstone Builder* (February 1946): 7, IX-13–1, AMC; CO Girl quote in Summer Service Unit Evaluation, Peace Section Data Files, IX-12, pronto 1, "Women's Service Unit Poughkeepsie Questionnaires," AMC.

39. Quotes from CPSers in the Shenandoah valley in "United We Stand," *Sky-*

liner 1 (October 1943): 9, IX-13-1, AMC; polling data in Paul Albrecht, "Civilian Public Service Evaluated by Civilian Public Service Men," *MQR* 27 (January 1948): 12–13; Lancaster CO quoted in "On the Subject—Conscription and War," Questionnaire distributed by Camp Committee of Lancaster Conference, reply by John L. Byer, Amos Horst Papers, LMHS.

40. Arnold Reimer to Fast, October 15, 1940, Fast Papers, MLA-MS-49, Box 1, File 6.

41. Fast to Reimer, October 19, 1940, Fast Papers, MLA-MS-49, Box 1, File 6; Incident from MCC camp newsletter from "CPS men discuss the future," *Snowliner* 1 (October 14, 1942): 3, IX-13-1, AMC; "the puttery work we have here" from Arlene R. Yousey, *Strangers and Pilgrims: A History of Lewis County Mennonites*, 196; Oral Interview, Keith Sprunger with Esko Loewen, October 9, 1973, Schowalter Collection, MLA.

42. Selective Service quoted in Wherry, *Conscientious Objection*, 26–27; on creation of relief training schools, see Gingerich, *Service for Peace*, 305–11. Kreider's experience in Oral Interview, Keith Sprunger with Robert Kreider, November 24, 1987, Schowalter Oral History Collection, MLA, interview notes; and "On Disappointment," *MCC Bulletin* 2 (July 22, 1943): 2. To be entirely accurate, the China unit was a joint program of MCC, AFSC, and the Brethren Service Commission but was under AFSC's administration; Kreider was thus technically dispatched by AFSC.

43. Interview, Juhnke with Fast, October 19, 1978, Schowalter Collection, MLA, transcript p. 13; on MCC's creation of mental hospital units and the numbers serving in them, see Gingerich, *Service for Peace*, 213–14.

44. On MCC's decision to segregate the Gulfport unit, see Sibley and Jacob, *Conscription of Conscience*, 158; and Grimsrud, "An Ethical Analysis," 172–73. Incidents at Mulberry in Interview, Linscheid with Bartel, Schowalter Collection, MLA, notes p. 9; incident at camp near Orlando in "July 4, 1944," *Box 96* 1 (July 1944): 1, camp newsletters, IX-13-1, AMC.

45. On Rustin's visits, see "Standin' in the Need of Prayer," *Rising Tide*, undated, p. 5; "Negro Pacifist Visits," *Weeping Water News Drops* 1 (November 1942): 1; for growing racial awareness, see "Brotherhood Month," *Box 96* 1 (February 1945): 2; "Editorial," *Yellowstone Builder* (February 1945): 2; all in IX-13-1, camp newsletters, AMC; also see "Mennonites and the Race Question," *MCC Bulletin* 3 (January 22, 1945): 1. Gaeddert to Miller, December 20, 1942, Gaeddert Papers, MLA-MS-50, Box 2, File 12. Very little, apparently, came of this suggestion. Incident at Camp Camino in Interview, Kroeker with Unrau, October 27, 1989, Schowalter Collection, MLA.

46. Supervisor's quote from William Keeney, "Experiences in Mental Hospitals in World War II," *MQR* 56 (January 1982): 9. Mental hospital anecdotes taken from oral interviews, David Kaufman and Richard Flemming with Henry Fast, May 16, 1973, transcript pp. 50–51; and David Haury with William Keeney, June 14, 1973, transcript pp. 8–9; both in Schowalter Oral History Collection, MLA.

47. Cherokee, Iowa, unit paper *Release*, quoted in "Applied Non-Resistance," *CPS Bulletin* 5 (May 2, 1946): 2; postwar confessions of orderly in Willard Lindscheid to Gingerich, October 6, 1947, Hershberger PPC Papers, I-3–5.7, Box

36, AMC; see also Ivan Mullet to Gingerich, October 23, 1947, same box; "Herbert Bentch Trial," *CPS Bulletin* 5 (June 27, 1946): 1.

48. "United for Peace," *Pike View Peace News* 2, (April 17, 1943): 2, IX-13–1, AMC; "For This Cause," *High Sierra Vistas* 1, (October 1943): 5, IX-13–1, AMC; Dallas Voran, "Making the Vision Live," *CPS Bulletin* 5 (April 18, 1946): 4.

49. Oral Interview, Kurt Goering with Edna Ramseyer Kauffman, April 27, 1976, Schowalter Oral History Collection, MLA; "Committee Suggestions for COGs," August 14, 1943; and "Constitution," P. C. Hiebert Papers, MLA-MS-37, Box 15, File 141. For a longer and more detailed explication of the experiences of "CO Girls," see Goossen, "Conscientious Objection and Gender," 163–77.

50. Goossen, "Conscientious Objection and Gender," 163–69, Miller quoted p. 169; Interview, Goering with Kauffman, MLA. For the reasoning and evaluations of the participants, see MCC Peace Section Data Files, pronto 1, "Women's Service Unit, Cleveland: Applications and Evaluations; and "Women's Service Unit Poughkeepsie, Questionnaires." For notes to speakers, see "Committee Suggestions for COGs," August 14, 1943, P. C. Hiebert Papers, MLA-MS-37, Box 15, File 141.

51. Editorial, "CPS Symposium," *Gospel Herald* 38 (February 15, 1946): 883.

52. Interviews, R. Juhnke with Ediger, October 9, 1978; Sprunger with Kreider, September 7, 1987; both at Schowalter Oral History Collection, MLA.

53. In addition, at times Mennonite CPS men voiced discontent when assigned to thin beets, which they perceived as directly related to military needs. See Robert Kreider, "The 'Good Boys of CPS'" *Mennonite Life* 46 (September 1991): 8–10.

54. On quotes from Grottoes camp newspaper, see "For Conscience Sake," *Olive Branch* (December 19, 1942): 5, IX-13–1, AMC; for non-Mennonite camper in a Mennonite camp, see "History of Leonard Holden in Civilian Public Service," undated statement to Melvin Gingerich, PPC Papers, I-3–5.7, Box 36, File 85; Gaeddert, "Report on Camp Camino," August 18, 1943, Gaeddert Papers, MLA-MS-50, Box 2, File 11. Radical objector quoted in Grimsrud, "An Ethical Analysis," 103. For a general depiction of the hostility between radical COs and Mennonites, see Sibley and Jacob, *Conscription of Conscience*, 319–25; also see Grimsrud, "An Ethical Analysis," 164–72.

55. Gingerich, *Service for Peace*, 372–73; quotes from camp administrator are from Paul Albrecht to Gaeddert, January 23, 1946, Gaeddert Papers, MLA-MS-50, Box 3, File 16.

56. Howard Charles, "Peace Section: Thinking about the Atomic Bomb," *Gospel Herald* 38 (October 19, 1945): 569; "Statement to the Ministers Conference Of The Western District," undated 1945 memo, Fast Papers, MLA-MS-49, Box 26, File 236; Blosser interview, transcript p. 7, Hist. Mss 6–248, AMC; CO quoted in Daryl Frey, "The Powellsville Conference," p. 4, MCC Peace Section Data Files, "Conscription Institute, Powellsville, MD" IX-12 (no.1), AMC.

57. Hershberger to Edgar Metzler, January 5, 1960, Bender PPC papers, I-3–5.10, Box 52, AMC; Frank Olmstead to Fast, March 8, 1943, MCC Correspondence, "War Resisters League," IX-6–3, AMC; "Representative of War Resisters League Visits Camp," *Whispering Pines* 2 (June 2, 1942), camp newsletters, IX-13–1, AMC.

58. "I begin to wonder" from Orie Cutrell to Paul Erb, April 22, 1944; on recol-

lection of past Mennonite migrations, see Louis Lock to Erb, April 22, 1944; "We have compromised greatly" is Lee Kanagy to Erb, December 19, 1944; all in Hershberger materials, PPC papers, I-3–5.7, Box 36, File 87, AMC. Lancaster CPS man is Albert Miller, response to questionnaire from the Camp Committee of the Lancaster Conference, March 4, 1946, Amos Horst Papers, LMHS.

59. "Lincoln abolished slavery" is Roland Stucky to MCC, November 16, 1944, MCC Correspondence, "Campers' attitudes towards conscription," IX-6–3, AMC. On responses to MCC concerning postwar conscription, see "Symposium on Post-war Conscription," *MCC Bulletin* 3 (October 22, 1944). "We cannot be too careful" from Francis Smucker to Gaeddert, October 21, 1944; "Are we compromising Christian ideals?" from David Anderson to Robert Kreider, October 8, 1944; both in MCC Correspondence, "Campers attitudes towards conscription," IX-6–3, AMC.

60. Melvin (Gingerich) to Guy (Hershberger), undated note, Hershberger materials, PPC Papers, I-3–5.7, Box 36, file 87, AMC.

61. Oral Interview, Roger Juhnke with Elmer Ediger, October 9, 1978, Schowalter Oral History Collection, MLA.

62. On MCC's understanding of the conscription institutes, see "Notes on Conscription Institute," Powellsville, Maryland, February 24–25, 1945, p. 1, Hershberger Materials, PPC Papers, I-3–5.7, Box 36, File 48, AMC. For dialogue at Powellsville, see "Notes on Conscription Institute," p. 1 and Frey, "The Powellsville Conference," pp. 3–4, Peace Section Data Files, AMC; Dwight Weldy, "Powellsville Conference," *The Skyliner* 3 (March 1945): 3, IX-13–1, AMC. For the discussion at Camp Camino, see "Notes on Conscription Institute," Camino, California, April 8–9, 1945, p. 2–4, Hershberger Materials, PPC Papers, I-3–5, Box 36, file 48, AMC. It remains unclear whether these were direct quotes from Bender and others; since they were included in MCC's official summaries of the institutes, they are more likely paraphrases of the real remarks of the participants. I have include them as quotes to preserve the flow of the narrative.

63. Notes of Conscription Institute," Powellsville, p. 2, Hershberger papers, AMC; "Less interference by government" in Weldy, "Powellsville Conference," p.4. For quotes and analysis of Powellsville, see Notes of Powellsville Institute, p. 2–3; on Camino, see Notes of Camino Institute, pp. 3,8; on Medaryville, see "Conscription Institute," *Peace Sentinel* 4 (April 1945): 2, IX-13–1, AMC.

64. Daryl Frey, "The Powellsville Conference," MCC Peace Section Data Files, IX-12, pronto 1, "Conscription Institute, Powellsville, Maryland," AMC.

65. Frey, "The Powellsville Conference," pp. 1–6, Peace Section Data Files, AMC.

66. Seventy percent judged their work to have been "generally significant," for example; and over half even testified that their personal skills and abilities were "used quite well." A larger percentage, 81 percent, admitted that through CPS their understanding of nonresistance had "become more clear," and an equal number said they would register 4E if they had to do it again; see Albrecht, "Civilian Public Service Evaluated," 10–12.

67. For a more detailed treatment of Mennonite GIs in World War II, see Bush, "Military Service, Religious Faith and Acculturation," 270–81.

68. Oral Interviews, Kroeker with Buller, December 6, 1988; Shipley with

Koehn, October 17, 1988; Fred Fransen with Heinz Janzen, November 27, 1987; all in Schowalter Collection, MLA. For the response of St. Johns Mennonite Church, see Oral Interview, Brian Colatruglio with Fred Reichenbach, February 6, 1995, interview notes p. 2, deposited with Mennonite Historical Library, Bluffton College. In his examination of MC congregations in Oregon, Peterson has even suggested that, at least in this context, the draftee's congregational affiliation influenced his decision more than education, age, or occupation. The "conservative," more separated, less acculturated churches that he studied saw their young men opt for conscientious objection at a much higher rate than neighboring "liberal," more tolerant ones. According to Peterson, World War II not only measured nonresistance in the Mennonite churches, but "in a broader sense it tested nonconformity, a trait that noncompliance to the state depended on" ("Ready for War," 227–28).

69. On Eden Mennonite Church, see R. Juhnke, "One War—Three Fronts," 70; and Tim Schrag with Richard Schrag, October 20, 1974, Schowalter Oral History Collection, MLA. On Juhnke and Friesen, see Interviews, Roger Juhnke with Roland Juhnke, January 6, 1979; Preheim with Friesen, December 20, 1990; both in Schowalter Collection, MLA. On Alexanderwohl, see "Proposed Constitution of the Alexanderwohl Mennonite Church, Moundridge, Kansas," Fast Papers, MLA-MS-49, Box 26, File 236.

70. On Central Mennonite, see Orland Grieser and Ervin Beck, *Out of the Wilderness*, 162; on Oak Grove see J. Lehman, *Creative Congregationalism*, 258; for larger numbers in the MC Indiana-Michigan Conference, see Indiana-Michigan Conference, "Report on Present Status of Mennonites Who Accepted Military Service," in Mennonite Research Foundation papers, project 19A: Church Status of Men in Military Service, V-7–20, Box 7, AMC.

71. Melvin ——— to Leland Bachman, February 28, 1945, Illinois Mennonite Conference Papers, "CPS Committee Correspondence," II-4–3, Box 2, AMC. "Peace Problems Committee," undated sheet in Hershberger materials, PPC Papers, I-3–5.7, Box 36, File 35, AMC; Illinois conference' response cited in Hershberger, *The Mennonite Church in the Second World War*, 114–15.

72. "Report on Present Status of Mennonites Who Accepted Military Service," Mennonite Research Foundation Papers, V-7–20, Box 7, AMC; and Hershberger, *The Mennonite Church in the Second World War*, 117. In contrast, the Illinois Conference, with its emphasis on common confession and its relatively lax church discipline had, by 1949, been able to restore to membership 69 out of 83 veterans.

73. "Suggested Procedures," undated memo; "A Suggested Form of Service, WHEN OUR BOYS COME HOME, 1945"; "Statement to the Ministers Conference of the Western District," undated memo, all from Fast Papers, MLA-MS-49, Box 26, File 236.

74. On Tabor Mennonite Church, see Ruby Funk, *Peace, Progress, Promise*, 98–100; bitter veteran cited in Roger Juhnke, notes of interview with M——— J———, November 10, 1974, Schowalter Oral History Collection, MLA.

75. This entire story is taken from Oral Interview, Tom Penner with Oliver Stucky, October 11, 1990, Schowalter Oral History Collection, MLA.

76. The particularly dramatic nature of this account perhaps needs to be accom-

panied by the reminder that, as oral historians are quick to admit, such memories must be approached with a bit of caution. Especially when recounting memories that are decades old, human beings are quick to exaggerate, embellish, forget, or otherwise interpret events through the hazy filter of nostalgia. In this case, for example, it would be difficult or impossible to completely document the veracity of Stucky's account.

Yet there is one telling clue that should be considered here. In July 1944, *Yank* magazine, a weekly newspaper for GIs published by the army, printed several letters from readers in response to an article on conscientious objectors. One read, "I spent 1 1/2 years in CPS (Civilian Public Service) camps and six months as a hospital orderly, in a mental institution. I'm now in the Army, having asked to be inducted . . . Conscientious objectors in CPS camps not only donate their labor but also furnish their own clothes . . . Now, don't get me wrong: these fellows aren't asking for anything and, what's more, most of them don't want anything for their services. Its just one way for them to show their love of country. I've seen quite a number of Axis prisoners of war and must say they are getting a much better deal than the conscientious objectors, who are American citizens. I think they should get a break!" The letter came from "O'Reilly General Hospital, Mo.," and was signed by "Pvt. O. G. Stucky." The printed letter in *Yank* (July 21, 1994) accompanied correspondence from Paul Springer to Arthur Nafziger, July 25, 1944, Hist. Mss. I-272, Arthur Nafziger Papers, Box 1, File 9, AMC.

77. Former CPS man is Harold Blosser, in Blosser Interview, Hist. Mss 6–248, transcript p. 8, AMC.

78. This exchange between French and Fast in Interview, Juhnke with Fast, October 19, 1978, transcript p. 18, Schowalter Collection, MLA; Bender quoted in notes of Conscription Institute at Medaryville, Indiana, 5.

79. Kreider, "Environmental Influences" 256; Charles Report, 101.

CHAPTER 5:
THE DECLINE AND REVIVAL OF THE MENNONITE COMMUNITY

1. Guy Hershberger, "The Economic Life of the Mennonite Community," *Christian Doctrine*, quarterly supplement to the *Gospel Herald* 35 (August 20, 1942): 452; Paul Peachey, "Identity Crisis Among American Mennonites," *MQR* 42 (October 1968): 259.

2. Robert Wiebe, *The Search for Order*.

3. John R. Mumaw, "Current Forces Adversely Affecting the Life of the Mennonite Community," *MQR* 19 (April 1945): 101–2, 106, 100–116 passim; Melvin Gingerich, "Rural Life Problems and the Mennonites," *MQR* 16 (July 1942): 169; "Report of the Committee on Economic and Social Relations," to the Mennonite General Conference meeting, Kalona, Iowa, 1963, n.p., AMC, 91–92.

4. H. P. Peters, "The Future of the Mennonite Church," *The Mennonite and Christian Evangel* 11 (August 6, 1935): 3–5; Ed. G. Kaufman, "The General Conference of the Mennonite Church of North America," *Mennonite Life* 2 (July 1947): 43.

5. For an overview of the Mennonite community movement about the time of World War II, see Theron Schlabach, "To Focus a Mennonite Vision," in J. R.

Burkholder and Calvin Redekop, eds., *Kingdom, Cross, and Community*, 30–31. For examples of the kinds of paeans to Mennonite rural integrity delivered by these scholars, see Kollmorgen, "The Role of Mennonites in Agriculture," *Mennonite Community* 1 (January 1947): 18–20; and Baker, "The Meaning of Rural Life," *Mennonite Community* 1 (May 1947): 9–10. On the larger rural community movement from which Hershberger, Fretz, and others took their bearings, see David Shi, *The Simple Life: Plain Living and High Thinking in American Culture* (New York: Oxford University Press, 1985), 226–47.

   6. On Hershberger's thinking and influences, see Schlabach, "To Focus a Mennonite Vision," 30–31, 33–34; and Paul Toews, "The Concern Movement: Its Origins and Early History," *Conrad Grebel Review* 8 (Spring 1990): 116.

   7. Hershberger, "Maintaining the Mennonite Rural Community," *MQR* 16 (July 1942): 218–20; Hershberger, "The Economic Life of the Mennonite Community," 452–54. Also see Hershberger, "Questions on Mennonite Community Life: III. What are some changes taking place in Mennonite community life?" *Gospel Herald* 36 (March 30, 1944): 1107. This "Questions on Community Life" series provided Hershberger with a weekly column in the denominational organ through 1944 to pound away at such concerns.

   8. On Fretz's background and sociological understandings, see "New Series by Dr. J. Winfield Fretz," *The Mennonite* 57 (March 31, 1942): 3; Leo Driedger, "Mennonite Community Change: From Ethnic Enclaves to Social Networks," *MQR* 60 (July 1986): 377–78; Paul Toews, "Mennonites in American Society: Modernity and the Persistence of Religious Community," *MQR* 63 (July 1983): 244–45; Toews, "The Concern Movement," 116–18; and Oral Interview, Perry Bush with J. Winfield Fretz, June 8, 1994, deposited with Schowalter Oral History Collection, MLA. On Fretz's message to the church, see J. Winfield Fretz, "The Effects of Urbanization among the Mennonites," *Gospel Herald* (April 13, 1945): 28; Fretz, "Mennonites and Rural Life," *The Mennonite* 57 (March 31, 1942): 3; "Rural Family Life," *The Mennonite* 57 (April 28, 1942): 3; "Keeping our Boys on the Farm," *The Mennonite* 57 (April 21, 1942): 3. Stauffer quoted in William Stauffer, "Mennonites and their Environment," *The Mennonite* 57 (August 18, 1942): 6.

   9. On the Mennonite Heritage series, see Melvin Gingerich, *Service for Peace*, 311–12; on farm and community schools, see ibid., 311–12; Paul Erb, "A Vision and its Realization," *Mennonite Community* 1 (January 1947): 9; and Grant Stoltzfus, "The Farm and Community School: Where CPS Men Prepare for Service at Home," *Gospel Herald* 37 (April 14, 1944): 37, Stoltzfus quote.

   10. The 1941 quote in "Report of the Committee on Economic and Social Relations," to the Mennonite General Conference meeting, Kalona, Iowa, 1963, n.p., AMC, 91–92. See "The Conference on Mennonite Community Life," undated cover letter, CESR files, I-3-7, Box 2, AMC. For a brief summary of the birth of Mennonite Mutual Aid in this Mennonite community movement, see Schlabach, "To Focus a Mennonite Vision," 36.

   11. Fretz, "Conferences on Mennonite Cultural Problems," *Mennonite Life* 3 (July 1948): 9; for the initial issue of *Mennonite Life*, see Leland Harder, "Urbanization in the Mennonite Church," *The Mennonite* 74 (February 10, 1958): 84; on

the inaugural issue of *Mennonite Community*, see Hershberger, "Appreciating the Mennonite Community," *Mennonite Community* 1 (January 1947): 6–7. On the activities of the CESR, see Schlabach, "To Focus a Mennonite Vision," 36. In 1951 the Mennonite Church expanded the areas of concern and changed the name of the old Committee on Industrial Relations to the Committee on Economic and Social Relations (ibid., 32).

12. Miller's comment found in "The Program of the Mennonite Community of Tomorrow," partial transcript of Conference on Mennonite Community Life, Goshen, Indiana, March 16–17, 1945, Hershberger CESR Papers, I-3-7, Box 2, AMC.

13. John Stauffer, "Godward or Worldward—Which?," Exhibit VII, Mennonite General Conference Meeting Minutes, November 6, 1953, Hershberger PPC Papers, I-3-5.11, Box 60, AMC.

14. John K. Shover, *First Majority, Last Minority*, 33; Gilbert Fite, *American Farmers: The New Minority*, 25–26.

15. Fite, *American Farmers*, 66, 73–76. On the state of American agriculture in the depression, also see Carl Taylor, "Rural Life," *American Journal of Sociology* 47 (May 1942): 841–44. For developments during World War II, see Fite, *American Farmers*, 80, 87–88; Walter Wilcox, *The Farmer in the Second World War* (Ames: Iowa State University Press, 1947): 8–14, 55–56, 98–99, 249; Wayne Rasmussen, "The Impact of Technological Change on American Agriculture, 1862–1962," *Journal of Economic History* 22 (December 1962): 579; Shover, *First Majority, Last Minority*, 246.

16. Shover, *First Majority, Last Minority*, 152, 5; Fite, *American Farmers*, 115.

17. Fite, *American Farmers*, 115–19, quoted p.116; Shover, *First Majority, Last Minority*, 6. Kansas farmers cited in Wayne Rohrer and Louis Douglas, *The Agrarian Transition in America*, 113. One analyst has identified the early 1950s as a "major turning point in American agricultural history" because a number of factors—particularly two important changes in the IRS codes—coalesced then to create a much more favorable investment climate for corporate farming in the United States. The stage was thus set for an ensuing escalation in corporate farming activity. See Philip Raup, "Corporate Farming in the United States," *Journal of Economic History* 33 (March 1973): 279–81.

18. On the 1940 numbers, see Melvin Gingerich, "Are We Farmers?" *Gospel Herald* 42 (November 15, 1949): 1119; also see Grant Stoltzfus, "Forces Working Against Social and Economic Equality in Our Brotherhood," *Gospel Herald* 44 (July 10, 1951): 469–650. J. Howard Kauffman and Leland Harder, *Anabaptists Four Centuries Later*, 284. Leland Harder, "The Quest for Equilibrium in an Established Sect: A Study of Social Change in the General Conference Mennonite Church," (Ph.D. diss., Northwestern University, 1962), table 30, p. 300; Harder, *Fact Book of Congregational Membership, 1980–1981*, 18, MLA.

19. Gingerich, "Rural Life Problems and the Mennonites," 168; Fretz, "Mennonites and Rural Life: Keeping Our Boys on the Farm," *The Mennonite* 57 (April 21, 1942): 3.

20. J. Lloyd Spaulding, "The Changing Economic Base of the Economic Community with Special Reference to Certain Kansas Counties," Proceedings of the

Eleventh Annual Conference on Mennonite Educational and Cultural Problems, North Newton, Kansas, June 6–7, 1957, pp. 92–93, 94–95, MSHL. Statistics on Alexanderwohl taken from P. A. Wedel and Leland Harder, "The Effects of Urbanization Upon the Alexanderwohl Church," cited in Esko Loewen, "The Impact of Urbanization and the Disintegration of the Mennonite Rural Community," Farm Study Conference, Buhler Mennonite Church, Buhler, Kansas, April 21–22, 1958, pp. k-2–k-3, MSHL.

21. *Mennonite Weekly Review* quoted in Harley J. Stucky, "The Agricultural Revolution of Our Day" *Mennonite Life* 14 (July 1959): 137.

22. Paul Peachey, *The Church in the City*, 84; Harder and Kaufman, *Anabaptists Four Centuries Later*, 54, 284. Numbers from the late 1980s taken from J. Howard Kauffman and Leo Driedger, *The Mennonite Mosaic*, 36.

23. Harder, *General Conference Mennonite Church: Fact Book*, 37, 39, 18, 27, 29, MLA; Harder, *Fact Book of Congregational Membership, 1908–1981* 18.

24. On the postwar hopes of CPS men, see Fretz, "Post-War Needs and Plans of C. P. S. Men," *The Mennonite* 59 (April 11, 1944): 4. Broken down as to denomination, 26 percent of GC CPSers said they planned to continue their education, whereas 20 percent of MC COs did so; see Irvin Horst, "Postwar Rehabilitation of C. P. S. Men," *Gospel Herald* 37 (April 21, 1944): 50. On the monies provided by the Western District Conference, see "Report of the Peace Committee to the Fifty-Fourth Annual Session of the Western District Conference," 1945, n.p. MLA, 227; for funds from the GC as a whole, see Fretz, "Present Day Needs for Mutual Aid," 15; on monies made available by GC colleges, see Albert Gaeddert, "Providing Educational Opportunities for Our Ex-C. P. S. Men," *The Mennonite* 62 (December 30, 1947): 4. On memories of postwar Goshen College, see Oral Interview, Leonard Gross with Howard Blosser, Hist. Mss. 6–248, AMC.

25. Calvin Redekop, "Education and Social Change Among Mennonites," Philosophy of Christian Education Study for the Mennonite Church, Study Paper F, September 13–16, 1960, p. 13, Vertical File, MSHL. For the increased percentage attending college in the 1950s and 1960s, see "More people, More Students," *The Mennonite* 76 (April 11, 1961): 246; Adolf Ens, "Mennonite Students—Statistical Background," *Mennonite Life* 20 (April, 1965): 55; Harder, *Fact Book of Congregational Membership*, 10.

26. Joel Carpenter, "The Fundamentalist Leaven and the Rise of an Evangelical United Front," in Leonard Sweet, ed., *The Evangelical Tradition in America* (Macon: Mercer University Press, 1984): 275–76; George Marsden, *Fundamentalism and American Culture*, 194–95.

27. Bender, "Outside Influence on Mennonite Thought," in Proceedings of the Ninth Conference on Mennonite Educational and Cultural Problems, Hesston, Kansas, June 18–19, 1952, MSHL, 36, 37–41. Also see Rodney Sawatsky, *Authority and Identity*, 21–22.

28. J. Lawrence Burkholder, "Social Implications of Mennonite Doctrines," Proceedings of the Twelfth Conference on Mennonite Educational and Cultural Problems, Elkhart, Indiana, June 16–17, 1959, MSHL, 103; Harder and Kauffman, *Anabaptists Four Centuries Later*, 284. According to the 1970 census, Americans were 73.5 percent urban (defined as living in a town or city with a population

larger than 2,500). The five major Mennonite and Brethren in Christ groups that Harder and Kaufman surveyed were only 35 percent urban (ibid., 54).

29. Quote from 1939 Mennonite World Conference in P. R. Schroeder, "The Mennonite Church and her Youth," *The Mennonite* 51 (October 6, 1939): 1. On the relatively greater cultural openness of the GCMC, see James Juhnke, "Mennonite History and Self-Understanding: North American Mennonitism as a Bi-Polar Mosaic," in Calvin Redekop and Samuel Steiner, eds., *Mennonite Identity: Historical and Cultural Perspectives* (Lanham, Md.: University Press of America, 1988): 92–93; and Lauren Friesen, "Type 2: Culturally Engaged Pacifism," in John Richard Burkholder and Barbara Nelson Gingerich, eds., *Mennonite Peace Theology: A Panorama of Types* (Akron: Mennonite Central Committee, 1991): 15–25. Kaufman quoted in Kaufman, "The General Conference of the Mennonite Church of North America," 42.

30. Olin A. Krehbiel, "Mennonite Principles and their Application Today," *The Mennonite* 57 (May 12, 1942): 4.

31. Franconia bishop quoted in Beulah Stauffer Hostetler, *American Mennonites and Protestant Movements*, 271.

32. Stauffer, "Godward or Worldward—Which?" p. vii-5.

33. Gingerich, "Rural Life Problems and the Mennonites," 168–69; Mennonite "domino theory" from James Juhnke, *Vision, Doctrine, War,* 313. Also on this point see David Peterson, "Ready for War: Oregon Mennonites from Versailles to Pearl Harbor," *MQR* 64 (July 1990): 227–28.

34. "Report of the General Problems Committee, as revised by the Resolutions Committee, August 18, 1944," J. P. Graybill papers, Box 32, LMHS. Smucker to Bender, December 15, 1947, Hist. Mss. I-278, H. S. Bender Papers, Box 23, File 3, AMC. "Report of Concerns and Suggestions, given at special Bishop Board Meeting," East Petersburg, January 25, 1962, Lancaster Mennonite Conference, Bishops' Board Meeting Minutes, n.p., LMHS.

35. See Hostetler, *American Mennonites and Protestant Movements,* 295–317. Oral Interview, Perry Bush with Paul G. Landis, May 10, 1989.

36. Ibid.

37. Hostetler, *American Mennonites and Protestant Movements,* 267, 307–8, 309–16 passim.

38. The travails of Zion Mennonite Church are described in Hope Kauffman Lind, *Apart and Together,* 87–88. On the dissenters in an Idaho congregation, see H. N. Harder to Olin Krehbiel, Walter Gering, and P. K. Regier, May 3, 1954, Gaeddert Papers, MLA-MS-50, Box 6, File 46.

39. Oral Interview, Jim Schmidt with Walter Neufeld, January 28, 1981, Schowalter Oral History Collection, MLA.

40. John Drescher, Editorial, "Observations—So Called," *Gospel Herald* 66 (August 28, 1973): 664; Conrad G. Brunk, "Rediscovering Biblical Nonconformity," *Gospel Herald* 66 (September 25, 1973): 729.

41. J. H. Kauffman, "Tradition and Change in Mennonite Family Life," Proceedings of the Eleventh Conference on Mennonite Educational and Cultural Problems, North Newton, Kansas, June 6–7, 1957, 124–130, MSHL. Even more to the point, in the early 1970s, Harder and Kauffman's more extensive sampling

of five Mennonite denominations discovered that the rural-urban residence variable was not a strong predictor of other measurements of Mennonite faith and life (*Anabaptists Four Centuries Later*, 293).

42. J. Juhnke, "Mennonite History and Self-Understanding," 86–87. For a fine summary and analysis of the *Concern* pamphlets, see Toews, "The Concern Movement," 109–26.

43. On GC critiques of Bender's Anabaptist Vision, see Rodney Sawatsky, "Beyond the Social History of the Mennonites: A Response to James C. Juhnke," and James Stayer, "The Easy Demise of a Normative Vision of Anabaptism," in Redekop and Steiner, eds., *Mennonite Identity: Historical and Contemporary Perspectives*, 102–6, 109–14; and Leo Driedger and J. Howard Kauffman, "Urbanization of Mennonites: Canadian and American Comparisons," *MQR* 56 (July 1982): 269–90. Harder quoted in Harder, "Mennonite Mobility and the Christian Calling," 11.

44. "Report Of The Findings Committee," at the Study Conference on Christian Community Relations, Laurelville Camp, July 24–27, 1951, p. 1, Hershberger CESR Papers, Box 2, I-3–7, AMC.

45. Roy S. Koch, "Are Mennonites an Ethnic People?" *Gospel Herald* 55 (January 30, 1962): 100; on the level of responses to this piece, see Editorial, "Persuaded Mennonites," *Gospel Herald* 55 (May 29, 1965): 491. Rudy H. Wiebe, "For the Mennonite Church—A Last Chance," *The Mennonite* 79 (July 28, 1964): 467.

46. Walter Neufeld, "No Half a Christ," in Letters to the Editor, *The Mennonite* 83 (July 23, 1968): 487; Gary Schrag, "I Once Left the Mennonite Church," *The Mennonite* 84 (July 15, 1969): 453; Editorial, "Where is the Mennonite Ghetto?" *Sword and Trumpet* 35 (November 1967): 2–3.

47. On the decline of this older Mennonite community movement, see Schlabach, "To Focus a Mennonite Vision," 37–38.

48. J. Lawrence Burkholder, "The New Mennonite Community," *Mennonite Life* 27 (December 1972): 104–5.

49. See J. H. Kauffman, "Boundary Maintenance and Cultural Assimilation of Contemporary Mennonites," *MQR* 51 (October 1977): 236–40; Leland Harder, "An Empirical Search for the Key Variable in Mennonite Reality," *MQR* 45 (December 1971): 342–43, 348–51.

50. J. Howard Kauffman and Leo Driedger, *The Mennonite Mosaic*, 34–41, 65–86, 101, 163, 258. Also on this point, see Driedger, "Mennonite Community Change," 377–78; and Toews, "Mennonites in American Society," 244–45.

51. Hostetler, *American Mennonites and Protestant Movements*, 293; Bauman quoted in J. Howard Kauffman, "Changing Values on the Church Scene," paper presented at the annual meeting of the Association of Mennonite Mutual Aid Societies, Chicago, March 1, 1979, pp. 6–7, vertical file, Mennonite Historical Library, Goshen, Indiana (hereafter abbreviated as MHL); Cornelius Krahn, J. Winfield Fretz, and Robert Kreider, "Altruism in Mennonite Life," in Pitirim A. Sorokin, ed., *Forms and Techniques of Altruism and Spiritual Growth* (Boston: Beacon Press, 1954), 327–28; Frieda Barkman, "Responsibility of Distinctiveness," *The Mennonite* 86 (September 28, 1971): 568. In addition, Driedger's entire article, "Mennonite Community Change," 274–386, is required reading on this point.

CHAPTER 6:
NEW DIRECTIONS AND FORMS OF WITNESS, 1946–1956

1. Gaeddert to Rufus Franz, September 23, 1947, Gaeddert Papers, MLA–MS-50, Box 3, File 21.

2. For concise summary statements of the origins and shape of the National Security State, see Robert Borosage, "The Making of the National Security State," in Leonard S. Rodberg and Derek Shearer, eds., *The Pentagon Watchers: Students Report on the National Security State* (Garden City, N.Y.: Doubleday, 1970): 3–63; and Marcus G. Raskin, *The Politics of National Security*, 31–59.

3. Important assessments of the origins of the Cold War include Daniel Yergin, *Shattered Peace*; Stephen Ambrose, *Rise to Globalism;* Walter LaFeber, *America, Russia and the Cold War;* and Thomas Paterson, *On Every Front.*

4. On the Hitler analogy applied to the Soviet Union on a popular level, see Paterson, *On Every Front*, 76–77; and Les K. Adler and Thomas G. Paterson, "Red Fascism: The Merger of Nazi Germany and Soviet Russia in the American Image of Totalitarianism, 1930's-1950's," *American Historical Review* 75 (April 1970): 1046–64.

5. For numbers on military contracting and procurement, see Borosage, "The Origins of the National Security State," 24–27. For a summary statement of the extent of the "military-industrial complex" by the 1960s, see Seymour Melman, *Pentagon Capitalism*, 1–106; Eisenhower quoted p. 88. On the acceptance of the military projections of NSC-68, see Yergin, *Shattered Peace*, 400–408, statistics taken from p. 408; Ambrose, *Rise to Globalism*, 113–20, 126–31, statistics cited p. 126.

6. On the military and political attractions of atomic weaponry, see Gregg Herken, *The Winning Weapon*, 195–217, esp. 211–17; Yergin, *Shattered Peace*, 201–4, 337–41; Ambrose, *Rise to Globalism*, 70–72.

7. Herken, *The Winning Weapon*, 218–303; for the sole reliance on the bomb envisioned in "Offtackle," see pp. 295–97.

8. Richard Fried, *Nightmare in Red*, 59–86; Stephen J. Whitfield, *The Culture of the Cold War*, 9–25; Yergin, *Shattered Peace*, 284–286, Kennan quoted p. 284.

9. Charles DeBenedetti, *The Peace Reform in American History*, 138–57. Lawrence Wittner, *Rebels Against War*, 151–228. The best account of this nonregistration campaign (and of Korean War conscientious objection altogether) is Zelle Andrews Larson, "An Unbroken Witness: Conscientious Objection to War, 1948–1953" (Ph.D. diss., University of Hawaii, 1975), 80–109, 134–54.

10. Franz to Gaeddert, March 31, 1948, Peace Committee Papers, MLA-MS-4B, Box 7, File 114; "Resolution 61," at the 1950 General Conference Meeting, Freeman, South Dakota, August 23–30, 1950, General Conference Mennonite Church, General Conference Minutes and Reports, p. 271, n.p., MLA.

11. Hostetler incident described in Chris Graber to Guy Hershberger, May 8, 1963, Hist. Mss. I-171, G. F. Hershberger Papers, Box 12, File 9, "Hostetler, Danny," AMC.

12. Frank Epp, *Mennonite Exodus*, 351–408. As an example of the reporting of news of this persecution to American Mennonites, see Cornelius Krahn, "Menno-

nites the World Over: The Fate of the Molotschna Colony," *The Mennonite* 61 (August 27, 1946): 4.

13. Smucker quoted in "Minutes of the Peace Section Meeting, April 23, 1948, Chicago, Illinois," p. 2, Peace Section Minutes and Reports, IX-7–8, Box 1, AMC; H. S. Bender, "Let Us Go On," in *Report of the MCC Peace Section Study Conference*, Winona Lake, Indiana, November 9–12, 1950, p. 130, MSHL.

14. On the rise of New Evangelicalism, see Martin Marty, *Pilgrims in Their Own Land*, 411–14; Sydney Ahlstrom, *A Religious History of the American People*, 2:455–56; Mark Silk, *Spiritual Politics*, 54–69, 88–94. On the growth and message of Youth For Christ during World War II, see Joel Carpenter, "Youth for Christ and the New Evangelicals' Place in the Life of the Nation," in Rowland Sherrill, ed., *Religion and the Life of the Nation: American Recoveries* (Urbana: University of Illinois Press, 1990), 128–51.

15. On Graham's appeal to Virginia Mennonites in 1956, see Moses Slabaugh, "We went to hear Billy Graham," *Gospel Herald* 49 (October 23, 1956): 1012; the attractions of Youth for Christ rallies to Lancaster Mennonite youth taken from Telephone Interviews, Perry Bush with Henry Benner, May 9, 1989, and with Robert Neff, May 10, 1989, notes in author's possession.

16. Milton Lehman to Paul G. Landis, July 2, 1962, Lancaster Mennonite Conference, Peace Committee Papers, LMHS; Ford Berg to Paul Peachey, November 29, 1954, O. O. Miller PPC Papers, I-3–5.3, Box 26, AMC.

17. John Howard Yoder, "Toward a Sifting of Faith From Culture," *Mennonite Life* 19 (January 1964): 38; Peace Section chief Edgar Metzger to Peace Section Executive Committee, March 3, 1967, MCC Correspondence, "Inter-Office Peace Section Members, 1967," IX-6–3, AMC. On the Mennonite effort to witness to New Evangelicals with their peace position, see Perry Bush, "Anabaptism Born Again: Mennonites, New Evangelicals, and the Search for a Useable Past, 1950–1980," *Fides et Historia* 25 (Winter/Spring 1993): 26–47.

18. Statistics taken from Richard J. Barnet, *The Economy of Death*, 5; and Melman, *Pentagon Capitalism*, 4.

19. Melvin Gingerich, "The Mennonite Church in World War II: A Review and Evaluation," *MQR* 25 (July 1951): 185; Elmer Neufeld to Elmer Ediger, July 15, 1955, Western District Conference Committee on Peace and Social Concerns Correspondence, MLA-II-3, Box 1.

20. Rufus Franz, "Educating for Peace in our Churches," p. 1, Exhibit II, Minutes of the Mid-Year Peace Section Meeting, Chicago, October 17, 1947, IX-7–7, Box 2, AMC; Ford Berg to John Hostetler, August 12, 1948, Miller PPC Papers, I-3–5.7, Box 17, AMC; J. W. Fretz, "Toward a Revived Peace Position in our Conference," Eden Conference Papers, p. D-132, MLA; "too many of our college presidents" in Ford Berg, "The Christian Attitude and Technique toward Pending Universal Military Training Legislation," Exhibit IV, p. 3, "Minutes of the Mid-Year MCC Peace Section Meeting," October 17, 1947, p. 3, MCC Peace Section Minutes and Reports, IX-7–8, Box 2, AMC.

21. "Literature Report to the Peace Problems Committee, November 20, 1954," by Secretary (Paul Peachey), Hershberger PPC Papers, I-3–5.11, Box 59, AMC. Even with such an impressive array of material, Peachey's evaluation of this

literature judged it of marginal use to the denomination. The majority of it was too historical and scholarly to be much appreciated by the average lay person, he argued, and a survey of CO reading habits revealed to him that "our literature consumption is not very encouraging." For a larger explication of GC peace literature in the postwar years, see Samuel F. Pannabecker, *Open Doors*, 263–64; Minutes of the Peace Committee Meeting February 18–19, 1948, MLA-I-4B, Box 7, File 114.

22. MCC Peace Section News Letter, No. 19, February 23, 1948, 1–4, Vertical File, "MCC Peace Section," MSHL; "Attend the Nonresistance Conference in Your Community, July 4–5, 1953," Peace Committee Papers, Lancaster Mennonite Conference, LMHS.

23. Hostetler to Ediger, January 24, 1948, IX-6–3, MCC Correspondence, 1948, "Hostetler, John," AMC.

24. Ray Horst(?), Peace Team Report, Summer 1948, Miller PPC Papers, I-3–5.3, Box 19, AMC. On the influence of fundamentalism, see Ernest Lehman, "Summary of Reactions Regarding the Work of the Peace Teams," PPC Meeting, October 15, 1948, and John Hostetler's journal, entries for Fisher and Rantoul, Illinois, July 8–9, 1948, PPC Papers, I-3–5.4, Box 30, AMC; Peace Team member David Shank to John H(ostetler), September 5, 1949, PPC Papers, I-3–5.5, Box 31, AMC.

25. R. L. Hartzler, "The Church, the Gospel, and War: A Significant Study Conference," *The Mennonite* 68 (May 5, 1953): 278–79. Originally, the organizers had hoped for 75 people to attend; instead, the conference attracted over 300. Epp's comments in "Student Impressions," *The Mennonite* 68 (May 5, 1953): 279.

26. Robert Kreider in personal correspondence to the author, March 24, 1994, letter in author's possession. The GCMC's new denominational growth in the postwar years is summarized in James C. Juhnke, *Creative Crusader*, 258–59.

27. Robert Regier, "Attitude of Mennonite Youth toward Peace Teaching," *The Mennonite* 66 (August 7, 1951): 494–95.

28. Naomi Lehman, *Pilgrimage of a Congregation*, 93–95.

29. Ibid., 96–105; Jack (Purves) to Elmer (Ediger), August 19, 1957, "Letters, Personal," Ediger Papers, MLA (unprocessed materials); Oral Interview, Keith Sprunger with Lynn Liechty, March 4, 1988, Schowalter Oral History Collection, MLA.

30. "Report of the Special Study Committee Appointed by the Mennonite Peace Problems Committee," cover letter dated January 20, 1943, Miller PPC Papers, I-3–5.3, Box 17, AMC; Wilfred J. Unruh, "A Study of Mennonite Service Programs," prepared for the Institute of Mennonite Studies, Associated Mennonite Biblical Seminaries, Elkhart, Indiana, 1965, pp. A57–60, A85–89, LMHS. Elmer Ediger, "The Voluntary Service Program," *Proceedings of the Sixth Conference on Mennonite Cultural Problems*, Goshen, Indiana, pp. 31–2. Also see Ediger, Editorial, "Should the Church Administer a Program of Voluntary Service?" *CPS Bulletin* 4 (January 4, 1946).

31. Unruh, "A Study of Mennonite Service programs," pp. A92–94, A61, A109–10; For another history of VS, see John Unruh, *In the Name of Christ*, 294–308. On the Gulfport project, see David Haury, *The Quiet Demonstration*.

32. "Report of Special Study Committee on Mennonite Service Work Ap-

pointed by the Peace Problems Committee," 1946(?), Hist. Mss. I-324, Nelson Kauffman Papers, Box 4, File 35, AMC.

33. Vernon Neufeld, ed., *If We Can Love*, 26–27, 32–36; Reading 21, "Excerpts, Report of the Mental Hospital Study Committee to the Annual Meeting, December 28–29, 1945," in Cornelius Dyck, ed., *Witness and Service in North America*, 80.

34. Gingerich to Ediger, October 16, 1948, MCC Correspondence, "Gingerich, Melvin," IX-6–3, AMC.

35. "I. Mennonites: A Brief History of Mennonite Disaster Service," undated memo found in MCC Peace Section Data Files, IX-12, pronto 3, "Mennonite Disaster Service," AMC. Also on the founding of MDS, see remarks given by John Diller, January 2, 1971, reprinted in MCC News Release, "Mennonite Disaster Service 'in the Beginning,'" MCC Peace Section Data Files, IX-12, pronto 6, "Mennonite Disaster Service, 1968–1972," AMC. Mennonites at the time recognized the roots of disaster service in the CPS experience. For example, Boyd Nelson argued in 1961 that MDS was "born out of the deep concern of returning CPS men for a channel to carry on the type of service interest and activity that they had come to know during the war years"; see Report of MDS Coordinating Committee Member, March 21, 1961, MCC Peace Section Data Files, IX-7–12, "Mennonite Disaster Service, 1960–69," AMC.

36. "Harry E. Martens to William T. Snyder re Mennonite Disaster Service Meetings, July 25, 1956, Memo on Visit to Mt. Lake, Minnesota Area in the Interest of Establishing an MDS Unit in the Area," MCC Peace Section Data Files, IX-12, pronto 3, "Mennonite Disaster Service," AMC. Actually the quote is Martens' paraphrase of remarks given by the Rev. Walter Goering. As national disaster relief endeavors became increasingly tied into military-focused civil defense programs, MDS volunteers would need to separate their efforts accordingly (see chapter 7).

37. Larson, "An Unbroken Witness," (cf. fn. 9), 37, 41–5, 47.

38. Ibid., 59–60, 289; on the path to deferment in 1948, see pp. 37–48. On the later broadening of the CO definition, see John Whiteclay Chambers II, "Conscientious Objectors and the American State from Colonial Times to the Present," in Charles C. Moskos and John Whiteclay Chambers II, eds., *The New Conscientious Objection: From Sacred to Secular Resistance* (New York: Oxford University Press, 1993): 38–43. As Chambers has described, the *Seeger* and *Welsh* decisions opened the floodgates of conscientious objection to objectors, first from religious traditions other than the HPCs, and then once again to people motivated by more moral and "secular" reasoning. Yet from 1952 to 1967, reported Selective Service in 1967, of the roughly 11,500 COs in that era, 14% came from the Church of the Brethren, 3.8% came from the Society of Friends, and 67.2% came from the different Mennonite groups; see "Mennonites lead list of conscientious objectors," *The Mennonite* 82 (February 21, 1967): 122.

39. Initial MCC statement in Dirk Eitzen and Timothy Falb, "An Overview of the Mennonite I-W Program," *MQR* 56 (October 1982): 366. "We are put on our honor," in John Horst, Editorial, "The Draft," *Gospel Herald* 61 (July 17, 1948); Ediger, "Voluntary Service and the Draft," *The Mennonite* 66 (January 23, 1951): 58. "Resolutions passed at Western District Conference, October 18–20, 1950," 1950 Western District Conference Report, p. 53, MLA. Similarly, Ford Berg ar-

gued in 1948 that "our voluntary service program should be expanded and enlarged so that a greater number of brethren will be in this work than would be in the armed forces if they [were] drafted"; see Berg, "The Inescapable Responsibility in Accepting Deferments," *Gospel Herald* 41 (July 20, 1948): 667.

40. Minutes of Peace Section Meeting, Chicago, April 23, 1948, and Exhibit IV, "Statement Expressing Attitude Toward Deferment of CO's," MCC Peace Section Minutes, IX-7-8, Box 1, AMC; Minutes of MCC Peace Section Executive Committee Meeting, Chicago, January 16, 1951, MCC Peace Section Minutes, IX-7-8, Box 1, AMC.

41. Larson, "An Unbroken Witness," 157-65.

42. "Minutes of the Special Meeting of a Representative Group Called by the MCC Peace Section," Akron, Pennsylvania, July 21, 1950, MCC Peace Section minutes, IX-7-8, Box 1, AMC; Minutes of MCC Peace Section Executive Committee Meeting, Chicago, January 16, 1951, Exhibit 2, "Guiding Principles for Consideration in the Event of Passage of Legislation Calling for Service by Conscientious Objectors," MCC Peace Section minutes, IX-7-8, Box 1, AMC; Eitzen and Falb, "An Overview of the Mennonite I-W Program," 366-67.

43. On MCC's reticence to administer another CPS-type program, see "Minutes, Conjoint Meeting," March 18-19, 1949, Hershberger PPC Papers, I-3-5.11, Box 59, AMC; and Peace Problems Committee Report to 1951 Mennonite [Church] General Conference, p. 38, AMC. Also see MCC Peace Section Correspondence, IX-7-12, "Conscientious Objector Services, Ex-CPS Letters, 1950-1951," AMC.

44. Larson, "An Unbroken Witness," 168, 172. For an account of the NSBRO lobbying behind the I-W program, see Larson, pp. 155-82. A key issue was getting the language of the final draft bill changed from placing COs in "work of national importance" to "work contributing to the national health, safety, or interest." This permitted church groups to have their COs engage in the social service work that many in various voluntary programs were already engaged in; see Larson, pp. 167-68.

45. On the basic shape and founding of the I-W program, see Larson, "An Unbroken Witness," 192-94, 280-86. On the anecdote about the advertising for I-W men by one hospital, see "I-W Office," in *1959 MCC Workbook*, pp. D-1-D-2, MCC Workbooks, IX-5-2, AMC.

46. I-W Services Report in 1952 MCC Annual Report, p. 80, IX-5-2, AMC; J. S. Schultz, "Evaluation of the I-W Program: A Report on the Experiences of Mennonite and Brethren-in-Christ I-W Men," 1955, pp. 1-2, MSHL; Larson, "An Unbroken Witness," 227-29.

The church leadership initially expected that the majority of I-Ws would opt to serve in VS—an expectation that most Mennonite leaders frankly hoped for, since this would present an image of sacrificial Christian service. Yet once deferment had ended, the flood of applicants into VS proved more than the program could handle, sending most Mennonite I-Ws into regular, paid jobs, or "earning service." By 1953, only 10 percent of Mennonite COs served their I-W alternate service obligations in VS or PAX, its overseas equivalent. See the Relief and Services Committee, "Report of I-W Services to the 1953 Mennonite General Conference meeting at

Kitchener, Ontario," n.p., p. 34, AMC; "Appraising I-W," *Gospel Herald* 46 (November 10, 1953): 1067. Before long Mennonite I-W men would opt for earning service primarily out of much less altruistic reasons.

47. Schultz, "Evaluation of the I-W Program," 4; I-W man quoted in Larson, "An Unbroken Witness," 229. Even though most I-Ws lived and worked with other COs—Schultz found that two-thirds of his sample belonged to I-W units of ten men or more—the influence of a new and unfamiliar world must have been all-encompassing.

48. Quotes taken from "I-W Service—Kingdom of God work?" *One-W Mirror* 1 (June 3, 1953): 2–4. On polling data of I-Ws, see Schultz, "Evaluation of the One-W Program," 12.

49. Larson, "An Unbroken Witness," 294–99, Kosch quoted pp. 298; "Keeping them Mennonite" in Paul G. Landis, "From an I-W Council Member," *Gospel Herald* 56 (August 8, 1961): 693. At the same time, however, church leaders also began to recognize signs that some of this optimism might have been ill-founded, noting the independence of the men, their control over their own time, living arrangements and churchgoing, and the fact that the wide dispersion of I-W populations made it difficult for the church to further minister to them (see chapter 7). See Editorial, "Appraising I-W," *Gospel Herald*,46 (November 10, 1953): 1067, and Report of the Peace Section to 1954 MCC Annual Meeting, "I-W Services," p. 1, MCC Workbooks, IX-5–2, AMC.

50. Discussion, "What about the Noncombatant Position?" in Report of the MCC Peace Section Study Conference, Winona Lake, Indiana, November 9–12, 1950, p. 54, MSHL (hereafter abbreviated as "Winona Lake Conference Papers"); quotes from I-W man in "Why CO?" *One-W Mirror* 1 (August 26, 1953): 1. The situation in McPherson noted in J. Harold Sherk to Ediger, December 26, 1950, Peace Committee Correspondence, MLA-I-4, Box 62, File 1314.

51. Ex-CPS man David Nissley to MCC, January 14, 1951, MCC Correspondence, IX-7–12, "Conscientious Objector Services, Ex-CPS Letters, 1950–1951," AMC; "Do We Spend Too Many Week Ends at Home?" *One-W Mirror* I (June 17, 1953): 2–3 (Olsen citation); "I-W, What?" *One-W Mirror* I (January 28, 1953): 2.

52. "Report on Meeting of General Conference Peace and Service Committee of Districts and Board of Christian Service in Chicago, February 15, 16, 1955," Board of Christian Service minutes and reports, 1955, bound volumes, MLA.

53. "III. Summary," in "Report on the 1954 Draft Census," compiled by the Peace Problems Committee and the Mennonite Research Foundation, Peace and Social Concerns Committee Papers, Virginia Conference Archives, Box 1A5.b/5, MSHL. For the cross-tabulations of these numbers with factors of age, education, and occupation, see Floyd Metz, "Analysis of the Draft Census of the Franconia, Illinois, Indiana-Michigan, Ohio, South Central, and Pacific Conferences, January 1, 1952–April, 1956," pp. 2–3, Mennonite Research Foundation Files, V-7–22, AMC.

54. "Report of Peace Team Program" from Fairview, Michigan, July 8–10 (1949), PPC Papers, I-3–5.5, Box 31, AMC.

55. "Summary of Discussions: The Disciple of Christ and the State," pp. 27–28, Winona Lake Conference Papers, MSHL.

56. Guy F. Hershberger, "The Disciple of Christ and the State," pp. 53–57, Winona Lake Conference Papers, MSHL.

57. "Summary of Discussions: the Disciple of Christ and the State," pp. 28–29; and Hershberger, "The Disciple of Christ and the State," pp. 7–58, Winona Lake Conference Papers, MSHL.

58. Robert Kreider, "The Disciple of Christ and the State," pp. 63, 65; and J. Winfield Fretz, "Nonresistance and the Social Order," pp. 69–72; both in Winona Lake Conference Papers, MSHL.

59. "A Declaration of Christian Faith and Commitment, Adopted at a Study Conference on Nonresistance held by representatives of the Mennonite and Brethren in Christ Churches of North America, Winona Lake, Indiana, November 9–12, 1950" (Akron, Pa.: Mennonite Central Committee). "The only extensive inter-Mennonite theological document ever produced" from John A. Lapp, "The Peace Mission of the Mennonite Central Committee," *MQR* 44 (July 1970): 287. For a concise summary of the theological importance of this conference, see Leo Driedger and Donald B. Kraybill, *Mennonite Peacemaking*, 85–86.

60. For the MC statement, see "A Declaration of Christian Faith and Commitment with Respect to Peace, War, and Nonresistance," as adopted by the Mennonite General Conference at Goshen, Indiana, August 23, 1951, 1951 Mennonite General Conference Report, n.p., pp. 48–49, AMC. For the GC statement, see "A Declaration on Peace, War, and Military Service," as adopted at Portland, Oregon, August 22, 1953, General Conference Mennonite Church, 1953 Report from General Conference, pp. 269–71, n.p., MLA.

61. Basic description of UMT taken from "Message to the Churches," *The Mennonite* 67 (January 1, 1952): 14. For a fuller description and analysis of these anti-UMT campaigns in the churches, see Joe P. Dunn, "The Church and the Cold War: Protestants and Conscription, 1940–1955" (Ph.D. diss., University of Missouri, 1973).

62. "We need to take a stand" from Harry Martens, "The Christian Attitude and Technique Towards Pending Universal Military Training Legislation," p. 2, in Minutes of the Mid-year MCC Peace Section Meeting, October 17, 1947, MCC Peace Section minutes, IX-7–8, Box 2, AMC; anecdote about Mennonite solidarity during Smucker's congressional testimony in John A. Lapp, "The Peace Mission of the Mennonite Central Committee," 289.

Of course, in this opposition the more liberal GCMC was able to take a more open and aggressive political stance than the Mennonite Church. However fervent their opposition, leaders of this group still had to exercise care not to arouse a conservative outcry against excessive meddling in the state's affairs. For example, from 1950 through 1954, the GC *The Mennonite* carried fifteen different articles on UMT, many urging different forms of opposition, whereas the MC *Gospel Herald* exhibited nothing of the sort. Sometimes more vocal MCs ran into trouble in even a quiet opposition. The Lancaster Conference Peace Problems Committee defeated a 1952 motion by Amos Horst, for example, which would have endorsed an anti-UMT letter from the committee to their local congressman. See "Present Trends and Activities Among Mennonites in Their Approach to the State," Paper presented to the Bluffton Study Conference, July 15–18, 1954, MCC Peace Section Data Files, IX-7–2, Box 2; "Minutes of the Peace Problems Committee held at the Mennonite Home, January 7, 1952," Lancaster Mennonite Conference, Peace Committee Papers, LMHS.

63. H. S. Bender, "A Statement of Position to the Preparedness Subcommittee of the Armed Services Committee of the United States Senate on S–1, Universal Service and Military Training Act," January 29, 1951, vertical file, "MCC Peace Section," MSHL. Bender, "A Statement of Concern Regarding H. R. 2967 Amending the Universal Military Training and Service Act, submitted to the Sub-Committee on Reserve Forces of the Committee on Armed Services of the United States House of Representatives," March 1, 1955, vertical file, "MCC Peace Section," MSHL.

64. This was a debate reverberating entirely in the ranks of the GCMC. MCC and the MC Mennonites disposed of the issue rather quickly. Considering the matter in July 1948, MCC recommended all young men to register under the new draft law. Likewise, a special meeting of the Peace Problems Committee with the Industrial Relations Committee in March 1949 concluded that the way of nonresistance did not also call for nonregistration. See "Report from Committee of Five," Minutes of MCC Special Joint Session with Peace and Aid Sections, July 17, 1948, p. 5, Peace Section minutes and reports, IX-7–8, Box 1, AMC; "Minutes, Conjoint Meeting," March 18–19, 1949, Hershberger PPC Papers, I-3–5.11, Box 59, AMC.

65. Gordon Kaufman, "Should Mennonites Register for the Draft?" *The Mennonite* 63 (June 8, 1948): 4–5.

66. Dwight Platt, "An Open Letter to President Truman," *The Mennonite* 66 (March 27, 1951): 206–9; Platt, "All of these Traditions," *The Mennonite* 83 (May 28, 1968): 372. Other GC nonregistrants, besides Platt and Regier, included Ralph and Eldon Bargen.

67. Austin Regier, "The Faith of a Convict," *The Mennonite* 64 (February 15, 1949): 8; Erland Waltner, "Numbered with the Transgressors," *The Mennonite* 64 (February 1, 1949): 4.

68. Austin Regier, "Christianity and Conscription," *The Mennonite* 63 (November 30, 1948): 13–14.

69. Robert Hartzler, "The Christian and the Draft Law," *The Mennonite* 64 (September 6, 1949): 15; Paul Goering, "Should We Make Registration the Issue?" *The Mennonite* 63 (June 22, 1948): 3.

70. Ediger to Regier, December 27, 1948, and Loewen to Ediger, January 6, 1949, both in Ediger Papers, "Special Letters, etc." MLA (unprocessed papers); Franz to "Bro. Albert" (Gaeddert), February 2, 1949, Peace Committee Papers, MLA-I-4B, Box 7, File 114. On the PC's successful attempt to table Regier's resolution, see Items II and V, "Meeting of the General Conference Peace Committee at the time of the Council of Boards Meeting at Bloomington, Illinois, February 15–17, 1949," Fast Papers, MLA-MS-49, Box 26, File 235; and Resolution 67, motions presented to the General Conference Meeting, Freeman, South Dakota, August 23–30, 1950, n.p., p. 272, MLA.

71. Orie Miller, "Our Witness to Government," *Gospel Herald* 41 (March 30, 1948): 294–95.

72. Paul Peachey, "The Peace Study Conference at Bluffton College," *Gospel Herald* 47 (September 21, 1954): 897.

73. John Miller, "Are CO's Dangerous?" *Gospel Herald* 47 (February 16, 1954): 153.

CHAPTER 7: SPEAKING TO THE STATE, 1957–1965

1. Paul Landis, "From a I-W Council Member," *Gospel Herald* 54, (August 8, 1961): 693. In this discussion of the problems in I-W service, it is important to note that I am referring to the roughly two-thirds of Mennonite COs who entered "earning" I-W service—that is, those who took paying jobs in the civilian sector rather than entering volunteer ranks in the VS (domestic U.S.) or the PAX (overseas) programs. In these programs, the men only received a subsistence wage from the church.

2. Report of the Board of Christian Service to the 1953 General Conference triennial meeting, GCMC, Portland, Oregon, August 15–23, 1953, p. 190, General Conference Minutes and Reports, n.p., MLA. On complaints from I-W men, see Boyd Nelson, "I-W Work, Worship, Witness: For I-o Men—An Earning Position or VS—Which?" *Gospel Herald* 47 (January 12, 1954): 40.

3. Ralph Weber, "Aggressive Presentation of our Peace Position to our Constituency," filed with Ray Bair to "I-W Workshop Participants," February 8, 1957, Albert Gaeddert Papers, MLA-MS-50, Box 7, File 52; Mennonite pastors O'Ray C. Graber to Gaeddert, October 2, 1956, and Howard G. Nyce to Gaeddert, October 9, 1956, both in Gaeddert Papers, MLA-MS-50, Box 7, File 51.

4. Edgar Metzler, "Another Alternative for Draft-age Youth," *Gospel Herald* 52 (November 17, 1959): 997; Dick Martin, "I-W—Embarrassment or Challenge?" *Gospel Herald* 57 (March 31, 1964): 273; Paul Peachey, "Secretary's Report to the Peace Problems Committee on Summer Assignment, 1956," September 8, 1956, p. 2, Miller PPC Papers, I-3–5.3, Box 26, AMC.

5. Dirk W. Eitzen and Timothy R. Falb, "An Overview of the Mennonite I-W Program," *MQR* 56 (October 1982): 371.

6. I-W administrator Edgar Stoesz to William T. Snyder, October 30, 1959, IX-7–12, "I-W Study Correspondence," AMC; "Findings of the I-W Evaluation-Planning Conference," *Gospel Herald* 55 (May 21, 1957): 489. "Wild-oats period" in I-W Services Report by the Relief and Service Committee to the General Council of (MC) General Conference, September 26, 1958, p. 3, Hershberger PPC Papers, I-3–5.11, Box 60, AMC.

7. "Too many worldly things" from Peter Neufeld to Reinhart Peters, May 28, 1954, Peace Committee Papers, MLA-I-4B, Box 3, File 60; on I-W rumors and lawbreaking, see Memorandum, I-W Office in Elkhart to "All Pastors," April 17, 1959, IX-7–12, "I-W Correspondence, MBMC," AMC; Albert Gaeddert, "Does the I-W Program Have Possibilities?" *The Mennonite* 69 (November 23, 1954): 726. For a pastor's response, see response from T. L. Nussbaum, pastor of the Bergthal Mennonite Church, Corn, Oklahoma, to "Pre-Draft Mailing Questionnaire," December 27, 1956, Peace Committee Papers, MLA-I-4B, Box 5, File 82.

8. Gaeddert to Fred (Unruh), April 25, 1959, Peace Committee Papers, MLA-

I-4, Box 22, File 563; Wilfred Unruh, "Committee on Peace and I-W Report," to Board of Christian Service, December 3–6, 1957, p. A-33, Board of Christian Service Reports, bound volumes, MLA.

9. For a summary of these attempts, see Eitzen and Falb, "An Overview of the Mennonite I-W Program," 371–74.

10. Developments at the MC Relief and Service Committee meeting in 1959 in Editorial, "Concerns at Belmont," *Gospel Herald* 52 (November 10, 1959): 955.

11. On the situation in Denver, see Wiebe and Kaspar, "I-W Visitation Report," 11–12, 14–16; on the "Denver plan," see Eitzen and Falb, "An Overview of the Mennonite I-W Program," 374–75.

12. "Puts the church in the saddle" from Boyd Nelson to Dwight Wiebe, September 11, 1958, Peace Section Data Files, IX-7-12, "I-W Denver Unit Correspondence," AMC; "unacceptable relationship between church and state" in Wiebe to Peace Section VS & I-W Office, April 9, 1959, Peace Section Data Files, IX-7-12, "Denver I-W Unit Correspondence," AMC. Also see "Concerns at Belmont," 955; and Eitzen and Falb, "An Overview of the Mennonite I-W Program," 375–76.

13. "Report of the VS and I-W Committee to Board of Christian Service, November 30, 1962," Exhibit V in Minutes of the Peace Section Executive Committee meeting, December 8, 1962, Vertical File, "MCC Peace Section," MSHL; Eitzen and Falb, "An Overview of the Mennonite I-W Program," 380.

14. For a good overview of the need for equity when democracies resort to conscription, see Elliot Cohen, *Citizens and Soldiers*, 145–51, 162–63. On the dangers to equity posed by the baby boom, see Lawrence Baskir and William Strauss, *Chance and Circumstance*, 21–22.

15. Baskir and Strauss, *Chance and Circumstance*, 15–24.

16. Selective Service System, "Channelling" Memo, Document no. 56 in John Whiteclay Chambers II, ed., *Draftees or Volunteers*, 494–500, document quoted pp. 494, 499; also see Chambers' comments pp. 427–29. Baskir and Strauss, *Chance and Circumstance*, 14–16.

17. Ray Bair, "Concerns for the I-W Program," p. 4, with papers of the I-W Evaluation and Planning Conference, Elkhart, Indiana, April 9–10, 1957, MCC Peace Section Data Files, IX-7-12, "I-W Correspondence, MBMC," AMC; Paul Peachey, "Where do we go from here?" concluding address to "Our National Government and Christian Witness Seminar" Report, p. 54, MCC Peace Section papers, IX-7-2, Box 3, "Study Conferences and Papers, 1959–1973," AMC.

18. Metzler, "Another Alternative for Draft-Age Youth," 977–78, 997; and "Is Alternative Service a Witness for Peace?" *Gospel Herald* 55 (December 11, 1962): 1060.

19. Harold S. Bender, "When May Christians Disobey the Government?" *Gospel Herald* 52 (January 12, 1960): 25–26, 44.

20. Duane Friesen has made this point quite clearly in *Mennonite Witness on Peace and Social Concerns, 1900–1980*, 7.

21. "MCC Group Studies Christian Responsibility to the State," *Canadian Mennonite* (November 22, 1957): 5–6; "Report on Devotional Periods and Plenary Meetings at the Conference on "Christian Responsibility to the State," MCC Cor-

respondence, IX-6–3, "1957 Conference on Christian Responsibility to the State," AMC. On the cultural openness of GC Mennonites, see Lauren Friesen, "Type 2: Culturally Engaged Pacifism," in John Richard Burkholder and Barbara Nelson Gingerich, eds., *Mennonite Peace Theology: A Panorama of Types* (Akron, Pa.: Mennonite Central Committee, 1991), 21–24.

22. John H. Yoder, "The Nature of The Church's Responsibility in the World," pp. 5–6, the 1957 Christian Responsibility to the State Conference papers, pp. 5–6, MCC Peace Section Data Files, IX-7–12, Box 2, File 9, "Peace Conferences and Study Papers, 1957, Chicago," AMC.

23. Elmer Neufeld, "Christian Responsibility in the Political Situation," Paper Presented at the MCC Study Conference on the Christian Responsibility to the State, Chicago, 1957, reprinted in *MQR* 32 (April 1958): 146, 141–43, 152–53; Selective Service officer quoted p. 143, Neufeld quoted pp. 143, 153. Also on Neufeld's background, see Oral Interview, Perry Bush with Elmer Neufeld, February 26, 1995, deposited with Mennonite Historical Library, Bluffton College, Bluffton, Ohio (hereafter abbreviated as MHLB).

24. Neufeld, "Christian Responsibility," 161. In these observations, Neufeld struck an immediate chord. Summarizing the different evaluations he had heard from participants, Driedger declared that the paper "united all of us including the most conservative and most liberal"; see Driedger, "Christian Responsibility to the State Conference, Summary of fourteen reports handed in by GC representatives," undated memo, MCC Correspondence, IX-6–3, "Conference on Christian Responsibility to the State, 1957," AMC.

25. Peace Problems Committee, Report to Mennonite [Church] General Conference Meeting, Johnstown, Pennsylvania, August 23, 1961, Mennonite General Conference Papers, n.p., p. 43, AMC; Minutes of the Peace Problems Committee Meeting, October 8, 1959, Goshen, Indiana, pp. 2–3, Hershberger PPC Papers, I-3–5.11, Box 59, AMC. For a parallel discussion of the theological breakthrough emanating from a new Mennonite understanding of the Lordship of Christ, see Driedger and Kraybill, *Mennonite Peacemaking*, 117–24.

26. Edgar Metzler, "Toward the Year 2000: War, Peace and Nonresistance— Implications for the Mennonite Church," *Mennonite Historical Bulletin* 57 (January 1987): 2. On the theological developments at the Puidoux conferences and Mennonite participation there, see Beulah Hostetler, "Nonresistance and Social Responsibility: Mennonites and Mainline Peace Emphasis, ca. 1950 to 1985," *MQR* 64 (January 1990): 53–54. For the actual theological documents emanating from these discussions, see Donald Durnbaugh, ed., *On Earth Peace: Discussions of War/Peace Issues Between Friends, Mennonites, Brethren and European Churches, 1935–1975* (Elgin, Ill.: Brethren Press, 1978).

27. "Theses on the Christian Witness to the State, Report of a Subcommittee of the Peace Problems Committee of the Mennonite Church," June 22, 1960, pp. 14, 1–13 passim, Miller PPC Papers, I-3–5.5, Box 27, AMC. Also see Minutes of Peace Problems Committee Meeting, June 22–23, 1960, Lansdale, Pennsylvania, pp. 2–3, Hershberger PPC Papers, I-3–5.11, Box 59, AMC.

28. PPC Minutes, June 22–23, 1960, pp. 3–5; Lapp and Horst quoted in Driedger and Kraybill, *Mennonite Peacemaking*, 286n.

29. PPC Minutes, June 22–23, 1960, pp. 3–5. For a concise summary of this development, see Driedger and Kraybill, *Mennonite Peacemaking*, 122. Also on this theological breakthrough, see Richard Detweiler, *Mennonite Statements on Peace, 1915–1966*, 34–52.

30. "The Christian Witness to the State," a Declaration of Purpose and Commitment adopted by the Mennonite General Conference, Johnstown, Pennsylvania, August 23, 1961, 1961 Mennonite General Conference Papers, n.p., pp. 48–53, AMC (hereafter referred to as "the Johnstown declaration").

31. On the lack of opposition expressed to the declaration in its approval at Johnstown, see Hershberger, "Questions raised concerning the work of the Committee on Peace and Social Concerns [of the MC] and its predecessors," January 20, 1967, n.p, p. 69, Peachey/Hackman PPC Papers, I-3–5.13, Box 70, AMC (hereafter referred to as Hershberger, "Questions Raised"). Before the vote, Metzler worried that the statement had not received enough publicity to be fully understood by Mennonites. As a result, the delegates would either reject the statement outright at Johnstown or else on some future date "when the committee has occasion to implement the statement in some specific action, there will be unfavorable repercussions because the implications of the statement were not fully understood at the time of General Conference approval." Such worries were prophetic. See Metzler to Paul Erb, August 9, 1961, Edgar Metzler Papers, Hist. Mss I-775, "Peace Problems Committee Correspondence" (no box or file number), AMC.

32. Hershberger quoted in Committee on Economic and Social Relations, Report to the 1963 Mennonite [Church] General Conference, Meeting at Kalona, Iowa, 1963, Mennonite General Conference Papers, 1963, pp. 94, n.p., AMC; "Letter to President John F. Kennedy," from the Mennonite [Church] General Conference, Meeting at Johnstown, Pennsylvania, August 24, 1961, Mennonite General Conference Papers, n.p., pp. 59–60, AMC; Hershberger, "CPSC dissent," p. 19. On the PPC/CESR merger, see Peace Problems Committee and Committee on Economic and Social relations, Report to 1965 Mennonite [Church] General Conference Meeting at Kidron, Ohio, n.p., pp. 33–34, AMC.

33. J. C. Wenger, "Harold S. Bender: A Brief Biography," *MQR* 37 (April 1964): 117, 120.

34. For examples of such arguments, see Fretz, "Should Mennonites Participate in Politics?"; Loewen, "Church and State"; and Ediger, "A Christian's Political Responsibility," all in *Mennonite Life* 11 (July 1956): 139–44; and Harley Stucky, "Should Mennonites Participate in Government?" *Mennonite Life* 14 (January 1959): 34–38, 12.

35. *Christian Responsibility to Society: A Biblical-Theological Statement*, Church and Society Series, 2 (Newton, Kans.: Faith and Life Press, 1963), 3; "The Church and the State," revised December 15, 1961, p. F-2, in "Church and Society Conference Papers, October 31–November 3, 1961, Peace and Social Concerns Committee Papers, MLA-II-3-B4, Box 2.

In the fall of 1957, the Board of Christian Service created the Social Concerns Committee to provide leadership to GCMC activities emerging out of its growing social awareness. Since the existing Peace Committee had already focused on race relations, this new committee turned its attention to nuclear weapons. By the following year, however, the two committees' spheres of activities had overlapped so much that the church bureaucracy merged them together into a new Peace and Social Concerns Committee (hereafter abbreviated as PSCC). See Loewen to Erwin Hiebert, July 10, 1958, Board of Christian Service Correspondence, MLA-I-4, Box 47, File 1148; and Fast to "Friends," December 23, 1958, Board of Christian Service Correspondence, MLA-I-4, Box 28.

36. Edgar Metzler, "The Church and the Civil Defense Dilemma," October 30, 1962, MCC Peace Section Data Files, IX-7–12, "Civil Defense: Christian Attitudes Toward, 1942–1964," AMC.

37. Ibid. On the entrapment of MDS in airplane spotting, see Report of the Board of Christian Service to the 1956 General Conference triennial meeting, GCMC, Winnipeg, Manitoba, August 15–20, 1956, Minutes and Reports from the GCMC General Conference Meetings, p. 54, n.p., MLA. Metzler quoted in "Mennonite Disaster Service and Civil Defense," MCC News Service Release, September 20, 1961, MCC Peace Section Data Files, IX-12 (no.3), "Mennonite Disaster Service," AMC.

38. "Mennonite Disaster Service and Civil Defense," MCC News Service, September 20, 1961; "Statement of Position on Civil Defense and Disaster Services," Adopted by MCC Peace Section, January 18, 1962, Peace Section Data Files, IX-7–12, "Civil Defense/MDS, 1960–64," AMC; for discussion, see "Disaster Service and Civil Defense," Findings adopted by the Sixth Annual Meeting of Mennonite Disaster Service, Denver, Colorado, February 10, 1961. On "grave reservations," see Elmer Neufeld to Peace Section Members, March 3, 1961, Peace Section Data Files, IX-12 (no.3), "Mennonite Disaster Service," AMC; Beatrice Mennonite Church to W. W. Cook Sr., May 31, 1962, PSCC Papers, MLA-IA-4C, Box 3, File 26.

39. Hershberger, "Reflection on Capital Punishment Resolution," *Gospel Herald* 59 (February 1, 1966): 107; Minutes from MCC Peace Section Executive Committee Meeting, November 10, 1960, p. 9, Peace Section Minutes and Reports, IX-7–8, Box 2, AMC. Driedger, "Peace and Social Concerns Analysis," 1962, p. B-25; Minutes and Reports from General Conference triennial meeting at Bluffton, Ohio, 1959, p. 13. For the final resolution, see "A Christian Declaration on Capital Punishment," statement adopted at the 1965 GCMC triennial meeting, reprinted in *The Mennonite* 80 (April 27, 1965): 281–82.

40. Hershberger, "Questions Raised," 69–73; "Position on Capital Punishment," *Sword and Trumpet* 33 (Second Quarter 1965): 4. For discussion at Kidron, see "General Conference HI-LIGHTS," no. 4, Kidron, Ohio, August 27, 1965, Hershberger PPC Papers, I-3–5.11, Box 63, AMC.

41. "Peace Problems Committee and Committee on Economic and Social Relations," Report to the 1965 Mennonite [Church] General Conference, p. 27.

42. Lawrence Wittner, *Rebels Against War*, 240–68; Charles DeBenedetti, *The Peace Reform in American History*, 154–64.

43. J. R. Burkholder, "Radical Pacifism Challenges the Mennonite Church," January 1960, p. 14, Vertical File, "Burkholder, J. Richard," MSHL; Loewen to Erwin Hiebert, July 10, 1958, Board of Christian Service Correspondence, MLA-I-4, Box 47, File 1148.

44. "Notes on Biological Warfare," Neufeld to Peace Section Members and Others, September 30, 1959; and Neufeld to same, February 29, 1960; both in Peace Section Correspondence, IX-7–11, Box 1, AMC. Miller to Neufeld, March 9, 1960, Peace Section Correspondence, IX-6–3, "Peace Section," AMC; Miller to Hershberger, March 29, 1961, Hershberger PPC Papers, I-3–5.11, Box 61, AMC.

45. Jess Yoder to Peace Section Members and Others, July 24, 1959, Board of Christian Service Correspondence, MLA-I-4, Box 62, File 1321; Driedger to Neufeld, June 17, 1959, Board of Christian Service Correspondence, MLA-I-4, Box 83, File 1558; Driedger to Goering, July 22, 1959; *Western District News Bulletin* II (August 1, 1959): 1; and Burkholder, "Radical Pacifism" p. 2. It is impossible to know whether these letters had any real effect on the Air Force's decision.

46. "A Christian Declaration on Nuclear Power," 1959 General Conference triennial meeting, Bluffton, Ohio, pp. 24–25, n.p., MLA.

47. Loewen to Driedger, December 19, 1961, Board of Christian Service Correspondence, MLA-I-4, Box 47, File 1150; also see "We Protest," flyer and material written and distributed by Bethel students, same file; David Janzen and Kay Peters, "Students Protest in Washington," *Mennonite Life* 17 (April 1962): 63–64; James Juhnke, "Youth and Taxes," *The Mennonite* 77 (April 24, 1962): 286.

48. For example, for the *Gospel Herald*, see Irvin Horst, "Mennonites and the Race Question," 38 (July 13, 1945): 284; Editorial, "The Race Question," 41 (January 27, 1948): 75; Harry L. Kraus, "Will You Dare to be Christian?" 42 (May 10, 1949): 494–5; Hershberger, "Islands of Sanity," 46 (March 25, 1952): 293–4. In 1959 Gordon Dyck traced the rapidly increasing number of articles on race relations in *The Mennonite*, which began in earnest in 1945 and numbered 72 separate items from 1952 through 1959; see Dyck, "Growing Involvement," *The Mennonite* 74 (January 20, 1959): 39–40.

49. For a summary of Mennonite racism, see "Mennonite Race Relations: Still at a Low Point," MCC News Service Release, August 7, 1970, Peace Committee Papers, MLA-IA-4C, Box 6, File 77; Daniel Kauffman, Editorial, *Gospel Herald* 35 (January 7, 1943): 865; "The Way of Christian Love in Race Relations," Statement adopted by the 1955 Mennonite [Church] General Conference, General Conference Minutes and Reports, n.p., pp. 20–26, AMC.

50. Minutes from the Annual Meeting of the MCC Peace Section, December 27, 1956, p. 2, Peace Section Minutes and Reports, IX-7–8, Box 2, AMC. On the interesting setting at Woodlawn and initial Mennonite contact with the civil rights movement, see Driedger and Kraybill, *Mennonite Peacemaking*, 109–12, 127; and interview, Bush with Neufeld, February 26, 1995, MHLB. For examples of this cautious enthusiasm for King and his work, see the Peace Problems Committee, Report to the 1959 Mennonite [Church] General Conference, General Conference Reports and Papers, n.p., pp. 30–31, AMC; and Peachey, "Nonviolence in the South," *Gospel Herald* 50 (February 19, 1957): 177. At other times this analysis took on a much more paternalistic tone. The PPC's 1957 report to the MC General Conference, for instance, articulated their "special call . . . to help those experimenting with nonviolence to an understanding of Christian love" (1957 General Conference Minutes and Reports, n.p., p. 68).

51. Metzler, "The Mennonite Churches and the Current Race Crisis," *Gospel*

Herald 56 (August 6, 1963): 684; Hershberger to Metzler, January 8, 1959, Hershberger PPC Papers, I-3–5.11, Box 58, AMC; Edgar Metzler, "Notes on the F. O. R. Training Conference on Nonviolence, Jan. 12—Feb. 1, 1959," Hershberger PPC Files, I-3–5.11, Box 58, AMC; "First Southwide Institute on Non-Violent Resistance to Segregation, Atlanta, Georgia, July 22–24, 1959, A Report with Recommendations by Elmer Neufeld and Guy F. Hershberger," Vertical File, MSHL.

52. Hershberger, "Lessons from Anabaptist History for the Church Today," Papers Presented at the Conference on Race Relations, Atlanta, Georgia, February 25–26, 1964, Vertical File, "MCC Peace Section," MSHL. Hershberger, "Nonresistance, the Mennonite Church, and the Race Question," *Gospel Herald* 52 (June 28, 1960): 581.

53. Hershberger and Neufeld's civil disobedience in "Sharing Across the Color Bar," CORE News Release, July 24, 1959, Hershberger CESR Papers, I-3–7, Box 7, AMC; and Interview, Bush with Neufeld, February 26, 1995, MHLB. Burkholder's civil disobedience in Elaine Sommers Rich, "Harvard Professor Jailed in Civil Rights Test," *The Mennonite* 79 (April 28, 1964): 283–84.

54. "Peace Section Understandings and Concerns Related to the Vincent Hardings Assignment," Exhibit I, Minutes of Peace Section Meeting of January 18, 1962, Peace Section Minutes and Reports, IX-7–8, Box 2, AMC.

55. Hershberger quoted in "The Church Facing the Race Crisis," Board of Christian Service Discussion, December 4, 1963, p. 18, PSCC Papers, MLA-IA-4C, Box 1, "Civil Rights—Action and the Church, 1961–1971."

56. For examples of the kind of reports the Hardings sent to the Mennonite press, see "MCC Representative in Albany Arrests," *The Mennonite* 77 (August 14, 1962): 519–20; Vincent and Rosemarie Harding, "Pilgrimage to Albany," *The Mennonite* 78 (January 22, 1963): 50–53; "Harding Aided Birmingham Conciliation," *The Mennonite* 78 (June 25, 1963): 428; Vincent Harding, "First Steps in Birmingham," *The Mennonite* 78 (July 9, 1963): 438–43.

57. Snyder and Harding quoted in "Summary of Informal Consultation Regarding Recent and Projected Developments of Vincent Harding Assignment," August 25, 1962, MCC Headquarters, Akron, Pennsylvania, Amos Horst Papers, "MCC," LMHS. These quotations were not recorded verbatim. MCC VS Director Edgar Stoez to Edgar Metzler, August 14, 1962, "Vince Harding visit to Akron," MCC Correspondence, IX-6–3, "Inter-Office Peace Section," AMC.

58. Harding, "The Task of the Mennonite Church in Establishing Racial Unity," from Report of a Seminar on "Christ, the Mennonite Churches, and Race," April 17–19, 1959, Woodlawn Mennonite Church, Chicago, pp. 29, 31, MSHL.

59. Vincent and Rosemarie Harding, "Reflections on a visit to Virginia," May 1962, Vertical File, "Speeches and Reports," MSHL; Hershberger, "Mennonites and the Current Race Issue: Observations, reflections and recommendations following a visit to southern Mennonite churches, July-August, 1963," Vertical File, "Hershberger, Guy F.," MSHL; Lapp to Hershberger, August 13, 1963, Hershberger CESR Papers, I-3–7, Box 7, AMC.

In the beginning of discussion on the Atlanta VS unit that was to focus on racial problems, MCC administrators stressed they needed to "avoid offending" existing southern Mennonite missions, since all "to date are on a segregated basis." Once established, Harding was not as careful to avoid disturbing such manifestations of racism; see Edgar Stoez to Elmer Neufeld, September 27, 1960, MCC Correspondence, IX-6-3, "Peace Section Correspondence, 1960," AMC.

60. On GCMC racial activism, see Vern Preheim, "Staff Report" to the Board of Christian Service, 1963, p. B-21-22, bound volumes, MLA; and Report of the Peace and Service Committee to the 1963 (p. 55, 83-84) and the 1964 (p. 32) Western District Conference Meeting, n.p., MLA. On MC activism on racial issues, see Hershberger, "The CPSC . . . and its Predecessors," 16-18; and Hershberger, "CPSC . . . Dissent," 19.

61. "Report from MCC Peace Section Executive Secretary to Peace and Social Concerns Committee and Peace Problems Committee," October 18, 1963, p. 2, CESR Papers, I-3-7, Box 5, AMC; for Mennonite meetings on race issues, see "Record of the Meeting of Church Leaders for a discussion on racial and civil rights problems," Prairie Street Mennonite Church, Elkhart, Indiana, September 14, 1963, p. 3, Peace Section Data Files, IX-7-7, Box 1, AMC; and Editorial, "Race Relations Responsibility," Gospel Herald 57 (August 11, 1964): 683, 701. On the number of articles on the civil rights issue appearing in the Gospel Herald, see Driedger and Kraybill, Mennonite Peacemaking, 127. For a description of MC regional consultations on racial issues, see the PPC/CESR Report to the 1965 Mennonite [Church] General Conference Meeting, Kidron, Ohio, 1965, n.p. pp. 29-30, AMC.

62. Hershberger, "A Study of Church-State Relations," Gospel Herald 57 (October 13, 1964): 889-90; "Minutes of the Church-State Planning Committee sponsored by the MCC Peace Section," July 24, 1964, p. 1, Vertical File, "MCC Peace Section," MSHL.

63. "Why Are We Here?" Church-State Study Conference, Chicago, Illinois, October 7-9, 1965, pp. 1-2, Vertical File, "MCC Peace Section," MSHL.

64. "East Area, Church-State Study Group, Meeting no. 4, Akron, Pennsylvania," March 15, 1965, pp. 1-3, Peace Section Data Files (pronto 4), "Church-State Study," AMC; also see minutes from the meetings of "The State and Public Morality" study group, Scottdale, Pennsylvania, on January 9 and 23, February 6 and 12, and May 22, 1965, Peace Section Data Files, IX-12 (pronto 3), "Church-State Study," AMC.

65. Delton France, "King Comes to Woodlawn," The Mennonite 80, (September 28, 1965): 607; MC minister Lynford Hershey, "Souls and Civil Rights," Gospel Herald 58 (July 6, 1965); Sanford G. Shelter, "Is This Our Task?" Gospel Herald 58 (July 20, 1965): 629-30. For popular Mennonite support of this stance, see the "Readers Say" column of Gospel Herald for issues of August 17 and 31, September 7, October 5 and 26, and November 16, 1965.

66. "Many of our people were influenced" in Hershberger, "The CPSC . . . and its predecessors," 15-16, 18; "politically-minded more than we knew" in Hershberger, "Questions Raised," 68.

67. Ben Rahn to Stan Bohn, November 18, 1965, Western District Conference Papers, MLA-II-3-B4, Box 1.

CHAPTER 8:
DRAFT RESISTANCE, NONRESISTANCE, AND VIETNAM, 1965–73

1. Vincent Harding, "Our Crisis of Obedience," *The Mennonite* 81 (February 15, 1966): 110.

2. Stanley Krakow, *Vietnam: A History*, 171–72, Rusk quoted p. 179; George C. Herring, *America's Longest War*, 9–10.

3. For concise summaries of growing American involvement in Vietnam, see Stephen Ambrose, *Rise to Globalism*, 140–45, 200–30.

4. Ambrose, *Rise to Globalism*, 213–15; Herring, *America's Longest War*, 146–49; Robert L. Gallucci, *Neither Peace Nor Honor*, 47–49.

5. For concise summaries of Nixon's "Vietnamization" policy, see Herring, *America's Longest War*, 221–37; Ambrose, *Rise to Globalism*, 234–43; and Frances FitzGerald, *Fire in the Lake*, 506–24. Kissinger quoted in Karnow, *Vietnam: A History*, 596. Charles DeBenedetti, *An American Ordeal*, 327–28, 333; Nixon quoted p. 333. For bombing totals, see Ambrose, *Rise to Globalism*, 217.

6. Charles DeBenedetti, *The Peace Reform in American History*, 173–87, especially pp. 173–75, 179–82, 186–87, DeBenedetti quoted pp. 186; DeBenedetti, *An American Ordeal*, 103–311. Also see David McReynolds, "Pacifists and the Vietnam Antiwar Movement," in Melvin Small and William D. Hoover, eds., *Give Peace a Chance: Exploring the Vietnam Antiwar Movement* (Syracuse, N.Y.: Syracuse University Press, 1992), 56.

7. On increased numbers of conscientious objectors in the Vietnam War, see John Whiteclay Chambers II, "Conscientious Objectors and the American State from Colonial Times to the Present," in Chambers and Charles C. Moskos, eds., *The New Conscientious Objection*, 41–43. On draft resistance and evasion, see Lawrence Baskir and William Strauss, *Chance and Circumstance*.

8. Mitchell K. Hall, "CALCAV and Religious Opposition to the Vietnam War," in Small and Hoover, eds., *Give Peace a Chance*, 36–40. On Niebuhr's involvement, see DeBenedetti, *An American Ordeal*, 145. Robert Wuthnow, *The Restructuring of American Religion*, 145–50; Wuthnow quoted p. 149.

9. On the beginning of Lancaster Conference mission work in Vietnam, see Ira Landis, "State of the Church—1956 Edition," *Pastoral Messenger* 17 (July 1957): 1. For Metzler's reports home, see James Metzler, "Lines from the Front Line," *Missionary Messenger* 41 (December 1964): 12–13; Metzler, "Commentary—Asia," *Missionary Messenger* 42 (October 1965): 11, 23; Metzler, "This Is War!" *Missionary Messenger* 43 (May 1966): 12–13.

10. The number of MCC mission workers in Vietnam noted in Leo Driedger and Donald B. Kraybill, *Mennonite Peacemaking*, 127.

11. Minutes of Peace Section Executive Committee meeting, May 8, 1964, p. 4, Peace Section Minutes and Reports, IX-7–8, Box 3, AMC; Report of the Executive Secretary to the Peace Section Executive Committee, April 17, 1965, exhibit 1, Vertical File, "MCC Peace Section," MSHL; C. N. Hostetter and William T. Snyder to the President, July 11, 1966, MCC Correspondence, IX-6–3, "C. N. Hostetter, 1966," AMC.

12. "A Message from Mennonite General Conference to the Constituent Congregations concerning the War in Vietnam," papers from 1965 Mennonite [Church] General Conference Meeting, Kidron, Ohio, 1964, n.p., pp. 113–15, AMC.

13. "Vietnam Resolution" discussion and "Resolution on Vietnam," 1965 General Conference Meeting, General Conference Mennonite Church, n.p., pp. 12, 22, MLA.

14. Lapp, "How Should I Witness to the State?" *Gospel Herald* 59 (July 26, 1966): 659–61; Edgar Metzler, "Why I Oppose the War in Vietnam," *Gospel Herald* 60 (January 17, 1967): 62–63; Donald Sensenig, "The Missionary in Vietnam," *Gospel Herald* 58 (June 8, 1965): 490–91. On the increasingly sharp MC condemnations of the war, see, for example, Lapp, "I Am Distressed," *Gospel Herald* 63 (May 26, 1970): 473, on the invasion of Cambodia; and Drescher, editorial, "Bombing, Law and Order, and the Press," *Gospel Herald* 66 (January 16, 1973): 63, denouncing Nixon's Christmas bombing of 1972. Also see the heavy volume of readers' reactions to this editorial in subsequent issues.

15. Miller quoted in Beulah Stauffer Hostetler, "Nonresistance and Social Responsibility: Mennonites and Mainline Peace Emphasis, ca. 1950 to 1986," *MQR* 64 (January 1990): 63–64.

16. J. Paul Graybill, "General Council Report," August 28, 1967, J. P. Graybill Papers, Box 35, LMHS; John E. Lapp, "A Statement of Concern to the Armed Services Committee of the House of Representatives of the United States on Behalf of the Mennonite Central Committee," May 3, 1967, Peace Section Data Files, IX-7–12, "Conscription, 1967," (pronto 7) AMC; John A. Lapp, "Vietnam and Cambodia: What Can We Do?" *Gospel Herald* 63 (May 26, 1970): 480. On the emergency letter to MC pastors, see Hubert Schwartzendruber to "Pastor," January 2, 1973, Lancaster Peace Committee Papers, LMHS. On the "Pastoral Letter to the Religious Communities of America," see "Congressmen Urged to End Vietnam War," *The Mennonite* 88 (February 6, 1973): 88; and DeBenedetti, *An American Ordeal*, 345.

17. On Shelly's role, see David Harder, "An Editor and His Denominational Periodical, or Maynard Shelly and *The Mennonite*: 1961–1971," Bethel College student paper, 1982, pp. 42–44, MLA. For a summary of GC antiwar activity by 1966, see Stanley Bohn, "Background for Considering Next Steps in Vietnam Witness," October, 1966, Board of Christian Service Papers, MLA-I-4, Box 28, File 736.

18. "An Urgent Message to our Churches from the 1967 Council of Boards," *The Mennonite* 82 (December 12, 1967): 753–54. In 1972 MCC was receiving a vast increase in funds sent for relief efforts instead of for tax payments to the Internal Revenue Service. See "MCC notes increase in tax-refusal donations," *The Mennonite* 87 (May 9, 1972): 317.

19. On "Vietnam Christmas" see Snyder to MCC Executive Committee, November 11, 1971, Peace Section Data Files, IX-7–12, "Peace Section Assembly," AMC. In this program, many Mennonites saved money ordinarily spent on Christmas gifts and gave it to MCC for medical relief in North Vietnam. "Vietnam Consultation," undated paper, PSCC Papers, MLA-I-4C, Box 7, File 94. Also see

Bohn to Kreider, September 26, 1966, Board of Christian Service Correspondence, MLA-I-4 Box 45, File 1105. On the amount of aid given, see Report of the Peace Section, 1972 MCC Workbook, p. 110, IX-5-2, AMC.

Not all the churches, however, judged giving medical aid to citizens whose nation was currently engaged killing American GIs a good idea. As Markham Community Mennonite Church in Markham, Illinois, stated, "It would be an act of dishonor and demoralization to the people and armies of the U.S." See their questionnaire in "Mennonite Consultation by Correspondence on Vietnam," (hereafter referred to as "Vietnam Consultation"), PSCC Papers, MLA-I-4B Box 3, File 65.

20. On peace activism in the Goshen/Elkhart area, see Guy Hershberger, "Conscience of Society," *Gospel Herald* 61 (February 20, 1968): 150–51; and "Goshen Students Raise Fund Offered for North Vietnam," *The Mennonite* 82 (January 17, 1967): 39–40. For Mennonite peace activism elsewhere, see "Vietnam Witness Efforts: Case Studies in Peacemaking," undated paper, PSCC Papers, MLA-IA-4C, Box 7, File 95; and "Vietnam and Cambodia: Are Mennonites Acting?" *Gospel Herald* 63 (May 26, 1970): 479.

21. J. Otis Yoder to Peachey, February 11, 1966; and May 13, 1966; both in CPSC Minutes and Reports, I-3–5.14, Box 70, AMC. Report, Peachey to CPSC Members, March 9, 1966, CPSC Minutes and Reports, I-3–5,14, Box 70, AMC.

22. Hershberger, "Questions Raised," p. 76; Yoder's message to Virginia Conference pastors noted p. 76; Editorial, "On Vietnam," *Sword and Trumpet* 35 (First Quarter 1966): 2. Peachey to CPSC Members, March 9, 1966, CPSC Minutes and Reports; Peachey to Lapp, March 28, 1967, Peachey and Hackman CPSC Papers, I-3–5.13, Box 69, AMC.

23. On the Washington visitation concerning Vietnam in 1965, see Wilbert Shank to Edgar Metzler, May 11, 1965, Hershberger PPC Papers, I-3–5.11, Box 59, AMC. Peachey to CPSC Members, March 9, 1966, and J. Otis Yoder to Peachey, May 19, 1966, both in Peachey and Hackman CPSC Papers, I-3–5.14, Box 70, AMC.

24. John A. Lapp to Peachey, February 12, 1966, Peachey/Hackman CPSC Papers, I-3–5.13, Box 69, AMC. John A. Lapp was the son of CPSC chair and Franconia bishop John E. Lapp and at the time was teaching history at Eastern Mennonite College.

25. For Shelter on George Wallace, see Sanford G. Shelter, "Is This Our Task?" *Gospel Herald* 58 (July 20, 1965): 629–30; "Just how much is any Anabaptist going to become excited . . . "in Shelter, "Some General Remarks, for the Committee on Peace and Social Relations," undated but probably 1965, Peachey/Hackman CPSC Papers, I-3–5.13, Box 68, AMC. Shelter, Editorial, "American-Russian Scoreboard," *Guidelines for Today*, Series No. 2 (March-April 1969): 6. Editorial, "Disarming America—A Real Cause for Alarm," *Guidelines for Today*, Series No. 3 (May-June 1969): 2.

26. "Study of Church-State Relations," *Gospel Herald* 61, (March 12, 1968): 236; "The Preparatory Commission for Church-State Relations," *Gospel Herald* 62 (March 11, 1969): 235; "Report V, Committee on Peace and Social Concerns," to 1969 Mennonite [Church] General Conference Meeting, Turner, Oregon,

332

NOTES TO PAGES 235-238

Mennonite General Conference Papers, n.p., pp. 41–42, AMC; Burkholder quoted in Hostetler, "Nonresistance and Social Responsibility," 65; "The Committee on Peace and Social Concerns, Report to the Mennonite General Conference," (1971), PSCC Papers, MLA-IA-4C, Box 4, File 60.

27. Minutes of Peace Section Executive Committee Meeting, Chicago, September 1, 1966, pp. 2–4, Peace Section Minutes and Reports, IX-7–8, Box 3, AMC; Larry Kehler, "The State Needs the Christian Witness," *The Mennonite* 82 (January 10, 1967): 22–23.

28. The disjuncture between the December 1966 and January 1967 findings reports is noted in Driedger and Kraybill, *Mennonite Peacemaking*, 120–21. For the statement itself, see MCC Peace Section, "A Message to Mennonite and Brethren in Christ Church Leaders and Peace Committees," January 19, 1967, Peace Section Minutes and Reports, IX-7–8, Box 3, AMC.

29. On the founding of MCC's Washington Office, see Hershberger, "A Mennonite Office in Washington?" *Gospel Herald* 61 (February 27, 1968): 186; "Report and Recommendation Concerning a Washington Office," Exhibit 1, to MCC Peace Section Executive Committee Meeting, Chicago, January 18, 1968, Peace Section Minutes and Reports, IX-7–8, Box 3, AMC; and MCC News Service Release, "Washington Office for Peace," February 2, 1968, Peace Section Data Files, IX-7–12, "Washington Office, 1973–74," AMC. On the functioning of the new office, see *Memo* from the Peace Section—Washington Office 2 (January 1970); and (March–April, 1970).

30. Emmet Lehman to Franz, March 11, 1969, MCC Correspondence, IX-6–3, "Lehman, Emmet," AMC. Lehman was a member of the Peace Section governing board. For a deeper analysis of the fire the Peace Section came under by conservatives, see "Peace Churches Polarized by Peace Witness, "*The Mennonite* 84 (February 16, 1971): 102–3.

31. Grant (Stoltzfus) to John (Lapp), May 26, 1972, MCC Correspondence, IX-6–3, "Inter-Office Peace Section, 1972," AMC; Snyder to Lapp, June 6, 1972, MCC Correspondence, IX-6–3, "Inter-Office Peace Section, 1972," AMC; Reply from Salem Mennonite Church, in "Vietnam Consultation" papers, PSCC Papers, MLA-I-4B, Box 3, File 65.

32. Lapp to Peachey, November 24, 1965, Peter Wiebe to Peachey, undated but probably November 1965, both in Peachey/Hackman CPSC Papers, I-3–5.13, Box 69, AMC.

33. I-W administrator Jesse Glick to Peachey, November 5, 1965, Peachey/Hackman CPSC Papers, I-3–5.13, Box 69, AMC; John Lehman to Hackman, January 5, 1968, Executive Secretary Files, Howard J. Zehr Papers, I-I-4, "CPSC 1967–69," AMC.

34. Oral Interview, Jim Schmidt with Ronald Krehbiel, January 27, 1981, Schowalter Oral History Collection, MLA. For replies to *The Mennonite*, see Letters to the Editor, *The Mennonite* 81 (January 4, 1966): 13; 84 (March 11, 1969): 179–80. For replies to the Bethel Peace Club, see Mrs. A. A. Schmidt to "Vietnam Moratorium Committee," October 8, 1969; Chester Benfer to Peace Club Executive Committee, November 6, 1969; both in Bethel College Peace Club Papers, MLA-III-I-A, File 2.

35. John E. Lapp, "The Mennonite Witness to Evangelism and the Social Implications of the Gospel," Exhibit V-A, General Council Meeting, February 25, 1967, Peachey/Hackman CPSC Papers, Box 68, AMC; for observations of Mennonite fundamentalists from young Mennonite radicals, see *Peace Notes* 17 (October 1970): 4, Peace Section Data Files, IX-7–12 (pronto 7), "Inter-Collegiate Peace Fellowship," AMC.

36. Peachey to District Conference Peace Committee Officers, April 25, 1967, Peachey/Hackman CPSC Papers, I-3–5.13, Box 69, AMC; Wuthnow, *Restructuring of American Religion*, 145–150.

37. Lapp to Doug Hostetter, July 8, 1970, MCC Correspondence, IX-6–3, "Hostetter, Doug, 1971," AMC.

38. It is important to note here that—somewhat surprisingly, given the careful work invested in this activity in other wars—no Mennonite agency bothered to undertake a draft census to measure their youth's fidelity to the church's teaching during the Vietnam War years. MCC began one but apparently never finished it. Peace Section secretary John A. Lapp, for instance, characterized the draft census in 1972 as "a monument to unfinished business." In 1970 MCC sent Henry Dick to Vietnam to minister to Mennonites in military service there. In his report describing his visit, Dick reported that 30 percent of all the GCs were in the military. While he hadn't received "an official figure" from the GCMC headquarters, the MC numbers, he claimed, were "correct." Yet Dick provided no indication where he had found the numbers. The GC Board of Christian Service offered some rough numbers in 1971, claiming that the percentage of GC youth opting for conscientious objection rose from 51.8 percent in 1960 to 63.3 percent in 1970, though the board did not indicate where it had gotten these numbers. One could speculatively attribute the gain to the influence of an antiwar popular culture and also to increasingly effective denominational peace teaching. Both Mennonite groups held a number of "Peacemaker Workshops" in 1967–68, which were very well received. See Lapp to Hackman, March 24, 1972, Hackman CPSC Papers, I-3–5.16, Box 72, AMC; Report of the Board of Christian Service to the GCMC triennial meeting, Fresno, California, August 14–20, 1971, General Conference Minutes and Reports, General Conference Mennonite Church, n.p., p. 39, MLA; "Committee on Peace and Social Concerns, Executive Secretary's Report, March, 1968," CPSC Minutes and Reports, I-3–5.14, Box 70, AMC. For Dick's numbers, see Henry H. Dick to MCC Executive Committee, "Visit to Mennonite Men in the Military Service in Vietnam," April 14–22, 1970, MCC Executive Committee Minutes IX-5–1, Box 5, AMC.

39. Harding to Bohn, August 25, 1966, Board of Christian Service Correspondence, MLA-I-4, Box 39, file 900. For the joint CPSC/PSCC meeting, see "Minutes of a joint meeting of the Mennonite and General Conference Peace and Social Concerns Committees," St. Louis, November 17–18, 1967, Peace Section Data Files, IX-7–7, Box 1, AMC; and PSCC meeting minutes, St. Louis, November 17–18, 1967, Board of Christian Service Papers, MLA-I-4, Box 28, File 739.

40. Guy F. Hershberger, "Our Peace Witness—In the Wake of May 18," *Gospel Herald* 60 (September 12, 1967): 821; and same title (October 24, 1967): 963 (congressional quotes); Ivan Kauffman, MCC News Service release, "Congress de-

cides against more stringent CO provisions; influenced by Peace Section testimony," June 1, 1967, MCC Data Files, IX-12, (pronto 4), "the Draft," AMC (congressional quote). For an analysis of this affair in a wider context, see Harry Marmion, *Selective Service: Conflict and Compromise* (New York: John Wiley, 1968), 129–45.

41. On the establishment of the Washington Office as a direct result of the episode in Congress, see Hershberger, "A Mennonite Office in Washington?" 186; "Report and Recommendation Concerning a Washington Office," Exhibit 1, to MCC Peace Section Executive Committee Meeting, Chicago, January 18, 1968, Peace Section Minutes and Reports, IX-7–8, Box 3, AMC.

42. "Peace Walk Baffles Peace Church," *The Mennonite* 81 (December 13, 1966): 757–59; Terence Goering, "A History of the Bethel College Peace Club," Bethel College student paper, 1975, pp. 24–26, MLA.

43. "Peace Walk Baffles Peace Church," *The Mennonite* 759–765; Goering, "A History of the . . . Peace Club," 26–32; Vernon Neufeld to Peace Club, November 1, 1966, and "Repentance Walk and Mail Discipline," undated paper, both in Bethel College Peace Club Papers, MLA-III-I-A, File 1. Though by national standards this was a relatively mild protest, it generated a storm of controversy in Mennonite circles. Both the *Mennonite Weekly Review* and *The Mennonite* issued several analyses and editorials on the march, which were followed by a number of letters both supporting and condemning the march and Neufeld's decision to redirect it. Editor Shelly of *The Mennonite* was particularly supportive of the marchers and angry at Neufeld's intervention. Shelly later pointed to one editorial that alienated several people serving on *The Mennonite's* oversight board as having cost him the critical support he needed to withstand the many critics of his editorship and led to his forced resignation five years later. See Shelly, Editorial, *The Mennonite*, 81 (December 13, 1966): 764–65; and Harder, "An Editor and His Denominational Periodical," 63.

44. "Something is 'blowin in the wind'" in Delton Franz, "Report from the Peace Section Washington Office," Exhibit 2 to MCC Peace Section meeting November 22, 1969, Peace Section Minutes and Reports, IX-7–8, Box 3, AMC. On wider Mennonite student activism, see "Vietnam Witness Efforts," PSCC files, p. 6. On the Goshen teach-in, see "Program for the October 15 Vietnam Moratorium to be held on the Goshen College Campus," undated memo, Goshen College Peace Society Papers, V-4–10, Box 5, AMC. Data on antiwar activism at Bluffton taken from Oral Interview, Perry Bush with Greg Luginbuhl, August 29, 1995, MHLB.

45. Newspaper clippings and letter, Karl North to John _____, March 5, 1966, both in Goshen College Peace Society Papers, V-4–10, Box 1, AMC.

46. "For us the bell tolled," *The Mennonite* 84 (November 4, 1969): 662–63; Goering, "A History of the . . . Peace Club," 39–46; "Bethel College made my whole day," in Lynn Edwards to Robert Mayer, September 23, 1969, Bethel College Peace Club Papers, MLA-III-I-A, File 2. The fall 1969 protests at Bethel created a considerable headache for college administrators. As the focal point for both community and Mennonite dissent to campus activism, President Orville Voth heard a wide variety of objections while refusing to outlaw freedom of expression at Bethel. Particularly trying was a fundraising letter the Peace Club mailed to the

college's mailing list. While the appeal did raise enough money to send thirty-four of the activists to the national protest activities in Washington that November, it also alienated some of the college's key financial backers, including one wealthy individual that Voth had been cultivating for several years. See Voth to Peace Club Executive Committee and Sponsors, Memorandum, "Proposed meeting about fundraising," November 11, 1969, Peace Club Papers, MLA-III-I-A, File 3.

47. Maynard Shelly, "Ferment on the Mennonite Campus," *The Mennonite* 83 (December 31, 1968): 810–11, Bethel student body president Richard Friesen quoted p. 811. On the expulsion of *Menno-Pause* editor Sam Steiner and his three compatriots, see Melissa Miller and Phil M. Shenk, *The Path of Most Resistance*, 101–2. For the quotes by a college administrator, see Shelly, "Students in an age of rebellion," *The Mennonite* 84 (January 14, 1969): 22–23. Also see Shelly, "When students meet school power," *The Mennonite* 84 (January 7, 1969): 6–8. On gatherings at Bluffton, see Oral Interview, Bush with Luginbuhl, August 29, 1995, MHLB.

48. Paul Erb, "Gathered with a Purpose," *Gospel Herald* 62 (September 16, 1969): 802.

49. Doug Baker, "Turner, 1969," *Mennonite Draft Resistance Newsletter* 1 (June 1970), Peace Section Data Files, IX-7-12, "Mennonite Draft Resistance Newsletter, 1970–1972," AMC; Harold Bauman quoted in Mark Chupp, "Reconciliation Through Resistance: Mennonite Draft Resistance and the Mennonite General Conference, Turner, Oregon, August, 1969," Goshen College student paper, 1981, MHL, p. 32; Conrad Brunk, "Needed: A New Nonconformity," *Gospel Herald* 63 (October 20, 1970): 887.

50. James Juhnke, "Conflicts and Compromises of Mennonites and the Draft: An Interpretive Essay," in *Conscience and Conscription*, Papers from the 1969 Assembly sponsored by the MCC Peace Section, Chicago, November 20–22, 1969, Akron: MCC Peace Section, p. 31, MSHL.

51. J. H. Yoder, Memo, "Campus Peace Mission," February 9, 1970, CPSC Minutes and Reports, I-3–5.14, Box 71, AMC; Darrell Fast to Franz, Hackman, and William Keeney, April 22, 1969, IX-7–13, "Peace Section Washington Office Files, 1968–79," AMC.

52. MC pastor Peter Wiebe to Paul (Peachey), undated, probably fall 1965, Peachey/Hackman CPSC Papers, I-3–5.13, Box 69, AMC; "makes us easy to handle" in letter, probably from Dwight King to friends at Goshen College, undated, probably from fall 1967, Goshen College Peace Society Papers, V-4–10, Box 1, AMC; David Rensberger, Letter to the Editor, *The Mennonite* 85 (January 27, 1970): 63; Nathan Habegger, Letter to the Editor, *The Mennonite* (December 16, 1969): 765.

53. Oral Interview, Raymond Reimer with Alvin Beachy, November 10, 1972, Schowalter Oral History Collection, MLA; David Janzen, "Persecution and Peace News—what prophetic life kind of future," *Peace News* (August 18, 1972): 2, Bethel Peace Club Papers, MLA-III-I-A, Box 2, File 26; "denying them the only true way" in "Reflections on IPF Conference on Nationalism," *Peace Notes* 20 (April 1974), Peace Section Data Files, IX-7–2, Box 1, AMC; Wesley Mast to Richard Nixon, March 17, 1970, MCC Peace Section Data Files, "Draft Dodgers Per-

sonnel Files, K-Y, 1966–74," AMC; Michael Friedman, "Why I canceled my membership in the SSS," *The Mennonite Draft Resistance Newsletter* (October 1971): 4, Peace Section Data Files, IX-7–12, AMC.

54. Hackman to Howard J. Zehr, August 2, 1969, Zehr files, I-I-4, "Committee on Peace and Social Concerns, 1969–1971," AMC; Chupp, "Reconciliation through Resistance," 14–18, Lapp quoted p. 18.

55. Baker quoted in "Report XX, Response to Conscription and Militarism," 1969 Mennonite General Conference Papers, n.p., pp. 119–20, AMC.

56. "Report XX," 1965 Mennonite General Conference Papers, 119–120; also see Chupp, "Reconciliation through Resistance," 19–21, and Miller and Shenk, *The Path of Most Resistance*, 48.

57. Chupp, "Reconciliation through Resistance," 22–23, 26–29, 33–34, delegates quoted p. 22, 27, Brunk quoted p. 34. Brunk's role also described in Miller and Shenk, *The Path of Most Resistance*, 49–50. On Orie Miller's approval, see Miller to Hackman, August 22, 1969, MCC Correspondence, IX-6–3, "Interoffice Peace Section, 1969," AMC.

58. The challenge by the Bethel Peace Club at the 1969 sessions of the Western District Conference described in Shelly, "Mennonite Ghetto Faces Eviction," *The Mennonite* 84 (October 28, 1969): 645–46, Shelly quoted p. 645. For the resolution itself, see "Resolution on Christian Action," Minutes of Western District Conference Sessions, October 10–12, 1969, n.p., pp. 18–19, MLA. "The Anabaptist movement . . . "in "Report of the Peace and Social Concerns Committee," pp. 49–50, and Resolution no. 9, "Non-cooperation with Selective Service," pp. 16–17; both in Minutes of the 1970 Western District Conference Sessions, n.p., MLA. Also see Palmer Becker to James Gingerich et al, with enclosures, January 6, 1970, Western District Conference CPSC Papers, MLA-II-3, Box 1.

59. On the 1969 Peace Section assembly, see MCC News Service releases, "Peace Section Sponsors Consultation on Conscience and Conscription," December 5, 1969; and Omar Eby, "Chicago Consultation on Conscience and Conscription: A Personal Impression," November 28, 1969; both in Peace Section Data Files, IX-7–12, "Peace Section Assembly, 1969–1974," AMC. On the new GCMC peace statement in 1971, see Harold Regier to Rod Sawatsky, August 25, 1971, Commission on Home Ministries Files, MLA-IA-4, Box 5, File 155; and "Resolution 12, The Way of Peace," in Minutes and Reports, General Conference [triennial] Meeting, August 14–20, 1971, Fresno, California, General Conference Mennonite Church, n.p., pp. 18–21, MLA. Also see Larry Kehler, "Peace Tract adopted after friendly debate," *The Mennonite* 84 (August 31, 1971): 504–5.

60. On support given to draft noncooperators, see CPSC Meeting Minutes, November 19–20, 1969, and April 17–18, 1970, CPSC Minutes and Reports, I-3–5.14, Boxes 70–71, AMC. For quote from 1971 Peace Team member, see Bob Charles, "Team Evaluation Questionnaire," August 3–4, 1971, Peace Section Data Files, IX-7–12, "Peace Teams, 1969–1971," AMC. On support for draft noncooperators in Lancaster, see Minutes of the Peace and Industrial Relations Committee meetings, Lancaster Mennonite Conference, October 9, 1969, March 2, 1971, July 6, 1972, Peace Committee Papers, LMHS. CPSC secretary Hackman attributed the disproportionate number of resisters from Lancaster "to the fact that they have

not acculturated to the degree that some other conferences have and consequently have not found it as easy to compromise themselves on the matter of military conscription." See Hackman to Mark Peachey, July 28, 1972, Hackman CPSC Papers, I-3–5.16, Box 71, AMC.

61. "Put into jeopardy the work of the last fifty years . . . " from Reinhold Ewy, Letter to the Editor, *The Mennonite* 85 (January 20, 1970): 45; J. Ward Shank, "Readers Say" *Gospel Herald* 62 (November 4, 1969): 973.

62. J. Juhnke, "Mennonites and the Great Compromise," *The Mennonite* 84 (September 23, 1969): 562; J. Juhnke, "Conflicts and Compromises" 32–33.

63. Juhnke, "Mennonites and the Great Compromise," 562–63. Also see Juhnke, "Conflicts and Compromises," 32–33.

64. "Draft Resistance Makes the Scene," *The Mennonite* 84 (December 16, 1969): 760; Lapp quote here.

65. Observer quoted in Eby, "Chicago Consultation on Conscience and Conscription," p. 2.

66. Minister's statement to Peace Team noted in "Peace Section—1971," Report of the Peace Section in the 1971 MCC Workbook, p. B-4, IX-5–2, AMC; "harmful to our public image" in Ralph Kauffman, Letter to the Editor, *The Mennonite* 84 (November 18, 1969): 699; Vincent Harding, "Vietnam: What Shall We Do?" *The Mennonite* 80 (September 21, 1965): 583.

67. Hackman to Board of Congregational Ministries, "Report of Staff Activities," January 27, 1972, Hackman CPSC Papers, I-3–5.16, Box 71, AMC; on numbers of Mennonite draft resisters, see Miller and Shenk, *The Path of Most Resistance*, 13.

68. Brown quoted in "United States of America, Plaintiff, vs. Dennis Ray Koehn, Defendant, Proceedings of April 15, 1971," Dennis Koehn Papers, MLA-MS-137 Box 1, File 3 (hereafter referred to as "Koehn Trial Transcript), pp. 35, 47. For a short summary of Koehn's case, see Miller and Shenk, *The Path of Most Resistance*, 79–82.

69. Koehn Trial Transcript, pp. 46–55; Brown quoted p. 53.

70. Koehn Trial Transcript, April 15, 1971, p. 93; June 14, 1971, pp. 24, 28.

CHAPTER 9: TRANSFORMED LANDSCAPE, TRANSFORMED VOICES

1. Guy Hershberger to Members of the Mennonite [Church] General Conference Executive Committee, November 14, 1966, CESR Papers, I-3–7, Box 7, AMC. I have paraphrased this chapter title from Rhys Isaac.

2. "Peace Section—1974," 1974 MCC Workbook, p. 109, IX-5–2, AMC; Ray Geigly to James Hess, February 7, 1974, Lancaster Peace Committee Papers, LMHS.

3. EMC senior quoted in Jim Bishop, "Rapid Shift Seen in Student Mood," *Gospel Herald* 65 (April 11, 1972): 330; "look inward" and Bethel president cited in Lois Barrett Janzen, "Mennonite Colleges: The Look Inward," *The Mennonite* 88 (January 9, 1973): 22–23; David Janzen to "Peacemakers, Mennos, friends," April 8, 1972, Peace Section Data Files, IX-7–12, "Janzen, David, 1972," AMC.

4. For MCC's awakening to women's concerns, see Ted Koontz, "Peace Section Hears Women," MCC News Service release, April 13, 1973; and Koontz to MCC

Executive Committee, November 29, 1974, both in Peace Section Data Files, IX-7–12, "Task Force on Women, 1972–74," AMC; Memo, "Men, Women and Decision-making in Mennonite Central Committee," Peace Section Data Files (pronto 3), "Women, 1973–74," AMC; Dorothy Yoder Nyce, "Beginnings: Women's Concerns Desk," *MCC Peace Office Newsletter* (September/October 1992): 10; "MCC Peace Assembly 1973, The Interdependence of Men and Women," Peace Section Data Files, IX-7–12, "Peace Assembly, 1970–74," AMC. For MCs and women's concerns, see "Women in the Church: A Study Document," Authorized by the Mennonite Church General Assembly, August 7–12, 1973, Peace Section Data Files, IX-7–12, (pronto 3), "Women, 1973–74," AMC; and John Drescher, "Assembly 73," *Gospel Herald* 66 (September 4, 1973): 666.

5. On the GCMC and women's concerns, see "Changes Recommended in Relationship of Church and Women at GC Consultation," and "General Conference Structure Study," in Report Number 3 from the Peace Section Task Force on Women in Church and Society, December 1973, Peace Section Files, IX-7–12, "Task Force on Women," AMC.

6. MC pastor Don Blosser, "Coming to Terms with Our Mennonite Faith," *Gospel Herald* 66 (October 16, 1973): 785; "slow destruction of the old community," in Richard Showalter, "Communication, Community and Mennonite Culture," *Missionary Messenger* 44 (February 1970): 5; Menno Wiebe, "To Be or Not to Be Mennonite People?" *Mennonite Life* 28 (September 6, 1973): 68, 70, 91.

7. By the mid-1980s, the question of a Mennonite identity had particularly come to rivet the attention of Mennonite scholarship. See, for instance, Calvin Redekop's *Mennonite Society* as his own effort "to understand who the Mennonites are" (p. xi); and also Redekop and Samuel Steiner, eds., *Mennonite Identity: Historical and Cultural Perspectives* (Lanham, Md.: University Press of America, 1988) for a variety of scholarly viewpoints on this matter.

8. Robert Wuthnow, *The Restructuring of American Religion*, 132–72, passim.

9. James Longacre, "Letter of Concern to All," *Gospel Herald* 66 (July 17, 1973): 556.

10. Leland Harder and J. Howard Kauffman, *Anabaptists Four Centuries Later*, 158–62, 275–82, 288–89; J. Howard Kauffman and Leo Driedger, *The Mennonite Mosaic*, 45–46, 236–37, 239–41. It is important to note that this apparent "liberal" Mennonite orientation in urban areas was not due to some kind of deterministic acceptance of liberal/urban values once they moved to the city. One strongly antiwar Mennonite pastor, who himself moved in 1970 from a pastorate in a small Kansas town to one in the more urban environs of Wichita, recalled that the relatively anonymous urban environment allowed Mennonites more social space to express their dissent without alienating themselves from their neighbors. See Oral Interview, Jim Schmidt with Mel Schmidt, January 27, 1981, Schowalter Oral History Collection, MLA.

11. Both teams of sociologists included in their large sample members from three Mennonite groups other than the MCs and GCs. All three of these groups lay much further toward the political and theological right, particularly in their much greater affinity for fundamentalism. If they had confined their comments to the MC and GC Mennonites, these sociologists would certainly have needed to

temper their analysis somewhat. Moreover, they recognized the tenuous predictive power of such variables as rural-urban residence; while Mennonites rural or urban place of residence did correlate somewhat with other variables, in many cases this effect was very slight.

12. James Thomas to Paul Landis, February 9, 1970, Lancaster Peace Committee Papers, LMHS; Harder and Kauffman, *Anabaptists Four Centuries Later*, 282, 329–30; Kauffman and Driedger, *The Mennonite Mosaic*, 45, 77–78, 203–4, 254–55.

As this study has outlined, these differing political and theological understandings as reflective of a deeper response to acculturation were manifested repeatedly by events occurring through the 1960s. It was the young Mennonites who went to college, for instance, who took much of the lead in formulating an active Mennonite opposition to the draft and the war. In a more specific example, James Juhnke discovered that the lines of loyalty broke in an unfortunate direction for him as an antiwar Mennonite college professor running for Congress in 1970. A later student of Juhnke's campaign noted that Juhnke attracted the votes of younger, better educated, less doctrinally orthodox, and higher income Mennonites. Unhappily for Juhnke, such votes were by far outnumbered by those of older, less educated, and lower income Mennonites. His opponent, a conservative Methodist lay leader and a firm supporter of the war, received the majority of Mennonite votes. See Mark E. Stucky, "James C. Juhnke and Mennonite Political Involvement," Bethel College student paper, 1971, pp. 21–31, MLA; and Juhnke, "A Mennonite Runs for Congress," *Mennonite Life* 26 (January 1971): 8–11.

13. Guy Hershberger to John Oyer, October 9, 1953, Guy F. Hershberger Papers, Historical Mss. I-171, Box 10, File 8, "Oyer, John S," AMC; John E. Lapp, "The Mennonite Witness to Evangelism and the Social Implications of the Gospel," Exhibit V-A, General Council Meeting, February 25, 1967, Peachey/Hackman CPSC Material, I-3–5.13, Box 68, AMC.

14. Lapp, "The Mennonite Witness to Evangelism," pp. 2–3.

15. On the number of Mennonites attending the U.S. Congress on Evangelism in 1969, see John Drescher, "Evangelism receives fresh perspective and purpose," *Gospel Herald* 62 (October 7, 1969): 877–79; Lancaster bishop quoted in "What the U.S. Congress on Evangelism Meant to Me," *Gospel Herald* 62, (November 4, 1969): 966. On the number of Mennonite students at the late 1960s Urbana conferences, see "Mennonite Students Attend Illinois Missionary Convention," *Gospel Herald* 61 (January 16, 1968): 68; and "Urbana '70: Direction for Life," *Gospel Herald* 64 (January 19, 1971): 65. On the birth—or rather, rebirth—of evangelical social concern in the 1960s, see David Moberg, *The Great Reversal*; Donald Dayton, *Discovering an Evangelical Heritage;* and Richard Quebedeaux, *The Young Evangelicals.*

16. On "Probe '72" see "Mennonite Consultation on Evangelism," *Gospel Herald* 65, (February 15, 1972): 144; and "What Happened at Probe '72?" *Gospel Herald* 65 (May 2, 1972): 405–6. For the Holy Spirit festival at Goshen, see "Festival of the Holy Spirit Report," *Gospel Herald* 65 (May 30, 1972): 487; and on the missions conference in Virginia in 1972, see David Hostetler, "Mission 72 Harrisonburg—Transition," *Gospel Herald* 65 (July 18, 1972): 578.

17. On the program at Probe '72, see "What Happened at Probe '72?" 405; and Richard Blosser, "Consultation Points to Evangelism Impetus," *Mennonite Weekly Review* 16 (April 20, 1972): 1. Frank H. Epp quote from MCC pamphlet *Evangelism: Good News or Bad News?* (Akron: MCC Peace Section, 1973), in Hist Mss. I-171, Guy Hershberger Papers, Box 27, File 400. On missions and service activities of Mennonite churches, see "How Five Church Groups Share the Good News," *Gospel Herald* 65 (September 26, 1972): 780.

18. Harder and Kauffman, *Anabaptists Four Centuries Later*, 334–35, 133, 159; Kauffman and Driedger, *The Mennonite Mosaic*, 68–71, 173–75.

Admittedly, the two sociologists in 1972 also discerned a good deal of wavering in regard to the two-kingdom doctrine, especially among MC Mennonites. In spite of their own refusal to take part in war, for example, many respondents suggested that they thought war was right for others. Half the MC and 44 percent of the GC respondents agreed that "the Vietnam war was necessary as a means of stopping communism in Asia." Similarly, while only 21 percent of MCs and 26 percent of GCs affirmed the state's right to use capital punishment, 33 and 26 percent expressed uncertainty on this question. Solid majorities of GCs endorsed different measurements of political participation, but only a little more than half the MCs agreed that church members should witness to the state by writing to legislators or testifying before congressional committees. See Harder and Kauffman, *Anabaptists Four Centuries Later*, 133, 157–61.

19. Kauffman and Driedger, *The Mennonite Mosaic*, 70–78, 203–5, 253–56; also on this point see Leo Driedger and Donald Kraybill, *Mennonite Peacemaking*, 227–29, 241–44. Unfortunately, Kauffman and Driedger did not provide the actual percentages of church members identified as either "Anabaptist" or "Fundamentalist" for each Mennonite group. Thus it is impossible to gauge the relative strength of these positions in the MC and GC churches.

20. For this recent reaffirmation of draft noncooperation, see Mark Becker, "Mennonite Resistance to Draft Registration," *Mennonite Life* 40 (December 1985): 19–20. On the GC endorsement of war tax resistance, see Driedger and Kraybill, *Mennonite Peacemaking*, 131. On the joint MC-GC embrace of nonviolent resistance, see General Conference Mennonite Church and Mennonite Church General Assembly, *Justice and the Christian Witness* (Newton, Kans.: Faith and Life Press, and Scottdale, Pa.: Mennonite Publishing House, 1985), statement quoted pp. 35–36. For Christian Peacemaker Teams, see Driedger and Kraybill, *Mennonite Peacemaking*, 155–56.

21. It remains a supreme irony, of course, that such well-meaning and sincere people have either constructed, or given their tax dollars and tacit consent to the construction of a weapons system that, if ever employed, promises to commit a scale of evil that would render Hitler's mild by comparison. Perhaps this paradox has something to do with what the political philosopher Hannah Arendt termed the "banality of evil"; see Hannah Arendt, *Eichmann in Jerusalem: A Report on the Banality of Evil* (New York: Viking, 1963).

22. On the ethical problems that total war poses for people committed, not to pacifism, but to the Just War tradition, see John Howard Yoder, *When War Is Unjust*.

23. Charles DeBenedetti has summarized this point well. See "The American

Peace Movement and the National Security State," *World Affairs* 141 (Fall 1978): 118–29.

24. See Martin Marty, "On Being Prophetic," *Christian Century* 97 (May 14, 1980): 559.

25. Actually, this has recently been a point of some dispute. As a process of acculturation more directly drew Mennonites into national society, and as they thus entered more consciously into the ranks of American religious denominations, they stressed their own theological commonality with other conservative Protestants. A classic statement along these lines issued from Harold Bender, who affirmed in 1937: "All the American Mennonite groups without exception stand upon the great platform of conservative evangelicalism in theology, being thoroughly orthodox in the great fundamental doctrines of the Christian faith such as the unity of the Godhead, the true deity of Christ, the atonement by the shedding of blood, the plenary inspiration and divine authority of the Holy Scriptures as the Word of God." The problem with emphasizing such theological commonalities, a few Mennonite theologians have begun to argue, is that it promised to perpetuate the same kind of "two-track" theological mindset that, as noted in chapter 2, Theron Schlabach found operating among Mennonite fundamentalists in the 1920s. Such a worldview held that issues of atonement, salvation, and evangelism were primary in importance and were shared with other conservative Protestant groups. Mennonite distinctives like peace and social justice were secondary and not as key as salvation. Such a gradation of doctrinal versus ethical concerns, with ethics clearly secondary, was damaging a half-century ago and certainly eased the exodus of many Mennonites into fundamentalist ranks. Yet ethnic bonds held together the idea of classic Christology with notions of discipleship and nonresistance. See Bender, "Mennonites of the United States," *MQR* 11 (January 1937): 79; Theron Schlabach, *Gospel Versus Gospel, 167–194*.

Now that those ethnic understandings are rapidly dissipating, however, some scholars argue that Mennonites have a real problem in their theology, and one that needs to be addressed if they are to maintain their separate identity as a peace church. Theologian J. Denny Weaver has developed this point with some care and prescribed some remedies for it. Rather than simply fusing or combining classic evangelical formulations with Mennonite ethics, Weaver's solution argues that assumptions of discipleship and nonviolence provide different formulations of doctrines such as Christology and atonement. See J. Denny Weaver, "Narrative Theology in an Anabaptist-Mennonite Context," *Conrad Grebel Review* 12 (Spring 1994): 171–88; Weaver, "Christus Victor, Ecclesiology, and Christology," *MQR* 68 (July 1994): 277–90; and Weaver, *Keeping Salvation Ethical: Mennonite and Amish Atonement Theology in the Late Nineteenth Century* (Scottdale, Pa.: Herald Press, 1997).

26. At least they have rejected such patronizing dismissals on the ideological level. On the functional level, as in alternative service arrangements, these dismissals have proven more attractive.

27. Wuthnow, *The Restructuring of American Religion*, 5, 322.

28. Rodney Sawatsky, *Authority and Identity*, 20–23; John Howard Yoder, "Anabaptist Vision and Mennonite Reality," in A. J. Klassen, ed., *Consultation on*

Anabaptist-Mennonite Theology: Papers read at the 1969 Aspen Conference (Elkhart, Ind.: Council of Mennonite Seminaries, 1970) 7, 23–24.

29. Timothy L. Smith, "Religion and Ethnicity in America," *American Historical Review* 83 (December 1978): 1158, 1161; Eugene Genovese, *Roll, Jordan, Roll: The World the Slaves Made,* (New York: Random House, 1974).

30. This incident recounted from James Juhnke, "Anabaptists and the Flagpole," *The Mennonite* 86 (April 13, 1971): 242–43.

Selected
Bibliography

MANUSCRIPT COLLECTIONS

Archives of the Mennonite Church, Goshen College, Goshen, Indiana
Harold S. Bender Papers
Committee on Economic Relations Papers
Goshen College Peace Society Papers
Guy F. Hershberger Papers
Doug Hostetter Papers
Illinois Mennonite Conference Papers (Leland Bachman Correspondence)
Nelson Kauffman Papers
Mennonite Central Committee Correspondence
Mennonite Central Committee, Civilian Public Service Data Files
Mennonite Central Committee, Peace Section Data Files
Mennonite Research Foundation Papers
Edgar Metzler Papers
Arthur Nafziger Papers
Boyd Nelson Papers
Peace Problems Committee/Committee on Peace and Social Concerns Papers

Lancaster Mennonite Historical Society, Lancaster, Pennsylvania
Lloyd M. Eby Papers
J. Paul Graybill Papers
Amos Horst Papers
Lancaster Mennonite Bishops' Board Papers
Lancaster Mennonite Peace Committee Papers
Michael Wenger Papers

Menno Simons Historical Library, Eastern Mennonite University,
Harrisonburg, Virginia
Peace and Industrial Relations Committee Papers
Virginia Mennonite Conference Papers

Mennonite Library and Archives, Bethel College,
North Newton, Kansas
Bethel College Peace Club Papers
Board of Christian Service/ Commission on Home Ministries Papers
Elmer Ediger Papers
Henry Fast Papers
J. Winfield Fretz Papers
Albert Gaeddert Papers
E. M. Harshbarger Papers
Peter C. Hiebert Papers
Dennis Koehn Papers
Elbert Koontz Papers
Esko Loewen Papers
Western District Conference, Committee on Peace and Social Concerns Papers

BOOKS AND PAMPHLETS

Ahlstrom, Sydney. *A Religious History of the American People.* 2 vols. New York: Doubleday, 1975.

Ambrose, Stephen. *Rise to Globalism: American Foreign Policy Since 1938.* 4th rev. ed. New York: Penguin, 1985.

Bainton, Roland. *Christian Attitudes toward War and Peace.* Nashville: Abingdon, 1960.

Baskir, Lawrence, and William Strauss. *Chance and Circumstance: The Draft, the War, and the Vietnam Generation.* New York: Alfred A. Knopf, 1978.

Barnet, Richard. *The Economy of Death.* New York: Atheneum, 1969.

Board of Christian Service, General Conference Mennonite Church. *Christian Responsibility to Society: A Biblical-Theological Statement.* Church and Society Series no. 2. Newton, Kans.: Faith and Life Press, 1963.

Boyer, Paul. *By the Bomb's Early Light: American Thought and Culture at the Dawn of the Atomic Age.* New York: Pantheon Books, 1987.

Carter, Paul. *The Decline and Revival of the Social Gospel.* Ithaca, N.Y.: Cornell University Press, 1954.

Chambers, John Whiteclay II, ed. *Draftees or Volunteers? A Documentary History of the Debate over Military Conscription in the United States, 1787–1973.* New York: Garland Press, 1975.

————, and Charles C. Moskos, eds. *The New Conscientious Objection: From Sacred to Secular Resistance.* New York: Oxford University Press, 1993.

Chatfield, Charles. *For Peace and Justice: Pacifism in America, 1914–1941.* Knoxville: University of Tennessee Press, 1971.

Cohen, Elliot. *Citizens and Soldiers: The Dilemmas of Military Service.* Ithaca, N.Y.: Cornell University Press, 1985.

Crane, Conrad C., *Bombs, Cities, and Civilians: American Airpower Strategy in World War II.* Lawrence: University Press of Kansas, 1993.

Dayton, Donald. *Discovering an Evangelical Heritage.* New York: Harper and Row, 1976.

DeBenedetti, Charles, assisted by Charles Chatfield. *An American Ordeal: The Antiwar Movement of the Vietnam Era.* Syracuse, N.Y.: Syracuse University Press, 1990.

———. *The Peace Reform in American History.* Bloomington: Indiana University Press, 1980.

Detweiler, Richard. *Mennonite Statements on Peace, 1915–1966.* Scottdale, Pa.: Herald Press, 1968.

Driedger, Leo, and Donald B. Kraybill. *Mennonite Peacemaking: From Quietism to Activism.* Scottdale, Pa.: Herald Press, 1994.

Dyck, Cornelius J. *An Introduction to Mennonite History.* 3d. ed. Scottdale, Pa.: Herald Press, 1993.

———, ed. *Witness and Service in North America: The MCC Story.* Vol. 3. Scottdale, Pa.: Herald Press, 1980.

Epp, Frank. *Mennonite Exodus: The Rescue and Resettlement of the Russian Mennonites since the Communist Revolution.* Altona, Manitoba: D. W. Friesen and Sons, 1962.

Erb, Paul. *Orie O. Miller: The Story of a Man and an Era.* Scottdale, Pa.: Herald Press, 1969.

Fite, Gilbert. *American Farmers: The New Minority.* Bloomington: Indiana University Press, 1981.

FitzGerald, Frances. *Fire in the Lake: The Vietnamese and the Americans in Vietnam.* New York: Vintage Books, 1972.

Flynn, George Q. *Lewis B. Hershey: Mr. Selective Service.* Chapel Hill: University of North Carolina Press, 1985.

———. *The Mess in Washington: Manpower Mobilization in World War II.* Westport, Conn.: Greenwood Press, 1979.

Fried, Richard. *Nightmare in Red: The McCarthy Era in Perspective.* New York: Oxford University Press, 1990.

Friesen, Duane. *Mennonite Witness on Peace and Social Concerns.* Akron, Pa.: MCC Peace Section, 1982.

Funk, Ruby, ed. *Peace, Progress, Promise: A 75th Anniversary of Tabor Mennonite Church.* Tabor, Kans.: Tabor Mennonite Church, 1983.

Fussell, Paul. *Wartime: Understanding and Behavior in the Second World War.* New York: Oxford University Press, 1989.

Gaddis, John Lewis. *The Long Peace: Inquiries into the History of the Cold War.* New York: Oxford University Press, 1987.

———. *Russia, the Soviet Union, and the United States: An Interpretive History.* New York: John Wiley and Sons, 1978.

Gallucci, Robert L. *Neither Peace Nor Honor: The Politics of American Military Policy in Viet-Nam.* Studies in International Affairs No. 24, The Washington

Center of Foreign Policy Research. Baltimore: Johns Hopkins University Press, 1975.

General Conference Mennonite Church and Mennonite Church General Assembly. *Justice and the Christian Witness.* Newton, Kans.: Faith and Life Press, and Scottdale, Pa.: Mennonite Publishing House, 1985.

Gingerich, Melvin. *Service for Peace: A History of Mennonite Civilian Public Service.* Akron, Pa.: Mennonite Central Committee, 1949.

Goossen, Rachel Waltner. *Meetingplace: A History of First Mennonite Church of Normal, Illinois.* Normal, Ill.: First Mennonite Church, 1987.

Gordon, Milton. *Assimilation in American Life.* New York: Oxford University Press, 1964.

Grieser, Orland, and Ervin Beck. *Out of the Wilderness: A History of the Central Mennonite Church.* Grand Rapids, Mich.: Dean Hicks Company, 1960.

Harder, Leland. *General Conference Mennonite Church: Fact Book of Congregational Membership.* Copyright by Leland Harder, 1971.

———, and J. Howard Kauffman. *Anabaptists Four Centuries Later.* Scottdale, Pa.: Herald Press, 1975.

Haury, David. *The Quiet Demonstration: The Mennonite Mission at Gulfport.* Newton, Kans.: Faith and Life Press, 1979.

Herken, Gregg. *The Winning Weapon: The Atomic Bomb in the Cold War.* New York: Alfred Knopf, 1980.

Herring, George C. *America's Longest War: The United States and Vietnam, 1950–1975.* 2d ed. Philadelphia: Temple University Press, 1986.

Hershberger, Guy F. *War, Peace, and Nonresistance.* 3d ed. Scottdale, Pa.: Herald Press, 1969.

———. *The Mennonite Church in the Second World War.* Scottdale, Pa.: Mennonite Publishing House, 1951.

Homan, Gerlof D. *American Mennonites and the Great War, 1914–1918.* Scottdale, Pa.: Herald Press, 1994.

Hostetler, Beulah Stauffer. *American Mennonites and Protestant Movements: A Community Paradigm.* Scottdale, Pa.: Herald Press, 1987.

Johnson, Paul. *The Rise and Fall of the Great Powers: Economic Change and Military Conflict from 1500 to 2000.* New York: Vintage Books, 1987.

Juhnke, James C. *A People of Two Kingdoms.* Newton, Kans.: Faith and Life Press, 1975.

———. *Creative Crusader: Edmund G. Kaufman and Mennonite Community.* North Newton, Kans.: Bethel College, 1994.

———. *Vision, Doctrine, War: Mennonite Identity and Organization in America.* Scottdale, Pa.: Herald Press, 1989.

Karnow, Stanley. *Vietnam: A History.* New York: Viking, 1983.

Kauffman, J. Howard, and Leo Driedger. *The Mennonite Mosaic: Identity and Modernization.* Scottdale, Pa.: Herald Press, 1991.

Keim, Albert, and Grant Stoltzfus. *The Politics of Conscience: The Historic Peace Churches and America at War, 1917–1955.* Scottdale, Pa.: Herald Press, 1988.

Kingston-McLoughry, Edgar. *Global Strategy.* New York: Frederick Praeger, 1957.

LaFeber, Walter. *America, Russia, and the Cold War.* 2d ed. New York: John Wiley and Sons, 1972.

Lehman, James. *Creative Congregationalism: A History of Oak Grove Mennonite Church in Wayne County, Ohio.* Smithville, Ohio: Oak Grove Mennonite Church, 1978.

————. *Salem's First Century: Worship and Witness.* Kidron, Ohio: Salem Mennonite Church, 1986.

Lehman, Naomi. *Pilgrimage of a Congregation: First Mennonite Church, Berne, Indiana.* Berne, Ind.: First Mennonite Church of Berne, 1982.

Lind, Hope Kauffman. *Apart and Together: Mennonites in Oregon and Neighboring States, 1876–1976.* Scottdale, Pa.: Herald Press, 1990.

Lingman, Richard. *Don't You Know There's a War On? The American Home Front, 1941–1945.* New York: G. P. Putnam's Sons, 1970.

Manchester, William. *The Glory and the Dream: A Narrative History of America, 1932–1972.* 2 vols. Boston: Little, Brown, 1973.

Marsden, George. *Fundamentalism and American Culture: The Shaping of Twentieth Century Evangelicalism.* New York: Oxford University Press.

Marty, Martin. *Pilgrims in Their Own Land: 500 Years of Religion in America.* New York: Penguin, 1984.

Melman, Seymour. *Pentagon Capitalism: The Political Economy of War.* New York: McGraw-Hill, 1970.

Miller, Gordon. *To God Be the Glory: The Mennonite Witness in Iowa City, 1927–1977.* Copyright by Gordon Miller, 1977.

Miller, Melissa, and Phil Shenk. *The Path of Most Resistance: Stories of Mennonite Conscientious Objectors Who Did Not Cooperate with the Vietnam War Draft.* Scottdale, Pa.: Herald Press, 1982.

Miller, Robert Moats. *American Protestantism and Social Issues, 1919–1939.* Chapel Hill: University of North Carolina Press, 1958.

Milward, Alan S. *War, Economy, and Society, 1939–1945.* Berkeley: University of California Press, 1977.

Moberg, David. *The Great Reversal.* Philadelphia: J. B. Lippincott, 1972.

Mumaw, John. *Nonresistance and Pacifism.* Scottdale, Pa.: Mennonite Publishing House, 1944.

Neufeld, Vernon. *If We Can Love: The Mennonite Mental Health Story.* Newton, Kans.: Faith and Life Press, 1983.

Niebuhr, H. Richard. *Christ and Culture.* New York: Harper and Row, 1951.

Pannabecker, Samuel F. *Open Doors: A History of the General Conference Mennonite Church.* Newton, Kans.: Faith and Life Press, 1975.

Paterson, Thomas. *On Every Front: The Making of the Cold War.* New York: W. W. Norton, 1979.

Peachey, Paul. *The Church in the City.* Institute of Mennonite Studies Series no. 2. Newton, Kans.: Faith and Life Press, 1963.

Peachey, Urbane, ed. *Mennonite Statements on Peace and Social Concerns, 1900–1978.* Akron, Pa.: Mennonite Central Committee, 1980.

Perrett, Geoffrey. *Days of Sadness, Years of Triumph: The American People, 1939–1945.* New York: Coward, McCann and Geoghegan, 1973.

Polenburg, Richard. *One Nation Divisible: Class, Race and Ethnicity in the United States Since 1938*. New York: Penguin, 1980.

———. *War and Society: The United States, 1941–1945*. Westport, Conn.: Greenwood Press, 1972.

Quebedeaux, Richard. *The Young Evangelicals: Revolution in Orthodoxy*. New York: Harper and Row, 1974.

Raskin, Marcus G.. *The Politics of National Security*. New Brunswick, N.J.: Transaction Books, 1979.

Redekop, Calvin. *Mennonite Society*. Baltimore: Johns Hopkins University Press, 1989.

Rohrer, Wayne, and Lewis Douglas. *The Agrarian Transition in America*. Indianapolis, Ind.: Bobbs-Merrill, 1969.

Sanders, Thomas G. *Protestant Concepts of Church and State*. New York: Holt, Rinehart, and Winston, 1964.

Sawatsky, Rodney. *Authority and Identity: The Dynamics of the General Conference Mennonite Church*. North Newton, Kansas: Bethel College, 1987.

Schaffer, Ronald. *Wings of Judgement: American Bombing in World War II*. New York: Oxford University Press, 1985.

Schlabach, Theron. *Gospel Versus Gospel: Mission and the Mennonite Church, 1863–1944*. Scottdale, Pa.: Herald Press, 1980.

Sherry, Michael. *The Rise of American Air Power: The Creation of Armageddon*. New Haven: Yale University Press, 1987.

Shover, John K. *First Majority, Last Minority: The Transformation of Rural Life in America*. Dekalb: Northern Illinois University Press, 1976.

Sibley, Mulford, and Philip Jacob. *Conscription of Conscience: The American State and the Conscientious Objector, 1940–1947*. Ithaca, N.Y.: Cornell University Press, 1952.

Silk, Mark. *Spiritual Politics: Religion and Society in America Since World War II*. New York: Simon and Schuster, 1988.

Smith, Willard. *Mennonites in Illinois*. Scottdale, Pa.: Herald Press, 1983.

Toews, Paul. *Mennonites in American Society, 1930–1970: Modernity and the Persistence of Religious Community*. Scottdale, Pa.: Herald Press, 1996.

Unruh, John. *In the Name of Christ: A History of MCC and Its Service, 1920–1951*. Scottdale, Pa.: Herald Press, 1952.

Weigley, Russell. *The American Way of War*. New York: Macmillan, 1973.

Wherry, Neal M. *Conscientious Objection*. 2 vols. Washington, D.C.: Selective Service System Special Monograph no. 11, 1950.

Whitfield, Stephen J. *The Culture of the Cold War*. Baltimore: Johns Hopkins University Press, 1991.

Wiebe, Robert. *The Search for Order*. New York: Hill and Wang, 1967.

Wittner, Lawrence. *Rebels Against War: The American Peace Movement, 1941–1960*. New York: Columbia University Press, 1969; Philadelphia: Temple University Press, 1984.

Wuthnow, Robert. *The Restructuring of American Religion*. Princeton, N.J.: Princeton University Press, 1988.

Yergin, Daniel. *Shattered Peace: The Origins of the Cold War and the National Security State*. Boston: Houghton Mifflin, 1977.

Yoder, John Howard. *When War is Unjust: Being Honest in Just-War Thinking*. With an Introduction by Charles P. Lutz. Minneapolis, Minn.: Augsburg, 1984.

Yousey, Arlene. *Strangers and Pilgrims: A History of Lewis County Mennonites*. Copyright by Arlene Yousey, 1987.

Zaroulis, Nancy, and Gerald Sullivan. *Who Spoke Up? American Protest Against the War in Vietnam*. New York: Holt, Rinehart and Winston, 1984.

SECONDARY ARTICLES AND CHAPTERS IN BOOKS

Adler, Les K., and Thomas G. Paterson. "Red Fascism: The Merger of Nazi Germany and Soviet Russia in the American Image of Totalitarianism, 1930s–1950s," *American Historical Review* 75 (April 1970): 1046–64.

Becker, Mark. "Mennonite Resistance to Draft Registration," *Mennonite Life* 40 (December 1985): 19–20.

Bender, Harold S. "The Anabaptist Vision," *Mennonite Quarterly Review* 18 (April 1944): 67–88.

———. "The Mennonite Church." In *The Mennonite Encyclopedia*. Hillsboro, Kans.: Mennonite Brethren Publishing House, 1959, 3:614.

Boli-Bennet, John. "The Ideology of Expanding State Authority in National Constitutions." In *National Development and the World System*, edited by John W. Meyer and Michael T. Hannan, 222–35. Chicago: University of Chicago Press, 1979.

Borosage, Robert. "The Making of the National Security State." In *The Pentagon Watchers: Students Report on the National Security State*, edited by Leonard S. Rodberg and Derek Shearer, 3–63. Garden City, N.Y.: Doubleday, 1970.

Burkholder, John Richard. "Nonresistance." In *The Mennonite Encyclopedia*, Vol. 5, edited by Cornelius Dyck and Dennis P. Martin, 637. Scottdale, Pa.: Herald Press, 1990.

———. "Type 4: Apolitical Nonresistance." In *Mennonite Peace Theology: A Panorama of Types*, edited by Burkholder and Barbara Nelson Gingerich, 30–34. Akron, Pa.: Mennonite Central Committee, 1991.

Bush, Perry. "Anabaptism Born Again: Mennonites, New Evangelicals, and the Search for a Useable Past," *Fides et Historia* 25 (Winter/Spring 1993): 26–47.

Carpenter, Joel. "The Fundamentalist Leaven and the Rise of an Evangelical United Front." In *The Evangelical Tradition in America*, edited by Leonard Sweet, 256–88. Macon, Ga.: Mercer University Press, 1984.

———. "Youth for Christ and the New Evangelicals' Place in the Life of the Nation." In *Religion in the Life of the Nation: American Recoveries*, edited by Rowland Sherrill, 128–51. Urbana: University of Illinois Press, 1990.

Chambers, John Whiteclay II. "Conscientious Objectors and the America State from Colonial Times to the Present." In *The New Conscientious Objection:*

From Sacred to Secular Resistance, edited by Charles C. Moskos and John Whiteclay Chambers II, 23–46. New York: Oxford University Press.

Childress, James F. "Reinhold Niebuhr's Critique of Pacifism," *Review of Politics* 36 (October 1974): 467–91.

DeBenedetti, Charles. "The American Peace Movement and the National Security State," *World Affairs* 141 (Fall 1978): 118–29.

Driedger, Leo. "Mennonite Community Change: From Ethnic Enclaves to Social Networks," *Mennonite Quarterly Review* 60 (July 1986): 374–86.

———, and J. Howard Kauffman. "Urbanization of Mennonites: Canadian and American Comparisons," *Mennonite Quarterly Review* 56 (July 1982): 269–90.

Eitzen, Dirk, and Timothy Falb. "An Overview of the Mennonite I-W Program," *Mennonite Quarterly Review* 56 (October 1982): 365–81.

Farber, David. "The Counterculture and the Antiwar Movement." In *Give Peace a Chance: Exploring the Vietnam Antiwar Movement,* edited by Melvin Small and William D. Hoover, 7–21. Syracuse, N.Y.: Syracuse University Press, 1992.

Finer, Samuel. "State and Nation Building in Europe: The Role of the Military." In *The Formation of National States in Western Europe,* edited by Charles Tilly, 84–163. Princeton, N.J.: Princeton University Press, 1975.

Flynn, George Q. "Lewis Hershey and the Conscientious Objector: the World War II Experience," *Military Affairs* 47 (February 1983): 1–6.

Friedman, Leon. "Conscription and the Constitution: The Original Understanding," *Michigan Law Review* 67 (June 1969): 1493–1552.

Friesen, Lauren. "Type 2: Culturally Engaged Pacifism." In *Mennonite Peace Theology: A Panorama of Types,* edited by John Richard Burkholder and Barbara Nelson Gingerich, 15–25. Akron, Pa.: Mennonite Central Committee, 1991.

Hall, Mitchell. "CALCAV and Religious Opposition to the Vietnam War." In *Give Peace a Chance: Exploring the Vietnam Antiwar Movement,* edited by Melvin Small and William D. Hoover, 35–52. Syracuse, N.Y.: Syracuse University Press, 1992.

Harder, Leland. "An Empirical Search for the Key Variable in Mennonite Reality," *Mennonite Quarterly Review* 45 (December 1971): 331–51.

Hershberger, Guy F. "Biblical Nonresistance and Modern Pacifism," *Mennonite Quarterly Review* 17 (July 1943): 115–35.

———. "Harold S. Bender and his Time," *Mennonite Quarterly Review* 38 (April 1964): 83–112.

Hostetler, Beulah. "Nonresistance and Social Responsibility: Mennonites and Mainline Peace Emphasis, ca. 1950 to 1985," *Mennonite Quarterly Review* 64 (January 1990): 49–73.

Juhnke, James C. "A Mennonite Runs for Congress," *Mennonite Life* 26 (January 1971): 8–11.

———. "Conflicts and Compromises of Mennonites and the Draft: An Interpretive Essay." In *Conscience and Conscription: Papers from the 1969*

Assembly, Sponsored by the MCC Peace Section, 22–23. Akron, Pa.: MCC Peace Section, 1969.

———. "Mennonites and the Great Compromise," *The Mennonite* 84, (September 23, 1969): 562–64.

———. "Gerald B. Winrod and the Kansas Mennonites," *Mennonite Quarterly Review* 43 (October 1969): 293–97.

———. "Mennonite Benevolence and Revitalization in the Wake of World War I," *Mennonite Quarterly Review* 60 (January 1986): 15–30.

———. "Mennonite Church Theological and Social Boundaries, 1920–1930—Loyalists, Liberals, and Laxitarians," *Mennonite Life* 38 (June 1983): 18–24.

———. "Mennonite History and Self-Understanding: North American Mennonitism as a Bipolar Mosaic." In *Mennonite Identity: Historical and Contemporary Perspectives*, edited by Calvin Wall Redekop and Samuel Steiner, 83–79. Lanham, Md.: University Press of America, 1988.

Juhnke, Roger. "The Perils of Conscientious Objection," *Mennonite Life* 34 (September 1979): 4–9.

Kauffman, J. Howard. "Boundary Maintenance and Cultural Assimilation of Contemporary Mennonites," *Mennonite Quarterly Review* 51 (October 1977): 227–40.

Keeney, William. "Experience in Mental Hospitals in World War II," *Mennonite Quarterly Review*, 56 (January 1982): 7–17.

Keim, Albert. "Service or Resistance? The Mennonite Resistance to Conscription in World War II," *Mennonite Quarterly Review* 82 (April 1978): 141–55.

Krahn, Cornelius, J. Winfield Fretz, and Robert Kreider. "Altruism in American Life." In *Forms and Techniques of Altruism and Spiritual Growth*, edited by Pitirim A. Sorokin, 309–28. Boston: Beacon Press, 1954.

Kreider, Robert. "The Historic Peace Churches Meeting of 1935," *Mennonite Life* 31 (June 1976): 21–24.

Krippendorff, Ekkehart. "The State as a Focus for Peace Research." In *Papers XVI: The Rome Conference*, 47–53. Peace Research Society, 1970.

Lapp, John A. "The Peace Mission of the Mennonite Central Committee," *Mennonite Quarterly Review* 44 (July 1970): 280–97.

Marty, Martin. "On Being Prophetic." *Christian Century* 97 (May 14, 1980): 559.

McReynolds, David. "Pacifists and the Vietnam Antiwar Movement." In *Give Peace a Chance: Exploring the Vietnam Antiwar Movement*, edited by Melvin Small and William D. Hoover, 53–70. Syracuse, N.Y.: Syracuse University Press, 1992.

Metzler, Edgar. "Toward the Year 2000: War, Peace, and Nonresistance—Implications for the Mennonite Church," *Mennonite Historical Bulletin* 47 (January 1987): 2–3.

Morris, Cynthia Hastas. "Arkansas's Reaction to the Men Who Said 'No' to World War II," *Arkansas Historical Quarterly* 43 (Summer 1984): 153–77.

Niebuhr, H. Reinhold. "Why the Christian Church Is Not Pacifist." In

Christianity and Power Politics, edited by Niebuhr, 1–32. New York: Charles Scribner's Sons, 1940.

———. "Christianity and the Social Revolution." In *Christianity and the Social Revolution*, edited by John Lewis, Karl Polanyi, and Donald B. Kitchin, 442–72. New York: Charles Scribner's Sons, 1936.

Orser, W. Edward. "World War II and the Pacifist Controversy in the Major Protestant Churches," *American Studies* 14 (Fall 1973): 5–24.

Oyer, John. "Historiography, Anabaptist." In *The Mennonite Encyclopedia*, Vol. 5, edited by Cornelius Dyck and Dennis P. Martin, 378–82. Scottdale, Pa.: Herald Press, 1990.

Peterson, David. "Ready for War: Oregon Mennonites from Versailles to Pearl Harbor," *Mennonite Quarterly Review* 64 (July 1990): 209–29.

Rapoport, Anatol. "Changing Conceptions of War in the United States." In *American Thinking about Peace and War*, edited by Ken Booth and Moorhead Wright, 59–82. New York: Barnes and Noble, 1978.

Rasmussen, Wayne. "The Impact of Technological Change on American Agriculture," *Journal of Economic History* 22 (December 1962): 578–99.

Redekop, John. "Politics." In *The Mennonite Encyclopedia*, Vol. 5, edited by Cornelius Dyck and Dennis P. Martin, 711–14. Scottdale, Pa.: Herald Press, 1990.

Russell, R. R. "The Development of Conscientious Objector Recognition in the United States," *George Washington Law Review* 20 (March 1952): 409–48.

Sawatsky, Rodney. "Beyond the Social History of the Mennonites: A Response to James Juhnke." In *Mennonite Identity: Historical and Contemporary Perspectives*, edited by Calvin Wall Redekop and Samuel Steiner, 101–8. Lanham, Md.: University Press of America, 1988.

Schlabach, Theron. "Paradoxes of Mennonite Separatism," *Pennsylvania Mennonite Heritage* 2 (January 1979): 12–17.

———. "To Focus a Mennonite Vision." In *Kingdom, Cross, and Community: Essays on Mennonite Themes in Honor of Guy F. Hershberger*, edited by John Richard Burkholder and Calvin Redekop, 15–50. Scottdale, Pa.: Herald Press, 1976.

Siegel, Bernard. "Defensive Structuring and Environmental Stress," *American Journal of Sociology* 26 (July 1970): 11–32.

Smith, Timothy L. "Religion and Ethnicity in America," *American Historical Review* 83 (December 1978): 1155–84.

Stayer, James. "The Easy Demise of a Normative Vision of Anabaptism." In *Mennonite Identity: Historical and Contemporary Perspectives* edited by Calvin Wall Redekop and Samuel Steiner, 109–16. Lanham, Md.: University Press of America, 1988.

Steele, Richard W. "American Popular Opinion and the War against Germany: The Issue of Negotiated Peace, 1942," *Journal of American History* 45 (December 1978): 704–23.

Teichroew, Allen. "Mennonites and the Conscription Trap," *Mennonite Life* 30 (September 1975): 10–12.

Toews, Paul. "The Concern Movement: Its Origins and Early History," *Conrad Grebel Review* 8 (Spring 1990): 109–26.

———. "Fundamentalist Conflict in Mennonite Colleges: A Response to Cultural Transitions?" *Mennonite Quarterly Review* 57 (July 1983): 241–56.

———. "The Long Weekend or the Short Week: Mennonite Peace Theology, 1925–1944," *Mennonite Quarterly Review* 60, (January 1986): 38–57.

———. "Mennonites in American Society: Modernity and the Persistence of Religious Community," *Mennonite Quarterly Review* 63 (July 1983): 227–46.

———. " 'Will a New Day Dawn from This?' Mennonite Pacifist People and the Good War," *Mennonite Life* 45 (December 1990): 16–22.

Weaver, J. Denny. "Christus Victor, Ecclesiology, and Christology," *Mennonite Quarterly Review* 68 (July 1994): 277–90.

———. "Narrative Theology in an Anabaptist-Mennonite Context," *Conrad Grebel Review* 12 (Spring 1994): 171–88.

Wenger, J. C. "Harold S. Bender: A Brief Biography," *Mennonite Quarterly Review* 38 (April 1964): 113–20.

Yoder, John Howard. "Anabaptist Vision and Mennonite Reality." In *Consultation on Anabaptist-Mennonite Theology: Papers Read at the 1969 Aspen Conference*, edited by A. J. Klassen, 1–46. Elkhart, Ind.: Council of Mennonite Seminaries, 1970.

———. "The Contemporary Evangelical Revival and the Peace Churches." In *Mission and the Peace Witness*, edited by Robert Ramseyer, 68–103. Scottdale, Pa.: Herald Press, 1979.

Zeitzer, Glen. "The Fellowship of Reconciliation on the Eve of the Second World War: A Peace Organization Prepares," *Peace and Change* 3 (Summer/Fall 1975): 46–51.

UNPUBLISHED MATERIAL

Becker, Mark. "Men and Women Who Dare to Say No: Mennonite Resistance to Draft Registration," Bethel College student paper, 1985, MLA.

Chupp, Mark. "Reconciliation Through Resistance: Mennonite Draft Resistance and the Mennonite General Conference, Turner, Oregon, August 1969," Goshen College student paper, 1981, MHLG.

Franz, Roberta. "Mennonite Preaching on the Vietnam War," Bethel College student paper, 1972, MLA.

Goossen, Rachel Waltner. "Conscientious Objection and Gender: Women in Civilian Public Service During the Second World War," Ph.D. diss., University of Kansas, 1984.

Goering, Terence. "A History of the Bethel College Peace Club," Bethel College student paper, 1975, MLA.

Grismrud, Theodore G. "An Ethical Analysis of Conscientious Objection to World War II," Ph.D. diss., Graduate Theological Union, 1988.

Harder, David. "An Editor and His Denominational Periodical, or Maynard Shelly and *The Mennonite*: 1961–1971," Bethel College student paper, 1982, MLA.

Harder, Leland. "The Quest for Equilibrium in an Established Sect: A Study of
    Social Change in the General Conference Mennonite Church," Ph.D. diss.,
    Northwestern University, 1962.
Juhnke, Roger. "One War–Three Fronts: Kansas General Conference
    Mennonite Response to World War II," Bethel College student paper, 1975,
    MLA.
Juhnke, William. "A World Gone Mad": Mennonites View the Coming of War,
    1938–1939," Bethel College student paper, 1966, MLA.
Larson, Zelle Andrews. "An Unbroken Witness: Conscientious Objection to War,
    1948–1953," Ph.D. diss., University of Hawaii, 1975.
Robinson, Mitchell. "Civilian Public Service During World War II: the
    Dilemmas of Conscience and Conscription in a Free Society," Ph.D. diss.,
    Cornell University, 1990.
Sawatsky, Rodney. "The Impact of Fundamentalism on Mennonite
    Nonresistance," MA thesis, University of Minnesota, 1973.
———. "History and Ideology: American Mennonite Definition Through
    History," Ph.D. diss., Princeton University, 1977.
Schmidt, Daryl Dean. "War is Sin? Mennonite Preaching on War, 1940–1945,"
    Bethel College student paper, 1966, MLA.
Stucky, Mark. "James C. Juhnke and Mennonite Political Involvement," Bethel
    College student paper, 1971.
Unruh, Wilfred. "A Study of Mennonite Service Programs," prepared for the
    Institute of Mennonite Studies, Associated Mennonite Biblical Seminaries,
    1965.

ORAL INTERVIEWS

Blosser, Howard and Eva. Interview by Leonard Gross, March 26, 1986.
    Historical Mss. no. 6–248, Archives of the Mennonite Church, Goshen,
    Indiana.
Fretz, J. Winfield. Interview by Perry Bush, June 8, 1994. Deposited with
    Schowalter Oral History Collection, MLA.
Gratz, Delbert. Interview by Bill Barberee, February 13, 1995. Deposited with
    MHLB.
Habegger, Loris. Interview by Perry Bush, June 10, 1994. Deposited with
    Schowalter Oral History Collection, MLA.
Landis, Paul G. Interview by Perry Bush, May 10, 1989. Salunga, Pennsylvania.
    In author's possession.
Luginbuhl, Darvin. Interview by Melissa Bratt, February 7, 1995. Deposited
    with MHLB.
Luginbuhl, Greg. Interview by Perry Bush, August 29, 1995. Deposited with
    MHLB.
Neufeld, Elmer. Interview by Perry Bush, February 26, 1995. Deposited with
    MHLB.
Reichenbach, Fred. Interview by Brian Colatruglio, February 6, 1995. Deposited
    with MHLB.
Schowalter Oral History Collection, Mennonite Library and Archives, North
    Newton, Kansas.

Index